PERSUASIVE COMMUNICATION

PERSUASIVE COMMUNICATION

THIRD EDITION

ERWIN P. BETTINGHAUS

Michigan State University

HOLT, RINEHART AND WINSTON

New York • Chicago • San Francisco • Atlanta • Dallas • Montreal • Toronto • London • Sydney

Library of Congress Cataloging in Publication Data

Bettinghaus, Erwin Paul, date
    Persuasive communication.

    Bibliography: p.
    Includes index.
    1. Persuasion (Psychology).   I. Title.
BF637.P4B4   1980   303.3'4   79–27798

ISBN: 0–03–089959–1

0 1 2 3 4 039 9 8 7 6 5 4 3 2 1

PREFACE

Persuasive Communication explores the ways in which people try to influence the behavior of others. It is specifically concerned with persuasion through communication—with the deliberate attempts people make to change the attitudes, beliefs, values, and actions of those around us. To be human is to want change. We want more money from a boss, less interference in our private lives, or more help from a teacher. We want people to work harder or to work less hard. We want people to believe what we believe or to believe more firmly in an already held belief. The tool that people use to achieve change is most frequently persuasion.

Persuasion takes place when one attempts to change the attitude of a friend toward a favorite political candidate, when a manager tries to improve the productivity of an employee, when students attempt to change the university they attend, and when the President of the United States attempts to convince the electorate that he should be reelected. This book describes the process of persuasive communication as it occurs in many different situations and analyzes communication sources, messages, channels, and their influence on the behavior of audiences.

The basic approach taken in this text is behavioral, and the basic data is derived from the literature of the behavioral sciences. Many of the examples of persuasive communication situations have been drawn from contemporary situations in public life; others are taken from experimental studies that were designed to illuminate specific aspects of the subject. The study of persuasion has not been limited to a single academic discipline. The literature discussed in this volume comes from scientific research in communication, psychology, social psychology, sociology, psycholinguistics, and anthropology.

In taking a behavioral approach to persuasion, an author always leaves himself open to the accusation that he is unethically teaching people how to manipulate each other. In fact, there is very little discussion of the ethics of persuasion in most of the chapters. This does *not* mean that ethical considerations should not enter into the use of persuasion. On the contrary, the techniques we suggest, the examples we use, the studies we cite and the advice we give, all are implicitly tied to a set of ethical decision points that every communicator must make.

As an author, I do not feel that I can make all of the ethical decisions for each of you. I cannot tell you when to engage in persuasion and when to refrain from persuasion. I cannot anticipate what causes will prove to be "good" causes that should be supported by your best persuasive efforts, and what causes are inherently "bad" causes that persuasive communication should not be used to support. What I can do is to be ethical in my own behavior, and to strongly urge that each of you also be careful to consider the ethics of a situation before you act.

The ethical question is so important to the overall behavior of human beings that we examine it in some detail in the first chapter of the book. The absence of a detailed discussion of ethics in the other chapters should not lead any reader to feel that the topic is not of real importance. Success in persuasive communication must be based on a series of decisions, each having its roots in the central question of what is best for mankind.

This is the third edition of *Persuasive Communication*. Much has happened in the dozen years that have passed since the first edition was thrust into the hands of students all over the country. Many of those changes have been captured in this latest edition, but our field has grown so fast that one cannot hope to be exhaustive about the field of persuasion in any single volume. The interpersonal theories that form the basis of much of our research in communication have been broadened and strengthened. We can have far more confidence in their application to persuasion. We know far more about the effects of the mass media than we did in 1968, and much of that knowledge is reflected in this edition. The chapter on the use of communication in formal organizations has been greatly changed by the addition of materials on network analysis. The chapters on message organization and on the use of language have been changed to reflect current knowledge. Despite the number of changes that have occurred over the years, the basic approach to persuasion is still the same. Persuasion utilizes communication to influence the behaviors of people. All of us—speakers, writers, readers, and listeners—must improve our understanding of persuasion if we are to be effective citizens of this society.

It is simply impossible to list all the family, friends and colleagues who have contributed to my knowledge about persuasive communication. I mention a few people below, and readily acknowledge that I am leaving out many others who also helped make this volume a success. My decision to enter the field of communication was largely the responsibility of Professor Halbert E. Gulley, for many years at the University of Illinois and just recently retired as Chairman of the Department of Speech Communication at Northern Illinois University. Dr. David K. Berlo brought me to Michigan State University, nurtured the first ten years of my academic career, and influenced my thinking about almost every topic in this book. Professors Gerald R. Miller, Randall Harrison, Everett Rogers, Bradley Greenberg, and R. Vincent Farace have all contributed their ideas to this volume through their own papers and scholarly efforts. Professor Michael Burgoon read every word of the draft of the book, and its final form and structure were significantly sharpened through his efforts.

I owe a particular debt to Mrs. Barbara Haslem, who managed my office in such fashion that I was able to concentrate on book writing and not on administrative matters for the better part of a year. Mrs. Debbie Jahangardi completed the typing in a remarkably short period of time, satisfying all deadline requirements.

Finally, I must acknowledge the help of Mrs. Pat Dart, who assisted me with the index for this edition, and the assistance of my wife, Cay, who provided a climate conducive to the research and writing process.

E.P.B.

East Lansing, Michigan
December, 1979

CONTENTS

ONE

PERSUASION AND COMMUNICATION

"Take me to the movies!" "Vote for Senator Smart." "Our taxes are too high, and we must reduce them." "Gays have rights, too." "I'm a person. Please treat me like one."

All of these are messages, messages sent from one person, or group of persons to another person or group of persons. Each of them asks that some change take place in a receiver's attitudes, beliefs, or behavior. We call such messages *persuasive messages*, and their use in our society is the basis for this book.

Persuasion is an important part of the daily life of every human being. What we eat, what we wear, who we listen to, what music we prefer, what church we go to, and who we will vote for are all behaviors that are largely formed and continue to be maintained through persuasive communication. In fact, persuasion is used so frequently, and is so pervasive a part of our daily life that we often fail to recognize when we use persuasive communication or when we are exposed to it.

Persuasion has always been important in human societies. The Greeks made it a foundation stone of their early democracies. The English Parliament devised careful rules for its use in decision making. Persuasion, however, has never been as important as it is today. The United States is characterized by a cultural pluralism present in few other societies. It is, in fact, a land of minorities with young, old, black, white, brown, rich, poor, educated, uneducated, men, women, children, religious, unionized, and hundreds of other possible divisions. Pluralistic societies can exist and prosper only when there are methods of obtaining consensus judgments, or at least majority judgments on the issues that confront the society and its members.

In other societies, in other times, methods of achieving uniform behavior and common directions have been different. Minorities within the society were relatively weak, easily identified, and usually small in number. The majority members imposed their views on the minority or they eliminated the minority from participation. Thus Nazi Germany attempted to solve the "Jewish problem" by eliminating the Jews, and medieval Spain attempted to solve its "religious problem" by eliminating all heretics. In most recent times, news accounts suggest that Cambodia is attempting to stifle all dissent by simply eliminating all dissenters.

Societies do not have to kill their minority members in order to achieve consensus. In the United States, we denied members of minority groups the right to vote, or to hold political office. We segregated them into ghetto areas where they would be no "trouble." We denied them jobs and education in order to dilute their influence. Regardless of the moral implications of our past behavior, such methods worked only when there were very few minority members in the society. When there are over 20 million blacks in a country of 230 million people, the old methods *cannot* work. Morally and ethically, moreover, the old methods should not work.

What does work then? This book argues that persuasion must and will become a primary force in our society. If we are in agreement that increased participation of all people is desirable, we must also agree that other forms of social control are undesirable. Force, murder, segregation, discrimination, exile, and war are no longer available as permissible means of achieving the consensus that is required in any society before decisions can be made and actions can be taken.

What then, is left? Cushman and Miller state the case succinctly:

> If people are to be free to formulate new alternatives and evaluate a wide variety of opinions, then we must not only allow, but encourage independent invention and judgment. However, if society is to function effectively and justly, then we must organize out of many diverse alternatives and opinions a capacity for consensus prior to significant public action. Persuasion is one of the few satisfactory methods for resolving this dilemma.[1]

One might argue that persuasion is not essential to a pluralistic society if the various elements of that society can somehow operate independently, with each group forming its own judgments, making its own decisions, and taking its own actions. The Union of South Africa is attempting to try out such a solution through the development of quasi-independent "homelands" for a number of its black citizens. In the political and economic climate of the 1980s, one can certainly argue that that attempt is doomed to failure. It is doomed largely because the members of the society are not independent of one another, but closely linked to one another. Certainly in the United States today, no group, no faction, no minority, no individual can be truly independent. We are all highly interdependent. One can no longer pick a piece of ground, defend it against all comers, and expect to be self-sufficient. Each one of us depends on others for education, food, clothing, transportation, and health. From the time we arise in the morning until we retire at night we are dependent on the actions that others take.

It is no longer possible for a nation to survive without the actions of other nations. The United States needs tin from Bolivia, diamonds from South Africa, and oil from Saudi Arabia. Japan made the radio you listen to, Brazil grew the coffee you drank this morning, and Australia may well have provided the wool for the sweater you are wearing. A century ago, if a nation needed raw materials from another country, it was still feasible to consider the use of military force in order to secure the resources. If the world has learned anything in the past thirty years, it is that military intervention doesn't work very well. There are other means to achieve action, and we shall be discussing the use of strikes, boycotts, marches, and so forth, as alternatives to persuasion. Our interdependence, however, is becoming so strong that persuasive communication is increasingly becoming the only acceptable means of social control. We must all come to a better understanding of the use and effects of persuasion.

COMMUNICATION AND PERSUASION

People *want* to communicate. Any time an innovation promising better communication comes along, millions of people rush to buy it. Fifteen years after television was introduced, the nation was saturated with television sets. Cable television services have no trouble obtaining subscribers, even when normal reception is excellent in an area. Almost any popular book promising better communication between husbands and wives, or parents and children enjoys large sales. People join encounter groups, T-groups, communes, Dale Carnegie courses, and public speaking courses in large numbers in the attempt to improve their communication skills. Corporations spend billions of dollars each year in order to communicate with potential buyers of their products.

Many attempts have been made to define human communication. At the simplest level a communication situation exists whenever one person transmits a message that is received by another individual and is acted upon by that individual. When a teacher walks into a room and says "Hello!" to a student who looks up and smiles, the teacher is engaging in a simple form of communication. He is acting as a *source* of communication, using symbols or stimuli that have shared meanings for individuals, as a *message* to be delivered or passed along some *channel* to someone who is serving as a *receiver* of communication.

These four elements—source, message, channel, and receiver—are present in every communication situation. As situations become more and more complicated, the basic elements remain, although we may have more than one source, more than one receiver, many messages spread out over time, and several different channels being used. As communication situations become increasingly complex, the models we must derive to explain those situations also become more complex. Such elaborations have been provided by Berlo,[2] Gerbner,[3] Schramm,[4] Westley and MacLean[5] and Shannon and Weaver.[6] Each of these writers was interested in describing the basic ingredients of particular types of communication situations. Their descriptions are not identical, and the point of view they take toward communication varies, but all include the four basic elements of source, message, channel, and receiver.

Persusasion always involves communication. To come to some understanding of the difference between "a communication situation" and "a persuasive communication situation," let us contrast two situations: The first is the one we used to illustrate communication, where a teacher walks into a room, and says "Hello!" to a student. For the second situation, imagine that same teacher walking into a room and saying, "Will you go to the library for me?" The student in the first situation looks up and smiles. In the second, the student looks up and says, "Of course. What do you need from the library?" In both situations, there is a source of communication and a receiver of communication. In both situations, there is a message being transmitted, and the use of an oral channel to transmit the message. In both situations, the receiver makes a response to the message. The major difference seems to lie in the intent of the source. The first situation is one in which the source does not expect any specific reaction from the receiver; the second, however, is one in which the source hoped that the receiver would respond in a particular way to his message. The *intent* of the source was to change the behavior, or influence the behavior of the receiver in a specified manner.

There is general agreement that the variable of *intent* is what distinguishes persuasive communication from other communication situations. *The Random House Dictionary* says that persuasion implies ". . . influencing someone's thoughts or actions."[7] Andersen says that "Persuasion is a communication process in which the communicator seeks to elicit a desired response."[8] Scheidel, in writing about persuasive speaking, says that it is ". . . that activity in which speaker and listener are conjoined and in which the speaker consciously attempts to influence the behavior of the listener by transmitting audible and visible symbolic cues."[9] Each of these definitions emphasizes that persuasion ought to be thought of as a conscious effort at influencing the thoughts or actions of a receiver. Any message might have an effect on the behavior of any recipient of the message, whether the effect was intended or not. For example, you might overhear someone saying to another, "That movie is one of the best I've ever seen. It is an absolute must." Although the message was not intended for you, you might well decide to see the movie as a result of hearing a remark not meant for you. We do not wish to label such situations as persuasive communication situations, although many of the elements of such situations are similar to persuasive situations. The argument has sometimes been made that since the effects of persuasive communication are frequently impossible to distinguish from outcomes of other communication situations, the insistence on *intent* as a necessary condition of persuasion makes little sense. We argue that it is necessary to preserve intent because we wish to include an ethics of persuasion as an essential part of the process. Obviously, if persuasion cannot be distinguished from any accidental communication situation, it is difficult to urge speakers and writers to some standard of ethical behavior in the message they create. Furthermore, concentrating on those situations which involve *specific*

intent on the part of communicators, we are better able to offer advice to those who are the recipients of persuasive communication as well as to those who wish to engage in persuasive communication.

This book, therefore, is concerned with those situations in which people deliberately produce messages designed to elicit specific behavior or influence specific attitudes on the part of a receiver or group of receivers. As a minimal condition, to be labeled as persuasive, a communication situation must involve *a conscious attempt by one individual to change the attitudes, beliefs, or behavior of another individual or group of individuals through the transmission of some message.*

All communication is not persuasion, but all of us do engage in persuasion, and we are all exposed to persuasive messages. When General Motors shows a television commercial in which a pretty girl is driving a new Pontiac through a beautiful forest, they are engaging in a persuasive attempt to sell automobiles. When a bread company dramatically lists the ingredients in their bread, and says they thought you would like to know, they are engaging in persuasion. When a man knocks on your door and asks you to sign a petition to lower taxes, he is attempting to be persuasive. When the President of the United States goes on national television to ask for controls on inflation, he is sending you a persuasive message. When a consumers affairs advocate sends a message telling you to beware of certain advertising practices, persuasion is taking place. When the State Chairman of the Democratic Party is asking for more support for a candidate you voted for, a persuasive message has been sent. All of these, and countless more, are examples of persuasive communication.

PERSUASION IN THE 1980s

Whether we are on the receiving end, or engaged in sending messages, we tend to look at persuasion as a one-way street, that is, we do not take the other person into account. Until very recently, most scholars and researchers have also viewed persuasion as a one-way process. The model that has most frequently been studied imagines that a receiver's attitudes have been determined. Then the receiver is exposed to a persuasive message; and after the message has been sent, the receiver's attitudes are measured again. If there is some change in attitude in favor of the message, we say that persuasion was successful. In similar fashion, experiments are designed that expose a receiver or receivers to messages asking them to take some specific action. After the message is sent, the experimenter waits for a period of time, and then checks to see whether the receivers actually did what the message asked them to do. Again, the message is judged to be successful if some significant proportion of the audience actually did vote for the candidate, attend the movie, or buy the product that the message advocated. This concept of persuasion as an essentially one-way process pervaded most of the experimental literature in the field until very recently.

The concept is no longer adequate. If we are to understand persuasive communication, we must extend our research and knowledge beyond this simple model. Persuasion must be viewed as an interactive process. At the same time a source is sending a message, the source is being influenced by the actions of the receiver for whom the message is intended. Messages are not sent in vacuums, although much of our research is conducted as if all possible effects were due to very simple causes. Both source and receiver are typically influenced by each other, as well as by the activities that take place long before the message is actually sent. The realities are that sources and receivers are interchangeable, that when I am trying to persuade you to my point of view, I am also trying to understand your point of view, and am exposed to your message to me. We are trying to persuade each other.

The results of an interactive view of persuasion can be seen in the ways we judge the effectiveness of persuasion, in the models used to conceptualize persuasion, in the variables identified as important, and in the situations we attempt to study. Let us look at an illustration of how a real life persuasive situation might differ from some of the experimental models developed and used in the past.

A real estate developer bought a large tract of ground across a highway from an area consisting of large, expensive single family dwellings. After studying his new tract of land, the developer sought permission to build a large apartment complex on the site. The apartments were intended for low income families, and for the elderly poor. In seeking permission from the city council to build his apartments, the builder sent a message which stressed the importance of housing for the poor and the elderly.

Residents in the area across the highway were incensed at the builder's plans. They stormed the city council meeting, and argued through their spokesman that the proposed building plans would lower their property values, cause ecological harm to the area, increase traffic unnecessarily, and add to the burden of school taxes because of the increased number of school-aged children that would be coming into the area.

Some of the city council members asked the builder whether he would consider putting a smaller number of units on the property. One city council member suggested that more expensive condominiums would be more appropriate. Spokesmen for the area residents were asked for data they might have to support the charge of serious ecological damage. At the end of the long meeting, the council members postponed a decision on the matter until there had been an opportunity to gather further data and to hear from other interested citizens.

If we had considered this persuasive communication situation as a one-way process, we would have listened to the builder make his presentation, and then recorded the immediate responses of the city council members. We would have made a judgment about the success or failure of the presentation on the immediate responses of the council members; but the situation was obviously far more complicated than that. Various city council members were speaking from time to time, and those messages had an effect on the area residents as well as on the builder and his staff. The area residents listened to the builder, and modified their presentations, and their behavior, as a result of the builder's messages. The point should be clear. In the decade ahead, there will be situations in which persuasion can be viewed as a one-way process. But the primary persuasive situations that all of us are going to be concerned with will focus upon the mutual persuasive efforts of people and nations working together to build better interpersonal relationships and better societies.

BASIC FACTORS IN PERSUASION

Our first approach to defining persuasion was based on a traditional model. That model is no longer sufficient. To be complete, we must extend our definition to include those communication situations in which people actively seek to find a consensus point on which they can base mutual actions. Thus, in subsequent chapters, we will consider two kinds of situations:

1. Those communication situations which involve a conscious attempt by one individual to modify or intensify the attitudes, beliefs, or behavior of another individual or group of individuals through the transmission of some message.
2. Those communication situations in which two or more individuals each consciously attempt to modify or intensify the attitudes, beliefs, or behavior of each other through mutual interaction.

Whether we examine one-way or two-way persuasive communication situations, the effectiveness of persuasion depends on the *nature and extent* of the changes experienced by individuals in the situation. A selection of the major factors which might account for persuasive changes is difficult. In any given situation, seemingly trivial factors may play a decisive role. In studies conducted by Gerald Miller[10] on the use of video-tape in the courtroom, the importance of these factors can be noted. In one situation, the experimenters were testing whether a woman claiming a back injury was persuasive with the simulated jury under a number of different circumstances. In one of the experimental situations, however, a jury member noticed that the woman was wearing high heels. The jury member convinced the rest of that panel that the woman had to be lying, because someone with a serious back injury would not be able to wear high heels. The audience change was thus due not to the actual message that had been sent, but to a factor that originally appeared to be completely unrelated to the experimental condition. Obviously, it is impossible to take account of all such minor factors in looking at persuasive communication, nor would such an accounting be of much help to the individual interested in improving skills.

Different receivers are affected differently by the same persuasive message. Thus an examination of the differences between receivers is in order. Some may be demographic in nature, such as, differences in age, sex, education, race, or occupation. A second set of factors may be psychological in nature and include such influences as motivation to respond, cognitive balance, and various personality factors.

Of central importance to our analysis is the fact that differences between sources affect persuasion. Study after study has demonstrated that when two different sources send exactly the same message, receivers do not respond in identical fashion to the two sources. Thus we shall be looking at source credibility, social power, societal role, relationship to the receiver, and various demographic characteristics as factors in persuasion.

When people are exposed to messages, they are most likely to be affected by the topic or content of the message, but it is also important to examine the effects of systematic variation in the appeals or arguments used, the organizational structure of the message, the language characteristics embodied in the message, and the stylistic design of the message.

The term "channel" has been defined in several ways in the research literature and its use and breadth were thoroughly explored by Berlo.[11] The research literature concerned with persuasion focuses on messages delivered in a face-to-face situation versus messages with some interposition between the source and receiver such as television, radio, or newspapers.

Finally, we have to look at persuasive communication from the standpoint of the social situation in which it occurs. Obviously, there is infinite variation in the kinds of situations within which communication *can* take place. Only a few such variations have been carefully studied. Included are situations where persuasion occurs in the presence of a group of individuals, where the setting is either familiar or unfamiliar to the receiver, where the situation is pleasant or unpleasant, and settings involving formal organizations such as a corporation or the city council.

Basic factors in persuasion thus include
1. similarities and differences between sources and receivers,
2. variations in the content of messages,
3. variations in message organization or style,
4. differences in the channels used to conduct persuasion,
5. differences in the nature of the situation in which persuasion takes place.

Each of these factors can be expected to produce differential responses on the part of receivers, and should trigger different kinds of messages on the part of sources. It is the extremely large number of possible outcomes that makes persuasion both so difficult and so interesting.

THE EFFECTS OF PERSUASION

Persuasion is linked to changes in attitudes, beliefs, or behavior. In the examples used thus far, the inference might be drawn that the effects of a persuasive message are always immediately observable. Such a conclusion is seldom justified in real life persuasive communication situations. Imagine listening to a speaker who advocated raising taxes in order to build an addition to the local high school. Before the speech, a listener might declare flatly, "No more taxes! I am tired of all these people coming here and asking for more money." The speech is dynamic, and the speaker has taken great care to point out how each member of the community will benefit from the proposed new addition. After the speech, our listener says, "I'm still opposed to more taxes, but that guy was really great. He could sell iceboxes to Eskimos."

The speaker did not succeed in getting our listener's vote with that one speech, but do we want to say that the speech had *no* effect? Certainly *something* had happened to the listener as a result of listening to the speech. The effect or outcome was not precisely what was intended, but one can well imagine that the listener would have an even greater change in attitude if exposed to more messages about the proposed school addition. This change in attitude toward the speaker is an outcome that can be traced directly to the speech, and is an effect related to the speaker's original intention. Such a change may not result in immediate differences in the way the listener behaves, but the initial effect could lead to future changes that would finally lead the listener to vote for a tax increase. The effects of persuasive messages cannot completely be assessed in terms of immediately observable behavior.

Rosenberg and Hovland[12] suggest that persuasive effects can be looked upon as involving *attitudes* as general predispositions to response, and can be classified as either changes in *cognition*, changes in *affect*, or changes in *behavior*. Figure 1.1 illustrates the relation of attitudes to other changes, and provides an index of external change. The general concept of attitude will be looked at more closely in the succeeding section, but before making such a detailed examination, it will be helpful to look at the three main types of change, and the ways in which changes can be identified.

Cognitions include the concepts we have, the beliefs we hold about various attitude objects, the values we place on objects and beliefs and the perceptions we have of the world around us. Typically, changes in cognitions can be identified by the verbal statements that people make after being exposed to a persuasive message, or by changes in the perceptions they have about some attitude object. For example, imagine that you are asked before a speech what you think about legalizing marijuana use in the United States. You state that you are completely opposed to any change in the laws which govern marijuana use. Then you listen to a speaker talk about the possible advantages of legalizing pot. After the speech, you are again asked what you think. If you reply that the speaker has not changed your mind, the conclusion would be that your cognitions had not changed, and we would say so on the basis of your verbal statements. If, on the other hand, you now say that there is merit in legalizing the use of marijuana, we would conclude that a cognitive change had taken place. The change would be indicated by the change in your verbal statements.

It is frequently difficult to attribute changes in cognitions directly to changes in verbal statements or directly to persuasive messages. People may express different opinions on a topic at varying times. They may change their cogni-

tions, and their statements as a result of thinking about the topic, getting further information about the topic, listening to a neighbor talk about it, or feeling pressured by someone else. If the individual happened to listen to a persuasive speech, and then said something that indicated a change in cognitions, the inclination would be to attribute the change to the speech. Actually, there could have been many reasons for the change, but determining the exact causes of cognitive change is always difficult.

Cognitive changes can also be indexed by changes in perceptions, that is, the way in which individuals see the world around them. Such indicators of change can be illustrated by a simple example. Imagine looking at a picture containing some "hidden objects." You look intently at the picture, but fail to spot any of the objects. Then a friend says, "Look at the upper left-hand corner next to the tree trunk." You do so and find a hidden tennis racket. The chances are very good that when you look at the picture again, the tennis racket will seem to almost leap out of it. Your perceptions have been changed as a result of the message telling you where to look.

Perception changes are not limited to such simple examples as tennis rackets hidden in pictures. A man may drive through a New York slum and see the people as dirty, ragged, drunken derelicts. After he listens to a speech from a social worker in that area, he may begin to see the same people as sober and dressed in clean, worn clothing. Several months ago, I listened to a man describe how he had changed his perceptions and thus his cognitions. He told of an incident in which his car had broken down on a lonely road. While he was standing rather helplessly next to the car, another car stopped, and two young men climbed out. They were dressed in somewhat ragged clothes, their hair was extremely long, and the speaker began to fear that he might be held up and robbed. Instead, the youths offered to help him, and did so. My informant reported that the ". . . boys spoke very politely, and when I drove off, I even forgot that their hair was long." This was a perception change, and such perception changes toward people and events are an important effect of persuasive messages.

In later chapters, we shall argue that persuasive communicators frequently will be unable to obtain action changes from a group of receivers, but it may be possible to get receivers to change their cognitions, and thus help to lay the groundwork for future messages that *will* successfully argue for action changes.

Affect changes are harder to describe. These are changes in our emotional states. Most people cannot tell us exactly how they feel, but when an experience is responsible for producing an emotional change, they know that the change has occurred. Affect changes are changes in mood, in emotions, and they may be indicated by laughing, crying, shivers running up and down the spine, and similar bodily events. In some cases, the psychologist working in the laboratory can show changes resulting from the presentation of messages through the use of instruments for detecting changes in heart rate, blood pressure, galvanic skin response, and sweating. Outside the research laboratory, such instruments are not available, and scholars must depend on verbal statements from receivers about emotional changes and the extent to which a particular persuasive message produced the change.

Regardless of the difficulties in indexing affect changes, there is ample evidence that these changes can result from persuasive communication. Examples may be noted when someone exclaims, "I cried at the ending of that movie," or "His speaking sent shivers up and down my spine," or "That book really discourages me." Fund raisers for charitable organizations frequently send persuasive messages attempting to make listeners or viewers feel sorry for the victims that a charity has been set up to help. For years, the Easter Seal campaign has been based on a poster showing a small, attractive, but crippled child. The obvious intent of the campaign is to produce a sympathetic reaction on the part of receivers that will then be translated into writing a check for the campaign. Note that it is frequently a very delicate set of decisions that has to be made. If the child chosen for the poster is extremely ugly, or very badly crippled, there is a chance that the affective reaction will be one of revulsion, or the feeling that "the poor thing would be better off dead." Such a reaction does not lead to large contributions. At the other end of the spectrum, there is the risk that the child chosen will be too attractive, or will not have a visible defect. There the reaction might well be: "That child is better off than my own children. They don't need any of my money." In either case, one of the intentions of the communicator is to produce an appropriate emotional reaction in a receiver.

A sampling of research into variables affecting the success of persuasion shows that there are few studies that directly examine affect changes. The problems in measuring these changes make research into this type of persuasive effect extremely difficult. These difficulties, however, should not lead to the conclusion that such effects are absent or unimportant. In fact, unplanned affect changes may sometimes result in inhibiting some of the persuasive effects desired by a persuasive communicator. Ignoring potential affect changes is done only at the risk of jeopardizing the entire persuasive effort.

Finally, *behavior* changes resulting from persuasion must be discussed. In one sense, *any* observable changes in behavior, including changes in the nervous system and verbal statements, could be called behavior changes since the individual is doing something, but it is helpful to distinguish between cognitive changes, emotional changes, and other types of overt, easily observable behavior. Getting an individual to agree, cognitively, that racial segregation is bad is far easier than getting that same individual to agree to stand on a street corner and hand out leaflets about racial segregation. Getting someone to actually stop drinking is far more difficult than getting that same individual to simply agree to stop drinking. Behavior changes, then, are changes in overt, physical actions that may result from attending to a particular persuasive message.

Behavior changes may become the focus of a persuasive communication situation. Helping clean up a river, marching against the construction of a nuclear power plant, buying nonpolluting soaps, putting a sign in the window advocating abortion reform, voting for additional school taxes, or joining a march on the Board of Trustees to protest sexism in faculty hiring are all examples of behavior changes that might be desired by persuasive communicators. In each case, an assessment of the situation must take into account the relationships that exist between what the receiver is doing now, what the source wants done, what message the source is going to transmit, and finally what changes in behavior actually occur after the message has been transmitted. The changes in behavior are best assessed by direct observations of the receiver, but in some situations, results may be able to be assessed by the verbal statements made by the receiver.

Cognitive, affective, and behavioral changes are not easily separated into three distinct and mutually exclusive categories. In almost any situation involving persuasive communication, combinations of effects will be noted. A man may vote for a bond issue and at the same time talk to a friend about how important the schools are. He is exhibiting both a behavior and a cognitive change. I can be emotionally stirred by a speech, and also make a contribution to charity. You can be exposed to a television commercial, laugh at the commercial, and buy the product three days later. In these situations, it is difficult to make clear distinctions between the various types of effects that may occur as a result of a persuasive message. The careful communicator, however, will plan strategy ahead of time, and take into account all possible effects before presenting a set of messages to a group of receivers.

ATTITUDES AND BELIEFS

In Figure 1.1, we show that all the possible effects of persuasion stem from changes in *attitudes* and *beliefs*. Before the communicator can expect a receiver to change a behavior, our model says that there has to be a corresponding change in an attitude or a belief. A clear understanding of what is meant by an attitude or a belief is thus central to an understanding of the persuasive communication process. We shall be using both terms frequently, as all of our current models and theories about persuasive communication rest on an understanding of the concepts of belief and attitude change and on the way in which these concepts are revealed in observable responses.

Attitudes are an individual's likes and dislikes, while *beliefs* express the relationships we see between two or more events, or people, or the relationships between events and characteristics of those events. Thus, I can express an attitude by saying "I like Ford cars," and can express a belief by saying "I believe that Ford cars are very durable." Note that my statements are only *expressions* of the underlying attitude or belief. Both attitudes and beliefs are nonobservable, cognitive states. No one has ever seen, heard, tasted, touched or smelled an attitude or a belief. Attitudes and beliefs are conceptual bridges between what an individual *does* and the cognitive processes that lead him to do it.

Although we cannot directly observe an attitude or a belief, we can find out about it. This is done by *making inferences* from the observable behavior of an individual to what we think the person's internal state might be. One man hits another in a bar, and we infer that negative feelings are being displayed. Two people walk up to one another, smile, and shake hands, and the observer infers that positive attitudes are being displayed. In many cases, we make inferences about an individual's attitudes and beliefs from the verbal statements that are made. Atti-

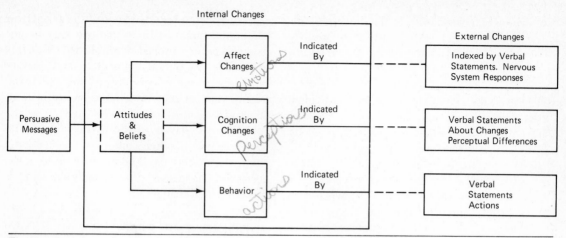

Figure 1.1

tudes are indexed in statements such as "I like Doonesbury," "That movie is excellent," or "Black is beautiful." Beliefs relate things, and might be inferred from statements like "College students are too liberal," "Taxes are far too high," and "All students must have a general education." In each of these statements, it is not the attitude or belief that is being observed. The existence of an attitude or belief is being inferred from the verbal statement or from the overt behavior.

Attitudes and beliefs, then, reflect an individual's psychological processes. Attitudes are described in terms of the favorability or unfavorability of the evaluation made by an individual of an object, person, or event. Beliefs index the relationships that individuals "see" in their environment.

It should now be obvious why the behavioral scientist is interested in attitudes and beliefs. The scientist postulates a positive relationship between attitudes and beliefs and cognitions, affect, and behavior. If you hold a highly favorable attitude toward General Motors, a commercial designed to sell Buicks ought to have more impact on you than if you have a neutral or negative attitude toward Gen-

eral Motors. If I hold a highly favorable attitude toward you, I am more likely to seek your company, would be more willing to spend time talking to you, and would be more likely to listen to your persuasive messages. If the positive relationship we postulate actually exists, attitudes can serve as a predictor of how likely an audience is to take some action as a result of a persuasive message, or how much resistance there is likely to be.

The relationship between attitudes and beliefs and the behavior a person exhibits is positive, but there is no one-to-one correspondence. Merely possessing a favorable attitude is not a sufficient guarantee that a particular kind of behavior will result. For example, imagine that a person holds extremely unfavorable attitudes toward certain minority groups, particularly blacks and Jews. If we give the person a paper and pencil test to assess attitudes toward these two groups, we may find that the individual consistently tells us that blacks are lazy, incompetent, and distasteful. In similar fashion, the person may view Jews as grasping, greedy, and stingy. The results of the paper and pencil test would suggest that the person is also likely to behave negatively toward both blacks and Jews.

It is, however, very unlikely that such an individual *will* exhibit overt, physical hostility when meeting a black person on the street. In fact, if we were to look only at overt, physical behavior, it would be difficult, if not impossible, to tell the extremely prejudiced individual from any other person. In our overt relationships with other people, we are restrained by attitudes and beliefs about the legal system, by fear of reprisals, by worry about the responses of others, and by many other psychological processes that serve to mediate between attitudes, beliefs, and overt behavior.

If attitudes and beliefs cannot be seen, if they can only be inferred from observable behavior, why talk about them at all? Why not talk only about what can be directly observed, that is, verbal statements or overt actions? Why not merely observe persuasive attempts and then note whether the receivers behave according to the intentions of the source? One reason why we retain these conceptual bridges lies with the nature of the research that has been performed by behavioral scientists interested in persuasion. Imagine that I make a speech to a group of people in which I advocate voting against a proposed new shopping mall. After listening to me, the audience goes home. How can I find out whether they behaved any differently? I could follow each one into the polling place and ask whether the person voted in favor of the mall or not? I could follow each one around the city and see whether any made statements opposing the mall. Such checking would constitute an attempt to observe individual reactions to persuasion within a "natural" setting. The difficulties, probable illegalities, and the huge expenses inherent in any such undertaking are apparent.

On the other hand, I could have the audience answer a short questionnaire about their attitudes and beliefs regarding the mall after I finished making my speech. The answers given would provide at least some indication, even if a weak one, about the ways in which the audience members might behave once they enter the voting booth. Many of the persuasive communication situations that we seek to understand occur in social situations in which it is impossible to obtain immediate and private estimates of the effects of the message being transmitted. In such situations, the estimate of effectiveness must be made by looking at the subsequent behavior of the participants to detect changes in their opinions, perceptions, emotions, or actions. The assumption is, however, that changes in attitude and belief always precede other changes.

JUDGING THE EFFECTS OF PERSUASION

Ultimately, persuasive communication must be judged in terms of its effect on the participants. Was it successful? Did it fail to achieve its goal? This may seem like an easy task, but it is seldom so easy. The end result of most persuasive campaigns, and indeed of most persuasive messages, seems to be that little can be detected. With rare exceptions, any changes that are detected in laboratory experiments seem to be quite temporary in nature, with the receivers rapidly returning to their original opinions and actions.[13] Were such persuasive attempts failures? A more careful examination of the dimension of success or failure is needed.

One dimension of the effects of persuasion is obtained by assessing the correspondence between the intentions of the source and subsequent behavior of the receiver. When an editorial asks its readers to change their attitude toward admitting Communist China to the United Nations, and later questionnaires suggest that there has been no change in their attitudes, the editorial would seem to have been a failure. When a mayor asks the people of a community to vote for him, and they turn out in huge numbers to do so, his campaign seems to be a success.

Using this criterion of the degree of correspondence between the stated intentions of the source and an assessment of the subsequent behavior of a receiver would seem to be a simple matter. Unfortunately, it is not. Norman Thomas repeatedly ran on the Socialist ticket for the presidency of the United States. He never won and, in fact, never came close to winning. All the messages he transmitted during his campaigns were seemingly directed toward the securing of votes for his candidacy. By the criterion of complete correspondence between intentions and achievements, Norman Thomas was a failure as a persuasive communicator. Few historians, however, would be willing to judge him a failure. They note that Norman Thomas was among the first to espouse a number of ideas that are now familiar parts of the American political and economic scene. They point to the number of proposals that are now planks in the platforms of other political parties and other political candidates. His messages failed in their immediate intent, but their long-range impact was great.

The National Association for the Advancement of Colored People was formed in the first years of this century. From its inception the NAACP advocated better treatment for black citizens. They long concentrated their efforts on the system of segregated schools in the South. For years, their words seemed to fall on deaf ears, if one judges their efforts by the number of schools that were desegregated. Was the organization a failure? Certainly not if you judge the results by events occurring since 1954 when their efforts helped lead to the Supreme Court decision declaring segregated school systems unconstitutional.

Judgment of the effects of persuasion cannot be based entirely on the immediate, short-range effects of messages that pass between participants in persuasion, regardless of the stated intentions of the source. Those intentions can be used as guidelines, but not as the sole criterion. There are many situations in which the immediate effects from a message are impossible to discern, but where an analysis of the situation after a period of time will show some effects of the original message.

A second criterion for judging the success of a persuasive message is the degree of change that is secured. Sales messages are one of the best examples we can use to illustrate this situation. Jane Jones is demonstrating a new food processor in the local department store. A crowd of twenty-five people is watching as she demonstrates the appliance, and tries to sell it to the audience. Her chances of getting all twenty-five members of the audience to buy a machine are obviously very small. How many machines does she have to sell before the message can be considered effective? To more than half the people? Less than half? Only one? If no one rushes up to buy one of the processors, do we consider Jane a failure? Should we fire her? The difficulties in making an immediate assessment are obvious. Some members of the audience might go home, think about the demonstration, talk to their friends and neighbors, and finally buy a processor two months later. If the store had fired Jane in the meantime, most of us would agree that an injustice had been done.

Persuasion must be judged in terms of gradations of success. One end of the scale may represent no change at all in any of the participants to the situation along any of the dimensions we have discussed. At the other end of the scale, we would find that all of the participants in the situation have changed in ways which reflect their mutual desires to find common ground on which decisions and actions are possible. Most outcomes of persuasive communication fall between these two extremes.

The final criterion we must use in judging the success or failure of persuasion is the level of difficulty of the task. Advocating a tax reduction is easier than advocating tax increases. In many districts in the South, a Democratic candidate usually has an easier time in winning an election than a Republican. If you are advocating strong efforts to control crime, your task may be easy, since few people are in favor of increased crime. If you are in favor of federal payments for abortions through welfare, however, you are likely to have a far more difficult time. Not only are there many opponents to changes in the current laws governing the use of federal funds for abortions, but the attitudes of most people toward abortion are firmly fixed. Getting an audience to change firmly fixed attitudes is more difficult than getting agreement on a position that seems to support attitudes weakly held. The difficulty level of the communicator's task can be assessed by comparing the initial position of a receiver on a particular topic to the position desired by the communicator. If the change in attitude desired is large, successful persuasion will be more difficult to achieve than if the source wants the receiver to change only a small amount from a currently held position. Imagine two persuasive communicators, one delivering a message to a receiver very firmly set in an attitudinal position, and the other delivering a message to a receiver with only weakly held attitudes toward a topic. If both communicators are successful in obtaining attitude change, we might wish to say that the first communicator was more successful than the second because the task was more difficult to accomplish.

Three criteria must be considered in judging persuasive communication. Situations can be assessed in terms of the *nature of the correspondence* between the intentions of the participants, the *degree of correspondence* between the intentions of the source and the subsequent behavior of the receiver, and the *difficulty level* of the task being engaged in. All three criteria are necessary if we are to properly assess the success or failure of persuasion.

THE ETHICS OF PERSUASION

Persuasion is a field for scientific research, a field similar to those disciplines which study political behavior, mental illness, or juvenile delinquency. Few object to the psychologist who is interested in trying to cure the psychotic, the criminologist working at the preven-

tion of crime, or the historian trying to understand the causes of war. Many people, however, have objected to the study and practice of persuasion. The term itself seems to suggest something not quite pleasant, something unfair or dishonest. People have always objected to the manipulation of others, whether by physical force, or by the force of words playing on the emotions. This concern about the power of persuasive communication arose early in man's recorded history, and philosophers from Aristotle to David Hume to John Stuart Mill have addressed themselves to some of the philosophical problems arising from the recognition that persuasion can be a powerful tool in the hands of man.

The most serious charge against the use of persuasion comes from those who argue for "openness" in the communicative relationships between people. This position can be recognized in a number of identifiable phrases. Proponents will say: "Let it all hang out;" "Just give them the facts;" "Don't tell me what to do, let me make up my own mind;" or "I'm a person, not something to be manipulated." The argument is intriguing, because it appears to equalize the status of everyone without lowering the worth of anyone. Certainly the argument deserves exploration, and there are several reasons why it would seem reasonable to reject the "openness" position as universally desirable.

First, we should note that the proponents of such a position are engaged in persuasion when they attempt to get others to adopt their own position. We would not want to say that such persuasion is bad, but it does seem ironical that the very people who argue against persuasion are dependent upon its use to get their position adopted.

Second, the type of communication called for in an open communication situation is frequently contradictory. Johennsen[14], for example, says that what is wanted is "free expression," but at the same time one should not use "value judgments that stifle." If there are types of communication that are to be avoided, can we argue that expression is really "free." In fact, what has evolved in open communication situations is a style of communicating that *does* overtly imply more trust in receivers, but the style is by no means completely "free" in the sense that one can say or do anything one wants to. In a later chapter, we shall argue that this style is, for certain types of communication situations, very persuasive.

Finally, we would argue that to refuse to persuade is to abdicate one's responsibility to society.[15] If you think something needs doing in the community, do you not have the responsibility to attempt to persuade others to your point of view? Those who say, "Just give them the facts, and let them make up their own mind," deny that responsibility. A more ethical approach would be one that argued the responsibility of every individual to examine data, draw conclusions, and then use persuasion as the tool for obtaining a consensus within the society.

In advancing the arguments against the openness position as an extreme position, we do not mean to deny some of its aspects. We believe firmly that more honesty, more trust in each other, more use of data, and greater faith in the value of each human being are goals not antithetical to reliance on persuasion as a major ethical tool for societies to adopt.

A second major charge against the use of persuasion is that it can be used by "evil" people and for "bad" ends. The charge is undoubtedly correct, but any tool can be used for either the benefit or detriment of society. Those who would limit persuasion because it could be used for evil ends sometimes go beyond the mere charge. They also argue that we ought not to teach persuasion, ought not do research which has the hope of improving persuasive attempts, ought not to write about persuasion. The charge is that the results of research, the books, and the courses might be taken by people who would use them unwisely, or unethically, or immorally.

The charge is a difficult one to answer simply. We shall attempt to do so by fashioning a series of related questions, and answering them.

1. Can persuasion be used for evil ends? Of course it can, but so can driving a car, firing a gun, or taking aspirin. So can medicine, law, banking, accounting, or plumbing be used for bad purposes by individuals determined to do so. No one would argue that we should close all medical schools because they have the potentiality of being used wrongly. A more rational suggestion is that we keep the medical school, and place some restrictions on the way in which people may practice medicine. With regard to persuasion, our society has argued the same way. The advertiser is allowed to attempt to persuade people to buy his product, but we make him legally responsible for the safety of the product.

2. When we teach about persuasion, do we put power over others in the hands of those we teach? Yes, we do, but we do so also when we teach a child how to write, teach a college student how to take a blood sample, or teach a soldier how to use a bayonet. Everyone who goes to school to learn how to be a farmer, banker, doctor, engineer, salesman, lawyer, plumber, or auto mechanic has acquired information that will help in controlling the lives of others. Knowledge is always powerful, but its power to control depends on the exclusivity with which it is held. If only a few knew how to persuade others, persuasion would be a very powerful weapon indeed. When everyone knows how to use persuasion effectively, and knows how to evaluate the persuasive messages that are received, persuasion becomes far more a tool, and less a weapon.

3. Does the use of persuasion lead to manipulation, and thus does it make people into objects? Persuasion is an attempt to control one's environment and people are an important part of that environment. If you mean by "manipulation" the changing of the behavior of others

through conscious attempts to change their behavior, persuasion does result in manipulation. Having said that, we might examine the original question a bit more closely. The use of the word "manipulation" has come to have a very negative meaning. If we substituted the word "education" or "socialization" or "rehabilitation" for the term manipulation, no one would worry about the association of persuasion with any of the three concepts. Yet each of them can be defined as conscious attempts to change the behavior of others. Society regards education, socialization, and rehabilitation as positive in nature. We all attempt to control the environment around us. We wouldn't be living organisms if we didn't, and persuasion is but one way we use to fit ourselves within our society.

4. Can we protect people against persuasion? Our answer here has to be: not completely. Unless we bar all communication between people, human beings are always going to attempt to persuade and to be persuaded. If one person speaks and another listens, there is a probability that persuasion will occur. We can, of course, pass laws forbidding certain types of persuasion, as we have done in the case of advertisements and product claims. That kind of limitation, however, covers only a very small number of possible communication situations. A better solution to the problem is to teach all people to use persuasion effectively, and to recognize and be able to evaluate persuasion when it is being used on them. The more information people have about persuasion and persuasive techniques, the better is the likelihood that people can increase their resistance to would-be hucksters. If this were done, there would be no need for laws or rules governing the use of advertising or product claims.

The original question was whether we should teach, study and write about the use of persuasion. The answer is yes, but it is a conclusion arrived at only after considering the alternatives. There are alternatives, and mankind has tried and keeps trying almost all of them. The Palestine Liberation Organization engages in terrorism against Israel, because they claim that persuasion hasn't worked. The Symbionese Liberation Army found that no one listened to their plans for restructuring the world, so they kidnapped Patty Hearst in order to force the world to listen. A dictator in Latin American finds people opposed to his policies, so he arrests all his opponents in order to silence their persuasive attempts. The alternatives to persuasion include whips, chains, bribes, tortures, murder, and warfare. In the short run, at least, the alternatives are just as effective, and perhaps more effective at shaping human behavior than persuasion. Surely, no one wishes to argue that any of the alternatives are a more desirable method for shaping a society than persuasion, even though they might be more effective.

We must do everything we can to promote the use of persuasion, and to make more people aware of the impact of persuasion on their daily lives. If we all become more effective sources and receivers of persuasive communication, mankind may eventually be able to stop using the alternatives to persuasion.

RESPONSIBILITIES

The remainder of this book views persuasion from the standpoint of a behavioral scientist. As such, it presents practical suggestions to the potential speaker, writer, reader and listener. Such knowledge implies certain responsibilites that sources and receivers have to themselves, to other people, and to society. A few of these responsibilities are outlined below:

1. Develop some expectations about ethics and morality. I am not an advocate for any particular moral code or any specific set of ethical standards. I do argue that every individual ought to have carefully developed a set of ethical standards and a set of expectations regarding ethical conduct. I do argue that each of

us should know what our standards are and how we wish to apply them in various situations. In particular, I do argue that when we use persuasion, we should do so from a position consistent with the set of ethical and moral standards we have.

2. Know all you can about persuasion. You do not normally attempt to use an electric drill without finding out where the switch is and what the drill can do. Persuasion is also a tool, and you ought to know what the effects are likely to be if you use this tool.

3. Establish for yourself some criteria for making decisions. Decision making is an important part of the persuasive process, and you ought to understand the ways in which decisions are made. Persuasion is used in communicating decisions about a topic. If the decision you make in regard to the topic is a poor one, your persuasive efforts may or may not be successful, but most probably, the long-range effects are not likely to be desirable.

We all act as both source and receiver of persuasive messages. Most of our formal education, however, has gone toward training us to be better sources of communication, and we are far more likely to want to communicate than to be communicated to. Yet the fact remains that we act as receivers of communication far more than we are able to act as a source of communications. We listen to the radio, read the newspaper, listen to other people, and view the television set many more hours a day than we engage in actually putting out messages. Here are some suggestions to help you predict the kinds of effects that particular persuasive messages are likely to have on you:

1. Know what your own biases are. We cannot know exactly how we will react to each persuasive message we face, but we can make ourselves aware of some of the types of arguments to which we react favorably or unfavorably. I know, for example, that I am likely to be taken in by the salesman who promises that an appli-

ance will be "long-lasting." I tend not to examine other aspects of the product if I have been assured that it will last a long time. Others may react to a message promising easy cleaning, or attractive decor. Every receiver should make the kind of self analysis that will enable the prediction of the kinds of effects that particular persuasive efforts are likely to have.

2. Know your source. You are exposed to newspapers, magazines, television, radio, neighbors, friends, and relatives. It is manifestly impossible for you to become an expert on all the problems that face you. You will have to depend on the perceived credibility of the people with whom you communicate. The development of credibility can be based on relatively casual knowledge, or on a fair amount of knowledge. The more people can find out about each other from sources of information that are available, the better off they are likely to be.

3. Become a collector of information. As you listen to the messages available to you, your predispositions toward listening to one message and refusing to listen to another message may make if difficult for you to make final decisions based on all available information. If, however, you constantly collect information from all kinds of sources, and of all degrees of reliability, you can include this information as an important part of the decision-making process. People are going to receive information differently, but perhaps they should fight against the tendency to narrow down what they listen to and read.

Nations, cultures and societies have evolved over the centuries through the measures they take to control the behavior of individuals within the society. A country can allow great diversity to exist within its borders, but there must be some situations in which all members of the society behave in the same way. A simple example is driving a car. A country just cannot allow some people to drive on the left side of the road, and some on the right. Either is completely allowable, but not both at the same time. In order to secure that necessary conformity, societies develop educational campaigns, methods of child socialization, and the use of law. Most such efforts grow out of the specific values that a society places upon the acts and customs of individuals. For example, in Sicily, the man who murders his wife's lover may receive a term of three years in jail, while the man who robs a train may receive a life sentence. Different values have led to different laws and customs.

Not every society has the same values, and there is no culture, nation, or society that cannot be improved, nor any that is not constantly changing. It will become obvious that I am in favor of using persuasion as the major tool of making changes in our society. I regard the development of persuasion as one of the major steps we can take to avoid war, crime and repression. Persuasion, however, is not the only tool a free society needs in order to grow, to change and to develop the necessary uniformities of behavior that all societies require. Compromise, mediation, arbitration, compliance, law and custom are other valuable tools of society. In order to aid in the development of persuasion as a major tool, there are steps we need to take:

1. **Protect persuasion by law and by custom.** As a nation, we pride ourself on freedom of speech, and it can be argued that we need not protect one form of communicaton more than is already provided for in our Constitution and by our laws. That protection, however, is always fragile and sometimes uncertain. There are always groups of people who would nibble away at the protections we have given to free speech, and a continual recognition of the value of persuasion to the operation of a democratic society is in order.

2. **Encourage the acquisition of knowledge.** Many people object to persuasion on the grounds that successful persuasion frequently uses emotional appeals. It does so successfully only when people have no other basis for judg-

ment. In an age of specialization, we have developed more and more knowledge as a society, but the amount of knowledge that is available to any one individual has beome increasingly limited. This has the effect of preventing the average citizen from fully participating in the decisions required in the society. In an agrarian society of 100 years ago, each citizen had much in common with all other citizens. Deciding where a road should be placed could be done by pooling the common knowledge (or common ignorance) of all the people within the area to be served by the road. Today, batteries of engineers, city planners, computers, and construction companies are required, and the input of the people in the area seems less and less needed.

I cannot offer any complete solutions to a problem that has always vexed democratic societies, and increasingly plagues the highly technological society we live in. A beginning might be to define a "core" area of knowledge that all citizens need. This core area might include information about the ways in which decision making occurs in a technological, democratic society, and about the role of communication in the decision making process.

3. Learn how to teach rationality. In later chapters, we will examine evidence that shows how people do not behave rationally or logically in many communication situations. The evidence seems overwhelming that we are not born as either logical or rational, but perhaps ways of teaching rational decision making can be found.

4. Keep an open society. Before World War II, the Japanese government wished to convince its citizens that Japan was being discriminated against by the Western Powers. The government succeeded to an amazing degree in uniting its population. Scientists suggested that one possible reason for the success was that the people were asked to turn in all short-wave radios for the war effort. Being an island nation, the populace was effectively shut off from the possibility of any contradictory messages being received. This example points to the necessity for

any society to remain open. When all points of view can be expressed, when all available information can be assessed by a citizenry, the probability increases that rational decisions can be made.

Our country has always vacillated between the pressures to keep an open society and those to close the society more and more. We pass open meeting laws, and the Freedom of Information Act. But as soon as we pass the law, others within the society argue that people do not need to know so much, that we may weaken ourselves by disclosing too much information. I must come down on the side of openness in society. I think it is required for rational decision making, and for the successful operation of persuasive communication.

5. Develop and protect the mass media within society. The population of the United States is growing, and will continue to grow for many years. The larger the population, the harder it is to communicate with all citizens of the country. Yet as the population grows, it will become more and more necessary that all citizens have the kinds of information needed for rational decision making. The mass media can be used primarily for entertainment, or they can be of major assistance in education and transmission of information. In this society, we have come down harder on the side of entertainment than on the side of education, and that is regretable. If we are to keep our society an open one, we must increase the ability of the mass media to reach all of the population with news, information, discussions, debate and arguments about the affairs of the nation. To push the media in that direction is a constant task.

These are some of the responsibilities that I see for all of us if we are to be able to use persuasion effectively—responsibilities for sources of communication, for receivers of persuasion, and for our society as a whole.

SUMMARY

Persuasion is a form of human interaction. It takes place when one individual desires some particular response from one or more other individuals and deliberately sets out to secure that response through the use of communication. It also takes place when two or more individuals agree to communicate cooperatively in an attempt to reach a consensus on which decisions and actions can be based. Persuasion has always been a tool used by societies to secure social changes, but we argue here that it has the potentiality of becoming the major tool for solving problems and arriving at a consensus for the pluralistic society in which we live.

In this chapter, we have defined persuasion, and placed it within a communication framework. We have noted some of the major factors that help determine the success or failure of persuasive communication situations. The nature of the anticipated effects on a receiver exposed to persuasion was discussed, and methods for judging those effects were noted. Finally, some suggestions for an ethics of persuasion and the responsibilities of communicators within our society were outlined.

FOOTNOTES

1. D. Cushman and G.R. Miller, "New Directions in Forensics: Two Useful Communication Constructs," *American Forensics Association Journal*, (In Press).
2. D. K. Berlo, *The Process of Communication*, (New York: Holt, Rinehart, and Winston, 1960), pp. 40–72.
3. G. Gerbner, "The Interaction Model: Perception and Communication," in J. Ball and F. Byrnes, eds., *Research, Principles and Practices in*

Visual Communicatio Research, Principles and Practices in Visual Communication, E. Lansing, Mich.: National Project in Agricultural Communication, 1960, pp. 4–15.

4. E. Schramm, "How Communication Works," in W. Schramm, ed., *The Process and Effects of Mass Communication*, (Urbana, Ill.: University of Illinois Press, 1954), pp. 3–26.
5. B. H. Westley and M. S. MacLean, Jr., "A Conceptual Model for Communication Research," *Journalism Quarterly*, vol. 34 (1957), pp. 31–38.
6. C. Shannon and W. Weaver, *The Mathematical Theory of Communication*, (Urbana, Ill.: University of Illinois Press, 1949), pp. 4–6.
7. *The Random House Dictionary of the English Language*, (New York: Random House, 1967), s.v. "persuasion."
8. K. Andersen, *Persuasion Theory and Practice*, (Boston, Allyn & Bacon, 1971), p. 6.
9. T. Scheidel, *Persuasive Speaking*, (Glenview, Ill.: Scott, Foresman and Co. 1967), p. 1.
10. Gerald R. Miller, Michigan State University, personal communication, 1978.
11. D. K. Berlo, pp. 63–70.
12. M. J. Rosenberg and C. I. Hovland, "Cognitive, Affective, and Behavioral Components of Attitudes," in C. I. Hovland and M. J. Rosenberg, eds., *Attitude. Organization and Change*, (New Haven, Conn.: Yale University Press, 1960), pp. 1–14.
13. For an example of a study which does report long term effects see: M. Rokeach, "Persuasion that Persists," *Psychology Today*, vol. 5, No. 4 (September 1971), pp. 68–92.
14. R. L. Johennsen, "The Emerging Concept of Communication as Dialogue," *Quarterly Journal of Speech*, 1971, vol. 57, pp. 373–82.
15. This responsibility is discussed in detail in H. W. Simons, *Persuasion: Understanding, Practice and Analysis* Reading, Mass: Addison-Wesley, 1976), pp. 35–38.

TWO

DEVELOPING ATTITUDES AND BELIEFS: LEARNING AND COGNITIVE CONSISTENCY

The model of persuasion we have advanced postulates that changes in attitudes and beliefs are necessary before changes in emotions, cognitions and behavior can occur. The fact that we emphasize *changes* in attitudes and beliefs suggests that all of the parties to persuasive communication situations already have a set of attitudes or a series of beliefs even before they are exposed to persuasive messages. How do people obtain the attitudes they have? What kinds of beliefs do people have? Can we improve our understanding of persuasion by finding out how attitudes and beliefs are developed? This chapter looks carefully at these questions, and concludes that both learning and cognitive consistency are processes directly related to the development of attitudes and beliefs.

Attitudes are the feelings of liking and disliking we have for things in the world around us. Thus you may like dogs, chocolate cake, flowers, the Republican Party, your communication professor, and your mother. In similar fashion, you may dislike snakes, dormitory food, rainy days, football games, and your high school principal, and you may be neutral, toward tennis matches, labor unions, short hair, broccoli, the salesman at the clothing store, and foreign cars.

Some attitudes are held with deep intensity. We may be attracted to a mother, a boyfriend, or a wife with such intensity that all else pales by comparison. We will do anything to be with these people, and would believe anything they say. At the other end of the spectrum, we may dislike spiders so much that we get physically ill at the very sight of a spider. Other attitudes are held more lightly. We may enjoy seeing Robert Redford on television, but it doesn't ruin our day if we happen to miss a particular show. We like chicken, but if beef shows up on the menu, we will eat that as well.

The examples we have used suggest that not everyone has the same attitudes. One person doesn't dislike insects, while another is very unhappy at any contact with any insect. One person loves steak, while the next person is a vegetarian. These individuals have had different sets of experiences. Individuals who can't stand the sight of spiders may have seen their mother recoiling from a spider when they were young, or had a spider bite, and heard their father talking about the "ugly little creatures." The individual who does not mind spiders may not have had the same kind of experiences. It is through the experiences of life that we eventually develop the attitudes and beliefs we hold.

A single experience is all it takes for attitudes to begin to form, but we would expect those attitudes to be weakly held unless the experience was a very powerful one. A child bitten at an early age by a large dog might need only one such experience to develop highly negative attitudes towards dogs, but most of the attitudes we hold intensely have been formed after many experiences. Attitudes are formed not only as the result of direct encounters with the world around us, but also through the indirect impressions we receive from others talking or writing about events. The child may never have seen a ghost, but may have very real attitudes about ghosts after hearing older brothers and sisters talk about them. Once we have formed our basic set of attitudes, we use the attitudes as a kind of filter that determines how new attitudes are going to be formed. This set of attitudes we call a *frame of reference*, and it helps govern our behavior.

The development of a set of reference frames is based on both genetic and environmental factors. The child is not born as a *tabula rasa*, a clean slate. Certain characteristics that influence the development of an individual's attitudes and eventual reference frames include eyesight, hearing, height, basic intelligence

level, and energy level. Later experiences certainly modify some of these inherited characteristics, but they do help play a role in developing frames of reference.

Despite the presence of genetic factors, environmental factors play the major role in the development of attitudes. Children are engaged in gathering information about the world from the minute they are born. They receive information about the world from their parents, brothers and sisters, aunts and uncles, friends, neighbors, and teachers. Children learn about trees, frogs, dogs, cats and cars. They are given information about their community, their church, and their country. They learn about democracy and communism. They have pleasant and unpleasant experiences. A child learns to avoid the neighborhood bully, and to be attracted to a nice kid down the block. Each time the child has an experience, interacts with the world, or learns something, the frame of reference is further developed.

The information we gather is not perceived as a "blooming, buzzing, confusion." Our brain operates in such a way that the information we receive is placed into structures of related information. We develop structures about nature, people, education, churches, and governments. By the time we are adults, these structures have become extremely complex. When the child has a new experience, the experience may cause a sweeping change in behavior because a new frame of reference has been started by the experience. On the other hand, when an adult has a new experience, it seldom causes a major change in behavior. Rather, the new experience is simply added to an already existing set of attitudes, and only minimal change may result.

Reference frames are not composed of simple attitudes alone. The *beliefs* we hold are also part of the reference frames we have. Following Rokeach,[1] we view beliefs as simple propositions or statements that can be preceded by the phrase, "I believe that. . . ." All of us have many different beliefs. For example, I believe that the world is round, that world population control is necessary, that Michigan State University is a wonderful place to teach, that blacks and women are discriminated against in our society, that students should not cheat on exams, and that man will someday reach the stars. Whenever individuals profess to see some relationship between two events or objects or people, or between some event and a characteristic of the event, we say that they hold a *belief*. In the beliefs just cited, just as in our attitudes, there seems to be considerable variety. The belief that the world is round is a different type of belief from the belief that man will reach the stars. How can we distinguish between these two beliefs?

We can distinguish between beliefs in two ways. First, we can attempt to see whether different beliefs can be classified with respect to what they tell us about the world around us. Thus, my belief that the world is round is a *descriptive* belief statement. It makes a statement about the world, and could be examined as to its truth or falsity. My belief that Michigan State is a wonderful place to work is an *evaluative* belief. It says something about what I think is good or bad. And my belief that students should not cheat on exams is a *prescriptive* belief. It makes a statement about what I think should happen, or about what I think people should do.

A second way of classifying beliefs is in terms of how difficult a belief would be to change through the use of a persuasive message. For example, I can think of no arguments or evidence that would make me change my mind about my belief that the world is round, yet an individual source who knows mathematics and physics might be able to put together an argument that would make me modify my belief that man *will* someday reach the stars to a belief that it *is improbable* that man will ever reach the stars. The first belief, however, is so firmly a portion of my belief structure, was acquired so early in life, and is taken so much for granted that nothing is going to disturb it. Both Rokeach[2] and Bem[3] suggest that one of the organizing features of beliefs is a "central-peripheral" dimension.

Figure 2.1 illustrates this view of an individual's belief structure. Highly *central* beliefs, such as: "The world is round;" "Water is heavier than air;" and "I believe what my eyes see;" form the core of any individual's belief structure. We acquire our most central or "primitive" beliefs very early in life. Furthermore, we continue to strengthen these beliefs as we go through life, and continuously validate them from our experiences.

Rokeach suggests that there are two types of central beliefs. For one type, there is complete agreement within the society that the belief is correct. The belief that "rocks fall to the ground when dropped" is an example of a primitive belief that everyone within a society would agree upon. The other type of highly central belief is illustrated by expressions such as: "I believe in God;" "Black cats bring bad luck;" and "I am basically a nice person." These are beliefs that are held very strongly by individuals, but there may not be consensus among members of a society as to the validity of these beliefs.

A second layer of beliefs illustrated in Figure 2.1 is comprised of those connected with *authority*. Children learn that they can trust some individuals and not others. They learn to place

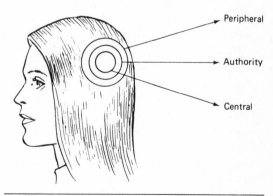

Figure 2.1 Belief System

faith in what their parents and teachers tell them. They learn that the President of the United States ought to be believed, but that Russian and Chinese leaders are less trustworthy. Our beliefs about authorities lead us to categorize others either as *positive* or *negative* authorities. We place faith in the statements of positive authorities, and tend to disbelieve what negative authorities tell us.

Our beliefs about authority are firmly held. They do shift slowly over time, but for an adult, changing such beliefs is difficult. Authority beliefs are less firmly held than central beliefs, but they help govern to whom we will listen and whom we will respect.

Finally, we can talk about *peripheral* beliefs. Beliefs such as: "Long hair is attractive on a man;" or "Harvard is the best university in the United States;" or "Steak is best when it is cooked rare;" or "CBS has the best news programs on television;" are examples of peripheral beliefs. Peripheral beliefs can be divided into two categories. Some of our peripheral beliefs are derived from central, more primitive beliefs. Thus, the individual who holds that abortion is wrong may have arrived at that belief from a more central belief that all human life is sacred. On the other hand, many peripheral beliefs do not seem to be based directly on more central beliefs. They seem to arise from an immediate set of experiences. My belief that CBS has the best news programs may be simply a matter of taste, and not based on any other beliefs.

The frames of reference we build up are composed of the attitudes we have and the beliefs we have. Because each of us has different sets of experiences, (even identical twins) each of us has frames of reference at least slightly different from the frames of every other person. If there were absolutely no predictability in the way reference frames are developed and organized, the persuasive communicator would have a very difficult time in finding appropriate messages. Attitudes and beliefs do not develop in completely random fashion, however,

and the reference frames that are eventually formed from our attitudes and beliefs can also be used to make predictions about the effects of persuasion. Beliefs are formed along a central-peripheral set of dimensions, and this organization allows us to make predictions about the probable effects of persuasive messages.

First, *the more central the belief, the more resistant will individuals be to changes in the belief*. If your persuasive goal demands that the receiver change a central belief, it is very unlikely that success will come easily or come at all. The difficulty of changing a primitive belief through persuasion is greatly magnified if the belief is one that has consensus within the society. Imagine, if you will, trying to get someone to change a belief that "the world is round." Changing a central belief that does not have consensus within the society is difficult, but it may be somewhat easier for the communicator. For example, few people change their belief in the existence of God as a result of a persuasive message. These central beliefs are so deeply ingrained into our reference frames that little can be done to change them. Perhaps better advice to the persuasive communicator is that these central beliefs can frequently be used as supporting arguments in messages advocating change in other beliefs. Wars have been justified many times by the argument that "God wants it."

Beliefs based on authority are also resistant to change, but not to the extent that central beliefs are. The individual who believes through long experience that "policemen are always trustworthy," may have that belief weakened if an example of "police brutality" is witnessed. The life-long Republican sometimes does change parties as a result of messages attacking the leaders of the party.

Peripheral beliefs are subject to change. Individuals can change their beliefs about hair styles, about the importance or lack of importance of environmental pollution, about abortion reform, about increased taxes, and about the quality of universities. These beliefs are constantly undergoing shifts and changes as a result of the persuasive messages that are encountered by the receiver. It is with the peripheral belief system that the persuasive communicator will have the best success.

The second major implication of our analysis of belief structures is that *those beliefs that are derived from central beliefs are more resistant to change than those beliefs that exist only as peripheral beliefs.* We have suggested that many peripheral beliefs are derived from more primitive beliefs. In a study conducted in 1953, I found that students tended to believe that the President of the United States was a most trustworthy figure, regardless of who was president.[4] When the President was quoted as favoring compulsory arbitration of labor disputes to one audience, there was more attitude change than when a labor leader was quoted as favoring compulsory arbitration. Rokeach[5] found that primitive-based beliefs are more resistant than beliefs based on authority, and authority-based beliefs are in turn more resistant than those entirely peripheral in nature.

This principle holds another implication for persuasion. When a belief held by an individual rests on a more central belief, it may be necessary to change the more central belief before it is possible to change the peripheral belief. Abortion reform is a good example. In order to change the stand of an individual who is opposed to legalized abortion, it may be necessary to change that individual's attitude toward the value placed on human life. Thus, a message directed only toward the peripheral belief may not succeed unless it is accompanied by messages directed toward the more central beliefs that are the foundation of the receiver's beliefs.

The third implication for persuasion to be drawn from our analysis is that *the more central the belief which is changed, the more widespread will be the changes in the remainder of the individual's belief structure.* The central beliefs we hold are connected to many peripheral beliefs. If I believe in God, I may also believe in the Bible as an authority, in ministers as mediators between God and myself, in tax exemption for churches, in the desirability of using public funds for church-supported schools, and in the legality of prayer in the public schools. Each of these beliefs may have been derived from the central belief in God. Now what might happen if the individual should change the belief about the existence of God? Imagine that something traumatic happens to the individual, a sudden death of a wife or child. If that event results in the individual's changing a central belief, we might expect the individual to also change the peripheral beliefs which derive from the primitive belief.

This third principle suggests that the persuasive communicator may find that a desired change will also produce unexpected changes in other beliefs. It is frequently impossible to predict whether this secondary change will be favorable or unfavorable to the communicator's cause. The communicator who is able to effect a change in a receiver's beliefs about the value of compulsory government health insurance, may find that the receiver has also changed beliefs about the role of physicians in the health care system.

Our beliefs are being formed from the first time we interact with the world around us. Like attitudes, the beliefs we develop become part of our frames of reference. Some beliefs are supported by extensive interaction with the world around us. Others are arrived at after a single experience. In similar fashion, attitudes and beliefs are built up into reference frames that may be very extensive and govern many of the everyday actions of a receiver, or may be sketchy, incomplete, and brought into play only on rare occasions. People do not discard the reference frames they have when an attitude or a belief has been changed. Rather, they simply adapt the changed attitudes or beliefs to the already existing reference frames in such a way as to cause minimal disturbance to the frame of reference.

The fact that individuals do not discard the frames of reference they have acquired but simply adapt those frames makes sweeping persuasive changes difficult to obtain. Consider racial prejudice. If an individual believes that members of a particular minority group are dirty, lazy, stupid, and troublesome, meeting someone from that reference group who is not dirty, lazy, stupid, and troublesome will not result in drastic changes of the original frame of reference. The new information will be assimilated into the original frame, but the belief pattern might now be: "Members of that minority group are dirty, lazy, stupid, and troublesome, except for Joe Jones, who is almost like me." Many encounters with many Joe Joneses are necessary to produce basic changes in the frame of reference used to evaluate messages about a given minority group.

The difficulties that are encountered in persuasive situations can be partially assessed by looking at the nature of the relationship between a reference frame and a message containing new information. Several situations are possible:

1. If the individual's frame of reference is extensive and relatively complete, new information that is contrary to that frame will produce few noticeable changes in behavior. In fact, it may seem as though the material is not being perceived at all. In such a situation, the communicator either has to be able to bring a new frame of reference into play or has to continue communicating until enough information has been added to force changes in the receiver's attitude structure.

2. If a frame of reference is extensive and relatively complete, new information that is not contrary to the frame serves to strengthen the frame. For example, if a man is a firm believer in safety measures to protect lives in the home and factory, he is also likely to be an individual who will be easily persuaded that seat belts save lives.

3. If an individual's frame of reference is sketchy and still incomplete, new information contrary to the frame serves further to increase the entropy, or level of uncertainty that the individual holds towards the message. The new information will not normally result in the abandonment of an incomplete frame but will make less likely the application of the frame as a decision-making tool in future situations. For example, most people in the United States do not have very much information about the People's Republic of China. What they do have is generally somewhat negative. When President Nixon announced in 1971 that he was going to visit China, there was no immediate swing in attitude favoring China. Rather, there seemed to be more of a "wait and see" attitude, which persisted until more information had been obtained by the visit.

4. If a frame of reference is sketchy and incomplete, new information that is not contrary to the frame serves to decrease entropy or uncertainty. The frame of reference, when completed by new information, will become a major decision-making tool for the receiver. For example, most people in the United States have developed a reference frame which suggests that they are against pollution. These reference frames, however, are not very well developed. People do not have specific technical information about the subject. When they encounter a stream filled with empty beer cans, or a speaker who tells them how many pollutants they breathe in every minute, that information may serve to strengthen their reference frame so that they view further information about pollution with heightened awareness.

Individuals do not view life through a single reference frame. Each of us has developed many different reference frames, covering different subjects and parts of our environment. What mechanisms govern the way in which a reference frame will be developed? We have suggested that the attitudes and beliefs that are part of an individual's reference frame have developed as a result of experience, and we ought to expect differences. Beyond the varying sets of experiences people have, however, there are some psychological principles that help govern the development and utilization of different reference frames. Two such mechanisms, *learning* and *cognitive consistency*, seem of major importance in helping determine just how attitudes and beliefs will be developed, and thus the nature of the frame of reference that will result.

LEARNING

Most people have a common understanding of what is meant by the term "learning." Everyone agrees that children have to *learn* how to walk, read a book, ride a bicycle, drive a car, and eat with a knife and fork. This common-sense definition can be extended to a general definition of learning as *the process by which some aspect of human behavior is acquired or changed through an individual's encounter with events in the environment*.

Early, "one-way" views of persuasion paid relatively little attention to learning as a vital part of the persuasive process. The assumption was made that the individual had already learned and simply was reacting to whatever message was being presented by a source. An interactional, "two-way" view of communication cannot ignore learning. If you are trying to convince a college advisor to let you bypass one of the basic courses in order to let you enroll for a more advanced course, it will probably be necessary to educate the advisor as to your own background and the experiences you have had that would allow you to skip the basic course. The advisor, on the other hand, may have to tell you some things you didn't know about the materials in the basic course that will be required in order to perform satisfactorily in the advanced course. To successfully engage in interactional persuasion, all parties must frequently engage in communication designed to improve understanding, that is, designed to have all parties to the situation *learn*.

Over the years that psychologists have been interested in the process of learning, many elaborate theories of learning have been developed and tested. We cannot in this volume, discuss any of the major theories in detail. Rather, we shall attempt to isolate and discuss those theories that seem most applicable to persuasive communication.

Basic to all theories of learning is the assumption that there is an explainable or predictable relationship between *stimuli* and *responses*. A "stimulus" can be defined as any event which can be perceived by the organism. Thus, in a persuasive communication situation, the message serves as a stimulus. The source serves as another stimulus, as does the physical setting for the situation. A "response" can be defined as anything which the receiver does as a result of perceiving a stimulus. Thus the original category scheme we defined in Chapter 1 of changes in affect, cognition, and behavior covers the kinds of responses which we might be interested in. We should note again that attitude changes are needed before any of the other kinds of change might be expected to take place.

The persuasive communicator normally wants to elicit a specific response from a receiver or group of receivers. The communicator can present a message and then wait passively until a receiver makes an appropriate response. Or the source can present a message under such conditions as to lead the receiver to an appropriate response. These two different approaches have been termed *instrumental* learning and *conditioned* learning. The distinction between the two is important to the remainder of our discussion, and further elaboration is in order:

1. In *instrumental* (also referred to as "operant") learning situations, a stimulus is presented to an organism, and when the correct or desired response has been made, some reinforcement or reward is given in order to either fix or strengthen the response. In instrumental learning situations, the theory suggests that if the organism makes several incorrect responses that

are not rewarded and then makes a correct response that is rewarded, the probability is increased that the organism will repeat the correct response if the same stimulus is presented.

2. In *conditioned* learning situations, a stimulus that has already been tied by the organism to a rewarding response is presented to the organism along with an unfamiliar stimulus. After a number of trials, the new stimulus should elicit the same response as the original stimulus. This is the famous "Pavlov's dog" situation, where it is established that the presentation of food elicits salivation from the dog. Then the food is presented along with a bell, and after a number of trials, ringing the bell alone will elicit a salivation response from the dog.

Persuasive communication makes use of both types of learning situations illustrated in Figure 2.2. A fund-raising agency sends several letters urging that an individual donate money to some charity. If the individual eventually does send a contribution, the fund raisers immediately send a letter of thanks, and perhaps a small token of appreciation such as a pin or a ball point pen. This is an example of instrumental learning, and the follow-up letter and gift are designed to be the reinforcing agent. Note that the receiver does not receive a letter of thanks or a gift until *after* making a donation. Note also that the re-

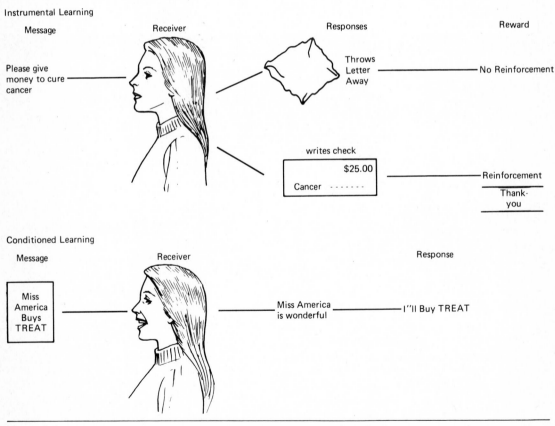

Figure 2.2

ceiver would not receive any reinforcement if a donation were made to some other charity. It is only when the response made is exactly the one desired by the source that any reward is given.

Conditioning principles are also frequently used by persuasive communicators. The advertiser knows that men are attracted to pictures of pretty girls, and that children like toys. So the advertiser presents a picture of his product being shown next to a pretty girl in a magazine, or shows a breakfast food that has a small toy in the box on a children's television program. The assumption is that the product will be seen as tied to a stimulus that is already rewarding to the receiver, and the sale of the item will thus be enhanced.

Learning theories are concerned with the connections between responses and specifiable stimuli. Some theories are concerned with an analysis of response probabilities and pay minimal attention to the cognitive state of the individual organism making the response. Such theories have been labeled stimulus-response (S-R) learning theories. Other theorists insist that any analysis of response probabilities must be based on an analysis of the internal state of the individual organism, as well as on an analysis of the stimuli and responses present in a given situation. Such theories have been called stimulus-organism-response (S-O-R) theories. The theoretic orientation of this book leans toward the latter type of theories, and our presentation owes much to the early work of Clark Hull[6] and Charles Osgood.[7]

Individuals differ in the ways in which they learn any given response, and differ in the ways in which they perceive any given stimulus. One person may perceive a stimulus and quickly assimilate it into an already existing frame of reference. Another person may not assimilate it as rapidly, and the stimulus will need to be repeated several times before it is firmly built into a frame of reference. Thus the persuasive communicator must be aware that the probability of a particular response being learned, and thus becoming part of an individual's frame of

reference, will vary widely among the audience members. Three principles help explain some of the different responses made by receivers exposed to exactly the same message.

1. *Individuals differ in their ability to respond.* This principle implies that when two people receive the same message, their responses may be different simply because they differ in their ability to respond. Imagine a message urging people to take a wonderful ten day vacation to England. Even though many people may wish to take the trip, it is likely that only a few would have the money. Attitudes and beliefs may be changed for all, but the final behaviors will be different.

A second implication is that repetition of the message may be helpful. Because people differ in their ability to respond, one person may understand the message after a single repetition, while another may require two or three repetions before being able to understand the message. We should caution, however, that simple repetition is maximally effective after only a few repetitions. Repeating a message many, many times may not strengthen the responses of those people who saw or heard the message the first few times, and may even alienate receivers.

The principle that people differ in their ability to respond should be an obvious one, yet communicators seem to frequently forget it. How many times has someone remarked, "I've told them and told them, but they never learn."? All of us know that people have different abilities, that children cannot do what adults can, that attention spans differ, and that not everyone can be an Olympic champion. Yet in communicating, we frequently forget that differences in ability may make one receiver view a message quite differently from another.

Imagine attempting to talk to a landowner about the necessity of cleaning up a river because of a high bacteria count. If the landowner has had little formal education, has never studied bacteria, and is seriously worried about the new property assessment that will be required, successful persuasion will be extremely difficult. Messages will have to be tailored to the landowner's ability to understand.

2. *Individuals differ in their readiness to respond.* This principle states that regardless of our intelligence, ability, or capacity, we are more likely to respond at one time than another. Some people just cannot operate at full efficiency early in the morning. Others have a period immediately after lunch or dinner when they are not very attentive to any messages. In other cases, people become readier to respond when they perceive a need for something. Imagine two men sitting in the living room watching a television advertisement for a new car. One person has a four year old car, while the other man bought a new car just three months ago. The readiness principle would predict that, other things being equal, the individual with a four year old car is readier to respond favorably to the advertisement than the man with the almost new automobile.

The persuasive communicator will have difficulty in determining when an individual is likely to be ready to respond to any particular message. There are some questions, however, that may help in determining the optimum time to present a message. Is the receiver paying attention? Are the physical surroundings such that they will not detract from the communicator's message? Has there been any attempt at "preteaching"? The term "preteaching" refers to the messages that may be sent ahead of time to give the receiver the necessary background for an understanding of the source's message. People will always differ in their readiness to respond, but if we can answer "yes" to these questions, we make the task of the persuasive communicator just a bit easier.

3. *Individuals differ in their motivation to respond.* If a man locks you in a room for two days with no food and then sends a message offering to feed you on the condition that you marry his daughter, your agreement to do so may be said to be motivated by hunger. There are a number of *motives* or *drives* that help to determine the nature of a response made or the frame of reference brought into play when a message is attended to. Some of these drives are *biologically* determined, such as hunger, thirst, pain avoidance, and sex. Other motives are *learned* such as preservation of health, loyalty to country, duty, competition, gregariousness, and desire for money. Learning is facilitated when the receiver is made to feel that a message is appealing to a particular motive.

In animals other than man, biological motives seem to be the strongest motives affecting behavior. With human beings, however, biological motives are less important. The persuasive communicator is seldom in a position where the audience can be deprived of food or water for two days prior to the speech.

Why, then, are biological motives important if we can seldom use them directly in persuasion? The answer lies in what people have *learned* about biological motives. People respond to messages about food even when they are not hungry, because they have learned that food is important to them. A picture of a beautiful steak can cause a man to salivate, even though his last meal was an hour ago. The television viewer is impressed by an advertisement for a particular beer, not because the viewer is thirsty at the time, but because the viewer has learned to react positively to thirst situations and to appreciate different types of drive-reducing stimuli. We should note, however, that while every individual viewing a beautiful picture of a steak may be expected to react in some fashion, those receivers that are actually hungry will be likely to respond more intensely than those who are not hungry. For persuasive communication, the utilization of biological motives is based largely on the ways that people have learned to react to stimuli appealing to those motives.

Our responses to persuasive communication are governed far more by learned or social motives than by biological motives. The experiences we have as members of a family, a school system, a nation and a culture provide all of us with motives that become extremely important to the ways in which persuasive communication is viewed. For example, in one family, competition in sports and family games may be strongly emphasized. We might expect that children from that family would have stronger motivation to competition than would children from a family where cooperation was stressed and not competition.

Responses to learned motives differ in strength with differences in the receivers and with differences in the individual motive. In our society, the motive to affiliate is a strong one for many people. A message urging people to join a particular group and experience the fellowship of the group may be highly success-ful, while a similar message given in another culture would have little motivational effect. A person who has acquired a strong motive to compete may be attracted by a message promising that the receiver can be "first" in some skill, activity or event. For other receivers, an appeal to loyalty, or friendship, or cooperation may prove to be a stronger motive.

People do differ in their motivation to respond. To be successful in effecting a change in the frames of reference of various individuals, the communicator must use different appeals, with different strengths, and with various repetitions.

The three principles discussed above, different ability to respond, different readiness to respond, and different motivation to respond, are principles governing all learning situations. They help in explaining how frames of reference are developed, as well as helping predict the nature of the responses that receivers are likely to make in persuasive communication situations. When the persuasive communicator knows exactly what responses are desired from a receiver, learning theorists suggest three principles to assist in the task.

4. *Reinforcement is helpful in establishing response.* This is the principle of reward and punishment that has already been discussed briefly in describing instrumental learning. The little girl who is given a cookie after tying her shoes correctly is more likely to tie them correctly in the future. The man who is encouraged to vote in favor of opening his neighborhood to minority groups is more likely to do so if he can be shown that there are some advantages to doing so. The reinforcement principle cannot be stressed too strongly. Many scientists believe that learning is *never* fixed or completed until some reinforcement has been given.

People do not all react to the same reward. For one individual, praise given after completion of a desired response is sufficient to insure future repetition of the behavior. For another, a direct monetary reward may be necessary. A third person may have learned the art of self-reward after a satisfactorily completed task, and no extrinsic reward is necessary.

Many of the problems the persuasive speaker today is concerned about are difficult to link to appropriate rewards. What are the rewards for reducing racism? For controlling pollution? For legalizing marijuana? For legalizing abortion? Look at the case for legalizing marijuana. Imagine that you are trying to convince the city council to legalize pot. What are the reinforcements you can offer? If none can be found appropriate to your audience, the chances of their responding favorably are much lower.

Individuals differ in the number of times they need reinforcement in order to continue to maintain a desired response. For some, every two or three times may be sufficient; for others, every twenty times may be enough. The frequency with which reinforcement is offered will remain one of the crucial decisions that must be made.

Reinforcement may be either positive or negative. A positive reinforcement is anything that increases the probability of a desired response when it is added to the learning situation. A negative reinforcement is anything that increases the probability of a desired response when it is removed from the learning situation. In laboratory situations, it is easy to provide both positive and negative reinforcers. Thus one can reward the rat that ran the maze correctly by giving food as a positive reinforcement, and one can turn off a bright, disturbing light in the cage as a negative reinforcer when the rat performs appropriately. In real life situations, negative rewards are more difficult to apply. The teacher can praise the student who learns the correct lesson, but what kind of things can the teacher remove from the situation as a negative reward? What can one do to the person who refuses to vote for needed school taxes? Finding a negative reinforcer for this situation is difficult. Perhaps the best that can be done is to say, "You'll be sorry when we have to close the schools, and you have the kids home all day." The history of the use of this statement and similar negative rewards is not very encouraging. Both positive and negative reinforcements have an effect on learning, but positive reinforcement seems to produce better results than negative reinforcement in most of the persuasive communication situations that have been studied. There are some theoretical questions about the exact role of reward and punishment in learning, but for persuasion, the social byproducts of learning under positive reinforcement situations seem to be more favorable than under negative reinforcement conditions.[8]

How can the persuasive communicator insure that reinforcement will be used correctly to secure the desired response? Imagine that Joe Salesman wants Mr. Smith to buy a new product—a different dandruff shampoo. The buying responses that Mr. Smith can make to the product are: (a) to buy the product; (b) to buy a competing product; or (c) not to buy any such product. Joe Salesman first has the problem of entering Mr. Smith's frame of reference in such a way as to attract his attention to *any* message he presents. If this is done successfully, Joe Salesman can then suggest that his product is the best on the market. He can suggest that his competitors' products will not be long-lasting and will not give Mr. Smith complete protection from dandruff. He can suggest that the shampoo also leaves the hair looking wonderful, and thus that Mr. Smith is more likely to be attractive to the people he associates with. He can emphasize the low cost of the shampoo. Let us assume that Mr. Smith eventually does buy the product. If Mr. Smith finds that using the shampoo does have some of the benefits claimed by Joe Salesman, the probability is increased that he will continue using it until a message for a presumably better product is encountered. If Mr. Smith does not find the rewards that Joe Salesman claimed, he will either begin using a competing shampoo or will buy none at all. Joe Salesman, then, like all persuasive communicators, has two tasks. He must select reinforcements to mention in the message that will attract the receiver's attention and reinforcements to help insure that the receiver will take the desired action. The selection of appropriate rewards is one of the most important, and one of the most difficult tasks with which the persuasive communicator is faced.

Reinforcement, then, is important in insuring that a particular stimulus will be assimilated into a frame of reference by a receiver and in fixing desired responses.

5. *In learning, active participation is better than passive participation.* This principle is useful whether you are engaged in a traditional persuasive campaign, or are engaged in mutual persuasive attempts with another individual. Billy Graham does not merely *ask* people to make a "decision for Christ." He asks people to rise from their seats and go to the front of the room. The active participation of an individual in the learning process facilitates the response desired.

This principle must be underscored. Many contemporary campaigns, worthy of great support, have failed because the participants in persuasion were given nothing to do. We argue with a friend, "Pollution is bad. We must all reduce pollution." We say, "Abortions are necessary if we are to control population growth." Then we stop communicating, assuming that because we have made a short speech, we have done our job. The message, however, may not have been assimilated into a frame of reference, nor even responded to, because we had failed to tell the receiver exactly what *he* or *she* could do to stop pollution, or achieve abortion reform.

This principle seems obvious if you think about trying to teach a child to ride a bicycle, ice-skate, or play golf. Imagine trying to learn any of these skills merely by reading a book on the subject. Yet many of today's communicators expect an audience to change health habits, improve schools, or improve race relations with no participation other than listening. The great tax revolts of the past few years, starting with the passage of Proposition 13 in California in 1978, are an example of the great degree of motivation that people have to participate in events. Many social scientists argue that large sections of the population are disenchanted with government and voted for Proposition 13 because they felt they personally were not being asked to participate in the political process. Obtaining active participation in a project is perhaps the best method of facilitating the development of favorable responses toward a topic.

6. *Meaningful responses are learned more easily than meaningless ones.* This is another principle that seems obvious, but examples exist to show that communicators sometimes forget to make their demands meaningful to the receiver. In 1966, Medicare became part of the American scene. Originally, everyone over the age of sixty five who signed up for the program by March 31, 1966, was to be covered under the program. Those who did not sign up by that time would have to wait more than two years. Many people signed up, but many others did

not. The main emphasis in the messages sent out by the government was that people sign up by a particular date. Relatively little attention was given in the many messages to telling receivers just *what* Medicare would do for them. For many receivers, this was probably a meaningless message. They did not possess any frame of reference the "signing up" message could be referred to. Eventually, the deadline had to be extended, and the officials concerned began directing attention to the reasons why people should sign up, thus finally tying Medicare to the original message.

It should be noted that meaningfulness is a concept much like reinforcement. It must be defined in terms of the receiver of a message, not in terms of what the source thinks is meaningful. For example, to one individual, "tax reform" may mean eliminating the property tax in favor of an income tax. To another, however, the same "tax reform" may mean abolishing all taxes. Learning is better accomplished when the materials the persuasive communicator wants learned are made meaningful to the receiver.

The three principles discussed above are related to the initial development of frames of reference, as well as to the initial learning of a particular response. The persuasive communicator, however, is also interested in the long-range effects of messages. Joe Salesman wants Mr. Smith to buy the product the first time in order to try it. But Joe isn't a very good salesman if he stops with messages advocating a single purchase. Joe Salesman should be interested in responses becoming *habitual* for the receiver, and frames of reference becoming strengthened so that they are consistently used by the receiver. For Joe Salesman to be completely successful, Mr. Smith should reach for the same brand of shampoo every time. Habits are developed over a period of time, with repeated stimuli being presented, and the correct responses being rewarded. A graph of the way a habit is formed might look like the one in Figure 2.3. The persuasive communicator who is

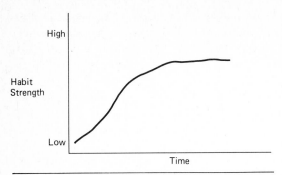

Figure 2.3 The Formation of Habits

interested in the development of habitual responses will find some principles available.

7. *As the number of rewarded repetitions of the response increases, the probability that the response will be made increases.* Many persuasive messages and campaigns have an immediate and apparently successful conclusion. People do become stirred up about racism in their community. People do call on their city officials for better pollution controls. As time passes, however, the response to repeated messages lessens and eventually disappears or becomes attached to another stimulus. Either *extinction* of the original stimulus-response relationship has taken place because the individual no longer finds it satisfying, or a *transfer* of the response from one stimulus to another has occurred.

Rather constant vigilance is needed to avoid extinction or transfer effects. Students at American colleges and universities have recently been given more say in the decision-making bodies of the institutions. If these privileges are not constantly exercised, they will inevitably be lost.

8. *The time interval between response and reward must be kept short for effective building of habit patterns.* When there is a long delay between the time a desired response is made to a particular stimulus and the time the receiver perceives the reinforcement to the response, the probability that the response will be repeated is lowered. If the time interval is long, other responses will have occurred more recently, and the reinforcement is likely to be transferred to a more recent stimulus. If the stimulus is intended to affect a particular frame of reference, but the reward is given when another frame of reference has been brought into play, the original frame will fail to be strengthened.

When children are very young, the effects of applying this principle are easy to see. The child who is rewarded at suppertime with a piece of candy for correctly tying a pair of shoes in the morning is not likely to connect the two events. The reward should have been given immediately after the child tied the shoes correctly if it was to have maximum effect. As adults, we are more able to engage in delayed gratification, the ability to wait for our rewards. Every student attending college has shown an ability to delay some rewards, that is, students are willing to train for a number of years rather than enter the work place immediately. Even as adults, even though delayed gratification *can* be successfully used in persuasive messages, habit strength is increased if the reward or reinforcement can be tied immediately to the sitmulus.

9. *Habit formation is facilitated when stimuli are presented in isolation.* The persuasive communicator who has to compete for space in the newspaper or has to sandwich the message in between many other messages on the radio will have a more difficult time in securing desirable responses than if able to present the message in the absence of other messages. We are all faced every day with many, many competing messages. The television set, the demands of parents, wives, husbands, roommates, employers, the radio blaring in the next room, all compete for our attention. The chance of any persuasive message getting through is very low. If all of us could present our persuasive messages when there was nothing else competing for the receiver's attention, our task would be easy.

Since that is seldom possible, we must strive to eliminate as many sources of competing messages as possible, or make our message stand out above all others.

In interactional situations, this principle is even more important. If you and your roommate have a problem to settle, it is usually difficult to do so in the dining room or over the blare of a stereo set. If you would like to be able to borrow the car from your father, it may not be possible if you ask him when all your brothers and sisters are in the same room. One of the major reasons the Symbionese Liberation Army was able to convince Patty Hearst to "come over" to their side was that they eliminated all other sources of information, and effectively isolated her from all competing stimuli.

It may not always be possible to find a situation where all competing stimuli are absent. But unless isolation can be obtained, persuasion will be difficult, and results less certain.

10. *The complexity of the response desired affects the ease of habit formation.* It is much harder to make correct piano-playing habitual than to make correct shoe-tying habitual. It is much harder to obtain a change in attitude in favor of a complex set of zoning regulations than a change in favor of a bill to place a sign at the edge of the city welcoming strangers. In 1968, at Michigan State University, the Academic Council, composed of faculty members, passed a regulation declaring that students should sit on faculty decision-making bodies. This change was accepted without very much debate, but it took three full years before the operating legislation was finally passed by that same body. It was easy to declare in favor of increased student representation, but to get everyone to agree on the specifics of the complex measures designed to select the students was far more difficult.

Complexity has to be looked at in another way. In training a seal to play "America" on a set of horns, the trainer cannot expect to teach the animal the entire song, and then have the seal practice the entire song. The trainer first proceeds to break the song down into its individual notes. He rewards the seal with a piece of fish when it has played the first correct note. When the seal plays the first and second notes, it gets another piece of fish, and so on to the final stage when the animal finally can play the whole sequence of notes.[9]

Many tasks can be broken down into smaller units, with better results. The first stimulus, when assimilated, helps strengthen the frame of reference so that the second step will be received more favorably, and that step in turn facilitates the third step. Our mythical Joe Salesman might well be advised to design his messages in such a way that the first message merely tries to attract interest in the product, the second asks that the receiver adopt a favorable attitude toward the product, the third attempts to persuade the receiver to come into the store, the next message argues for a first purchase of the product, and the final set of messages is designed to make the buyer want to buy the product again and again. Joe Salesman, of course, has counterparts in many fields. The politician follows a similar path. Courtship and marriage patterns in the United States are designed in steps that look very much like the pattern followed by Joe Salesman, and some people have even argued that marriage failures can frequently be traced to a failure to follow a pattern similar to the one we have outlined.

When the response desired by a persuasive communicator is very complex, even receivers who respond favorably to the message will form habits far more slowly and with less stability than those individuals who respond to messages advocating simpler responses. Complex intentions on the part of the communicator are best broken down into simpler parts to facilitate the formation of reference frames, and the eventual formation of habitual responses.

11. *Individuals tend to generalize the responses they make.* Generalization is a common phe-

nomenon in learning situations. It can be illustrated easily by an example from animal learning. Imagine that a cat has been trained to come for food when a certain bell is rung. It is very likely that a bell slightly higher or slightly lower in tone will also produce the same response in the cat, but a bell which is much higher or lower will not produce the response. This is *stimulus generalization*, the making of the same response to slightly different stimuli. *Response generalization* is an analogous phenomenon in which slightly different responses are made to the same stimuli.

This principle explains many of the effects seen in persuasive communication. Political parties are highly dependent on the phenomenon of generalization for their very existence. The Democratic Party, for example, wants voters in the voting booth to identify any candidate under the Democratic Party banner as having the same characteristics as all other candidates under the same banner. The names of the candidates, that is, the stimuli, are different, but the response desired is the same. The amount of generalization that exists with respect to either of the two major political parties seems to have declined in recent years, and some analysts suggest that the importance of the parties themselves has also declined along with the lack of stimulus generalization that has occurred. A similar example can be seen in the efforts of many of the large multinational corporations to establish a single trademark. Corporations such as ITT, TransAmerica, and CitiBank have spent thousands of dollars attempting to identify and then publicize an appropriate trademark that is to be attached to all of their products. The intent is that favorable responses about one product will be transferred to any other product bearing the same label.

It is fortunate that we do generalize. If generalization did not occur, the speaker could elicit learned responses from a receiver only when exactly the same message was repeated. This is seldom possible. There is significant evidence that generalization effects can be strengthened or weakened by reinforcement. To establish a class of responses to the same stimulus (response generalization), the source must provide reinforcement for all of the responses that fit the intent of the communicator. To establish a single response to a class of stimuli (stimulus generalization), the source must insure that the single response is reinforced whenever it is made to any of the desired stimuli and that it is not reinforced for any other stimulus. Our brief description of this problem may make it sound simple. In fact, finding and applying appropriate reinforcements in any generalization situation is a difficult task for any advertiser or for any persuasive communicator.

Through selective reinforcement relatively wide ranges of either stimulus or response generalization can be made. Furthermore, through selective reinforcement the receiver can be made to respond to only a single, very narrow range of stimuli. This phenomenon is called *discrimination*, and again, it has an important place in persuasive communication. The advertiser who has to sell a particular brand of soap product is a good example. Grocery store shelves are lined with many soap products, all claiming to perform much the same function. The advertiser's task in such a situation is to insure that the buyer is reinforced not only for buying soap but also for buying one particular brand of soap. Sometimes the advertiser offers special prices. At other times coupons may be offered, but the attempts are to force the buyer to discriminate between products.

Generalization and discrimination are phenomena that occur in many persuasive communication situations. They can be changed, strengthened, or weakened by selective types of communication and selective reinforcement on the part of the source.

12. *Providing information about receiver performance leads to improved performance*. This principle is particularly important to the interactive view of persuasion that we have been

trying to develop. The acquisition of language and the ability of the individual to develop intrinsic rewards leads to an ability to use information about a performance to correct the performance for subsequent presentations. Thus, if we can systematically inform receivers about the quality of the responses being made, the information can be used to improve future responses.

Providing the receiver with information about a set of responses not only helps improve the receiver's responses, it also helps strengthen the frame of reference. The receiver may not have developed a highly structured frame of reference about the topic under discussion. Providing additional information helps accomplish this. Several months ago, an ecologist made a speech about pollution. He gained considerable support from his audience. They were "with him." Then he offered to take them on a walk through the city, where they were to show him what they had learned about pollution. As they walked, he asked people to help him identify some of the sources of environmental pollution in the area. They did so, and then he asked them to walk back over the same route with him. This time, he pointed out all the conditions they had missed. It was a dramatic performance, and when their own performance was corrected, the audience members were able to sharpen their appreciation of the problems he had originally pointed out. Rewards are important to successful learning, but human response can be improved if the individual can be told how to improve.

Before persuasion can be successful, people have to acquire a frame of reference which will let them attend to the message. The development of a reference frame depends upon the acquisition and assimilation of information. This is largely controlled by the process of learning. Once a reference frame has been developed, it can only be changed by the learning of new materials that force the person to make behavior changes. Whether we are concerned with persuasion in the traditional sense, or whether we are concerned with those interactional situations where mutual persuasion is taking place, learning, and the application of learning theory principles is important.

Our examination of the role of learning in persuasion is far from complete. We have mentioned only those principles that seem to have high relevance to persuasion. Furthermore, learning theories are not the only theories for explaining human behavior. Many theorists criticize learning theories for what they see as a very simplistic stimulus-response model. Critics argue that learning theories do not take into account psychological mechanisms within the individual that may *not* require reinforcement. In fact, we shall now examine a class of theories that suggests that people sometimes respond in ways that seem to be against their best interests. Regardless of the criticism to which learning theories have been exposed, all behavioral scientists agree that the role of reinforcement in determining response to new situations and new people is extremely important. There is also general agreement that the principles we have discussed are important in determining response to persuasive communication. The student wishing to learn even more about learning will find that the bibliography at the end of this book lists a number of sources pertaining to learning and learning theory and the role that learning plays in the development of responses.

COGNITIVE CONSISTENCY

One of the major charges against classical learning theories is that they fail to recognize the importance of the mediation activities the mind engages in between the time a stimulus is perceived and a response is given. There is a whole class of theories referred to as "cognitive" theories that see the mind as a vital mechanism which organizes the messages it receives into meaningful wholes. Cognitive theories argue that the brain does not simply respond to those stimuli that are reinforced while rejecting those stimuli that are not reinforced. Instead, the argument is made that the mind is constantly at work organizing the stimuli that are perceived into patterns.

Some of the most important cognitive theories have been termed "consistency theories." A person does not perceive the world as a series of completely unrelated stimuli. When a new event is recorded by the individual, the stimulus is processed within existing frames of reference. The trend of this processing is toward *minimizing the internal inconsistencies* among the items that form the frame of reference. Furthermore, the fact that we tend to form consistent reference frames means that our responses —emotions, cognitions, and actions—also tend tend to occur as consistent responses to other behavior. Because the pressure toward consistency seems to be important in shaping our reference frames as well as our responses, some elaboration of consistency theories as they apply to persuasive communication will be helpful to communicators and receivers.

Consistency theories were first propounded during the early 1940s, although the roots for such theories undoubtedly go back much further.[10] Since World War II, the various cognitive consistency theories have provided one of the most fruitful areas of study within communication and the behavioral sciences.

The term "cognitive consistency" is used in this book to cover a number of specific theories which we have tried to apply to different types of persuasive communication situations. Although the various consistency theories have unique aspects, all the theories are based on the common premise that inconsistency is somehow unpleasant or painful or distasteful, and that the tensions created by this unpleasant state will lead to attempts to reduce the tensions. Festinger refers to consonance and dissonance,[11] Osgood to congruity and incongruity,[12] Abelson and Rosenberg to consistency,[13] and Heider to balance and imbalance.[14] The psychological mechanism that is being studied appears to be much the same for all these researchers. We have, therefore, chosen to label the general psychological mechanism as *cognitive consistency*, while recognizing that there are differences between each theory.

The research literature on cognitive consistency theory is very extensive and would fill several volumes the size of this one. Rather than attempt to review the entire body of research literature, we have chosen to present examples of the major theories as they may be used to illustrate persuasive communication. It may appear to the reader from the examples we use that scholars are in complete agreement, since the examples tend to look so reasonable that no one could disagree with the example. That is not always the case. We should note that a number of scholars have reservations about how far consistency theories should be applied to human behavior.[15] Many of the early theorists we cite in this section felt that consistency theory could be applied to a broad range of human activities. Today, the trend seems to be to develop somewhat more limited theories, applicable to very carefully defined situations. Eagly and Himmelfarb suggest that one of the major reasons for the shift to more limited theories is because research could not support the generalizability of these theories to a very wide range of behavior.[16] These are valid criticisms, and the reader should keep them in mind when reading this section. We have chosen descriptive examples that are closely related to persuasive communication and in which the evidence does seem to support a consistency explanation. The theories certainly do not explain all communication behavior.

Talking with One Another

Perhaps the simplest of all communication situations is when Mr. A talks to Mr. B about some object or concept, which we can call X. In a persuasive communication situation, imagine President Blue of Imaginary University talking to Joe Cool, a student leader, about allowing alcohol on campus. It is an interactive situation. Both Blue and Cool are attempting to convince the other that he ought to change his position. Can we make any predictions about the changes in attitude and response that are likely to emerge from this situation?

This type of situation has been called by Newcomb the "AtoBreX" situation.[17] To study it effectively, we have to consider the relationships which might exist between Blue and Cool with respect to the subject of alcohol on campus.

Figure 2.4 shows the possible sets of attitudinal relationships that can occur in this persuasive communication situation. There are six such relationships that are meaningful to our discussion. For example, in (a), the first situation diagrammed, the three relationships with which we are concerned can be described by saying that Blue likes Cool, that Cool likes Blue, and that both feel favorably to having alcohol on campus. The situation is balanced. Blue will probably not have much effect on Cool's attitudes, since he and Cool already agree. If there is going to be a change in behavior as a result of their discussion, it will probably be to strengthen the resistance of both individuals to outside communicators, such as the Board of Trustees, who might differ with their positions. Their resistance might increase because both have received new information which is consistent with an already existing belief structure. Increasing resistance to change is, of course, an important goal in persuasion, and is facilitated by the type of situation shown in (a).

Another balanced situation is shown in (d), except that neither Blue nor Cool are in favor of alcohol on campus. Again, we might expect persuasion to strengthen belief, and increase resistance to change. Still a third balanced situation is shown in (e), although the situation is more important than (a) or (b) if persuasion is considered. Here, Blue is opposed to having alcohol on campus, and Cool is in favor of it. Both Blue and Cool have tangled in the past,

and have come to have an extreme dislike of one another. But the situation *is* balanced. Both Blue and Cool are in the position of disliking someone who has a different viewpoint. There is no pressure to change attitudes or behavior, and we would predict that the meeting will be short, perhaps stormy, and that both parties will come away with no change in their original attitudes.

An unbalanced situation is shown in (b). Blue and Cool find themselves on the same side of the fence, but past experience has led them to dislike one another. If our theory is correct, we should find pressures to change affecting both Blue and Cool. How can they change? They could change their feelings toward one another, and become more positive. That would move them over toward the situation shown in (a). Or Blue could change his mind about the topic. He could say to himself, "If Cool is in favor of alcohol on campus, there must be something wrong with it. I'll go slow on this one." Again, the shift is toward a more balanced state.

A second type of unbalanced situation is shown in (c). Past experience has led Blue and Cool to have considerable respect for one another, but they find themselves on opposite sides of the topic. Here we predict that there should exist a spirit of cooperation between the two individuals. There should be a mutual changing of attitudes, so that the eventual result will be a position somewhere between the two original positions. Note that we said that there *should* be a spirit of cooperation. It is quite possible that, if the topic is very important to either Blue or Cool, balance will be obtained by changing their feelings toward each other. Balance is restored, but persuasion is unsuccessful, and the problem that brought Blue and Cool together in the first place is not solved.

In (f), we have another unbalanced situation, perhaps a common one. President Blue is in favor of alcohol on campus, but over the years, he has come to have respect for Cool, who works hard at being a student leader. Cool, on

Figure 2.4 Attitudinal Relationships

the other hand, is also in favor of alcohol on campus, but has achieved a strong dislike for President Blue. There are going to be changes in the situation because it is unbalanced. Cool could also change his mind about Blue, which would produce the best of all situations from a persuasive communication standpoint. But Cool could also change his mind about the topic, and say to himself, "If Blue is for it, I must be wrong. We can't allow Blue to have alcohol on campus." This may not be the normal prediction, but it would restore balance.

There are other possible situations than the six I have described. We leave it to the reader to examine the other possibilities, and work out the possible outcomes.

Our analysis of these relatively simple communication situations suggests that persuasion is facilitated in some of the situations but will be difficult in others. There are, however, some other outcomes that are possible. Look again at (f). Here we suggested that Cool can restore his balanced state by changing his attitude toward alcohol, but he can also restore balance by changing his attitude about Blue. How can we predict which event will occur? *Attitude change will occur about the object which is the less highly valued.* If Cool's attitudes about alcohol on campus have been developed over a long period of time and are embedded within a strong frame of reference, while his attitudes toward Blue are less well developed, he can be expected to change his attitude toward Blue before he will change his attitude about the topic.

In any of the unbalanced situations we have described, there will be pressures to restore balance to the situation. There are, however, some possible changes that have the *appearance* of restoring balance, but which do not actually do so when considered over time. In (c), if Cool and Blue are allowed to talk freely to one another, and if persuasion is allowed to continue between the two, it is quite possible for Cool to arrive at a position in which he distorts Blue's position. The close interaction between the two

has strengthened Cool's liking for Blue. This puts more pressure on Cool to balance his attitudes about alcohol with those of Blue. In effect, Cool may distort Blue's real position to make it fit within his own frame of reference. Such a reaction does have the effect of restoring balance, but when time passes and Cool discovers that Blue really does have the negative attitudes he says he does, the unbalanced state returns. Such distortion is relatively common and must be avoided by the communicator.

Balance can also be restored through the process of *dissociation*. Blue and Cool like each other. They could get along for a long time if they never talked about alcohol on campus and confined their conversation to topics on which they are in agreement. If Cool is really interested in achieving his goal, however, he will eventually have to introduce the subject, and the pressure will once again fall on Blue to balance the situation. If Cool continues to push his materials on Blue, the final type of disassociation will occur. Blue will refuse to meet with Cool. There is such a difference between their positions that they dissociate from one another. Such a reaction may be found in labor-management disputes, disputes between husbands and wives, between teachers and students, and between nations. Dissociation may allow an individual to balance his own cognitions, but it represents a failure in persuasion where the goal is to reach common agreement.

Our discussion about cognitive balance may make it seem a completely passive process, but persuasion is not always a matter of presenting material to a receiver and awaiting the subsequent judgment of that material by a receiver. Evidence suggests that the balance mechanism works in simple one-way communication situations. The example we have used of a situation which involves interactive communication, however, is far closer to reality for most of us. Interactive persuasive communication situations always involve the attitudinal relationships that obtain between all the individuals engaging in the relationship. The pressures in such a persuasive situation are toward reaching a consistent position for all participants.

In the situation we have used, only two people were involved. There are, of course, many interpersonal communication situations which involve only two people, but cognitive consistency may apply equally to situations which involve more than two. In that case, it is necessary to take into account the attitudinal relationships that obtain among all of the people involved. For example, in the case of Joe Cool and President Blue we were able to illustrate the possible cases fairly easily. Imagine that the situation also involved Mary Jackson, a student who is opposed to liquor on campus and Trustee Barbara Allen, who says that she is neutral on the matter. How many possible situations would we have to take into account when we add people and topics to a persuasive communication situation? It is easy to see that as the number of people and topics increases, the difficulty of making predictions also increases. If many people are involved, the task becomes impossible, and we must turn to other methods of gaining information about the possible reactions of receivers.

Regardless of the number of receivers involved, the pressures toward balance implies that compromises may take place, and that prior analysis of the situation may help indicate how those compromises will be achieved.

Attention to Competing Messages

Every year millions of Americans are faced with the task of purchasing a new automobile, buying a house, voting for political candidates, deciding whether to vote for increased school taxes, or simply evaluating the editorials they read in the newspaper. In each of these situations, several different messages are likely to be available to the individual. The Ford Motor Company sends a message extolling the virtues of a Ford; General Motors argues for a Chevrolet; and Volkswagen tells you that the only

way to go is with a Rabbit. The incumbent state senator tells you that he should be reelected, while his opponent tells you that the incumbent ought to be turned out of office in favor of himself. One editorial tells us that our community needs more business and fewer people trying to obstruct the growth of business, while the competing paper argues for a moratorium on new business until the community has solved its sewage problem.

If the persuasive speaker could know which messages were more likely to be attended to, it would make the task much easier. In similar fashion, if we could predict what messages were most likely to be attractive, we might have a better chance of guarding against poor decisions. Consistency theory reasons that changes in the frame of reference and changes in responses should be in line with making cognitive structures more consistent. In the case of competing messages, basic works by Festinger,[18] Brehm and Cohen,[19] and McGuire[20] attempt to specify some of the factors which might control this situation. The problem can be illustrated by looking at the process of buying a car.

Elizabeth Dawson has just graduated from college and has been hired by a large chemical company to work in their public relations office. Elizabeth has moved to the city where she is to begin work, and soon realizes that she must have a car. The plant is located far from any housing, and she can quickly see that recreation on weekends will depend on being able to get away from the city. So Elizabeth begins looking for an automobile.

It is at this point that the problem of competing messages begins to raise its ugly head. Several questions are of interest to the persuasive communicator in this situation. To which messages is Elizabeth most likely to listen? What factors are likely to guide Elizabeth in making a choice of automobile? After Elizabeth has made a choice and purchased one of the competing models, how is she likely to behave toward other messages regarding automobiles? Our theory allows us to make predictions about each of these questions.

Perhaps the biggest decision that Elizabeth faces will be one of price. As a newly hired graduate, it is not likely that she will be able to afford an extremely expensive car, so the chances are that she will quickly rule out automobiles that are in the upper price brackets. Our theory says that she will stop paying much attention to messages about Cadillacs or Lincolns. Even after Elizabeth has decided on the price range she *can* afford, however, there are still likely to be several different makes and models which fall within that price range. For each model there will be a lot of persuasive literature and many different advertisements to which she will be exposed. In addition, Elizabeth faces a barrage of competing information from salesmen and the comments of friends and relatives. These conflicting claims and messages provide, according to Festinger, a *dissonant* situation for the receiver. Dissonance theory states that Elizabeth will, in this situation where she is "just looking," be willing to look at many different kinds of literature, view all the television advertisements, and pay attention to anyone that has something to say about automobiles. Elizabeth is in an *information gathering* phase, and if our theory is correct, she will be willing to gather information from all the sources she can.

After talking to many people, and reading all the literature she can get, Elizabeth is going to have to make a decision, and order her car. That decision is going to be made in light of the evidence she has collected, and her feelings about the people who acted as sources of information. If there is an individual in whom she has great trust, it is very likely that the recommendations of that person will be very influential. This is in line with the importance of authority beliefs that we discussed in the beginning of the chapter. She might reject Volkswagen because someone convinced her to "buy American." At any rate, the eventual decision Elizabeth makes is going to be one consistent with her own frames of reference and the messages she has been exposed to.

Finally, the discussions are over, and Elizabeth signs an order for a new automobile. She has made a *choice*, and in so doing, she has finally lowered the tensions that arose because she was faced with competing information. What is her behavior going to be now that the decision has been made? Dissonance theory suggests that now she will be quite selective in the materials she reads about automobiles. She will not read or listen to messages about the cars she did not choose, unless the messages point out faults in the cars she could have chosen, but did not. The theory also suggests that Elizabeth will continue to be receptive to information about the automobile she did choose, but only *positive* information. Information which might indicate that she made a bad choice will not be received or sought out.

We have used our short example to show that dissonance theory purports to be able to predict the communication behaviors of individuals before a choice is to be made, to help in predicting what choice will be made, and to tell us what communication behaviors the individual will engage in after a choice has been made. Obviously, many things could have happened to make us miss our predictions. If Elizabeth was going to have to get a loan from her parents for the automobile, the preferences of her parents may have played a larger role in the final choice than her own. The availability of a repair department close to her home may have weighed heavily in the final decision. Our example merely illustrates a number of factors that are of importance to persuasive communication, and that can be extended beyond the car-buying example.

First, an individual is placed in a dissonant situation whenever faced with a choice in which the elements are perceived to be an *inverse relationship* to one another. Smoking is a good example. Smoking is pleasurable, but, smoking may also cause lung cancer. If people do not know that smoking may cause lung cancer, they may continue to choose to smoke with no psychological tension. The frames of reference such people hold about smoking are relatively simple, and there are no conflicting elements within those frames. What happens to such individuals when a report comes out that makes it clear that smoking *is* related to increased risk of lung cancer? Our theory says that when people become aware of such discrepant information, dissonance results, and there will be attempts to reduce it. There are different ways to reduce dissonance in this situation, and we may expect that different people will use different methods. Some may decide to quit smoking, an act that does reduce the dissonance. Others may decide that the pleasures of smoking outweigh the dangers of lung cancer, and that decision also reduces dissonance. Still others may decide that the risk of lung cancer is fairly large, but that the danger of gaining weight and increasing the risk of a heart attack is even larger, and thus it is still better to smoke. Again, dissonance is reduced. Note that an outsider may not at all agree with the mental gymnastics used by any of the people in our example, but each of the ways we have cited in which dissonance may be reduced is perfectly compatible with individual frames of reference. If nothing else, the example should tell a persuasive communicator that it may not be enough to just "give people the facts." The communicator may have to steer the receiver in the direction desired by the source.

Second, the *magnitude* of the dissonance that is present will be a function of the importance of the elements or stimuli that are involved, the intensity with which attitudes are held toward the elements and the number of elements involved. For example, Mr. Mason enjoys two television programs, both of which are programmed into the same time slot. Mr. Mason is in a dissonant relationship in this situation, but it is not really an important decision for him to make, so the amount of dissonance he will experience should be relatively small. One would imagine that the persuasive communicator would have an easy time persuading him to watch one show as opposed to the other. On the other hand, imagine the cognitive tensions arising in Mr. Rivers when he realizes the conflict he has over a new job with a major firm. During his college years, Mr. Rivers worked long and hard on campus to achieve a cleanup of the river running through campus. His interest in ecology and a clean environment is very high. Just before accepting the job, he finds that his prospective company has been cited by the federal government as a major polluter. In this situation, we expect the magnitude of the dissonance that Mr. Rivers will experience to be extremely high. Mr. Rivers knows that he needs a job, but the past four years have been spent in building a frame of reference in conflict with the type of job he now finds himself considering.

How can Mr. Rivers reduce the dissonance that he is experiencing? He could, of course, turn down the job. That would reduce dissonance, but if jobs are very hard to find in his field, turning down the job is not going to reduce dissonance. A more likely course of action would be to accept the job, and tell himself that he will be able to work to change the company's practices and image. That does reduce dissonance, but it does so only as long as the individual feels that he is making progress. A. similar kind of situation is found when a woman marries a man who drinks, smokes, gambles, or does anything else that the woman disapproves of. She justifies her actions by the belief that she "can change him for the better." Her dissonance level may be high, and we expect her actions to be extreme, producing a large change in her frames of reference. In general, when the magnitude of the dissonance is very high, the probability of sweeping changes in the person's frame of reference is also high, *if* the individual is to succeed in reducing the dissonance. When dissonance is low, persuasion is more likely to be successful, because it may take only minimal information to change the situation, and thus reduce dissonance.

A third factor of importance to persuasion is the relationship between *choice* and the consequent of choice, *commitment*. Commitment to the various elements of a situation is an important requisite for the occurrence of significant dissonance. An individual can hold conflicting frames of reference, but if there is no public commitment to any of the frames, there is little dissonance produced when the inconsistency is pointed out. If, however, such conflicting reference frames are held, and a person is publicly committed to one of the frames, great dissonance may result. Thus the magnitude of the dissonance and the consequent expected attitude change increase as the degree of inconsistency between reference frames and public commitment increases.

The importance of such commitment can be seen in our educational system all across the United States. Many people in the northern tier of states applauded the Supreme Court decision of 1954 which called for an end to segregated schools. The news was full of state governors and legislators who announced that they were completely in favor of the decision, and veiled comments were made about those Southerners who came out in opposition to the Court's decision. That attitude prevailed throughout much of the 1960s and early 1970s. Today, however, courts have moved beyond the early stage, and have called for an end to *de facto* segregation in many large Northern cities. Most such plans call for the massive use of bussing. The same individuals who welcomed the original Supreme Court decision now find themselves in a highly dissonant situation. They may *not* be in favor of having their children ride busses. They may be in favor of neighborhood schools. In the past, they could be generally in favor of integration and also in favor of neighborhood schools. In city after city, however, people are being forced to make a choice between integration and neighborhood schools. The dissonance produced in attempting to make that choice is threatening to tear our society apart. Our theory tells us that the amount of dissonance produced would be less if people had not earlier committed themselves to public support of integration. Finding ways to reduce that dissonance consistent with the demands of the law and the courts has occupied the time of many persuasive communicators in the past few years, and promises to be a continuing problem in the next few years. The problem is increased because of the degree of public commitment in past years.

A final factor relating to dissonance may be termed *exposure* to inconsistency. All of us hold some conflicting frames of reference, some conflicting attitudes and beliefs. We continue to hold them until the inconsistency is made known to us. When that inconsistency is made known to us, we can predict that there will be pressures in the direction of greater consistency. Rokeach,[21] has demonstrated that this can occur. He obtained attitude and value ratings from a number of students about the topics of "equal rights" and "civil rights demonstrations." Then he went back to the students and showed them that most students ranked "freedom" first and "equality" sixth. At the same time, he showed the students that low rankings were given to "equality" by those students who said they were unsympathetic to civil rights demonstrations. Following this demonstration, the students were given a statement about the rating task they had originally done. They were told that they and their friends who had participated in the experiment seemed to be interested in their own freedom, but that they were obviously not interested in freedom for others. The students were then thanked for their help, and asked to think about the implications of the various rankings.

Three weeks later, the students were tested again. The results were generally what we would expect from a cognitive consistency theory framework. Students who had ranked both "equality" and "freedom" high showed little attitude change. Students who had ranked both concepts equally low also showed little change. Students who ranked "equality" high and "freedom" low, however, showed a significant shift of attitude by ranking their attitude about civil rights demonstrations higher. Rokeach tested again after a three-to-five month period, and found that there had been even more of a shift toward balancing the two sets of attitudes. This experiment suggests that the persuasive communicator can sometimes change attitudes in the desired direction by simply exposing the inconsistencies between two frames of reference and allowing the receiver's cognitive consistency mechanisms to work at closing the gap.

People do seek to reduce the amount of dissonance they experience when faced with competing messages. One of the consequences of an open society, such as we now live in, is that there are many competing messages on many topics. Our research frequently uncovers situations in which a persuasive message seems to result in attitude change, but when a later check is made, the individuals have moved back to their original attitudinal position. This is likely to happen because there are competing messages that result in later changes in position. Successful persuasion cannot stop with a single, apparently successful message. When a persuasive communicator succeeds in getting a receiver to make a choice favorable to the communicator's position, the next step is getting the receiver to continue to support that choice. Just as Joe Salesman needs to send messages to keep people coming back to the store, the source that has succeeded in getting the receiver to adopt a position that was dissonantly held can aid in fixing the decision more firmly for the individual by "postdecision communication." Such messages offer receivers even more reasons why their choices were good ones. The automobile company that Elizabeth chose invariably makes use of this technique after the new car is delivered. Elizabeth will get a letter congratulating her on picking the particular car she did, will list the features that made her choice a wise one. One might think that Elizabeth would not be interested in automobile literature after just buying a new car, but our theory suggests that she *will* be interested in any materials that tend to confirm the choice she made.

Every day, messages compete for our attention. They ask us to work for abortion reform, support open admissions, believe in ideas, buy cars, and watch certain television shows. Which messages are listened to, how they are acted upon, and what the consequences are of such decisions, are not random behaviors performed by receivers. Rather, they are complex decisions, explainable in part by a cognitive mechanism which makes us look at the world as a constant whole.

Linking Sources and Messages

Thus far in our discussion of consistency theories, we have been concerned with the cognitive relationships that might obtain between *all* of the basic elements in a communication situation: source, receiver and message. Osgood and Tannenbaum[22] suggest that the consistency mechanism will come into play *any* time the individual receiver is faced with a source delivering a message. They ask, "What will happen when an individual who holds one attitude toward a source and another attitude about a topic sees the source linked to the topic in a message?" Imagine the receiver who holds a very positive attitude toward Governor Jones and also holds a very negative attitude about increased gasoline taxes. Under most circumstances, holding two such attitudes would not at all be unusual for anybody. Osgood and Tannenbaum, however, wonder what would happen if that receiver saw a big headline in the newspaper reading, "GOVERNOR JONES COMES OUT IN FAVOR OF INCREASED GASOLINE TAXES." This message is inconsistent or *incongruous* for the receiver, and they suggest that there will have to be changes in the receiver's frames of reference to accommodate the perceived incongruity. What could happen to reduce the incongruity in this example? The

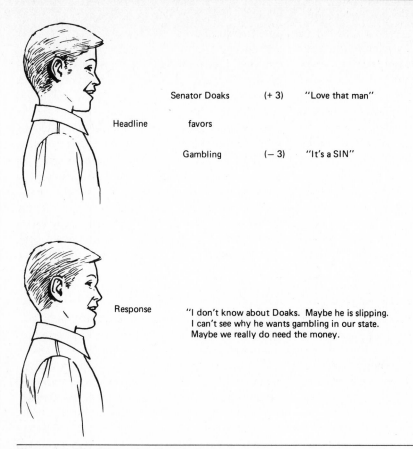

	Senator Doaks	(+ 3)	"Love that man"
Headline	favors		
	Gambling	(− 3)	"It's a SIN"

Response "I don't know about Doaks. Maybe he is slipping. I can't see why he wants gambling in our state. Maybe we really do need the money.

Figure 2.5 The Congruity Situation

receiver could lower the favorable attitude originally held toward Governor Jones, or raise the attitude held about increased gasoline taxes. Either of these two changes would make the reference frame consistent again. Another possible solution would be to change attitudes about both topics, or become neutral about both topics. The receiver could also refuse to believe the headline, and thus refuse to believe that any inconsistency existed. Any of these changes on the part of the receiver would result in congruity in the situation, but it is easy to see that not all of them would be equally desirable from the standpoint of the persuasive communicator.

The data that Osgood and Tannenbaum present, as well as other data that has been gathered on this topic,[23] suggests that the *most likely* outcome will be that the receiver's attitudes toward Governor Jones will become slightly less positive, while attitudes toward increased gasoline taxes will become slightly more positive (Figure 2.5). If the receiver saw only the one message, we might expect that attitude change as a result of the message will be temporary in nature, and that the attitudes involved will move back toward their original position after a period of time. If, however, the receiver continues to see stories in which Governor Jones advocates increased gasoline taxes, the inconsistency in attitudes will become more and more apparent to the receiver and there will be stronger and stronger pressures to reduce the perceived incongruity. If there were no other elements involved in the situation, the theory predicts that the final attitudinal position for the receiver would be neutrality toward both source and topic. In essence, the receiver should move from an original position of strong attitudes toward both source and topic to one that says, "I don't know what to believe about either the source or the topic."

In real persuasive communication situations, neutrality is not likely to be the final result. In the case discussed, Governor Jones is certainly going to be associated with topics other than his stance on increased gasoline taxes. The Governor may be making speeches on decreasing the property tax, improving the environment, getting more business to come into the state, and many other topics. If these topics are ones about which the receiver also has a favorable attitude, the effect will be a tendency to keep attitudes toward Governor Jones positive. The net effect of all of these messages is to dilute the effect of any one message.

The reader may wonder why we mention the congruity principle when our example suggests that it may not have much effect in many situations. There are some situations where the principle may have powerful effects. There are some receivers that are "single issue" voters. Some people care only about the abortion issue. If a candidate isn't "right" on that issue, that type of voter is going to vote *no*, even if the candidate is "right" on every other issue in the election. Some political scientists feel that there is an increasing number of such voters. In fact, in the 1978 elections, far more money went to support groups advocating a single issue than went to the two major political parties.

A second example where the congruity principle may be expected to be extremely important is the situation where a single issue becomes of overriding importance to the majority of the populace. Such was the situation with former President Nixon and the war in Viet Nam. It made little difference what other topics Nixon espoused. People judged him by his stance on the war, and he lost popularity accordingly. In both of these situations, the congruity principle may play an important part in persuasion.

The congruity principle suggests that speaking about an unfavorable topic is not likely to produce immediate results for the communicator. Rather, a long campaign, during which the persuasive communicator may temporarily lose personal popularity, is likely to be required if long-term changes in the receiver's frames of reference are to be affected. Second, the communicator of an unfavorable topic has to prepare for a campaign which will run longer than a campaign for a topic that is likely to be favorably received. This is frequently seen in political life. The politician does not wish to be attached to an unpopular cause immediately before an election, but after reelection, the politician knows that there are a number of years in which to change voters' attitudes about an unpopular topic. Although sponsoring an unpopular cause may temporarily lower the politician's own personal popularity, there is time to gain personal popularity before the next election by having the politician be associated with some popular measures. The congruity principle also suggests that the persuasive communicator with but a single cause may fail to attain the goal. If the goal is unpopular, and there are no other topics to offset the effect of an unpopular topic, the persuasive communicator's own popularity will be diminished, and there may be little that can be done to achieve the persuasive goals.

We have described the Osgood and Tannenbaum situation separately from other cognitive consistency situations, but the mechanism that is at work in the congruity situations is the same cognitive mechanism that is present in the dissonance situation and in the "AtoBreX" case. The general base for all consistency theories is the idea that whenever an individual is placed in an unbalanced situation, there will be tension experienced, and attempts made to reduce the tension. All consistency theories can be classified as drive-reduction theories of behavior. The force for changes in behavior is inconsistency, a force providing powerful motivation to reduce tensions. Attempts at tension reduction will result in changes in the individual's reference frames, and thus in changes in the responses the individual makes to persuasive communication.

One final note ought to be added before we end our discussion of consistency theories and their application to persuasion. At the beginning of our discussion, we suggested that not all social scientists agreed on the importance of consistency as a psychological mechanism. This area of disagreement deserves further mention. Certainly, most psychological theories have their detractors as well as their supporters. Consistency theories are no exception. They have been opposed on methodological grounds by Chapanis and Chapanis[24] and Lott.[25] More important, from our standpoint, is the development of a school of thought arguing that man also seeks the novel, the unpredictable, and the complex. This approach, presented by writers such as Berlyne[26] and Fowler[27] argues that while it might be true that there is a tendency to balance the information we receive, it is also true that there is a tendency to seek the unexpected, look for the novel, and enjoy the complex. They suggest that a desire to seek the "novel" is not compatible with the desire to keep reference frames stable and to balance the information we receive. McGuire[28] argues that the two theories, while apparently somewhat contradictory, may both be true. We may seek the novel or the new, for example, as a way of balancing a reference frame that is causing tension. We may use the novel as a way of justifying beliefs that educated men and women ought to be open to new ideas. Perhaps the best conclusion we can make is that there is no serious threat to the importance of balance theories as a predictor of human behavior from novelty theories. The persuasive communicator, however, should note the tendency to seek the novel, since it may be very useful in composing a persuasive message.

SUMMARY

Human beings are constantly receiving information about the world around them. Our senses convey a steady stream of bits and pieces of information which allows us to decide whether we will put on a raincoat in the morning, cross the street to a store, vote for a tax increase, or execute any other element of our daily lives. The bits of information we receive do not come into sensory channels in random fashion. From the time we are born until the time we die, our mind is in the process of fashioning a set of complex frames of reference. These frames help determine what we will attend to, what we will come to believe in, whom we will like and dislike, and how we will respond to the messages to which we are exposed.

The frames of reference we develop help determine how we will behave in persuasive communication situations. Our reference frames are composed of attitudes and beliefs, and successful persuasion is linked to changes in attitudes and beliefs. Regardless of the type of persuasion in which we are interested, two major areas are of significance to us. We must understand the ways human beings learn and acquire new information. If persuasion is to be successful, the individuals participating may have to acquire new information before they can change existing attitudes, opinions, emotions or actions. Similarly, various theories of cognitive consistency seem applicable to persuasion. Individuals tend to try to achieve consistency in the way they respond to messages and to other people. The attempts we make to achieve consistency are important indicators of the potential outcomes of any persuasive communication situation.

FOOTNOTES

1. M. Rokeach, *The Open and Closed Mind*, (New York: Basic Books, Inc., 1960). See also: M. Rokeach, *Beliefs, Attitudes and Values*, (San Francisco: Jossey–Bass, 1968).
2. Rokeach.
3. D. Bem, *Beliefs, Attitudes and Human Affairs*, (Belmont, Calif.: Brooks/Cole Publishing Co., 1970).
4. E. Bettinghaus, "The Relative Effect of the Use of Testimony in a Persuasive Speech upon the Attitudes of Listeners," (M.A. thesis, Bradley University, 1953).
5. M. Rokeach, *Beliefs, Attitudes and Values*, pp. 22–61.
6. C. L. Hull, *A Behavior System: An Introduction to Behavior Theory Concerning the Individual Organism*, (New Haven, Conn.: Yale University Press, 1951).
7. C. E. Osgood, *Methods and Theory in Experimental Psychology*, (New York: Oxford University Press, 1953), pp. 299–599.
8. E. R. Hilgard, *Theories of Learning*, (New York: Appleton–Century Crofts, 1956), pp. 485–88.
9. B. Ballantine, *Wild Tigers and Tame Fleas*, (New York: Holt, Rinehart, and Winston, 1958), pp. 139–54.
10. For discussion of early work on consistency theories, see W. McGuire, "The Current Status of Cognitive Consistency Theories," in *Cognitive Consistency*, ed. S. Feldman, (New York: Academic Press, 1966), pp. 2–4.
11. L. Festinger, *The Theory of Cognitive Dissonance*, (New York: Harper and Row, 1957).
12. C. E. Osgood, P. Tannenbaum and G. Suci, *The Measurement of Meaning*, (Urbana, Ill.: The University of Illinois Press, 1957), pp. 189–216. See also, C. E. Osgood and P. Tannenbaum, "The Principle of Congruity in the Prediction of Attitude Change," *Psychological Review*, vol. 62 (1955), pp. 42–55.
13. R. P. Abelson and M. J. Rosenberg, "Symbolic Psycho-Logic: A Model of Attitudinal Cognition," *Behavioral Science*, vol. 3 (1958), pp. 1–13.
14. F. Heider, "Attitudes and Cognitive Organization," *Journal of Psychology*, vol. 21 (1946), pp. 107–112. See also F. Heider, *The Psychology of Interpersonal Relations*, (New York: John Wiley & Sons, 1958).
15. See for example N. P. Chapanis and A. Chapanis, "Cognitive Dissonance: Five Years Later," *Psychological Bulletin*, vol. 61, (1964), pp. 1–22; D. O. Sears and R. P. Abeles, "Attitudes and Opinions," *Annual Review of Psychology*, vol. 20 (1969), 253–88; and R. B. Zajonc, "Cognitive Theories in Social Psychology," in G. Lindzey and E. Aronson eds., *The Handbook of Social Psychology*, 2nd ed. vol. 1 (Reading, Pa.: Addison-Wesley, 1968), pp. 320–411.
16. A. H. Eagly and S. Himmelfarb, "Current Trends in Attitude Theory and Research," in S. Himmelfarb and A. H. Eagly, eds., *Readings in Attitude Change*, (New York: John Wiley & Sons, 1974), pp. 595–601.
17. T. M. Newcomb, "An Approach to the Study of Communicative Acts," *Psychological Review*, vol. 60 (1963), pp. 393–404.
18. L. Festinger, *The Theory of Cognitive Dissonance*.
19. J. W. Brehm and A. R. Cohen, *Explorations in Cognitive Dissonance*, (New York: John Wiley and Sons, Inc., 1962).
20. W. McGuire, "Cognitive Consistency and Attitude Change," *Journal of Abnormal and Social Psychology*, vol. 60 (1960), pp. 345–53.
21. M. Rokeach and G. Rothman, "The Principle of Belief Congruence and the Congruity Principle as Models of Cognitive Interaction," *Psychological Review*, vol. 72 (1965), pp. 128–42.
22. C. E. Osgood and P. Tannenbaum, "Prediction of Attitude Change," pp. 42–55.
23. See E. P. Bettinghaus, "The Operation of Congruity in an Oral Communication Situation," *Speech Monographs*, Vol. 28, August, 1961, pp. 131–42; P. H. Tannenbaum, "Mediated Generalization of Attitude Change via the Principle of Congruity," *Journal of Personality and Social Psychology*, Vol. 3, 1966, pp. 493–99; P. H. Tannenbaum and R. W. Gengel, "Generalization of Attitude Change through Congruity Principle Relationships," *Journal of Personality and Social Psychology*, 1966, Vol. 3, pp. 299–304; and P. H. Tannenbaum, "The Congruity Principle: Retrospective Reflections and Recent Research," in R. P. Abelson, E. Aronson, W. J. McGuire, T. M. Newcomb, M. J. Rosenberg, and P. H. Tannenbaum eds., *Theories of Cognitive Consistency: A Sourcebook*, (Chicago: Rand McNally, 1968), pp. 52–71.
24. N. Chapanis and A. Chapanis, "Cognitive Dissonance: Five Years Later," pp. 1–22.
25. B. Lott, "Secondary Reinforcement and Effort: Comment on Aronson's 'The Effect of Effort on the Attractiveness of Rewarded and Unrewarded Stimuli'," *Journal of Abnormal and Social Psychology*, vol. 67 (1963), pp. 520–22.

26. D. E. Berlyne, *Conflict, Arousal, and Curiosity*, (New York: McGraw Hill, 1960).

27. H. Fowler, *Curiosity and Exploratory Behavior*, (New York: Macmillan Co., 1965).

28. W. McGuire, "The Current Status of Cognitive Consistency Theories," pp. 35–38.

THREE

SUCCESSFUL PERSUASION: PREDICTING INDIVIDUAL RESPONSE

If you prepare a persuasive message, and then direct it toward a number of receivers, it is likely that the results will show that some people are dramatically affected by the message, others are affected to a lesser degree, and some people do not seem to be at all affected. Even if you have attempted to carefully ascertain what the original attitude level of the audience is, and have determined that everyone receiving the message does have the ability to respond, you can expect differences in the way people behave. What causes people to respond to a message in different ways? How can the source predict how a person is likely to respond to any message?

Communication scholars and other behavioral scientists have been interested in questions about individual response to messages for some time. After all, being able to make even *some* predictions about the ways in which people are likely to respond to a message would be of tremendous help to a source. Just think of some of the many situations in which the ability to predict would be of use. Will my boy friend or girl friend respond favorably to an invitation to a concert? What will my communication instructor do if I ask her to postpone the midterm examination? What will my boss do if I ask him for a raise?

Making such predictions is admittedly difficult. None of the theories we are going to discuss below are foolproof in any sense of the word, but each of them approaches the interpersonal persuasive situation from a slightly different point of view, and each of them has proven to be a useful way of making predictions about human behavior. Our three approaches use *personality theory*, *attribution theory*, and *social exchange theory*. Each of them is appropriate for communication situations involving only a few people. In the next chapter we shall examine theories that help in making predictions about larger audiences.

PERSONALITY THEORY

This is the age of Psychological Man. Everybody seems to be interested in psychology. Newspapers carry columns about human behavior, popular songs try to interpret our behavior, and a number of popular magazines are devoted to the analysis of human behavior. Business and government spend large sums training their personnel in management methods based on psychology. In view of this emphasis, it is not surprising to find studies indicating that psychological differences between individuals may be important in determining the ways in which persuasive messages are received.

A large unabridged dictionary contains approximately 18,000 words to help differentiate between people. That huge number is an example of the importance we place on being able to catalog each person as an individual. Some of these words refer to physical differences between individuals, words such as tall, bald, heavy, young, and well-dressed. Others refer to an individual's affective orientation toward some person, such as interested, attentive, angry, fearful, sad, loving, and jealous. Finally, some of our trait words refer to firmly structured, persisting, cognitively oriented differences in the ways in which people face the world. We call overt behavior that indicates the presence of one of these structured differences "personality", and use the structures to make predictions about future behavior. Personality structures include such cognitive organizations as aggressiveness, need achievement, dogmatism, egotism, rigidity, and anxiety. This section examines personality traits and their relation to communication.

One may wonder why it is helpful to consider personality as a variable after just having discussed the nature of belief systems. After all, personality structures are belief structures. They form part of the reference frames that we all develop. Personality structures, however, are organizations of beliefs and attitudes that become pervasive for the individual, and thus tend to affect the way in which the individual will behave in many kinds of situations.

The average person uses personality terms many times a day, and uses them rather casually. Everyone has heard statements similar to the following: "Joe, you've got to have an open mind on this subject;" or "I think Hilda has an inferiority complex;" or "Don't you think Sam is a bit aggressive, you know, too pushy?" A little thought shows why the psychologist tends to be disturbed by such relatively casual use of technical terms. Having an "inferiority complex" lies in the mind, but it is certainly impossible for anybody to actually look inside the mind of anyone else. Determining personality is necessarily done through a process of *inference* by which conclusions about an individual's probable orientations toward people, objects, and events are drawn from observable behavior. One of the major problems in defining personality characteristics is the necessity to decide what kinds of behavior ought to be observed in order to make an assessment of personality.

A second problem is the fact that personality is a *dyadic* concept. We must distinguish between *monadic* and *dyadic* concepts. The statement "Jim is six feet tall," is a monadic statement. It can be made with no reference to another individual. Monadic statements do not depend for their truth or falsity on any relationship to other individuals or events. To say, however, that "Jim is a superior student," is different. The notion of a "superior student" is a dyadic concept, since if Jim is superior, there must be individuals who are inferior to him. In other words, dyadic concepts have to take into account relations between people or events. Personality is a dyadic concept. An individual is aggressive only because there are other people who are less aggressive. One individual can be considered highly motivated, only after we have considered a group of people and found others less motivated.

The fact that personality is a dyadic concept

also influences the ways in which we measure and assess personality. Three different methods of making some assessment of personality can be described.

1. The first approach to studying personality is one that attempts to assemble a rather complete description of an individual's actual behavior patterns in different situations, and then to draw up a composite estimate of the individual's personality. Imagine that we are interested in doing this type of analysis on Elizabeth Dawson. We might attempt to find out how she behaves in large social groups. Does she interact freely, or does she tend to withdraw to a smaller group of people? How does she behave under stress conditions? Does she tend to get frightened when taking tests? From these and many other observations, the scientist attempts to write a comprehensive description of Elizabeth's personality and make predictions of the ways in which she will behave in a particular situation. The persuasive communicator who is skilled in observation will find this to be an important tool. The emphasis, however, must be on the word "skilled." Most of us do not make very accurate estimates of behavior, although most of us will not admit that our judgments are really not very good. Our tendency is to judge others based totally on our own experiences, and we are thus inclined to miss important bits of data. Many observations are necessary before conclusions about an individual's personality can be drawn with confidence. Even when a trained psychologist is making estimates of personality based on observations of behavior, the correlations between such estimates and later behavior are not very accurate.[1]

2. A second general approach makes use of *projective tests*. This method is the one most closely associated with popular conceptions about personality testing. The Rorschach Ink-Blot Test is an example of a projective test. In the Rorschach Test the psychologist asks an individual to look at a series of various ink-blots and then to tell the psychologist what has been seen. The answers given are assumed to be related to the type of personality possessed. Projective tests are of little use to the persuasive communicator. It takes a highly trained individual to administer and interpret projective tests. Furthermore, such tests have been most useful in identifying individuals with serious mental illnesses. Most persuasive communicators do not find themselves in situations with receivers who exhibit such extreme behavior.

3. The most widely used approach utilizes *personality inventories* of various types. These tests consist of a number of statements about which an individual indicates attitudes or feelings. Examples of the type of statements that might be in a personality inventory include:

a. Certain religious sects whose beliefs do not permit them to salute the flag should be forced to conform to such patriotic action, or else the sects should be abolished.
b. It is a mistake to allow any Japanese to enter the army where he would be free to commit sabotage.
c. A large-scale system of sterilization would be one way of breeding out criminals and other undesirable elements in our society and so raise its general standards and living conditions.
d. We are spending too much money for the pampering of criminals and the insane, and for the education of inherently incapable people.[2]

These are examples from an older test used to measure ethnocentrism. Today, we would use updated examples, but the principle is the same. The answer to any one question is relatively meaningless, but when an individual's entire set of answers are compared to the answers of a large number of others, meaningful comparisons can be made.

Each of the three methods we have discussed has certain advantages and disadvantages. In persuasion, the use of direct observation, and the use of personality inventories seems to have the most value. We should look at some of the studies that have attempted to isolate the relationships between personality traits and persuasibility. We cannot cover all the studies that have been done, but we can focus on those areas which seem to have the most applicability to the persuasive communicator.

Self-Esteem

One of the most pervasive aspects of personality is the way in which people look at themselves. A person displaying *high self-esteem* will typically appear to be confident, optimistic, and competent. The person will display few feelings of inadequacy, will not feel socially inhibited, and will not exhibit a high degree of anxiety. Both in behavior and in testimony, people with high self-esteem face the world with good impressions of themselves. In contrast, individuals with *low self-esteem* will admit to being anxious in decision-making situations, will tend to be pessimistic, may not appear to be competent, and may testify that they do not feel confident in social situations. Such individuals are always consulting others before making decisions, or taking a position on a topic.

If John Jones has low self-esteem, he ought to be more willing to agree with the opinions of others, since he has little confidence in his own opinions. Thus, we can hypothesize that individuals with low self-esteem should be more persuasible (more easily persuaded) than an individual with high self-esteem.

Most of the available research tends to support this hypothesis. Divesta[3] suggests that when individuals are threatened with a loss of self-esteem, they tend to prefer their own judgments to those of others. Janis,[4] in some early research, suggested that adjustment factors such as feelings of social inadequacy, inhibition, and depression, all indications of low self-esteem, are related to high persuasibility. Janis and Field,[5] measured self-esteem by asking the

subject about his feelings of inadequacy, his social inhibitions, and his test anxiety. Again, they provide support for the hypothesis. Janis and Rife,[6] followed up the Janis and Field study by looking specifically at an audience of individuals in a mental institution. The results showed again that low self-esteem is related to high persuasibility. This study is important in that the investigators were able to test an audience which exhibited these personality characteristics to a high degree.

Another group of studies shows that self-esteem is, indeed, a dyadic characteristic. Cohen[7] has demonstrated that people with low self-esteem are more susceptible to persuasion when they perceive the source as having high self-esteem than when they see the source as having low self-esteem. A study by Leventhal and Perloe[8] further shows the dyadic nature of the self-esteem variable. They conclude that subjects with high self-esteem are influenced by messages that are cast in an optimistic and buoyant tone, while subjects who were low in self-esteem were more susceptible to messages that have a pessimistic and threatening tone. Neither the Cohen study nor the Levanthal and Perloe study contradicts the hypothesis that self-esteem is related to persuasibility, but they do suggest that this is a complicated variable, in which the relationships between the message and all parties to the situation must be taken into account if an accurate prediction is to be achieved. In the examples we have been using, the levels of self-esteem are generally not at the extreme level. People who test out at extreme levels of self-esteem, whether it be high or low, behave more like each other with respect to persuasion than do people who fall into the moderately high or moderately low self-esteem category. Self-esteem thus exhibits a curvilinear relationship with persuasibility, and we might expect to find individuals exhibiting very high self-esteem and very low self-esteem to be persuasible.

One important question is whether it is possible to alter a person's resistance to persuasion by altering their self-esteem. If I work with a receiver and send messages designed to raise self-esteem, will that receiver subsequently be less persuasible? The evidence generally supports a relationship between self-esteem and persuasibility. Miller and Burgoon[9] review the literature and suggest that raising self-esteem is a fairly effective way of increasing a receiver's resistance to a subsequent message when the subsequent message is relatively simple. They suggest that if the message is a complex one, raising self-esteem does not seem to have the same result, and making predictions is more difficult.

Self-esteem is an important variable, because it is one in which some estimates can be made by simply observing receivers as they work and interact with others. Individuals with low self-esteem behave less confidently than others. They ask for advice more than the individual with high self-esteem. They seem to worry more about what they are doing. Such individuals are more likely to be susceptible to persuasive messages.

Anxiety

One of the factors making up a personality structure is the degree of *anxiety* exhibited in various situations. Anxiety may be displayed by feelings of tension, apprehension, uncertainty or panic in everyday encounters with situations and events. We are *not* concerned here with that level of anxiety that becomes so severe that it is an indicator of emotional disturbance. We *are* concerned with the types of tension that all of us experience when meeting new situations, or making important decisions. The research suggests that individuals who experience relatively high anxiety levels about decisions are less susceptible to persuasion. Nunnally and Bobren[10] have shown that individuals with high anxiety tend to show low interest in persuasive messages regardless of the message form. Since persuasion has to depend on initial attention to the message, this study

supports the hypothesis. Janis and Feshback,[11] and Haefner[12] worked with strong and weak fear appeals in a series of messages and showed that when strong fear appeals are used and the receivers are highly anxious, less persuasion occurs. When weak fear appeals are used, the difference between high-anxiety and low-anxiety individuals tends to disappear, but there is still some indication of defensive reactions to the message.

What can be said about persuasion and completely normal levels of anxiety? All of us experience some mild tension and uncertainty when facing the new or the unexpected. In fact, such feelings may be a characteristic of any important decision-making situation, and thus of many interactive situations that people face. In general, our evidence suggests that persuasion may be *better* received in such situations. There may be an increase in the general readiness to respond to communication. People respond because they feel that the messages being received might contain information which would reduce anxiety. Thus, we would expect parties in a situation which requires mutually satisfactory solutions to be more willing to compromise and to reach out for a solution. Doing so will reduce anxiety for both parties. Anxiety, like self-esteem, seems to exhibit a curvilinear relationship to persuasion. Individuals having very high levels of anxiety and very low levels of anxiety seem to be less persuasible than those people who fall into the more normal range.

In offering practical advice regarding the variable of anxiety, it should be pointed out that making an estimate of the anxiety level of a large audience is usually not possible. After all, an audience is composed of many members, each approaching the situation with a different degree of anxiety at the time of the speech. In small, two- or three-way communication situations, however, individuals have some chance to work together, and it is easier to get some estimate of the amount of anxiety others are displaying.

Dogmatism

Milton Rokeach and his associates have been studying a personality characteristic they refer to as "open-mindedness".[13] They use the term "closed-minded" and "dogmatic" as synonymous, and they suggest that these terms refer to the ways in which individuals tend to approach people, ideas, beliefs, and messages. Dogmatism has been shown to be a pervasive personality trait affecting many aspects of an individual's behavior. Our discussion of the open and closed mind emphasizes the centrality of belief to show the importance of this personality trait to the understanding of persuasive communication.

An open-minded individual, one who is not highly dogmatic, tends to be able to bring various belief structures together for purposes of comparison. There is little discrepancy in the beliefs held by such an individual. The individual will tend to have an optimistic outlook about the way in which the world is put together, will not hold that authorities are absolute determiners of policies, will not believe that decisions made today will hold forever, and will tend to view information along a very broad time perspective. The open-minded individual does not compartmentalize beliefs. Open-minded people are more willing to be exposed to controversial materials and are also more willing to express themselves about material that might be contrary to their own attitudes.

In contrast to open-minded people, closed-minded or dogmatic individuals tend to compartmentalize the beliefs they hold, and to be very reluctant to compare various beliefs. Dogmatic people are more likely to be pessimistic about the future of the world, more inclined to believe in the absolute correctness of authorities, and inclined to reject messages from people that are not in agreement with the authorities in which the dogmatic person believes. The closed-minded person is inclined to take a very narrow view of the world's problems.

A number of studies have related dogmatism to persuasibility. One major characteristic of the highly dogmatic individual is a heavy dependence on authority as a source of personal attitudes and beliefs. If an authority the dogmatic individual believes in supports a particular position, the dogmatic individual tends to also believe that position. In a study by Bettinghaus, Miller, and Steinfatt,[14] receivers were asked to judge the logical validity of syllogisms. Some syllogisms had been presented as coming from a source valued positively by the receiver, and some were attributed to negative sources. The results showed that the highly dogmatic subjects made more errors when the syllogisms were attributed to a negative source than to a positive source. This result did not hold true for the individuals classified as "low dogmatic." The more open-minded individuals tended to evaluate the messages on their own merits, rather than on the recommendations of trusted authorities. In another study, Powell showed that closed-minded individuals had difficulties in separating the ideas presented in a message from the authorities who supported or rejected the ideas.[15]

The implication of these studies for persuasion is clear. People who are highly dogmatic can be expected to be more persuasible in those situations where the ideas presented are supported by authorities in whom the individual places trust, and less persuasible in situations where the ideas presented are supported by or linked to authorities in whom little trust is placed. People who are not highly dogmatic are less likely to have a belief in an authority linked to a belief in an idea. Such open-minded individuals are better able to evaluate the ideas in a message apart from the sources of those ideas or the supporters of those ideas.[16]

Dogmatism has further implications for persuasion. The evidence suggests that the open-minded individual is able to relate new ideas to existing reference frames and is able to more easily make adjustments in those frames. Thus a persuasive message which suggests changes away from the status quo, that is, argues for sweeping changes in the social order, ought to be more successful with receivers who are open-minded than with those who are closed-minded. The highly dogmatic person holds beliefs very closely, and is unwilling to allow changes in those beliefs. The highly dogmatic person is unwilling to entertain messages which point out conflicts in belief structures. For example, it is inconsistent to believe that smoking causes lung cancer and to still continue to smoke. We ought to expect more attitude change from a message pointing out this discrepancy and urging people to stop smoking when it is presented to open-minded receivers than to closed-minded receivers. Closed-minded receivers hold beliefs in a compartmentalized fashion, and are unwilling to bring inconsistent beliefs together to reconcile them.

Receivers cannot be divided into two separate groups, dogmatic and nondogmatic. Most people have varying degrees of dogmatism, and only a few fall at the extreme ends of the dogmatism scale. Nevertheless, many people can separate their friends into those who tend to be open-minded individuals and those who lean more toward a closed-minded position. Attaining some knowledge of this personality characteristic will help in predicting how an individual is likely to react to new ideas which might be suggested, to the use of evidence in a message, and to the use of supporting materials.

Authoritarianism

For twenty-five years, psychologists have been conducting research on individuals who possess in varying degrees what has been termed the "authoritarian personality." The emphasis in this work has been on the reaction of certain personality types to situations involving racial and religious minorities. Many persuasive communication situations also involve attempts to reduce prejudice, involve the use of sources representing minorities, or are directed toward members of minority groups. Thus, the work originally presented by Adorno and his colleagues in *The Authoritarian Personality*[17] seems applicable to the general study of persuasive communication.

Basically, people possessing an authoritarian personality tend to be highly reliant on the moral authority of their own reference group, tend to adhere fairly rigidly to middle-class values, and become preoccupied with the relative power and status of other people and with their own power and status. Such people tend to make absolute judgments regarding the values they hold, and to see the world in black and white. They are not easily swayed by messages that might seem to contradict the beliefs they have or the authorities they rely on, despite the judgments of others that the message is rational and logical. Furthermore, the highly authoritarian personality tends to identify with individuals in the groups that appear to have power. The authoritarian personality tends to have the same beliefs as the leaders of those groups, and may reject and act prejudiced and hostile toward individuals in other groups.

An analysis of individuals who seem to have highly authoritarian personalities would suggest that their reaction to persuasion will depend on their reactions to factors other than the merits of the ideas presented. Rohrer and Sherif,[18] for example, examined the reactions of individuals to messages about blacks. They report that while individuals who are not high on the authoritarian scales tended to be persuaded by the ideas in the messages they read, the subjects who were high authoritarians tended to be persuaded by the authorities presented in the messages. This was true for the high authoritarians regardless of whether the message they read was problack or antiblack. The controlling factor in this study seemed to be the dependence of the high authoritarian on the infallibility of the authority figures cited in the messages. The high authoritarian, then, seems to be highly reliant on the authority dimension of the belief structure, and needs to link beliefs about authorities to peripheral beliefs.

Harvey and Beverly[19] point to one of the possible reasons for the kinds of attitude change typically found when differences between high and low authoritarians are noted. In their study, they found that high authoritarians changed in the direction of the position advocated by a high status source to a significantly greater degree than did low authoritarians, but that the high authoritarians could not reproduce the points made in the speech with the same degree of accuracy as could the low authoritarians. Again, the reported attitude change seemed to be the result of the perceived status and power of the source, rather than the strength of the message itself. Similar results have been reported by Paul[20] and Weiss,[21] on the basis of their studies of authoritarianism and attitude change.

Our description of the closed-minded personality and the authoritarian personality suggests that there is undoubtedly some overlap between the two kinds of constructs. The correlations, however, are not complete, and many researchers feel that we are dealing with two different personality factors. Studies of the authoritarian personality were originally directed toward explaining racial and religious prejudice. The authors of *The Authoritarian Personality* suggest that prejudice can be explained in part as a reaction against an "out-group". For high authoritarians, belief and trust is placed only in members of the groups to which they belong. Other groups are rejected, and rejected in such ways that negative actions are taken against members of the out-groups. The persuasive communicator who wishes to secure favorable attitudes toward minority groups might find the task facilitated by making use of trusted authorities to carry the persuasive message to particular receivers. An example of this situation occurred when the conservative wing of the Republican Party was willing to accept Richard Nixon's opening the door to Com-

munist China, although that group refused to accept any other person who argued in favor of such a step. If it is not possible to make use of a trusted source as an actual communicator, then the persuasive communicator might well be advised to design the message in such a way that these authority figures are quoted in the message as favoring the proposed attitude change.

Merely possessing a highly authoritarian personality does not necessarily mean that a person will be more persuasible. Authoritarianism seems to be linked to the use or nonuse of authorities, and is not necessarily related to persuasion in all situations. Understanding authoritarianism as a personality factor and using those particular kinds of messages which emphasize the endorsement of trusted authorities ought to result in more successful persuasion.

The Need for Achievement

David McClelland and his associates[22] have been working for twenty years to clarify a personality variable they refer to as an individual's "need for achievement" or "n-achievement." McClelland measures n-achievement by having individuals write short themes about pictures of individuals working and talking with other people. The themes are scored for the number of "achievement" themes the subject writes into a description of the situations. McClelland reports that his scoring system is now so well developed that his scorers almost never disagree regarding the scoring of an individual's replies.[23] The replies an individual makes indicate his rank on the n-achievement scale.

McClelland's work has been extended in many different directions. He has related this variable to economic success in underdeveloped countries, to the question of whether n-achievement can be trained into an individual, and to the relationship between a child's need for achievement and the parents' achievement need. Our concern, of course, is with any possible relationship between this variable and persuasion.

Individuals who possess a high need for achievement in our society tend to be entrepreneurs, always trying to improve themselves, and trying to do so by their own personal efforts. Such individuals are seemingly driven to more efficiency, to attempting to solve problems and pit themselves against any challenges that might be placed in their paths. Yet people with a high n-achievement are not gamblers; they seem to want to solve the problems they encounter with methods that take the risks into account. On the other hand, individuals who score relatively low on this variable are more artistically sensitive; they will take more risks and they lead a less worried life. Lower socioeconomic class families tend to produce more individuals who score low on n-achievement, but so do individuals from the upper classes. High n-achievement is a characteristic of middle-class parents and middle-class children. This does not mean that other individuals will not exhibit high n-achievement. But the trait is found more frequently among the middle class.

The relationship between the n-achievement variable and persuasibility seems to lie in the nature of the *topics* chosen for persuasion and the appeals used in the message. We might expect that message topics that seem to promise an advance in a person's personal status, economic condition, or power would have a special appeal for the receiver scoring high in n-achievement. On the other hand, we might expect that topics that imagined the receiver giving up something for the benefit of the larger society might not be as successful with the person who is very high in n-achievement. When the persuasive communicator can use a set of appeals that challenges the receiver to action, appeals to the receiver's ability to use personal effort, or offers the possibility of personal gain at moderate risk, the appeals ought to be successful with that receiver who is characterized by having high need for achievement.

Most of the personality variables we have discussed are related as much to the receiver's perceptions of the source and to the authority figures associated with the message as they are to the message itself. Our studies show a clear relationship between the topics used in persuasion and the appeals built into the persuasive message, and thus, do provide the persuasive communicator with considerable predictive power when interacting with certain people.

Personality variables result from the development of reference frames. They are longstanding, pervasive, well organized ways in which the individual tends to view the world. They may not be brought into play by the receiver for *every* communication situation, but in the long run, the type of personality an individual develops will be extremely influential in determining who is listened to, who can be of influence, what topics are likely to be listened to, what appeals will be influential, and finally, how the receiver will respond to the persuasive communication situation.

ATTRIBUTION THEORY

One of the major objections to personality theory is that it takes highly trained individuals to make accurate estimates of personality structures. There are areas in which a source can expect to make useful predictions about personality, but it is certainly the case that going beyond that fairly elementary level is a job for the trained professional. *Attribution theory* argues that *any* time we observe the behavior of others, we will attempt to *attribute* that behavior to *personal* factors or to *situational* factors. An example will help illustrate this point.

Imagine that you have a close friend whom you haven't seen for several weeks. Then you both meet at a large party. You spot your friend across the room, and raise your hand in greeting, but there is no response from your friend. So you call across the room, and again there is no sign of a response. Finally, you start to make your way across the room, through the mass of people, in order to confront your friend in person. When you arrive there, the friend is gone. Attribution theory attempts to explain what you are likely to think and do as a result of perceiving your friend's behavior. For example, you might wind up feeling that the friend is angry with you and has purposely stopped communicating with you. That inference attributes the behavior to the person, since you are concluding that the friend's behavior was something that could be personally decided. On the other hand, you might conclude that the crowded room and the noise were responsible for your friend not seeing you and thus not responding to the messages you sent. That conclusion attributes the behavior to the situation.

The example we have used is a simple one, but it should serve to illustrate the central aim of attribution theory which is an explanatory vehicle for human behavior. It should also demonstrate just why attribution theory is relevant to persuasive communication. In the example, we suggested two possible explanations for the friend's behavior. The reader might very well suggest that either or both of these explanations is incorrect. If we had continued examining the behavior of the friend, we probably would have become better and better at understanding that behavior. If we were obliged to engage in constant interaction with that friend, and had to send persuasive messages to him, our ability to formulate messages should improve as our ability to predict behavior and dispositions improves. Thus one major goal of attribution theory is *to improve the persuasive communicator's ability to predict what the receiver is likely to do in the future.*

Attribution theory is based on *perception*. An individual must be able to perceive the behavior of another before making any attributional inferences about that behavior. For our purposes, then, the theory is especially useful for those persuasive communication situations that involve the face-to-face interactions of people with one another. Husbands talking to wives, roommates working together, teachers working with students, or a city council debating a new ordinance are all examples of the type of situation where attribution theory seeks to improve understanding of human behavior, and the ability to predict that behavior.

Attribution theory grew out of the work of Fritz Heider as it was expounded in *The Psychology of Interpersonal Relations*.[24] Heider tried to set down the conditions in which observers (sources) would observe the behavior of actors (receivers) and then make estimates as to the reasons for such behavior. Thus attribution is closely related to consistency theory, and depends on the assumption that when one person observes the behavior of another, there will be pressures to understand that behavior and to account for it. H. H. Kelley,[25] and Jones and Davis[26] have provided further insights into the nature of attribution theory. The reader who wishes a succinct account of attribution theory will find Shaver's *An Introduction to Attribution Processes*[27] very useful. In this short account, we attempt only to outline the framework of attribution theory and concentrate on those aspects that seem to best apply to persuasion.

The attribution process must start with an observation of the actions taken by someone else. The observer may view the actions in person, or through some medium such as television, film, or even through the newspaper. In our account, we shall concentrate on the observations of receivers by sources made prior to sending persuasive messages. The observations that sources make can be made first hand, as they would be by individuals working together in face-to-face situations, or they may be derived through the accounts of others. If later attributions are to be accurate, and predictability is to be high, it is important that as much first hand information be gained as possible. When the source has to get information from others, or has to obtain it by making inferences as to what the behavior was, the probability that misinterpretations will take place is greatly increased. Misinterpretations lower the probability that accurate attributions will be made.

The second step the source must take is to attempt to separate that behavior of the receiver which is important to later attributions from that which is attributionally meaningless. Imagine that you are sitting across the table from Mike Barker. You watch his behavior for a half-hour period. During that time, he sneezes several times, scratches his head, continues breathing noisily during the whole half hour, and smokes two cigarettes. Although there may be special situations in which any of these activities might be informative to the source, in general, we would have to label each of them as attributionally uninformative. Each of these activities would seem best judged as habitual behavior such as cigarette smoking, reflexive behavior such as breathing, or involuntary behavior such as sneezing. Attribution theory does not wish to argue that knowing about such behavior is useless. In fact, the persuasive communicator may very well find the fact that an individual smokes cigarettes a useful piece of information to have in certain situations. None of these activities, however, appear to be *intentional* in nature, and attributional theorists argue that only behavior that appears to be intentional on the part of the receiver is to be considered as attributionally meaningful.

Let us look again at Mike. This time we shall discard all the observations we have made of Mike breathing, sneezing, and smoking, but we will be very much interested when Mike suddenly picks up a textbook and begins reading and making notes about his reading. This behavior appears intentional, and once we can make that determination, it will be possible to begin to attribute the behavior either to some personal disposition or to some environmental or situational disposition.

Before attempting to move on from the determination that a behavior is intentional, and, therefore, useful to us, we should note that it is quite possible for us to have made a mistake in actually describing the intentional nature of the behavior. For example, we might say that Mike is "studying" when he picks up a book and begins writing. Someone else might say that he is "just fooling around," while a third person

might argue that Mike is just "pretending to read while actually writing a note to his girl friend." Obviously, we would make different attributions about Mike's behavior depending on the way in which the behavior is actually described. For that reason, it is important to be as accurate as possible in describing behavior, and to avoid making any personal judgments about the behavior in the actual description. Step two, then, is to isolate and describe the intentional behaviors of the receivers we are interested in.

The final step of the process is to make a *dispositional attribution* about the receiver's behavior. Note again that the type of attribution we make may be either personal or situational. In our example, we may decide that Mike has picked up his book and begun reading because he is genuinely interested in learning the material in the book. That would be a *personal disposition*, and can be contrasted with the inference that Mike picked up the book because he saw everyone else around him engaged in similar behavior. We would label that type of conclusion as environmental or situational in nature.

At this point one may well ask just what difference it makes whether we make a personal dispositional attribution or an environmental dispositional attribution, or in fact, whether we make any judgments at all. The case of Mike Barker can again serve to illustrate the usefulness of attribution theory. Imagine that you are a book salesman, and you wish to sell Mike some books. If you watch his behavior, and infer that his picking up the book and reading it is a result of his genuine love for scholarship, you would design a message which would ask Mike to buy your books because they will help him improve his grades and learn a new body of material. If, however, Mike actually performed his actions because of the situation in which he found himself, the appeal to scholarship is not likely to be successful.

People make both situational and personal attributions. But some people tend toward making personal attributions more than situational, while other people have the opposite tendency. Thus one person may assume that all the situations encountered are as a result of the fact that, "Everyone is out to get me." Someone else may go through life assuming that, "The world is against me. I'm just unlucky." The type of persuasive strategies we use to approach these two individuals will be quite different. In the case of the person who habitually makes personal attributions, we might be quite successful in hinting that we know "who" can make a difference in the person's life. An appeal to authority ought to be more successful with people who tend to make personal attributions, while such an appeal might not have the same effect on those who tend to make situational attributions. We can use the attribution process to make predictions about the way in which people will behave generally, and to develop communication strategies accordingly.

There are other social situations that may be important to the persuasive communicator, and that can further serve to illustrate the importance of the attribution process. Are criminals a product of their environment, or is there a set of personal characteristics that "makes" people commit crimes? Making that judgment may be extremely important in attempting to deal with the subject of juvenile delinquency in a persuasive message. When your boy friend makes a pass at you after a date, is he doing so because of a genuine interest in you, or because the situation is such that a pass seems appropriate? If you are sitting with a small group of voters in your community and attempting to persuade them to vote "yes" on a ballot item proposing an increase in the property tax to fund an expanded school program, how should you interpret their responses? Are they saying "yes" to you because of a personal disposition that does represent what they will do in the voting booth? Or do they say "yes" because of the presence of others, and their apparent agreement is a situational response that may not be replicated in the voting booth? These and similar examples suggest that making attributions *is*

important to an understanding of human behavior. The examples also suggest that it is not always easy to make accurate attributions. Only practice and the constant checking of predictions against behavior will result in success.

Attribution theory is an important tool for the persuasive communicator to have and to use. All of us make attributions as a result of observing the behaviors of others. Few of us attempt to carefully examine the attributions we make and to test our accuracy over many situations and many encounters with people. Attribution theory suggests that we can improve our understanding about the behavior of others, whether the others are sources to whom we are exposed or receivers we hope to reach with our messages. Making observations, determining intentions, and then making dispositional attributions is a process that all can engage in and improve upon.

SOCIAL EXCHANGE THEORY

Both personality theory and attribution theory can be described as essentially "one-way" theories. The theories themselves do not formally take into account the interactive linkages between people. The source can make predictions about the behavior of the receiver without considering the effect that the source may be having on that behavior. *Social exchange theory* is different. This theoretic position is based on the belief that one can best understand the behavior of people by considering the behavior of *both* source and receiver. Thus it is a *dyadic* rather than *monadic* theory. It is also different because it rests on a foundation of learning theory, and thus all of the principles that we discussed in Chapter 2 are relevant to exchange theory. What makes exchange theory different from other social learning paradigms is that it considers human behavior to be like money, goods and services. Behavior can be offered for exchange, and the vendor and the buyer both take into account the "cost" of the behavior and the "reward" associated with the behavior. Just as learning theory assumes that the amount of the reward offered is directly related to the probability that a response will be made, social exchange theory assumes that the strength of the reward is responsible for the way in which the individual will behave. Learning theory assumes that difficult behavior will be learned less easily than easy behavior, and in similar fashion, social exchange theory assumes that behavior with high cost will occur less frequently than behavior with low cost.

A simple example will help in our understanding of social exchange theory. Imagine that Joe Cool, the student leader we mentioned in the last chapter, turns his attention from President Blue to Mary Johnson, an attractive senior in social science who has been working with Joe on a campaign to permit alcohol on campus. Joe is attracted to Mary, and decides to ask her for a date. He thinks about his finances, and then at the next meeting of their committee, he gets Mary off to one side and says, "Mary, you have been wonderful on the committee. I'd love to take you out for dinner and a flick." At this point, we have a classic social exchange situation. What is Mary's answer likely to be? The theory says that Mary's answer and her subsequent behavior can be explained in terms of a cost versus reward analysis.

Mary will examine the costs of going out with Joe. And there *will* be costs. She may have to buy a new dress, or at least will have a cleaning bill for a dress she already owns. She will have to take time off from studying, perhaps a minimal cost, but a cost nevertheless. She will have to decide how it will affect other men she dates if she is seen for a whole evening with Joe Cool. She will have to spend the entire evening talking to Joe, and that is a psychic energy cost, if nothing else. She will have to decide whether Joe will want her to do anything more in the future with him, and whether she wants to become further engaged. Those will be some of the costs that she will have to con-

sider. But there are rewards as well. She will get away from dorm food for one evening. She will get to see a movie that she won't have to pay for. She will get to talk to someone other than her roommate. She may find Joe Cool to be extremely interesting and may develop a longtime relationship. She may find it rewarding to be seen with a student leader. Social exchange theory suggests that Mary will make her decision by weighing the costs or efforts she will have to go through against the rewards that are perceived, and then make a decision to accept or not to accept the date.

Social exchange theory does not rest on the type of relatively simple example presented above. It has grown out of the work of several social psychologists and interpersonal communication researchers. In particular, the works of Thibaut and Kelley,[28] Homans,[29] and Blau[30] have led to the current understanding of social behavior as exchange. The reader will also find the book by Chadwick-Jones[31] to be an extremely useful summary of the relevant research. Much of that research has been based on careful studies using a number of psychological "games", or situations in which people can show how they might behave in certain social situations. The classic design for social exchange research is based on the game called "Prisoner's Dilemma." Luce and Raiffa describe the basic game:

> Two suspects are taken into custody and separated. The district attorney is certain that they are guilty of a specific crime, but he does not have adequate evidence to convict them at a trial. He points out to each prisoner that each has two alternatives: to confess to the crime the police are sure they have done, or not to confess. If they both do not confess, then the district attorney states he will book them on some very minor trumped-up charge such as petty larceny and illegal possession of a weapon, and they will both receive minor punishments; if they both confess they will be prosecuted, but he will recommend less than the most severe sentence; but if one confesses

and the other does not, then the confessor will receive lenient treatment for turning state's evidence whereas the latter will get "the book" slapped at him.[32]

There are many variations of the prisoner's dilemma game, utilizing various types of rewards or punishments depending on the nature of the situation being tested. Figure 3.1 shows a typical kind of matrix for the situation mentioned above.

An examination of each of the cells in the prisoner's dilemma game will be helpful in understanding social exchange theory and its relation to persuasion. Why should either prisoner confess? The message is clear. If both prisoners stick together, the worst that can happen is that both will serve one year each. One might assume that all pairs of prisoners would always opt for cell (4), and would remain silent regardless of the persuasive messages being sent to them. The problem is that neither prisoner can talk to the other one, and the rewards to be gained by confessing are substantial. If Prisoner A gives in, confesses and implicates his partner, he serves only half as much time as in cell (4). That might not be enough incentive, but Prisoner A is aware that if he does not confess, and Prisoner B does, he will serve twenty years, an extremely high "cost" when placed against the possibility of getting off with six months. The message strategy that the district attorney must

use is obvious. The district attorney must emphasize the weak nature of the other partner. He must carefully point out the high risks being taken, and the length of time that twenty years in the slammer represents. On the other hand, the district attorney must never mention the possibility that both prisoners might confess, because the possibility of a ten-year sentence is also a high cost behavior, and might be viewed as no different than a twenty-year sentence.

Obviously, there are many other variations of this game. For example, we could change cell four to read "get off free" for both prisoners. What might we expect to happen when the reward for not confessing is raised with respect to the possible costs of confessing. The message strategies will obviously have to be changed, and the percentage of people responding by confessing or not confessing will also change.

The study of social exchange theory has utilized the prisoner's dilemma format or any of the hundreds of different variations that can be developed from this basic design, and then determined how people actually behave when confronted with the situation. How many people will give up a small reward in order to obtain a much larger reward even when the chance of losing is increased by so doing? How many people will "throw over" a partner in the hopes of obtaining a lesser punishment or a larger reward for themselves? Our concern,

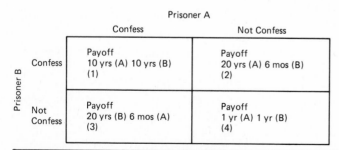

Figure 3.1 The Prisoner's Dilemma Game

however, is with the manner in which social exchange theory relates to persuasive communication, and many of the intricacies of the theory must be ignored in order to concentrate on persuasion.

Let us return to our example of Joe Cool and Mary Johnson. As we discussed this example, we made the implicit assumption that the behavior of Mary could be predicted in terms of costs and rewards, but nowhere did we consider the role that Joe played in the situation, nor did we discuss the effect on persuasion of Joe's own analysis of the costs and rewards of making an initial offer, or the costs and rewards of their mutual behavior in subsequent situations. Prisoner's dilemma suggests that we could have made a far more accurate estimate of the situation if we had included Joe in our analysis. If we had included an analysis of the costs to Joe of asking Mary out, together with an accounting of the benefits that Joe would gain, we might have been able to predict whether Joe would have even initiated the offer to Mary. Joe might have considered the possible embarrassment of Mary's saying "no." He might have thought about the effect on his campaign workers if he seemed to be favoring one person over another. He might have worried about the possible long-term financial costs if this date became a success. If we had had an accurate analysis of Joe's assessment of the situation as well as Mary's assessment, we would have been in a better position to predict whether Joe would have entered into the situation at all, and if he did, what Mary's behavior was likely to be. None of the other theories we have discussed offer such clear cut opportunities to examine an entire situation, taking into account the behavior of both source and receiver.

Social exchange theory offers us the opportunity to make suggestions to both the source and the potential receiver about situations involving persuasive communication.

For the source we can suggest the following:

1. Make an analysis of the costs versus the benefits for any persuasive message you might send. This is really seldom done by persuasive communicators. They tend to look only at potential rewards if successful, and seldom assess costs of making an exchange, or make an analysis of the potential disadvantages. In all probability, there would be less communication if we all took the trouble to make such an analysis.

2. Make an analysis ahead of time of the costs versus the benefits for the receiver to whom the message is directed. Again, we think about the potential rewards to the receiver, but seldom attempt to estimate the costs. If we did, we might sometimes find that there are no circumstances under which it would be possible for the receiver to answer "yes" to our message. In that event, we must redesign the message to offer better reinforcement.

3. Make sure that your message specifies the reasons why it should be accepted. Many persuasive messages simply propose that the receiver take some action. The source hopes that the perceived reward is implicit in the message. Perception is selective, however, and it is frequently the case that the rewards the source sees so clearly in analyzing the task are misperceived or not seen at all by the receiver.

4. Be sure to consider the future effects of persuasion on both yourself and your receiver. We may make an analysis of a particular situation, and decide to proceed with our message. If, however, we had made an analysis of the potential effects of a receiver's behavior on our future behavior, we might not have decided to take the initial plunge.

In the same fashion that we give suggestions to the source about exchange considerations, we can also give some suggestions to the receiver:

1. Make sure that you analyze both costs and benefits before responding to any persuasive message. The most common fault is to look at the potential rewards, but to ignore the resultant costs. More people have wound up in bankruptcy court, or the loan office, or have

bitterly regretted a decision that was taken because only the possible rewards were recognized, and not the costs.

2. Attempt to ascertain what the source is getting out of the situation. Exchange theory makes the assumption that few, if any, people operate in a completely altruistic fashion. What does the source expect to gain? Will you, as the respondent to a message be rewarded in proportion to the rewards of the source? A receiver who asks these questions before responding can better assure that the people in the situation will make a social exchange that is equitable for all parties.

3. Examine the message carefully in order to obtain an accurate estimate of both costs and rewards. Many persuasive messages are carefully constructed to tell the receiver what the rewards are going to be for taking the recommended action, but few spell out the costs as carefully. The receiver should make an attempt to gain *all* the available information before jumping to some suggested action.

4. Attempt to assess future costs and benefits from taking a recommended action. This advice, recommended for the source, is equally appropriate for the receiver. Many of us act as a result of one message, without realizing that taking one action may require taking a series of actions extending into the future.

Social exchange theory, then, is another attempt to understand the behavior of people in interactional situations, and to be better able to predict those actions. It depends on the assumption that people will act in accordance with economic principles, making decisions based on an analysis of the perceived costs and perceived benefits. We must note that the word "perceived" is an important one. Social exchange theory does not claim that everyone will behave in exactly the same way when confronted by the same situation. One person may perceive the costs differently than another. One person may be willing to take large risks, while another attempts only to maintain a current position. One person's sense of loyalty in the prisoner's dilemma situation will result in decision after decision against what would seem to the outside observer to be in the person's best interests. Social exchange theory does provide another tool to both source and receiver in approaching the persuasive communication situation, a tool that allows understanding and prediction in dyadic situations.

SUMMARY

There are many different types of persuasive communication situations. Some of the most important are those situations involving interpersonal communication, where a communicator is talking to one or a very few people. Predicting the nature of the attitudes and beliefs that the receiver holds in that situation is extremely important to the communicator. In this chapter, we examined three theories designed to make it easier to make an accurate assessment.

Personality theory is based on the assumption that when our belief structures become relatively fixed, we may be able to identify the structures in terms of various personality characteristics. These personality categories can help the communicator in making predictions about the way in which people are likely to react in a communication situation.

Attribution theory is based on the premise that all of us make attributions as to the causes of behavior when we observe the behavior of those around us. The theory suggests that we tend to attribute behavior to either personal or situational dispositions. The communicator who can make a careful assessment of the attributions from which receivers will operate, can improve understanding and prediction.

Finally, we discussed social exchange theory, an approach to studying human behavior which concentrates on the analysis of the costs and benefits that sources and receivers can expect from engaging in communication. Suggestions to help both the source and the receiver improve the ability to predict behavior point to the usefulness of exchange theory to the persuasive communication process.

FOOTNOTES

1. N. L. Munn, *Psychology: Fundamentals of Human Adjustment*, 3d ed., (Boston: Houghton Mifflin Co., 1956), pp. 170–184.
2. T. W. Adorno and others, *The Authoritarian Personality*, (New York: Harper and Row, Inc., 1950), p. 106.
3. F. J. DiVesta and J. C. Merwin, "The Effects of Need-oriented Communications on Attitude Change," *Journal of Abnormal and Social Psychology*, vol. 60 (1960), pp. 80–85.
4. I. L. Janis, "Personality Correlates of Susceptibility to Persuasion," *Journal of Personality*, vol. 22 (1954), pp. 504–18.
5. I. L. Janis and P. B. Field, "Sex Differences and Personality Factors Related to Persuasibility," in I. L. Janis and C. I. Hovland, eds., *Personality and Persuasibility*, (New Haven, Conn.: Yale University Press, 1959), pp. 55–68.
6. I. L. Janis and D. Rife, "Persuasibility and Emotional Disorder," in I. L. Janis and C. I. Hovland, eds., *Personality and Persuasibility*, (New Haven, Conn.: Yale University Press, 1959), pp. 121–37.
7. A. R. Cohen, "Some Implications of Self-esteem for Social Influence," in I. L. Janis and C. I. Hovland, eds., *Personality and Persuasibility*, (New Haven, Conn.: Yale University Press, 1959), pp. 102–21.
8. H. Leventhal and S. I. Perloe, "A Relationship between Self-esteem and Persuasibility," *Journal of Abnormal and Social Psychology*, vol. 62 (1962), pp. 385–88.
9. G. R. Miller and M. Burgoon, *New Techniques of Persuasion*, (New York: Harper and Row, 1973), pp. 21–23.
10. J. C. Nunnally and H. M. Bobren, "Variables Governing the Willingness to Receive Communications on Mental Health," *Journal of Personality*, vol. 27 (1959), pp. 275–90.
11. I. L. Janis and S. Feshbach, "Effects of Fear-arousing Communications," *Journal of Abnormal and Social Psychology*, vol. 49 (1954), pp. 211–18.
12. D. P. Haefner, "Some Effects of Guilt-arousing and Fear-arousing Persuasive Communications on Opinion Change," (Ph.D. dissertation, University of Rochester, 1956).
13. M. Rokeach, *The Open and Closed Mind*. (New York: Basic Books, 1962).
14. E. P. Bettinghaus, T. Steinfatt and G. Miller, "Source Evaluation, Syllogistic Content, and Judgments of Logical Validity by High- and Low-dogmatic persons," *Journal of Personality and Social Psychology*, vol. 16, no. 2 (1970), pp. 238–44.
15. F. A. Powell, "Open- and Closed-mindedness and the Ability to Differentiate Source and Message," *Journal of Abnormal and Social Psychology*, vol. 65 (1962), pp. 61–4.
16. R. Vacchiano, P. Strauss, and L. Hockman, "The Open and Closed Mind: A Review of Dogmatism," *Psychological Bulletin*, Vol. 71, No. 4 (1969), p. 261.
17. T. W. Adorno and others, *The Authoritarian Personality*, (New York: Harper and Row, 1950).
18. J. H. Rohrer and M. Sherif, *Social Psychology at the Crossroads*, (New York: Harper and Row, Publishers, 1951).
19. O. J. Harvey and G. D. Beverly, "Some Personality Correlates of Concept Change through Role Playing," *Journal of Abnormal and Social Psychology*, vol. 63 (1961), pp. 125–30.
20. I. H. Paul, "Impressions of Personality, Authoritarianism, and the *Fait Accompli* Effect," *Journal of Abnormal and Social Psychology*, vol. 53 (1956), pp. 338–44.
21. W. Weiss, "Emotional Arousal and Attitude Change," *Psychological Review*, vol. 6 (1960), pp. 267–80.
22. For a review of n-achievement, see D. McClelland and others, *The Achievement Motive*, (New York: Appleton–Century–Crofts, 1953), and D. McClelland, *The Achieving Society*, (Princeton, N.J.: D. VanNostrand Co., 1961).
23. T. G. Harris, "Achieving Man: A Conversation with David C. McClelland," *Psychology Today*, vol. 4, No. 8 (January 1971), p. 36.
24. F. Heider, *The Psychology of Interpersonal Relations*, (New York: John Wiley & Sons, 1958).

25. H. H. Kelley, "Attribution Theory in Social Psychology," in D. Levine, ed., *Nebraska Symposium on Motivation*, (Lincoln, Neb.: University of Nebraska Press, vol. 15, 1967), pp. 192–238.

26. E. E. Jones and K. E. Davis, "From Acts to Dispositions: The Attribution Process in Person Perception," in L. Berkowitz, ed., *Advances in Experimental Social Psychology*, vol. 5, (New York: Academic Press, 1965), pp. 219–66.

27. Kelly G. Shaver, *An Introduction to Attribution Processes* (Cambridge, Mass.: Winthrop Publishers, 1975).

28. J. Thibaut and H. H. Kelley, *The Social Psychology of Groups* (New York: John Wiley & Sons, 1959).

29. G. C. Homans, *Social Behavior: Its Elementary Forms*, (New York: Harcourt, Brace, 1961).

30. P. M. Blau, *Exchange and Power in Social Life*, (New York: John Wiley & Sons, 1964).

31. J. K. Chadwick Jones, *Social Exchange Theory: Its Structure and Influence in Social Psychology*, (New York: Academic Press, 1976).

32. R. D. Luce and H. Raiffa, *Games and Decisions*, (New York: John Wiley & Sons, 1957), p. 95.

FOUR

SUCCESSFUL PERSUASION: PREDICTING GROUP RESPONSE

East Lansing, Michigan conducted a local election in 1976, a process repeated yearly in towns and cities all over the United States. Two members of the City Council were to be elected from a slate of four candidates who had survived the primary election. The nature of the persuasive messages developed by each of the candidates illustrates the problems to be discussed in this chapter.

Elections to the City Council are conducted on a nonpartisan basis, and candidates are not identified as either Republicans or Democrats. Thus candidates must make themselves and their programs known to the voters without having a party label on which to depend. East Lansing is also a university community, with several thousand Michigan State University students registered and eligible to vote in local elections, and several thousand townspeople also registered and eligible to vote.

Two of the candidates became known as the "liberal" candidates. They directed most of their time, attention, and messages toward the student voters. They called for stronger environmental protection laws, elimination of marijuana felony laws, and a hold on the construction of new businesses until serious housing problems could be solved. The other two candidates became known as the "conservative" candidates. These candidates had fewer contacts with students and more with the townspeople. They advocated measures to improve the business opportunities in the community, increased spending on city parking facilities, no change in the drug laws, and city services to homeowners.

Obviously, the two groups of candidates seemed to be appealing to what they felt were different beliefs and attitudes held by the varying groups of voters. Furthermore, many voters, as well as the news media, tagged the candidates with a label which represented perceived attitudes of the groups to whom the candidates appealed. Our problem in this chapter is to investigate the relationship between persuasibility and those characteristics which individuals possess as a result of their membership in particular groups.

Humans possess many attitudinal structures, and we have examined the development and change in these structures as people attend to the events in their environment. In the previous chapter, we looked at some theories that help in predicting what attitudes, beliefs, and behaviors are likely to be for individuals who are engaged with the source in face-to-face interpersonal communication situations. The three theories we discussed are most appropriate for those situations in which the source can learn from and observe the receiver over a long period of time. Such a period of observation is simply not always possible. Many times, a source faces an audience composed of many people, or of a few strangers. For example, candidates for the City Council in East Lansing frequently make use of neighborhood "coffee klatches" to carry their message. They find one person they know, and that person invites neighbors to meet the candidate. How is the candidate to be able to obtain some estimate of the attitudes and beliefs that the audience might have? Such situations are the topic of this chapter.

The development of reference frames is influenced by the *groups of people with whom an individual associates*. The people we associate with are constantly sending us messages, and we react to those messages. If you are a college student living in a dormitory on campus, the likelihood is that you will be receiving and acting upon many messages sent by fellow students. You cannot help but be influenced by these messages, and you will most likely become more like your fellow students than like your high school classmates who did not go to college and are working on a production line in a factory. The student living in a dormitory will be different from the student living at home with parents, or the one living in an apartment off campus. When you, as a college student, receive messages from any source, you are likely to respond to those messages with behavior colored by reference frames developed as a result of your association with other college students. The influence that groups have on the development of attitudes and beliefs is important information for the persuasive communicator.

REFERENCE GROUPS

When people behave in such a manner that their attitudes and beliefs seem to be dependent on their association with particular groups, we say that they have made use of a *reference group*. The term "reference group" is used to describe any group to which people relate their attitudes and beliefs. An understanding of reference groups is necessary to persuasion because frames of reference are built up, at least in part, as a result of contact with or membership in particular groups.

Reference groups serve two major functions. One function is that of determining behavior for an individual by setting group standards or norms of behavior. The second function of reference groups is to serve as a standard or checkpoint for making decisions about persuasive messages that have been recieved. The latter function is more closely related to our concern with persuasibility.

Kelley suggests that the use of a reference group as a standard or checkpoint is really a "comparison function." He says, "A group functions as a comparison reference group for an individual to the extent that the behavior, attitudes, circumstances, or other characteristics of its members represent standards or comparison points which he uses in making judgments and evaluations."[1]

Reference groups can be divided into a number of different types. One way of looking at reference groups is to divide them into *membership* and *nonmembership* groups. That is, they can be groups of which the individual is actually a member, such as a fraternity, the Junior Chamber of Commerce, the local Methodist Church, or the American Legion. They can also be groups of which the individual is not a member, but which serve as a standard that is used in making decisions. The college student who does not belong to a fraternity may use what he knows or thinks he knows about fraternities in making judgments on certain issues. A second, closely allied way of distinguishing between reference groups is described by Newcomb when he refers to *positive* and *negative* reference groups.[2] In terms of persuasive communication, a positive reference group is a group toward which an individual aspires. Thus for a given receiver, a message opposing socialized medicine might be viewed favorably by someone who wants to become a physician, since the receiver may feel that the reference group physician does not tend to view socialized medicine with favor. A negative reference group is one the individual opposes. To use the same example in reverse, an individual who believes that "all doctors charge too much," might oppose a message arguing against socialized medicine, taking the position that: "If doctors are against it, I'm for it."

Reference groups are only one kind of standard that receivers use to form frames of reference. Our discussion in previous chapters suggested that *any* information a person acquires may be used in the development of reference frames. The experiences that people have, the standards set by technology, by laws, by customs, and by education can be important in the development of reference frames. The experiences that we have may be enhanced, however, by associating with people who think them to be important. Thus associating with a particular group, or just learning that some group has spoken out on a particular topic, may make it likely that one attitude will be developed over another, or that one belief will be adopted and another denied. We are helped in making predictions about potential responses through a knowledge of an individual's reference groups. For this reason, further examination of the characteristics of various groups that can potentially serve as a reference group is warranted.

MEMBERSHIP GROUPS

Every individual belongs to many groups. Some kinds of group membership are those over which the individual has little or no control. These are *demographic groups*, or *involuntary groups*, and are indicated by such variables as age, sex, ethnic origin, and occupation. People cannot control how old they are, or whether they are born black or white. We might argue that the matter of being born at a particular time in history, or being born of parents of a particular race ought not to make any difference in individual beliefs and attitudes. The evidence suggests, however, that these demographic groupings *do* make a difference, because of the probability that individuals sharing demographic characteristics will also have increased interaction with one another.

The second type of membership group can be identified as that which people join voluntarily or over which they have at least some control. These are *voluntary groups* and include such associations as religious affiliation, social groups, and political groups. We shall discuss both demographic and voluntary groups and their relationship to persuasive communication.

If a man were to be described in terms of all the possible groups to which he belonged, the description would point to one and only one individual. To illustrate, there may be only one person in the United States who is a man, thirty-eight years old, a Methodist, a school superintendent, a father of seven children, married to a Wellesley graduate, a Republican, earning $25,300 a year, and an accomplished oboe player, but there are many people who are men, many who are school superintendents, and millions of Republicans. If these groups can be shown to produce distinct behavioral characteristics in an individual, and if the communicator can construct messages in such a way that the receiver will use one of the groups as a reference group, prediction of response is improved.

DEMOGRAPHIC GROUPS

Demographic groups include those associations over which the individual has little control. People cannot control which sex they are, what racial group they were born into, nor what age they are. We have some control over our religious affiliation, although the vast majority of people belong to the religious group that their parents belonged to, suggesting that even this group is set for many people. In examining demographic characteristics, we should remember that they can serve only as guides to the communicator. Predicting the characteristics of a particular audience from a knowledge of the demographic characteristics is very helpful as long as the persuasive communicator realizes that the predictions may well not fit any one specific member of the audience.

Sex

A number of studies suggest differences between men and women in the ways in which they react to persuasive messages. In general, these studies tend to show that women are more persuasible than men, although the findings are perhaps not as clear as we would like. Janis and Field,[3] in an early study, suggest that men and women differ in persuasibility, with women in their study being more persuasible. The differences between the sexes were small, but significant. A number of other studies also report that women are more persuasible

than men, across a wide range of topics.[4] Although there are a number of studies that do report such differences, there may be other reasons for the differences that seem to exist. For example, Abelson and Lesser[5] used grade-school children and reported that they did not find significant differences between boys and girls. This different finding is of considerable help to the communicator, since it might help explain why the differences we reported above do appear. Small children do not perceive, and are not trained to see, major differences between the sexes, but as a child grows, there are training differences, associational differences, and social differences between boys and girls that give rise to different attitudinal frameworks. Carmichael reports a study in which both men and women students were given messages that told them they were inferior students, and then they were exposed to a persuasive message. Another experimental group was sent messages telling them that they were excellent students, and that group was also then exposed to a persuasive message. The results showed no differences between men and women in terms of persuasibility for the group getting the information that they were excellent students. On the other hand, the group told that they were inferior students showed that the women in that group were more persuasible than the men.[6] Clearly, the results suggested that the variable of frustration and not sex was responsible for the change.

Another explanation for the differences in persuasibility may be that the topics used by the experimenters in the studies we have cited may have been oriented toward men rather than women. For example, imagine that the subject of a persuasive speech is compulsory arbitration of labor disputes and that the audience is composed of equal numbers of men and women drawn from a general population. The chances are that many of the men will have formed frames of reference about labor and labor disputes, since such interests have traditionally formed part of the male role in our society. When the speech is presented, striking attitude changes would not be expected from the men in the audience, since the information presented would have to fit into an already existing reference frame. For the women in our general audience, however, expectations are somewhat different. There will certainly be women in the audience who are members of labor unions, or who work with companies that are concerned with the arbitration of labor disputes. These women will already have formed reference frames about the topic, and their reactions to the message may be very much like those of the men in the audience. Many other women will not have built up an elaborate set of reference frames about labor–management problems, and their reactions may be more pronounced than the reactions of those members of the audience who do have such structured reference frames. Given equal attentivity on the part of all members of the audience, a researcher might find that women made more changes in their attitudinal structures than men, since they were moving from knowing very little about the topic to knowing at least the content of the speech, without, however, being able to evaluate it from a specific frame of reference. The conclusion of the researcher in this situation would be that women are more persuasible than men.

The example we have used suggests that caution must be exercised in making judgments about the persuasibility of any demographic group. Persuasibility is probably related more to the topic or the situation than it is to any set of personal characteristics. If we had changed the topic of the speech from compulsory arbitration to abortion, we might have found the opposite results, and would thus have concluded that men are more persuasible.

There are differences between men and women in terms of the attitudes and beliefs that are held, and those differences result in different reference frames, and thus in different predictions about reactions to persuasive messages, but the differences between men and women

arise largely because of the different role positions typically filled by the two sexes, and *not* because of any inherent differences in persuasibility. Furthermore, there is evidence that many of those traditional roles are changing. The growth of the National Organization for Women, the push by millions of Americans of both sexes to get the Equal Rights Amendment passed, and the opening of roles traditionally held by only one sex to both, argues that *role position*, not sex, may provide the best predictions in the future. If children are raised without constant attention to role differences, if schools attempt to educate boys and girls alike, if jobs are distributed equally among the population, such differences as do exist may be expected to disappear. Nevertheless, despite all of the reasons that can be cited for the differences, the evidence clearly shows that women are more persuasible than men. The gap may be closing, but knowledge of that gap can be of help to the persuasive communicator in planning a speech.

There are studies that suggest that some people within the society are paying less attention to the traditional divisions of labor between men and women. Bem[7] has investigated the "androgynous personality." He finds that those individuals who are able to assume both masculine and feminine roles do not conform in their attitudes or behavior to the ways in which men or women are *supposed* to behave. These studies suggest that the future might bring quite a different type of analysis for the variable of sex.

Sex and its relation to persuasibility has been discussed in some detail because it illustrates the problems that a communicator faces with many of the demographic variables. There may be no inherent reason why certain people should react differently to persuasive messages, but the available research says that they do. When the investigator finds that kind of situation, it is necessary to look beyond the variable in an attempt to understand the findings. For example, the polls show clearly that there are differences in attitudes between men and women on certain topics. Normally, however, there will be women whose reactions are the same as the majority of men, and men whose reactions will be similar to the majority of women. We can help improve predictability in this situation by attempting to isolate the type of jobs held, the educational level, or the role positions that could help account for the attitudes held. In such a fashion, the communicator can improve predictions to a level which is better than that which a simple prediction from a single variable would provide.

Regardless of whether you feel that there should or should not be any differences between the sexes in our society, the evidence we can gather from polls and from other studies suggests that there are attitudinal differences. Taking account of the differences will improve the persuasive messages that sources construct.

Age

Many young Americans feel that their elders are extremely rigid individuals who "can never change their minds." Many older Americans, on the other hand, feel that the younger generation consists of "wild kids" who irresponsibly change their opinions and attitudes at the drop of a hat. Are there real differences in the general persuasibility of different age groupings? When age groups are used by different individuals as reference groups, are there differences between the reference groups of the young and the old?

We have no studies that correspond exactly to the Janis and Field study examined in the previous section. One way of collecting data to make some inferences about potential persuasibility differences between various age groups is to look at the differences in beliefs and attitudes that researchers have found between parents and their children. A series of studies conducted by many researchers from the 1930s to the 1950s suggested that children tended to hold roughly the same kinds of attitudes as

their parents, although the young did not hold their attitudes with the same degree of certainty or intensity.[8] By far, the greatest percentage of children expressed the same political party preference as their parents in these comparison studies. Economic attitudes were somewhat the same, although there is wider variation than in the case of political preferences. Where there were differences between a college-aged youth and his parents, the differences were in the greater degree of liberalism expressed by youth. Old and young tended to differ slightly in their attitudes toward war, toward sexual practices, and toward communism.

The studies we have cited are all over twenty years old. A legitimate question to ask might be whether today's younger people are significantly different from older generations. Studies by Hess and Torney[9] and by Langton[10] indicate that teenage groups are becoming more unlike their parents. Not only are the young more liberal, a finding that hasn't changed much in many years, but they may also be rejecting the political party labels of their parents. Atkin,[11] for example, found that over 70 percent of college students at Michigan State University listed themselves as "independent."

With respect to sexual attitudes, the available data seems to indicate similar conclusions. Younger people seem to have tolerant attitudes toward what might be cited by their elders as deviant behavior. One cannot, of course, draw the conclusion that younger people actually differ in sexual behavior from their elders, but there is clearly an indication of more tolerance of homosexuality, of sexual intercourse before marriage, and of other practices that are objected to by an older generation. Another indication of differences in attitude between the old and the young is reported by Barrett, who states that "teenagers and their ways" is the most frequently cited area of annoyance to males seventy years of age and older.[12] These differences in attitude do not directly indicate that there are differences in persuasibility between the two groups, but our knowledge of reference frames would suggest that the older generations are less persuasible than the younger on many issues. Their reference frames are more complete, and the introduction of new information or ideas is not going to make the same impact on those frames as it might with an individual whose reference frames are less well developed. Both the differences in attitudes and the differences in persuasibility are of help to the communicator who needs to plan a persuasive message.

We could continue to examine some of the specific areas in which the attitudes or reference frames of individuals from varying age groups are different. The specific nature of the differences, however, changes from topic to topic, and from time to time. The evidence suggests that there are certain topics which seem to remain stable for age groups across time. One of the most famous sets of studies in sociology was the Middletown study of attitudes and beliefs in Muncie, Indiana.[13] The studies showed that there were differences between parents and children, but that those differences existed primarily for peripheral beliefs. Parents and children tended to hold similar beliefs about the existence of God, the importance of the family, and other highly pervasive beliefs. Children and parents, however, tended to differ about music, entertainment, and other areas of life that are not part of the central or authority set of beliefs. Most interestingly, the same town has been studied recently, using many of the same questions that were asked in the earlier studies.[14] Despite the passage of time, approximately the same differences between parents and children were found then as in 1924. Children tended to believe in God at the same level as fifty years ago. Peripheral beliefs were just as different in both studies. Young people in the second study tended to accept marijuana as desirable, while their parents rejected it. The researchers' overall conclusion was that Muncie had changed very little if one looked at central or authority based beliefs.

The differences were in peripheral beliefs, beliefs about ideas and topics and things that were not even in existence when the first studies were made.

What specific advice can we offer the persuasive communicator. There are two suggestions that might prove to be helpful. First, there are polls published every two or three weeks that try to describe current attitudes and beliefs of various segments of the population. Magazines such as *Psychology Today*, *Human Behavior*, *Time* and *Newsweek* routinely run stories about attitudes and beliefs of various age groups. These sources can be used to assist the communicator in making some estimate about current attitudes that might be held by people of various age groups.

The second suggestion comes from an examination of the way in which reference frames are developed. Because reference frames are developed through experience, it is likely that the older individual will have more firmly developed reference frames, and thus should be less persuasible than a younger person who may have only sketchily developed reference frames. The result is that exposure to, and acceptance of, any given persuasive message is likely to have a far greater impact on the young than it might on one who possesses relatively complete attitudinal structures.

There are differences between individuals of different ages. The variations may not lie in any inherent differences between the young and the old, but rather in the differences in the experiences people have, the different groups associated with, and the nature and kinds of attitudinal and information-processing structures the individual possesses.

Social Class, Education, Occupation, and Income

In one sense, the variables of social class, education, occupation, and income are not demographic variables in the way that age and sex are such variables. One might argue that individuals do have control over the educational level they attain, the social class to which they belong, their occupation, and income level. In actuality, however, these variables are all tied together, and in our society, are difficult to distinguish from variables such as age, sex, and race. Therefore, we shall treat them as most sociologists do—as demographic variables.

Although these four variables are frequently separated in research studies because people are asked different questions, the answers that people give tend to be highly correlated. The level of education that people have tends to determine occupation, which is highly related to income level, and that in turn to social class. Knowing that these relationships *are* intertwined suggests that we can make use of one of the variables as a standard against which to make at least *some* estimate of the others. Social class is the variable about which we have the most evidence, and a number of different studies indicate that there are important differences in attitudes and beliefs between the various class groups.

Lipset and Linz[15] suggest that individuals in the lower classes are particularly susceptible to information purporting to help them move into a higher class. A study by Short and Strodtbeck[16], however, suggests that this susceptibility is not a general characteristic, but applies only to messages purporting to tell the individual how to move into the next higher class, not to social classes two or more above the person's current level. This study illustrates some of the problems we have in making use of information about an individual's social class, education, or occupation. Short and Strodtbeck studied delinquent youths in several teenage gangs. Part of the data gathered concerned the feelings the boys had about the kind of family life they would like to have. The results indicated that the boys were unable to imagine a life much different from their own. If persuasive messages to these boys had emphasized the rewards to be gained from joining a country club or from an occupation requiring a college

degree, the chances are that the message would not have been effective.

One of the most complete studies of attitudes and social class differences was conducted by Tryon.[17] He took individuals living in different areas of San Francisco and divided them into three clusters along economic lines. He then looked at three attitude structures regarding politics and government, community enterprise, and state support of churches and welfare organizations. Tryon found significant correlations between the demographic clustering of individuals along economic lines and the three sets of attitudes he measured. Even more important for persuasion is his finding that the relationships tended to hold for different areas of the city over long periods of time, although there was much movement of individuals in and out of the three areas. Clearly, the differences produced in an individual's frames of reference through the different experiences associated with being in a particular social class are extremely important to the persuasive communicator.

Educational level is related to social class, income, and occupation, but there are some rather specific conclusions indicated by a consideration of studies relating education level to attitudes. In 1970, CBS News ran a series of programs reporting on an assessment of the attitudes of young adults in our society.[18] Individuals were divided into two groups: those who had completed high school and those with a college education. The study showed that there were wide differences between the two groups. In general, those with college training appeared more liberal than those without the college experience. They were more opposed to war, more in favor of abortion reform, more in favor of welfare reform, and more in favor of laws to control pollution. The college-educated group was also more unlike their parents in terms of attitudes than were those who had no college education. The experience of the individuals who had gone on to college obviously had enabled them to form reference frames which differed considerably from those of their parents and from those of contemporaries who did not go to college, and who had thus had a different set of experiences during the years that others spent in college.

Our discussion thus far suggests one important factor for the persuasive communicator to remember. The communicator in a traditional persuasive situation also has a particular educational level, has a particular occupation, and lives at some particular income level. The communicator's reference frames may be conditioned by past experiences on the job or in education in exactly the same way as receivers' frames are conditioned. The very fact that the source brings attitudes to the communication situation makes it difficult to put aside those attitudes and beliefs in order to accurately assess the attitudes and beliefs of others. One way of helping to overcome this tendency is to use evidence and data collected by others. There are many studies published each year about attitudes and beliefs, and many of those studies concentrate on the beliefs of particular social groups. We mentioned polls in the previous section, and these too, often concentrate on the responses of particular subgroups in the population. This data will help the communicator make predictions about the probable reception that messages are likely to have. Such studies can also help decide the level of difficulty, the organizational framework, and the language level that might be appropriate for a particular group of receivers.

Social class, education, occupation, and income level provide some of the very best predictors of an individual's possible reactions to any persuasive message. Certainly, there are going to be exceptions. There are college students who are not liberal. There are people holding blue collar jobs who are liberal. There are millionaires who always vote for Democrats, and people on welfare who vote for Republicans. These are exceptions to the general patterns of behavior that we expect will govern a receiver's approach to persuasion. When we are working with a large audience, the message is best cast to the majority set of attitudes and beliefs, not to the exceptions.

Religion

Over 50 percent of the American population is formally connected with a church, and an even larger percentage acknowledges having some set of formal religious beliefs. Like social class, the religious affiliations held by an individual tend to affect the ways in which responses are made to persuasive messages. Rossi and Rossi[19] asked a group of people in an industrial community in Massachusetts to designate the individuals and groups to whom they would go for advice or help in making decisions about local affairs. They also asked to whom the respondents had gone in the past. The results showed that Roman Catholics who had attended parochial schools named religious leaders 53 percent of the time. Catholics who attended public schools named religious leaders 43 percent of the time, while Protestants named such leaders only 22 percent of the time. In the second part of the study regarding advice actually given by leaders, the results showed that 24 percent of the Catholics who had attended parochial school claimed religious leaders had given them helpful advice, but only 18 percent of the Catholics and Protestants who had attended public schools claimed religious leaders had given them helpful advice.

The Rossi and Rossi study shows that religion is an important determiner of the ways in which persuasive messages will be perceived. Even though the percentages are significantly lower when the study asks what people were actually consulted than when it asks whether religious leaders ought to be consulted, the results show clearly that religion plays an important role in determining the frame of reference people use to judge particular questions.

Religion is a variable whose importance depends to a great extent on the *intensity* of belief and commitment, and not merely on a simple acknowledgement of a religious affiliation. Individuals from strongly fundamentalist religions tend to bring their religious reference frames into play in many areas in judging questions that arise. Thus their religious beliefs may affect their attitudes about education, taxes, politics, and war. Religion plays the dominant role in the life of these people, and their religion becomes the single most important reference frame they possess.

For most people, religiosity is not the most important reference frame they possess and use. People form early, central beliefs about religion, but do not bring these beliefs into play unless the topic is one closely associated with religion. Thus, the strongest opposition to abortion legislation in the United States has come from members of the Roman Catholic faith. Certainly, there are millions of others who oppose abortion, but the organized opposition has been largely from Roman Catholics. The communicator wishing to argue in favor of federal funds for abortions should be able to make predictions for this topic by knowing something about the religious affiliations of the audience. Most people in the United States would not see interest rates on home mortgages as at all related to religion, but there are fundamentalist sects who believe that any interest is usury and a violation of biblical injunctions. The point is that religion can be a powerful predictor of the attitudes and beliefs that people bring to the communication situation, *but* this element is far more varied in its importance than other elements we have mentioned, and more careful study and analysis of it is required.

Political Affiliation

Religion is viewed as a nonvoluntary membership group because many individuals seem to hold the religious views of their parents, and thus cannot be said to have adopted them in a completely voluntary manner. In the same fashion, our studies suggest that the political group to which an individual belongs is likely to be the same one chosen by his parents. This generalization doesn't hold true for all people, and there is considerable evidence that political alignments in the United States are changing. A far greater percentage of young voters today tag themselves as Independents or "weak" Democrats regardless of the political party of their parents. Political affiliation, however, still seems to be more of a demographic variable than a voluntary choice on the part of an individual.

The most popular concept of political differences in the United States is that Republicans are conservative and Democrats are liberal. Thus, a communicator might expect to find Democrats more easily persuaded on issues that represent changes in the direction of liberalism, and Republicans more easily persuaded on issues oriented toward conservatism. This concept probably has a good deal of merit, but there is a serious problem with the popular view. What constitutes liberalism and conservatism is subject to change on very short notice. In the elections of 1978, for example, one of the major issues across the country was tax cutting. This has typically been a strong Republican issue, but in 1978, the Democrats claimed the issue as their own, and were able to convince many people that they were as much in favor of tax cuts as their Republican opponents. As a result, the issue was not as important as other issues. Studies do show that voters feel that Democrats tend to support liberal causes, while Republicans support conservative issues, but those same studies also show that there is a great deal of overlap between the two parties. Furthermore, it is not easy to make predictions about the growing group of independent voters. There is, furthermore, a very large group of Americans who may label themselves as belonging to one or the other party, but who have no awareness of any of the issues that are considered important by party leaders.

Political affiliation is not an important reference frame for most individuals. This conclusion, however, can be refined to be of considerably more help to the persuasive communicator. Awareness of political issues and of political party stands on particular topics *is* high among those individuals who are active party workers. Furthermore, active party workers seem to use the party as a reference group more frequently.[20] For such audiences, political membership becomes a more significant reference group, and an awareness of it is extremely useful in persuasion.

Knowing the membership of those individuals who are not active in a political party, but who do list themselves as members of one of the political parties, may be helpful to the communicator. For example, quoting a top Democratic politician who does have high credibility to an audience of nominal Democrats is likely to be more persuasive than quoting a Republican.

There are many studies available to the persuasive communicator which can help in looking at the possible states of the receivers' reference frames. Gallup, Roper, Lou Harris and other polling firms frequently make surveys regarding receiver's attitudes about particular topics. Furthermore, their results are normally published with breakdowns which indicate how people sampled from various political groups feel about the topic, or how they tell the pollster they are likely to vote. The persuasive communicator should get into the habit of reading these surveys in newspapers and magazines in order to obtain some information that may be helpful in preparing messages, as well as in making predictions about the possible success of the messages.

Racial and Ethnic Groups

Every individual in the United States has a racial and ethnic background. We are white,

brown, black or yellow. We, or our fathers and grandfathers came from such countries as England, Japan, India, Mexico, the Congo, or Poland. We may be able to trace our ancestry back to a single foreign country, or to many countries, but we all belong to racial and ethnic groups.

For many Americans, the fact that ancestors of several generations back immigrated from England, France, or Sweden is of little importance in persuasion. Only on rare occasions will they bring that reference frame into play as important to a persuasive message. The persuasive communicator who knows the ethnic background of a particular audience may use that fact to gain the attention and goodwill of the audience, but it will probably have little to do with the eventual reaction to the speech.

Although racial and ethnic group identification does not play an important part for many Americans, many other millions do have racial and ethnic memberships that dramatically affect the way in which they approach persuasive communication and are affected by it. Black Americans, Mexican Americans, Jewish Americans, Polish Americans, Japanese Americans and other groups do have attitude and belief systems that are identifiable in part by their racial and ethnic background. This happens whenever people have been set apart in some manner from the rest of society, and thus base their attitudes and beliefs on associations with people of similar background, and not on their experiences in the mainstream of society.

The Mexican American can serve as a very useful example. First, the Mexican American has been set apart partially by the language difference. When Spanish is the first language for an individual and English a second language, associations with others are more likely to be developed with people who also speak Spanish. In addition, the Mexican American tends to live in neighborhoods with other Mexican Americans, partly as the result of discrimination, partly out of economic considerations, and partly from choice. The result is that this group of people does develop attitudes and beliefs which are different from those of other groups in the same community.

Many of our large cities still have ethnic pockets where individuals retain some of their old-world customs, beliefs and attitudes. Detroit, Michigan, like other large cities, exemplifies this type of racial and ethnic clustering. There are neighborhoods in which a large percentage of the inhabitants still speak Polish, listen to Polish language programs on the radio, go to churches in which Mass is conducted in Polish, and read Polish language newspapers. The same city also has neighborhoods which are largely populated by Black Americans; the people read the *Michigan Chronicle*, a black owned and operated newspaper, and tend to listen to one of the radio stations with programming by black personnel.

Detroit is, of course, not unusual. Similar examples can be found in almost every section of the United States. For a persuasive communicator to work successfully with a group of individuals who do maintain racial or ethnic identities, a knowledge of their racial or ethnic background may be extremely helpful in understanding their beliefs and attitudes. Reading a newspaper put out for an ethnic community may help. Talking to those who share similar backgrounds will aid the communicator in gaining information about the characteristics of the group for whom the message is designed.

What does the communicator do with the information? One of the easiest things to do is to use the information to make the audience feel that the source shares experiences with the audience. President John Kennedy made use of this technique when he began his famous speech to a group of citizens in Berlin, Germany with the phrase, *"Ich bin ein Berliner."* In similar fashion, President Carter used the same technique when he began a speech to a national convention of Black Americans by saying, "Brothers and Sisters." More difficult, but also more important, is the ability to ascertain whether there are any topics that should be avoided, or whether there is someone with high credibility who could be mentioned in a speech. Obtaining that type of important information is sometimes difficult, but it can greatly increase the communicator's chances of success.

One caution should be added to our discussion. It may not be needed, but it bears repeating to ourselves as persuasive communicators on frequent occasions. There is a natural tendency to treat anyone different from ourselves as in some way inferior. If this is our attitude, we may easily talk down to others, and have our message rejected. A group of thirty-two social scientists writing a brief for presentation to the United States Supreme Court points succinctly to the real reason for the apparent variations among people from different racial or ethnic groups:

> The available evidence indicates that much, perhaps all, of the observable differences among various racial and national groups may be adequately explained in terms of environmental differences. It has been found, for instance, that the differences between the average intelligence test scores of Negro and white children decreases, and the overlap of the distribution increases, proportionately to the number of years that the Negro children have lived in the North . . . fears based on the assumption of innate racial differences in intelligence are not well founded.[21]

There are certainly differences in persuasibility among the various racial and ethnic groups that make up the pluralistic society we have in the United States today. These differences exist because of different needs, different environments, different past experiences, and different associations. While people in the United States are probably more like each other than they are like the people of any other culture or any other nation, there are differences among us. Knowing something about the racial or ethnic composition of our audiences can help us improve the persuasive speeches we make to those audiences.

VOLUNTARY GROUPS

The membership groups we have discussed thus far are ones over which individuals seem to have little, if any control. Most people, however, also belong to reference groups they have voluntarily joined. These groups may be either formal, organized groups, or relatively informal groups. Both types need discussion.

Formal Groups

It has often been said that Americans are "joiners." Any look at the number of formal organizations available in even a small community bears out this observation. There are chess clubs, stamp clubs, Kiwanis clubs, fraternities and sororities, bridge clubs, child study clubs, and hundreds of other formal clubs or groups which people can join. These are all voluntary organizations. Each one has a roughly outlined set of goals and values it supports and defends. The chess club may provide better facilities for playing chess; the Kiwanis club may support a children's hospital; the bridge club may have been organized so that a group of people could enjoy themselves. We do not have to agree with all of the stated objectives and goals of the organizations of which we are members, but the probability is high that we will be influenced by those goals and by other members in the groups. If I join an organization dedicated to improving water quality in the river running through my city, it is a pretty good bet that I will be approachable on other environmental issues, and persuasible on those issues.

There are few empirical studies assessing the effects of social clubs on attitude change. Those by Newcomb[22] and by Homans[23] tend to support the proposition that social groups serve to direct decision making about persuasive messages. The members of an organization tend to influence the attitudes of each other member of the organization. Furthermore, people tend to join groups that espouse the same values as they hold. Thus the process of joining various groups produces constant reinforcement. Knowing what the values and goals are for a particular organization becomes of extreme importance when working with the members of that organization.

The kind of effect that membership in a social group will have depends upon the complexity and strength of the attitudinal structure associated with the group and the individual's particular association with it. Many boys join the Boy Scouts of America. The organization has a set of goals and stated values for each member of the organization to follow. These values include proper conservation practices. The probability is high that when an individual is actually with his Boy Scout troop on a camping trip, he will conform to the expectations of the organization and refuse to be persuaded by messages urging him to destructive practices. For some, identification with the Boy Scouts is so strong that it becomes a reference group even when they are not with the troop. For the majority of boys, however, absence from the troop is likely to mean that the Scouts will not be used as a reference group, and that persuasion which goes against Boy Scout values has a chance of being successful. In this case, the individual's identification with the group is weak, and it serves as a reference group only when the individual is with it.

What is true of the Boy Scouts is undoubtedly true of membership in other formal organizations. People are influenced by the organizations they belong to when they are in contact with it or are with other members, but the influence of the organization is lessened when the person leaves the group situation. Some organizations may exert only trivial influence on the attitudes of its members—a bridge club, for example. Others, like a fraternity, may have great influence on the formation of attitudes and beliefs. Knowing an individual's role in an organization can also help improve predictions about the influence of the group. For example, the attitudes of a club officer or a long-time member are more likely to reflect the objectives of the group, while a new member, or someone who is on the fringes of the group may have been influenced very little.

One variable which is helpful in predicting whether a person will use membership in a group as a reference point is the severity of initiation into the group. Many groups are fairly exclusive. The cost of belonging may be extremely high, thus limiting membership, or the procedures for nominating and selecting members may severely limit membership. The higher the costs of getting into a group, the more likely it is that the individual will use the group as a reference group. Joining a particular country club, or a social fraternity, or a professional group with high standards, or a small church group, may well lead the new member to quickly adopt the attitudes and values of that group, and to use those values in judging messages.

The fact that an individual is a member of a particular organization does not mean that the reference frames developed from membership in the club will be automatically brought into play whenever a persuasive message is delivered. It is a responsibility of the persuasive communicator to make the receiver aware of the relationship of the message to a particular reference group, thus raising the probability that that configuration will actually be used as a frame of reference.

Informal Groups

Every day, we are placed in informal group situations. It might be during a coffee break at work, in a dormitory bull session, talking to a friend as we walk down the street, or double dating with friends at a beer parlor. The informal groups may be temporary, with three or four people meeting for a short time, and never meeting again. These are of less interest to us than those sets of informal associations which are semipermanent, with groups of people meeting many times over a period of months and even years.

Undoubtedly, the temporary, transitory group associations we have do help determine some of the attitudes we develop, but making predictions about those influences is difficult, because of the very transitory nature of the associations. The more permanent associations people have with informal groups also help in determining attitudes and beliefs, and these are more predictable by the persuasive communicator.

Not all persuasive communications situations occur in large, formal group situations. In fact, if we were to keep a log of the number of times a day we are exposed to persuasion, we would find that the majority of the time it is our casual friends and acquaintances who are attempting to persuade us to go to a movie, have a beer, vote in a campus election, take a trip, buy a car, or date a particular girl. Our reactions to these messages are, in part, conditioned by the kind of social groupings we have formed.

Informal associations help to determine our norms or uniformities of behavior. This is brought about by social pressures to which we are subjected. In 1970, I did a study of preteenage smoking behavior in several cities in Michigan.[24] The results showed that for those children aged from nine to thirteen who smoked regularly, it was almost always the case that their parents, older brothers and sisters, and friends did also. Their associations determined this set of behavioral norms. One might imagine that any persuasive communicator attempting to convince these youths that smoking was harmful would have a difficult time if the youths' associates could not also be convinced.

A series of classic studies made by Asch[25] and Sherif and Sherif[26] supports the analysis of the importance of the group in influencing behavior. Their studies show that given the presence of a group, individuals will make statements which their eyes tell them aren't so. Their reactions to making judgments about the length of a line, or the distance a point of light moves are conditioned by what they think their group believes. These studies suggest that we have to take cognizance of both the formal and informal groups to which people belong before making predictions about their behavior.

For all of the membership groups to which we belong, the voluntary groups we join, the formal associations we make, and the demographic groups with which we are associated, there seems to be a set of relatively constant factors that governs behavior. Simple membership, however, in one group or another is usually not enough to insure that a particular receiver will utilize that membership as a reference group. Mr. John Doakes may be a member of the Junior Chamber of Commerce in his community, but merely knowing that fact may be of little use in making a speech about the necessity of building a new civic center in the community. Mr. Doakes may or may not react to the speech in a fashion that reflects the reference frame built up as a result of membership in the Junior Chamber of Commerce. If, however, the persuasive communicator mentions the support of the new civic center by some prominent member, the probability is strongly increased that Mr. Doakes will respond by making use of this particular reference group. The communicator *must* design the message in such a manner so as to insure that a desired frame of reference will be brought into play by the receiver.

NONMEMBERSHIP GROUPS

The discussion up to this point has concentrated on membership groups that are used as reference groups by people. Reference groups, however, need not be membership groups to be used in this fashion. Any nonmembership group used as a standard of comparison, either positive or negative, may be defined as a reference group for an individual. Suppose Mr. Royce is prejudiced against a minority or a majority group. It is quite possible that he will

judge persuasive messages by the standard of whether the group he dislikes is in favor of the idea presented or not. Mr. Royce is not a member of the group against which he is prejudiced, and may not have accurate information about what that group would or would not want in a particular situation. Nevertheless, this group serves as a reference group for Mr. Royce, and he makes judgments accordingly.

The definition of a nonmembership group and our example suggest two questions of interest. What can be said about the processes of selection of positive and negative nonmembership reference groups? What can be said about the relationship between an individual's use of a group as a reference group and the person's degree of knowledge about that group?

Selection of Nonmembership Reference Groups

A common belief is that everyone strives to be better than he presently is. Sometimes such a belief is expressed as "keeping up with the Joneses," "social climbing," or "status seeking." In terms of reference group theory, this belief would indicate that people may be expected to use groups to which they aspire, but do not belong, as positive reference groups. Conversely, groups to which the individual does not aspire and may want to avoid, are more likely to be selected as negative reference groups.

Siegel and Siegel[27] did a study using college women and compared their membership and nonmembership reference groups. They found that both types of groups were effective in helping to determine attitudes. The nonmembership groups used were ones to which the girls aspired, and these groups proved to be even more effective in determining attitudes and behavior than did the simple association groups to which the girls were assigned for purposes of the study.

Maccoby and her associates[28] conclude that people who wish to "move up" in social class are more likely to vote Republican than Democratic, thus, suggesting that such "climbers" are using groups to which they aspire as reference groups. In large corporations, rising executives behave as they believe immediate superiors would behave in similar situations.

The situation is analogous with negative reference groups. People use negative reference groups to judge persuasive communication by deciding whether the message will or will not be believed by the disliked group. The Communist Party, Jewish bankers, blacks, Democrats, Republicans, rich people, people on welfare, college educated "pinkos," jocks, and many other groups have been used as negative reference groups. In many cases, the usage may have nothing to do with the actual policies, if any, of the particular group serving as a negative reference group. The utilization seems to be based largely on the users concern about the "danger" posed by the particular group.

In selecting either positive or negative nonmembership referents, the receiver may be operating from a general frame of reference that is used in judging all messages regarding social change. Thus, interviews with members of the John Birch Society, a group of people generally labeled as highly conservative, suggested that the content of a message is of little concern when set against the supposed support of a negative reference group.[29] Members of that group would oppose a message that advocated the same things they advocated if it came from someone labeled as a liberal. They would use the argument that, "if so-and-so is in favor of it, it must not be a good idea." Obviously, there are extremists on both the right and the left who tend to view all messages from such general reference frames. Equally common, however, is the selection of a nonmembership group to judge specific topics. People might use the upper class as a reference group in deciding voting behavior, but use the people on the next block as a reference group to decide on the purchase of a new car.

Knowledge About Nonmembership Reference Groups

Individuals using groups to which they do not belong as reference groups sometimes seem to be putting words in the mouth of the other group. In the example of Mr. Royce, one group was used as a reference group, even though he did not seem to know much about its actual characteristics. Mr. Royce can be described as prejudiced in his attitudes toward this group. Studies of prejudice have been concerned with the problem of the amount and kind of information that individuals have about the groups toward which they feel prejudice.

When people use a nonmembership group as a negative reference group, we sometimes say that they are engaged in "stereotyping." There are three aspects of stereotyping:

1. Individuals in the group are all seen as possessing certain identifying characteristics.
2. Individuals in the group who engage in stereotyping all tend to agree on what those characteristics are.
3. There is little correspondence between the actual characteristics of the minority group and the attributed characteristics.

Stereotyping most frequently occurs with minority groups in a society. Gilbert[30] illustrated the problem by a study in which he asked Princeton University students to assign traits to a series of racial and ethnic groups. The results showed that the students felt that blacks were superstitious, Jews were shrewd, Germans were scientifically minded and industrious, the Irish were quick tempered, and the Turks were cruel.

Stereotypes tend to change as events change. During World War II, all Japanese were portrayed in cartoons and films as evil, with glasses and buck teeth. Their image has changed so drastically that when one of those early cartoon films appears on television it is difficult to tie current impressions with those in the film. Characterizations of the Chinese living on the mainland have begun to undergo a drastic change now that the Peoples' Republic of China is opening up to the world. Attitudes toward blacks and Mexican Americans have undergone broad changes in the past few years. Yet prejudice and its consequence, discrimination, remains, and the relative ranking of groups within American society stays much the same over the years, with many of the same kinds of misinformation being used to judge the conduct of others. Stereotypes can be changed somewhat, but large changes are extremely difficult to obtain. In any society, as long as there are perceived differences between groups, stereotyping, prejudice and discrimination are likely to exist. Their existence affects the ways in which people respond to persuasive messages and must be taken into account by sources and receivers.

Negative nonmembership reference groups have been discussed above largely because it is easier to find information about such groups, but individuals who use a positive nonmembership reference group may also lack accurate knowledge about that group. The teenage girl who bases her decisions on what her favorite musical group would do in a similar similar situation is a case in point, as is the ten-year-old boy who bases his life on that of his favorite football team.

Whyte, in describing the "corner boy society,"[31] suggests that the positive reference groups these men used were frequently ones about which they had no real knowledge. The "corner boy" study was done during the late 1930s and early 1940s, in a slum section of an eastern city. It could have been done today, since the same type of juvenile and teenage gangs exist today. The interactions between gangs from different streets in the same city, and between groups of slightly different ages point out the importance of reference groups. Few of the individuals in any group would

make decisions without checking with the members of their groups. If they did things that the group disapproved of, they were ostracized, and either left the group, or apologized to the group. The groups, however, all had some positive reference groups about which they knew little. They used the rich people or the college types as reference groups, and made their own decisions based on what they thought these positive reference groups thought, although their information was frequently lacking in accuracy. The poor in the United States develop stereotypes about the rich that are just as inaccurate as those the rich develop about the poor, although in any given communication situation, one group may be serving as a positive reference group, and the other as a negative reference group.

Receivers use the beliefs and attitudes derived from their own groups to judge the persuasive messages to which they are exposed. They also bring to bear attitudes about groups to which they do not belong. A set of guidelines may help in planning communication strategies to make use of what we have learned about reference groups.

UTILIZING REFERENCE GROUPS IN PERSUASIVE COMMUNICATION

People do not form all their judgments about persuasion on the basis of the reference groups they use. In succeeding chapters, we will examine other factors, and varying strategies regarding reference groups. Below, we offer advice on some of the ways the persuasive communicator may improve messages by taking account of the reference groups to which receivers belong.

1. When there is information about the probable reference groups of individuals, messages can call a particular reference group to the attention of the receiver. What the communicator intends to do in this situation is to focus attention on a reference group that is favorable

to the message. Thus, the probability that the receiver will utilize the group named as a reference frame by which to judge the message is increased.

2. Different groups have different values as reference groups to the receiver. Some are used more frequently than others. For many individuals, their family, church, occupational association, neighbors, and close friends are more important than political affiliations, veterans organizations, alumni groups, or other groups with which the individual does not have frequent contact. The persuasive communicator can use the probability that a particular group will be either an important or relatively unimportant group to the individual in planning the content of the message.

3. Many membership groups set certain standards of conduct for their members. These standards can be used to increase the probability that receivers will take desired actions. Fre-

quently, an occupational group will also set standards of behavior for its members. These standards can be invoked to enhance the probability that an individual will respond appropriately.

4. The physical setting for communication may increase the probability that one reference group will be used in preference to another. A man watching the Detroit Lions perform on the field is not likely to attend to any message he receives regarding the church to which he belongs. Communicators may have to arrange for appropriate physical settings in order to be successful with the message.

5. Sometimes a favored reference group can be quoted directly in a message, again enhancing response on the part of the receiver. Thus the student who belongs to a particular organization may respond favorably if the communicator uses a quote by another individual within the organization.

SUMMARY

Our frames of reference are built in many ways. The experiences we have as children, the books we have read, the friends we make, all contribute to the development of our frames of reference. These frames mediate the way in which we will view the world around us and the way in which we will listen to and react to persuasive messages. We are gregarious animals, and we tend not to live in solitude. We all associate with others, sometimes formally,

sometimes informally. Furthermore, these associations also help in the development of our reference frames. The people with whom we associate, and even those with whom we do not, form the reference groups we use as standards or comparisons in judging persuasive messages. Our study of the participants in persuasion cannot be complete without a discussion of the role played by reference groups.

FOOTNOTES

1. H. H. Kelley, "Two Functions of Reference Groups," in H. Prohansky and B. Seidenberg, eds., *Basic Studies in Social Psychology* (New York: Holt, Rinehart and Winston, 1965), pp. 210–14.
2. T. M. Newcomb, "Attitude Development as a Function of Reference Groups," in H. Prohansky and B. Seidenberg, eds., *Basic Studies in Social Psychology* (New York: Holt, Rinehart and Winston, 1965), pp. 215–25.
3. I. L. Janis and P. B. Field, "Sex Differences and Personality Factors Related to Persuasibility," in I. L. Janis and C. I. Hovland, eds., *Personality and Persuasibility* (New Haven, Conn.: Yale University Press, 1959), pp. 55–68.
4. B. T. King, "Relationships between Susceptibility to Opinion Change and Childrearing Practices," in Janis and Hovland, eds., *Personality and Persuasibility*, pp. 141–66; J. O. Whittaker, "Pa-

rameters of Social Influence in the Autokinetic Situation," *Sociometry*, Vol. 27 (1964), pp. 88–98; T. M. Scheidel, "Sex and Persuasibility," *Speech Monographs*, 30 (1963), pp. 353–58.

5. R. P. Abelson and G. S. Lesser, "The Measurement of Persuasibility in Children," in Janis and Hovland, eds., *Personality and Persuasibility*, pp. 141–66.

6. C. W. Carmichael, "Frustration, Sex and Persuasibility," *Western Speech*, Vol. 34, No. 4 (1970), pp. 300–07.

7. S. L. Bem, "Androgyny vs. the Tight Little Lives of Fluffy Women and Chesty Men," *Psychology Today*, Vol. 9 (1975), pp. 58–62.

8. T. D. Peterson, "The Relationship between Certain Attitudes of Parents and Children," in H. H. Remmers, ed., *Further Studies in Attitudes*, *Purdue Studies in Higher Education*, Series 2, vol. 37 (1936), pp. 127–44; C. Morgan and H. H. Remmers, "Liberalism and Conservatism of College Students as Affected by the Depression," *School and Society*, vol. 41 (1935), pp. 780–84; S. C. Fisher, *Relationships in Attitudes, Opinions and Values among Family Members*, University of California Publications in Culture and Society, 1948, vol. 2, no. 2; R. Bassett, "Opinion Differences within the Family," *Public Opinion Quarterly*, vol. 13 (1949), pp. 118–20; J. Himelhoch, "Tolerance and Personality Needs," *American Sociological Review*, vol. 15 (1950), pp. 79–88.

9. Robert D. Hess and Judith Torney, *The Development of Political Attitudes in Children* (New York: Anchor Books, 1967).

10. Kenneth P. Langton, *Political Socialization* (New York: Oxford University Press, 1969).

11. C. Atkin (Unpublished telephone survey of students at Michigan State University, East Lansing, Michigan, October, 1971).

12. J. H. Barrett, *Gerontological Psychology*, (Springfield, Ill.: Charles C. Thomas, 1972), p. 154.

13. R. S. Lynd and H. M. Lynd, *Middletown: A Study in Contemporary American Culture* (New York: Harcourt Brace and Co., 1929). also see R. S. Lynd and H. M. Lynd. *Middletown in Transition: A Study in Cultural Conflicts* (New York: Harcourt Brace and Co., 1937).

14. "Middletown Revisited," *Time*. Vol. 112, No. 16 (Oct. 16, 1978), pp. 106–09.

15. S. M. Lipset and J. J. Linz, "The Social Bases of Political Diversity In Western Democracies," unpublished manuscript reported in B. Berelson and G. Steiner, *Human Behavior: An Inventory of Scientific Findings* (New York: Harcourt, Brace

and World, 1964), p. 424.

16. J. F. Short and F. Strodtbeck, *Group Process and Gang Delinquency* (Chicago: University of Chicago Press, 1965).

17. R. C. Tryon, "Identification of Social Areas by Cluster Analysis: A General Method with an Application to the San Francisco Bay Area," *University of California Publications in Psychology*, University of California Press, 1955.

18. CBS News, Special Report on Youth, 1970.

19. P. H. Rossi and A. S. Rossi, "Some Effects of Parochial School Education in America," *Daedalus* (Spring 1961), pp. 300–328.

20. P. F. Lazarsfeld, B. Berelson and H. Gaudet, *The People's Choice* (New York: Duell, Sloan and Pearce, 1944).

21. "The Effects of Segregation and the Consequences of Desegregation: A Social Science Statement," *Minnesota Law Review*, vol. 37 (1953), p. 435.

22. T. Newcomb, "Attitude Development as a Function of Reference Groups: The Bennington Study," in E. E. Maccoby, T. H. Newcomb and E. L. Hartley, eds., *Readings in Social Psychology* (New York: Holt, Rinehart and Winston, 1958), pp. 265–75.

23. G. C. Homans, *The Human Group* (New York: Harcourt, Brace and World, 1950).

24. E. Bettinghaus, "Michigan Survey of Preteenage Smoking Behavior," mimeo Michigan Youth Council, State of Michigan, 1970.

25. S. E. Asch, "Effects of Group Pressure upon the Modification and Distortion of Judgment," in H. Guetzkow, ed., *Groups, Leadership, and Men* (Pittsburgh, Pa.: Carnegie Press, 1951).

26. M. Sherif and C. Sherif, *An Outline of Social Psychology* (New York: Harper and Row, 1956).

27. A. E. Siegel and S. Siegel, "Reference Groups, Membership Groups, and Attitude Change," *Journal of Abnormal and Social Psychology*, vol. 55 (1957), pp. 360–64.

28. E. Maccoby, R. Mathews and A. Morton, "Youth and Political Change," *Public Opinion Quarterly*, vol. 19 (1954), pp. 23–39.

29. John (Klempner) Bear, "People Who Write In: Communication Aspects of Opinion-Letter Writing," (Ph.d. Dissertation, Michigan State University, 1966).

30. G. M. Gilbert, "Stereotype Persistence and Change among College Students," *Journal of Abnormal and Social Psychology*, vol. 46 (1951), pp. 245–54.

31. W. F. Whyte, *Street Corner Society* (Chicago: University of Chicago Press, 1955).

FIVE

THE INFLUENCE OF THE COMMUNICATOR

Some communicators are better at persuasion than others. Two speakers can deliver exactly the same speech, and one speaker will be rated better than the other. Most receivers are aware of differences in the communicators they attend to, although they might not be able to specify why they feel as they do. They may say something like, "I don't know why! But I do know that some people have it, and some don't." If we were to push them a bit further, such receivers might give us reasons such as, "He is a smooth speaker;" "She sounds better;" "He looks great in that suit;" "She had all the better arguments;" "He sounded really honest and sincere;" or "He makes you stop and think." Even when persuasion is looked at as an interactive process, with two or more individuals attempting to persuade one another, the onlooker is usually impressed with the fact that few of these situations ever conclude in results that appear to be equal for both individuals. One person seems to compromise or to give up more than the other. One person will seem to have more influence on the final decision than the other. This chapter examines the communicator's role in persuasion, attempting to pinpoint what that quality is that some people have and others apparently do not. We shall look at ways in which communicators can improve their abilities as sources of communication and can thus become more influential with their audiences. Finally, we shall examine a series of studies that suggest that persuasion may be enhanced if we can get receivers to actively participate in the persuasive process.

The belief that the source of any message is important to the eventual effect of the message is not new. It can be traced at least to the ancient Greeks. Aristotle regarded the speaker as a force just as important as the receivers or the message. His observations are as pertinent today as ever:

> Persuasion is achieved by the speaker's personal character when the speech is so spoken as to make us think him credible. We believe good men more fully and more readily than others: This is true generally whatever the question is, and absolutely true where exact certainty is impossible and opinions are divided. . . . It is not true, as some writers assume in their treatises on rhetoric, that the personal goodness revealed by the speaker contributes nothing to his power of persuasion; on the contrary, his character may almost be called the most effective means of persuasion he possesses.[1]

Telling the communicator, as Aristotle does, that being effective means being a "good man," is of little help unless we also instruct the communicator on how to go about becoming a "good man," and thus a more effective source. Since Aristotle, many scholars have been concerned with the problem of improving the abilities of communicators wishing to engage in persuasive communication.

In examining research studies, it soon becomes obvious that there are a number of different strains of research that look generally at the problem of personal influence in persuasion. These research efforts have normally examined different types of communication situations, and different labels have been applied to each kind of research. In some studies, the influence variable has been labeled "ethos," in others, "source credibility," "status differential research," "opinion leadership," and "charisma." We take the position that, while there are differences in the situations studied and the research paradigms used, each of these labels has been attached to what is essentially the same variable. We shall, therefore, refer to the variable of communicator influence in persuasion as *source credibility*. This term has been most frequently used in recent research, and seems to be more applicable to the general persuasive situation than any of the other terms. We shall

first look at cases subsumed under the general heading of source credibility, and then look at more specific situations for which other terms have been used. A final section section of the chapter will examine the special case of "self-persuasion," a technique that may assist the communicator in achieving successful persuasion in certain situations.

SOURCE CREDIBILITY: THE GENERAL CASE

How can we be sure that the source of any message is having an influence on the receiver? Might any results of the speech or the article be attributed to the topic of the message, and not to the source. A hypothetical example will help in defining credibility, and in showing how we can know when a source is credible.

Imagine that a speech is prepared that calls for strong population controls. The speech is audio-taped. Then, researchers assemble two audiences randomly chosen from a city and find out what their attitudes are about family planning, birth control, and other topics associated with zero population growth. The investigators determine that there are no apparent differences between the two groups of people in their prespeech attitude toward population growth. Then the researchers let the two groups listen to the speech. For one group, however, the investigators announce the speaker on the tape as a nationally famous expert on family planning. For the other group, the researchers introduce the same tape by saying that the speaker is a student at the University of Michigan. After the tape is finished, the investigators again ascertain the attitudes of the two groups. The group that thought it had listened to an expert on family planning had changed more in favor of the topic than the second group. Since both groups heard exactly the same tape, and since the groups were similar in their original attitudes, the only conclusion that can be drawn is that the differences between the two groups must be due to a difference in perceived *credibility* between the two imaginary sources. This hypothetical example represents the basic paradigm under which much credibility research has been conducted. The experimenter holds the message constant, uses equivalent audiences, and then systematically varies the characteristics of the communicator in his effort to find out what factors attributable to the source are persuasive.

There are a number of early studies that clearly establish credibility as an important factor in persuasion. Haiman[2], in one of the earliest studies, used a design almost exactly like our hypothetical example, with the topic of a speech being socialized medicine, and the supposed speakers being Dr. Thomas Parran, the then Surgeon General of the United States, Eugene Dennis, Secretary General of the Communist Party of the United States, and an anonymous university sophomore from Northwestern University. The results showed significantly more change for the group that thought it was listening to the Surgeon General of the United States. In another early study, Hovland and Weiss[3] used written messages, and tested the credibility of both individuals and institutions, that is for example, J. Robert Oppenheimer, the physicist, and *Pravda*, the Russian newspaper. The result of their study again suggested that sources possessing more credibility for a given audience were more effective in persuasion.

In these and other early studies, the assumption was implicitly made that credibility is a single-valued variable and can be viewed much as we would view the variable of gender; that is, that people either are credible or are not. The studies also tended to suggest that it was relatively easy to determine who was credible and who was not. Our subsequent research does not support such a simplistic view of source credibility. Will the mayor of a city always be seen as more credible than a plumber? Imagine that the topic is concerned with the way in which the plumbing has been installed

in a new city building. The mayor makes a speech defending the adequacy of the installation. The mayor is opposed by one of the city's master plumbers who maintains that the job was badly done and that the city paid too much for the job. Will the mayor posess more credibility in this situation than the master plumber?

Credibility is not a single characteristic of an individual, such as age or sex. Neither is it represented by a set of characteristics such as socioeconomic position. *Credibility is a set of perceptions about sources held by receivers*. Thus we must determine whether an individual possesses credibility by asking potential receivers about the source. We cannot say that an individual either is or is not credible simply by looking at the clothes the person wears, or the position the person holds. Source characteristics, however, such as age, sex or socioeconomic status may affect the perceptions that a receiver has, and thus, such characteristics become relevant to the study of credibility.

If source credibility is dependent on the *perceptions* that receivers have, then we may expect to find that any given source could be perceived as highly credible by one receiver, and not at all credible by another. In order to ascertain just how a given receiver viewed a source, we could have to find some method of asking the person just what perceptions were held about a receiver. One way of going about this is to ask receivers to rate the source on a number of different characteristics. In such a fashion the researcher could discover just what factors seemed to be important in credibility and could also determine how credible a set of communicators were to a given audience.

Hovland, Janis, and Kelley,[4] suggest that credibility seems to depend on two factors: the *competence* or *expertness* ascribed to the source by the receiver, and the *trustworthiness* the receiver ascribes to the source. Andersen[5] suggests that receivers judge credibility in terms of a *dynamism* factor and an *evaluative* factor. McCroskey[6] reports somewhat similar findings, and labels his two factors as perceived *authoritativeness* and *character*. It is important to note that McCroskey did not include scales which might reflect showmanship or the dynamic qualities associated with speakers. Markham[7] did include such scales in his study of television newscasters, and reports three major credibility factors labeled as *reliable—logical*, *showmanship*, and *trustworthiness*.

Perhaps one of the most careful examinations of source credibility has been made by Berlo, Lemert, and Mertz.[8] Like Andersen and Markham, they followed procedures developed by Osgood and Tannenbaum[9] to measure connotative meaning, and applied these procedures as an analogous method to the systematic rating of varying sources. Essentially the method consisted of developing a set of polar adjectives such as: good–bad, right–wrong, and competent–incompetent, placing the adjectives at either end of a seven-point scale, and having groups of subjects rate a number of sources on each scale. The kind of scale used by Berlo and his associates is typified by Figure 5.1.

They investigated four types of sources: personally known sources, public sources that had no relationship to the topic, public sources associated with relevant topics, and public sources associated with irrelevant topics. In their preliminary studies as many as eighty-three different scales were used. Those scales that did not apply to the sources were discarded, and a total of thirty-five scales were used to rate twelve different sources. Each respondent was asked to rate all twelve sources on each of the thirty-five different scales. The ratings were then analyzed by the methods of factor analysis to find out whether they were common ways of judging sources.

The results of the Berlo, Lemert, and Mertz studies conform closely to some of the early studies. They suggest that there are three dimensions or factors which people use in judging the credibility of various sources. The first factor they identified was termed a *safety* factor. It seems analogous to the trustworthiness factor hypothesized by Hovland, Janis, and Kelley and by Markham. A second factor was labeled a *qualification* factor, which seems much like the expertness factor of Hovland, Janis, and Kelley and like McCroskey's authoritativeness factor. The third factor was labeled as *dynamism*. The third factor seemed less important than the first two, but did stand out as a separate and independent variable.

Almost every research study in credibility agrees on the existence of a safety or trustworthiness factor and a qualification or competence factor. There are, however, minor differences with respect to some of the less important factors. McCroskey, Jensen, and Valencia, for example, mention three additional components of *composure*, *sociability* and *extroversion*.[10] Their description of these factors does suggest their similarity to the dynamism factor identified by Berlo, Lemert and Mertz. Their discussion of these three factors, however, makes some use-

---

RICHARD NIXON

Safe	____	____	____	____	____	____	____ Dangerous
Qualified	____	____	____	____	____	____	____ Unqualified
Pleasant	____	____	____	____	____	____	____ Unpleasant
Fast	____	____	____	____	____	____	____ Slow
Competent	____	____	____	____	____	____	____ Incompetent
Dynamic	____	____	____	____	____	____	____ Lethargic

Figure 5.1
A Credibility Rating Scale

ful distinctions for the persuasive communicator. Before addressing some of the limitations of these studies, it will be useful to discuss the major factors in some detail. We shall combine the various third factors into a single category labelled as *personal characteristics*.

Safety

The safety dimension as reported by Berlo, Lemert and Mertz seems to be characterized by the use of scales having some relation to general personality traits. Thus, a communicator rating high on this factor might be described as kind, cogenial, friendly, warm, agreeable, pleasant, gentle, unselfish, just, forgiving, fair, hospitable, sociable, ethical, calm and patient. Any given source may not be rated highly on each and every one of these scales, but the receivers would have rated the source high on the majority of the scales. On the other hand, individuals perceived to have low credibility would tend to be rated at the other end of these scales. Such an individual might be rated as untrustworthy, cruel, or dangerous. Again, a particular source need not be rated as unsafe on each of these scales, but an individual scoring low on the safety dimension will generally fall toward the low end on the majority of the scales.

The safety or trustworthiness factor is a general factor. For topics that do not require a lot of expertise, or where the receiver does not have much specific knowledge, the safety factor tends to come into play. Many ministers have experienced the situation where a member of the congregation comes to seek advice on personal finances, health problems, or even advice as to the best school for the member's children. The minister is seen as trustworthy, although he may have no special qualifications in any of these areas.

Qualification

The qualification dimension consists of scales that are indicators of the impression the re-

ceiver has of the source's competence or training as it relates to the topic with which the source has been associated. It is assumed to be an independent dimension from either dynamism or safety, which means that knowing how individuals mark scales on the safety dimension for a variety of sources is of no help in predicting how they will mark scales on the qualification dimension. A person rated high on the qualification factor might be described as trained, experienced, skillful, informed, authoritative, able, and intelligent. Sources rated low on this dimension might be characterized by adjectives having the opposite meaning, such as untrained, clumsy, stupid, or inexperienced.

While the safety dimension seems to be a fairly general factor, the qualification or expertness factor is applied when people are faced with topics or situations where skill may be perceived as necessary. Thus, we might expect an individual to decide between two potential tennis teachers on the basis of their actual skill at the game. Obviously, we do not wish to argue that skill in playing a sport is the best factor in judging a teacher of that sport, but the evidence suggests that many people will call their perceptions of an individual's qualifications into play in such situations.

Personal Characteristics

Source credibility factors which fall into this third category tend not to be as important as either safety or qualification. When receivers do not have firmly fixed impressions about an individual's competence or trustworthiness, however, the receiver is likely to make a credibility judgment based on personal characteristics. Thus, an individual who stuttered or had a nervous mannerism might be rated low on composure. A person who came across as friendly would be seen as more sociable, while a person with a forceful vocal style might be perceived as dynamic or extroverted.

Personal characteristics may be more important to the persuasive communicator in situations where the audience is unfamiliar with the communicator. If I go to church and listen to a minister for the first time, and find the minister to be a very poor speaker, hesitant, slow, and introverted, I am likely to judge the minister on those personal qualities, and pay little attention to what is being said. After hearing the minister on many different Sundays, I am more likely to judge credibility on *what* is said, and actually ignore those personal characteristics.

Each of the three dimensions of source credibility has been discussed in detail. There seems to be general agreement among researchers that source credibility[15] is an important variable in persuasion. Some researchers suggest that it may take more than three dimensions to adequately characterize credibility, or that other measuring instruments are more appropriate.[11] Nevertheless, most of the research in this area does suggest that communicators can be characterized along various dimensions of credibility for a given audience. Our assumption is that if a potential source is rated by the receivers in an audience as highly credible, then that source will, *because of perceived personal characteristics*, have relatively more success in persuasive situations.

In real life, credibility is not an easy factor to isolate. Remember that *credibility is dependent on the perceptions of the receiver, and not necessarily on any actual characteristics of the source.* The local congressman will be perceived differently by strong Democrats and by strong Republicans. The president of a university may be perceived differently by faculty and by students. The head of the ALF–CIO will be perceived differently by union members and by management members. Many sources will be perceived as possessing neither very high nor very low credibility. They have not developed themselves along any of our three dimensions so far as receivers are concerned. If we ask whether there is some ideal source that might cut across the dimensions we have mentioned, we can turn to the work of Burgoon for an apt answer:

. . . a composite picture of a "high credible" source would be someone who is moderately competent, highly sociable, of good character, moderately composed and near neutral on extroversion. More specifically, the ideal source would be highly (i.e., near the extreme) responsible, reliable, honest, just, kind, cooperative, nice, pleasant, sociable, cheerful, friendly, good natured, and relaxed and only slightly (i.e., near neutral) expert, virtuous, refined, calm, composed, verbal, mild, extroverted, bold, and talkative.[12]

We cite this rather complete description because it nicely illustrates two of the major problems with source credibility and persuasive communication. The description is a general one. It could apply to a number of possible sources of a persuasive message, *depending on the perceptions of the individual receiver.* Thus in order to identify an ideal source, we do not look for sources. Rather, we ask receivers. The first problem then, is in finding out whether I, as a potential source, am likely to have credibility with an audience.

A second, and related problem, exists for those people who know, or suspect, that their credibility may be low or at least not high. Since the characteristics we have discussed are not ones that people are born with, it is reasonable for a potential source to ask, "How can I develop credibility?" It is easy to say, "Just live a good life; be moderate along these dimensions; and people will recognize your sterling character." We *can* go beyond this answer, and we will make some helpful suggestions after we look at some other research efforts closely related to source credibility research, but which examine some specific types of communication situations.

STATUS DIFFERENTIAL RESEARCH: PERCEIVED ROLE DIFFERENCE

People play a number of different roles as they go about the business of life. The same person may be a student during the day, and a husband at night. Another may be an office manager, a father, President of the Kiwanis Club, and an Elder in the church. Still, another person may be a mother and wife during the evening, a PTA president on the weekend, a Cub Scout den mother before supper, and a businesswoman from eight to five. Some of the roles that people play occupy large amounts of time, such as the job role, or the family role. Others are secondary and are assumed only on rare occasions, such as the role of voter, which people assume once a year, or even less frequently. When people occupy particular role positions, some of their behavior is predictable by the behavior prescribed for that role. The behavior that people exhibit in any role is thus composed of behavior stemming from unique personal characteristics and behavior determined by the nature of the role position. Mrs. James, an elementary school teacher, is expected to meet her classes on time each day. She is expected to teach a subject in such a way that her students will be able to pass standardized tests at the end of the year. She is expected to maintain discipline in her classes. She is expected to meet with parents once every term. Those are behaviors that are demanded of Mrs. James because of the role position that she is occupying, and we would expect to find great

similarities between Mrs. James and all other teachers in the same school. Not everything Mrs. James does as a teacher, however, is prescribed by the nature of the position. For example, Mrs. James may feel that her students should sit in a semicircle around her, and not in rows in front of her. Her own personal beliefs are responsible for that aspect of her behavior.

In persuasion, with either a one-way or a two-way relationship, what is important is not the actual role that any communicator or receiver is occupying, but the relationship between the roles of the source and the receiver. Each role can be described in terms of the *status* or prestige assumed to go with that role. The President of the United States has higher prestige because of his role than does the governor of a state. The foreman within an automobile plant has more status than does the worker on the production line. The college teacher has more status than does a high school or grade school teacher. When any two role positions are compared, it is usually possible to determine which one would be accorded higher status by a general audience. In the following table (Figure 5.2), a number of pairs of role positions are compared. Most receivers would agree on the relative role position rankings for the positions listed toward the top of the list. When we get to the bottom, however, the determination is

HIGHER STATUS	LOWER STATUS
President of the United States	United States congressmen
Mayor of New York City	Chief of Police, New York City
President, General Motors Corporation	Colonel, United States Army
President, Stanford University	Professor, University of Michigan
Policeman, city of Detroit	Fireman, city of Detroit
Master plumber	Carpenter
Boy Scout leader	Usher, Methodist Church
President, Parent-Teacher Association	Secretary, League of Women Voters
President, Chamber of Commerce	Chairman, Building Committee of Baptist Church
Senior, Michigan State University	Sophomore, Michigan State University
Prosecuting Attorney	Defense Attorney

Figure 5.2
Relative Role Position Rankings

much harder to make. For example, many students would automatically consider defense attorneys as having more prestige than prosecuting attorneys, while an audience of policemen might well rank the prosecuting attorney as higher than the defense attorney. For any given pair of role positions, however, a given receiver will tend to accord higher status to one.

The importance of the differential status attached to role positions is that the higher a receiver views the prestige of a given position, the more likely is the individual occupying such a position to be influential in a persuasive situation. In the Haiman study cited, the differences between a college sophomore and the Surgeon General of the United States is a perceived difference in the status of the two role positions.

A few years ago, the U.S. Public Health Service published a report dealing with the relationship between smoking and lung cancer. Many of the items in the report were not new and had been the subject of messages from a number of researchers. There was, however, little decrease in smoking as a result of these messages. Then the Surgeon General held a news conference at which he released the Service's report summarizing the various studies. As a result, a large number of individuals stated that they had stopped smoking (at least temporarily). Many things may help explain the apparent persuasiveness of the Surgeon General in this situation. The timing of the message, the length, the language used, the amount of publicity, and the size of the viewing audience are all factors that may have contributed to the effect of the message, but doubtless, the status associated with the Surgeon General's position was a strong contributor to the effect of the message. In fact, it may have been status alone in this case, and not the person actually occupying that position. Ask yourself whether you could name the Surgeon General. News stories of that era frequently did not feature the name of the person occupying the office. Headlines only reported something like,

"Surgeon General Links Smoking to Lung Cancer." The position provided the credibility to the reader, not the individual occupying the position.

Perhaps the best situation in which to be as a source is to occupy a position of high status *and* possess high personal credibility. In Michigan, for example, such an individual was one of the long time governors, William G. Milliken, who could speak from a position of high status, but who also possessed very high personal credibility, led Governor Milliken to victories when he was not a very good leader, were forced to declare openly that he was a "very nice guy." That personal stature, derived from both the status of his position, and his personal credibility led Governor Milliken to victories when many other members of his political party were going down to defeat. Status and credibility are linked, but the linkage is neither direct nor complete. A source can have high status and low credibility, or high credibility and low status. An example of the first situation might be former President Richard Nixon, who clearly had high status, but for many people, had no credibility. An example of the second kind of situation might be the small-town minister, who does not have high status, but whose personal credibility for members of the community makes him a highly influential person. We do pay attention to the messages we receive from sources who possess higher status than ourselves, but that influence can be increased or decreased by the personal credibility we perceive.

OPINION LEADERSHIP RESEARCH

The status attached to any given role position is not the only factor related to the influence a source may have in persuasive situations. Imagine a group of students collected in a dormitory lounge. They are listening to David Sharp, another student, argue that penalties for marijuana possession and use should be reduced.

David Sharp holds no official office. His status is no higher than that of any of the other students in the room. Yet after the speech, we find that most of the students agree with the speaker. Even those students who have been midly opposed to reducing penalties seem to have swung over to agreement with the position advocated by Sharp. What has happened? Was the message so well prepared and delivered? Or does David Sharp have something going for him that we are unaware of?

One such criterion may be whether a source is regard as an *opinion leader* by other members of a peer group. The pioneering study pointing to the importance of opinion leadership was made by Katz and Lazarsfeld.[13] They examined the effects of the mass media of communication on the attitudes and behavior of those who listened to radio and television or read the daily newspaper. Their initial conclusion, after presenting a message over one of the mass media and then measuring the effects of the message, was that there seemed to be little change in audience attitudes, but when they went back to the same group some weeks later, and again assessed attitudes, they found that there had been significant change. In looking for an explanation of the unexpected later shifts, they suggested that these individuals changed their attitudes only after they had talked to others in whom they had confidence. Katz and Lazarsfeld referred to the people conferred with as *opinion leaders*.

Opinion leaders do not seem to possess any specific characteristics to an extraordinary degree. They do not necessarily have better jobs, nor are there sharp status differences between leaders and other members of the group, but the David Sharps do influence opinion formation and attitude change. We shall not be concerned here with the first part of the situation that Katz and Larzarsfeld studied, that is, the transmission of information from the mass media, but we shall be concerned with whether particular individuals can be identified as opinion leaders who possess the credibility to make

them influential in persuasive communication.

A number of characteristics of the opinion leader are of use to the persuasive communicator. The most general way of describing opinion leaders is that they tend to serve as models for the group members. They are asked for their opinions, and their advice is listened to. There seem to be few characteristics that all opinion leaders possess, but there are some factors that are useful in predicting opinion leadership.

Opinion leaders tend to be better informed in those areas about which they are consulted. They are better informed about the information transmitted by the mass media, particularly when it concerns the subjects on which they are influential. Berelson and his associates were concerned with an election study and the determination of opinion leaders in a political situation. They reported that leaders were more interested in the election, were better informed about it, held stronger opinions about it, and were more concerned about the election than nonleaders.

One of the major factors that seems to emerge from the research is the amount of communication that is associated with being an opinion leader. Opinion leaders talk to more people than nonleaders. They know more people. They read more, listen more, and view more. They have more than one circle of acquaintances, although they may be opinion leaders in only one circle.

Opinion leaders vary, depending on the topic under consideration. The opinion leader for the political arena is not too likely to be the opinion leader for the latest in sports nor perhaps for the latest in stockmarket activities. The student opinion leader in the dormitory who was influential in changing attitudes about marijuana might not be as successful in influencing attitudes about student government.

Opinion leadership is a relative variable. Opinon leaders cannot be detected by the amount of education or social status they have, since this variable is a relative one. For a neighborhood where the average education is one year of high school, the opinion leader may have had three years of high school. Ten blocks away, there may be a neighborhood where the average number of years of schooling is one year of college, and the opinion leader on a topic might be a college graduate. The two opinion leaders probably cannot trade places and continue as opinion leaders with their new groups. Opinion leadership is defined by receivers, not sources. Within any particular group, the variables of education, social status, mass media usage, information level, and intensity of opinions will help to identify a potential opinion leader, but the process may have to be gone through all over again when look at a different group.

The reader may at this point think, "Now I know why President Kennedy or Martin Luther King were so influential. They had high credibility because they had high status." Leaders like Kennedy, King, Winston Churchill, or' Mao Tse-Tung need to be discussed apart from the ordinary run of influential people. There is a term for such individuals. They are said to possess *charisma*. The charismatic leader is one whose ability in persuasion and leadership seems to transcend any of the usual abilities of most individuals. Abraham Lincoln, Franklin Roosevelt, Adolf Hitler, and Ho Chi Minh have all been called charismatic leaders. Originally, the term was applied to mean the "qualities of those who claim or are believed to possess powers of leadership derived from some unusual sanction—divine, magical, diabolic—or merely exceptional individuals.[14] Today the term is usually removed from the realm of magic, but it is still used to refer to unusual credibility or to the unique personal influence of an individual. To say that someone has charisma is to say that he seems to possess characteristics that cannot be easily defined or explained, but which are considered relatively constant over many topics and for many different audiences.

Throughout history, individuals have appeared who possessed a charisma that led them to leadership of large groups. Demosthenes of Greece, Cicero of Rome, Gengis Khan of Asia, Guatama Buddha of the Far East, Disraeli of England and Gandhi of India are well-known examples. In each of these cases, the ability to produce changes in attitude and behavior through persuasive communication appears to be almost magical. Perhaps the best guess we have about the nature of charisma is that it is the possession of many dimensions of credibility by a single individual and possession of those factors to a greater degree than seen in other persuasive communicators. The student leader, the PTA president, the Chamber of Commerce leader, the state senator, the factory foreman, and the local physician can all improve their effectiveness in persuasion through an improvement in their perceived credibility, prestige, or status. Charismatic leaders, however, cannot be so easily produced. The charismatic leader is an individual whose effect on audiences and history is not easily explain by research literature.

Source credibility, status differential and opinion leadership are similar concepts. Each suggests that the source can have influence on the outcome of a persuasive message simply because of characteristics that receivers attribute to the source. Each line of research, however, it cast in slightly different ways, and thus deserves separate treatment.

POWER

Our discussion of the influence of the source makes the assumption that receivers have a free choice to change their attitudes or not to change their attitudes as a result of attending to a persuasive message. The credibility model does not destroy the notions of free choice that underlie the model. It simply suggests that receivers may be influenced in their choice by perceptions held about the source. There is another view of the relationship between source and receiver. This view holds that behavior in many communication situations is dependent on the *power* that one individual can exert over another. In fact, we can define power *as the ability that Individual A has to influence the behavior of Individual B.*

Two examples will help our understanding of power in certain situations. Why do students prepare term papers and turn them in on time? Why do those same students come to class on time, and submit to taking tests? A naive reader might argue that the student is motivated simply by a burning desire to learn, and that it is the desire for learning that makes the student willing to perform all kinds of painful and difficult tasks. An analysis in terms of power would suggest another explanation. It would suggest that the teacher has a certain power over the student. If the student wants to graduate from high school or wants to graduate from college, and wants the benefits·that that graduation will bring, then the student has to do what the teacher wants, since the teacher has certain powers over the student. In particular, the teacher has the ability, through the use of the power to give grades, to stop a student from graduating. Thus an analysis of the situation from a standpoint of power would conclude that the students behave as they do because of the perceived power that the teacher possesses.

Another example of personal power at work can be seen in the situation where a wife is beaten over a long period of time by a brutal husband. Sometimes, such a situation can exist for years and years. An outsider, making an analysis of the situation from a "free choice" perspective might conclude that the wife likes to be beaten. If we look at the same situation from the standpoint of power, the beating becomes understandable, even though still deplorable. The wife allows the husband to influence her behavior because she perceives the husband as having more power in the situation. She may feel that there is nothing she can do on her own, that she would starve or that the children

would starve if she left the brutal husband. In other words, she allows one kind of behavior, because she wishes to perserve her ability to perform other kinds of behavior.

Like some source credibility, power is dependent on the mutual perceptions of both the source and receiver. Emerson[15] emphasized the interdependency of individuals and pointed out that power comes from the situation, and not from any inherent characteristics of the source or the receiver. Emerson also pointed out in the same article that there are always attempts by people to equalize power differences between people. He suggests that such differences may be equalized by withdrawal from the situation by one party, by an attempt to increase the number of people in the situation so that there is more chance for equal power relationships, by the formation of coalitions to neutralize the power of one member of the group, and by attempts to gain status and thus lessen the effects of power. His point is that when there are perceived power differences between people, there will be attempts by those in power within the group to maintain that power, and attempts by others in the groups to reduce the power differences.

Power has to be discussed in specific terms, because one individual's power over another is usually not a universal relationship. As a teacher, I may have the power to reward you for class performance, and thus be able to influence your behavior in certain areas, but I do not have the power to tell you where you must live, or what you must wear. It may be that your parents have the power to influence your choice of living arrangements, but do not have the power to influence the church to which you belong. Power is not universal, and a very careful analysis has to be made of the sources of power for any specific communication situation.

Power is, like status and credibility, a relationship that exists between people *only* when it is perceived to exist. If neither source nor receiver admit that any power relationship exists, that variable cannot influence a communication situation. Another way of putting it is say that you have power over me only when I believe that a power relationship exists.

Jacobson,[16] in his excellent book *Power and Interpersonal Relations*, provides an analysis of many different kinds of interpersonal situations where power can operate to influence behavior. At the end of the volume, he provides a very useful set of forty-eight "power principles" derived from many different studies. Only a few of these principles seem directly related to persuasive communication situations, although many are indifectly related to persuasion. We discuss some directly related principles below:

1. The amount of communication is directly related to power. In any communication situation, the individual who can monopolize the amount of communication being presented is likely to have more power, and thus exert more influence.

2. The person in a persuasive communication situation with the most information about the topic will be the most powerful person. This suggests that the initial approach by a source may not be enough to influence change, *if* the receiver has more information than the source.

3. The more a source can promise to deliver to the receiver that which the receiver wants or needs, the more influence is likely to be exerted in the situation. This principle emphasiszes the need for an analysis of the audience before beginning persuasive communication.

4. In a group, people with less power communicate less frequently, but they tend to talk to people with more perceived power. This principle is related to the first principle we discussed, but turns the situation around to the receiver's viewpoint. The principle will help in making a prediction about the relative power held by members of the group.

5. To the extent that an individual has had a series of past successes which become known to the group, the individual will be perceived as having more power. This principle is directly related to the general credibility principles that we developed in the first part of this chapter. It suggests that power can be acquired sometimes if the group is informed about the source's past successess.

6. If there is a deviant member within the group, communication attempting to get that individual to conform will increase, until it becomes obvious that the person is not going to conform. At that point, communication will drop, and the individual will be isolated. This principle is closely related to some of the balance principles we discussed in an earlier chapter. The group can sometimes restore balance only be eliminating deviant members.

7. Groups with very sharp perceived power difference between members are likely to have poor social—emotional climates. Productivity in such groups may not suffer, but for long-term maintenance of the group, the power differences between the members of the group should be minimized. This suggests that it may be difficult to exercise strong power attempts and still hope to keep a group happy.

There are other principles that Jacobson cites, but they are more indirectly related to persuasion. Our analysis of social power, however, indicates that it may play a very important role in the success of persuasion, and particularly in the way in which the source is viewed by receivers. Power, like source credibility, is a dyadic variable. It makes little sense to talk about having high social power, if there is no one who has low social power. Power is also dependent on the perceptions that people have of one another. Whether I have or do not have power depends less on me than on the people with whom I am attempting to communicate.

SELF-PERSUASION: A SPECIAL CASE

The models of persuasion we have been discussing tend to assume that all persuasion requires both a source and a receiver, and that the source and the receiver have to be different people. The source sends a message, and the receiver absorbs the message and then reacts to it. This is a simplistic, passive view of the communication process. Receivers do assist in building their own reference frames, their belief systems, and in determining what behaviors they will engage in. Receivers do modify their beliefs and attitudes as result of observations made of their own behavior.

In persuasion, the fact that an individual's active participation can lead to changes in attitudes and beliefs has lead to an interest in *self-persuasion*. This model assumes that people can persuade themselves to take some action or to change some attitude, and that successful persuasion does not rest entirely on an individual being persuaded by another. The entire body of research literature in this area has been reviewed and synthesized by Miller and Burgoon[17]. Our concern in this volume will be with the ways in which self-persuasion occurs.

One major type of self-persuasion occurs when someone has been placed in a *role-playing* situation. A situation frequently studied is the use of role-playing to get smokers to stop smoking. Janis and Mann asked subjects to imagine that they had to tell someone else that they had to stop smoking because they had lung cancer.[18] The subject had to place himself or herself in that position, and try to find the words and actions that would be most appropriate to the situation. The results showed that those people who had been asked to role-play in this situation changed attitudes and behavior more than did subjects who merely listened to a message about the dangers of smoking. Although it may be difficult to find situations in which role-playing can be used as a persuasive technique, evidence suggests that it can be a useful tool in several kinds of persuasive situa-

A special case of self-persuasion is termed *counterattitudinal advocacy*. In this situation, an assessment is first made of an individual's prior attitudes toward some topic. Then, the individual has to be induced to present a persuasive message that conflicts with prior attitudes.

After the message is presented, we again assess attitudes toward the topic. If we find that those attitudes have shifted in the direction the individual advocated in the message and away from the prior attitudes, we say that counter attitudinal advocacy has been successful.

The efficiency of counterattitudinal advocacy has been demonstrated. Janis and King[19] show the difference between self-persuasion and passive reception of a persuasive message. They had students deliver a message that went against their prior attitudes. Another group of students formed the audience for the message. Then, the attitudes of both groups were measured again. The results showed that there was more change in attitude for the group that delivered the message than for the group that merely listened to the message. The implications for persuasion are clear. If we can find some way to make people encode their own messages about abortion reform, or pollution, or educational reform, they may be more persuaded then by any message which the communicator might deliver.

Why do receivers change attitudes and beliefs as a result of active participation in the persuasion process? Miller[20] carefully reviews four possible explanations. His concluding position agrees closely with my own. Each of the four positions has some evidence in favor of it, but taken alone, none of the positions seems sufficient to account for the evident success of counterattitudinal advocacy. We will briefly examine each of the four major theoretical positions that have been advanced to account for this phenomenon.

The first, and currently most popular position, involves balance theory, and particularly Festinger's account of dissonance theory. The individual has been induced to engage in the presentation of a counterattitudinal message. Mary Smith knows that she does not believe in abortion or abortion reform, but she is speaking in favor of abortion reform. This condition arouses dissonance in her. As a result of the conflicts which have been aroused, she changes her attitude toward abortion and abortion reform to better fit what she has been induced into saying. Thus she now believes what she has been saying.

The second explanation offered for self-persuasion can be termed the "incentive or reward interpretation." This explanation suggests that self-persuasion will not take place under all circumstances, even if the individual is engaging in the presentation of a counterattitudinal message. This explanation says that attitudes and beliefs will change only if the task is seen as positively rewarding by the subject. If the subject does not seek the task as rewarding, attitude change will not occur. To take a practical example, if John Jones is induced to give a speech favoring women's liberation, and he sees that the speech will improve his relations with his girl friend, or with his wife, he is more likely to change his attitudes in favor of women's liberation than if he can see no advantage in making the speech. The position is supported by studies by Janis and Gilmore,[21] and Elms and Janis.[22]

A third interpretation can be termed the "self-perception" interpretation. This position is straightforward. People change their attitudes because they see themselves behaving in certain ways and change the attitudes to fit the behavior. Thus, if we have the head of the local Junior Chamber of Commerce making a speech in favor of black capitalism, and we ask him after the speech whether he favors black capitalism, he answers, "Yes, I do. After all, I wouldn't make a speech in favor of black capitalism if I didn't favor it."

In an early study, Festinger and Carlsmith[23] paid subjects either twenty dollars or one dollar to convince other subjects to engage in a dull, nonrewarding task in which the subjects being paid had already been engaged. One would expect that the subjects paid one dollar would subsequently rate the task as more attractive than those paid twenty dollars, since the one dollar payment is so low that the subjects cannot really justify their support for the task to themselves. This is exactly what happened, but

it should be noted that both groups of subjects actually changed attitudes in favor of the dull task. Self-persuasion worked to change attitudes. This self-perception explanation is examined in detail by Miller and Burgoon.[24] The studies do not allow one to give an unequivocal explanation, but all of the studies utilizing some variant of the Festinger and Carlsmith situation do report attitude changes as a result of self-perception.

The final explanation offered can be termed the "functional analysis" interpretation. This explanation is closely related to a balance theory explanation, but differs from it in suggesting that certain types of conflict situations will not result in a change in attitude, while other types will. This position has been articulated by both Baron[25] and Kelman.[26] The functional analysis interpretation suggests that there are three kinds of situations: *moral, hedonic,* and *consensual validation* situations. In a moral situation, such as when a strong Roman Catholic is asked to espouse legalized abortion, little attitude change can be expected. The morality of the situation overrides any possible cognitive inconsistency that might arise. The hedonic situation arises when the individual has been asked to undertake a difficult, time-consuming counterattitudinal task. For example, we might ask James Joy to spend many hours preparing a paper on the effect of the eighteen-year-old vote. Even if James were initially against the eighteen-year-old vote, he might change his attitude because of the work involved in the task. In the consensual validation situation, a man might change his mind because he comes to believe that he was originally wrong. Thus, if we ask the man to prepare a speech opposed to his original beliefs, and tell him that he is doing something that everyone else believes in, this fact may cause him to shift his own opinions.

It is quite possible that none of these explanations are sufficient to account for attitude change in the counterattitudinal situation. It may be necessary to use parts of each interpretation depending on the nature of the situation we have. The four explanations leave unanswered one persistent question. How can we get people to engage in counterattitudinal advocacy in the first place? It is easy to insure these conditions in the laboratory study, but it is not as easy in the real-life situation There are several possibilities.

In small group situations, it may be possible to get members of the group to help study a problem by researching all sides of a problem, and then by presenting messages which complete the work of the group. In so doing, some people might find themselves on the opposite side of the argument, and change their position toward the side desired by the persuasive communicator. In some situations, it may be possible to convince someone to act as devil's advocate, and present the opposing view so that the group will have all of the arguments. Most college debaters, for example, do shift their attitudes as the season goes along. The shift is away from their original position and probably occurs as a result of having to present both sides of the argument in different debates. It may be possible to arrange a debate on an issue, in which the individual whom the communicator wishes to convince is asked to take a side opposite to previous beliefs. The situation might result in the desired attitude change. Finally, it is frequently possible to arrange to reward an individual for taking unfamiliar or unpopular side. This is particularly true in the sales situation, where the salesman may reduce the price, or may place an article for a trial period with a potential receiver. The very fact that the person feels rewarded in this situation may cause positive feelings toward the product or the situation.

Self-persuasion is a fact. It does occur, and it may help the persuasive communicator achieve a goal. In essence, the communicator is using the self-credibility of an individual to get the individual to change attitudes and behavior. Self-persuasion depends in part on the nature of the individual who is asked to participate, and it may depend on the nature of the topic involved. The basic element involved, in self-persuasion, however, is that receivers are more likely to change their attitude and beliefs when actively engaged in a task than when they are simply part of a passive audience.

IMPROVING THE INFLUENCE OF THE PERSUASIVE COMMUNICATOR

What help can we give the college student who does not want to spend the next twenty years waiting to acquire status? Can we help the new teacher who wants to make an impact on the school system? Can a housewife become effective in spite of the fact that she is not a well-known personality? The literature available does not allow a simple answer; rather, it indicates a series of suggestions and cautions:

1. In general, receivers do not ascribe negative characteristics to sources with which they are completely unfamiliar. Greenberg and Miller[27] found that when sources are not personally known to receivers, the sources are usually evaluated as positive rather than negative. They hypothesize that receivers may develop a cultural standard which in essence says, "I will remain open-minded, until I have seen or heard a source. Furthermore, I will err on the positive rather than the negative side." As an unknown source, then, we are at least not going into the persuasive communication situation with negative influence. If our influence becomes negative, it will be because of the way we handle the actual communication situation. The Greenberg and Miller findings suggest strongly that the beginning, unknown communicator is actually better off than the communicator who has already developed a negative image because of past actions.

2. Persuasive communication will be more effective if receivers view the source as being similar to themselves. This suggestion may help the beginning communicator locate audiences that will be receptive to the message. It

may also help the communicator realize that perceived similarity helps in those situations where the source can do something to appear similar to the audiences that are being approached.

Several types of studies support this suggestion. Everett Rogers reviews a number of studies in this area.[28] He suggests that "homophily," the condition of being similar to a receiver, is almost always more effective than "heterophily," the opposite situation, where the source and receiver perceive themselves as quite different. This homophily–heterophily distinction seems to exist across a large number of factors, including socioeconomic status, education, attitudes and beliefs. It may even extend to variables such as dress. The author, in collecting data for another purpose, measured attitudes toward individuals with "normal" college clothing such as slacks and sweaters, and sports suits, and toward "abnormal" dress, that is, dirty overalls and sweatshirts. The results showed that the abnormally dressed individuals were rated lower than were the more normally attired individuals. Today, slacks and sweaters might seem the abnormal mode of attire.

Rokeach[29] suggests that race may make a difference, but that race is not as important a variable as is the perception of similarity. Whites will prefer blacks if they see the black as being more like themselves than another white person. Again, similarity seems to be the preferred characteristic.

Through audience analysis, sources can isolate points of similarity between themselves and their audiences and can emphasize those items in the message. Through audience analysis, communicators can examine their own backgrounds and begin to make prediction as to the possible effects they might have on an audience. Perceived similarity is a powerful variable in determining the effects of persuasion.

3. A persuasive communicator is seldom completely unknown to an audience prior to communicating. Before the listener starts to listen, before the reader starts to read, and before

the viewer starts to view, they are making judgments about the source to which they are going to expose themselves. This suggests that it is not the first, momentary exposure to the source at the time of message transmission that is important, but the total set of impressions commencing from the time the receiver first becomes aware of the source.

We have already discussed the development of reference frames. We must remember that people are always viewed from within an already existing frame of reference. If the source seems to violate the receivers' expectations as to what sources should look like, talk like, and behave like, the probability is that the source will not be highly successful. The preconditions for persuasive communication are thus an important determiner of the eventual success of the message. If an introduction by a third party can help pinpoint characteristics of the source with which the receiver can identify, this step ought to be taken. In general the source will enhance credibility by taking steps to acquaint the audience with those personal factors that might be appreciated by an audience.

4. Status level has been shown to relate to persuasion. Most sources cannot raise their social status for a specific occasion, yet a receiver may associate a source with one organization and be completely unaware of the level that the source has reached in another organization. For example, imagine that a group of social workers is listening to Danny Kaye talk about the problems of orphan children in Europe. The social worker may well wonder just why she, a professional, should be listening to an actor, no matter how good, talk about a subject that has no connection with acting. If, however, Kaye had been introduced to the group with a mention of the international commissions dealing with children on which he has served as chairman, and a mention of the work he has been doing for the United Nations Educational, Scientific, and Cultural Organization (UNESCO), his status as perceived by the social worker might well have been improved and

his influence increased. In a local election in 1971, one of the candidates running for a City Council seat was a young, twenty-four-old resident of the city. There was some speculation that he was too liberal for the older voters. So at one of the campaign meetings, he wore his old Boy Scout uniform, complete with merit badges. He lost the election, but wearing the uniform had been an attempt to show older voters that his values were not appreciably different from theirs. A campaign manager might have suggested some other tactic to achieve the same result, but the candidate recognized the necessity of establishing credibility with an audience.

It has been my experience that there are few people who have absolutely no status at all. The fact that one is a college student may be important for the individual who has never been in college, or for the high school student who aspires to college. Having been a leader in a church youth organization may well enhance credibility with some audiences. It is one of the tasks of persuasive communicators to examine themselves in the continuing attempt to determine how they might relate to a receiver or group of receivers.

5. It is not possible to become an instant opinion leader. It takes time to work with a group until they recognize you as an opinion leader, and you then have the opportunity to influence them. We can, however, suggest what sources might do to make themselves into opinion leaders for a particular group. Most important perhaps, is a willingness to gather and dispense information. Opinion leaders must attend to the mass media, expose themselves to many different kinds of information, show a willingness to talk to others and to answer questions about interesting topics. Opinion leaders must digest information and then be willing to pass along that information to the members of the group.

Individuals serve as opinion leaders at the whim of the group, and they may move in and out of such an influential position as the group changes or the situation changes. Communicators can enhance their chances of being regarded as an opinion leader, thus, enhancing their persuasive influence, by behaving as an opinion leader would.

6. Credibility has been studied largely as it affects a receiver's prior images of the speaker, but the communicator must remember that credibility, and thus, influence, may well develop and change as a result of behavior during a speech. Brooks and Schneidel[30] had an audience rate the late Malcom X at various periods during a speech. The audience started with a somewhat low image of the speaker. There was a sharp rise shortly after the speech began, then a decline, another sharp rise, and then a final decline that lasted to the end of the speech. The final attitude toward Malcom X was lower than the image the audience brought with them as a result of the speaker's behavior during the speech.

Although this study has some methodological problems associated with the testing situation, it does illustrate the kinds of shifts that can take place during an individual's attention to any message.

Several studies support the conclusion that persuasive communicators can increase or decrease credibility as a result of their own behavior during a speech. Bettinghaus,[31] in 1959, had a group of speakers behave "properly," and behave "improperly," while making a presentation to a group of college students. Some of the speakers were told to lean sloppily on the podium, dress poorly, and generally behave as if they cared little for the audience. Others were told to make the best appearance they could. The results showed that the speakers who behaved more "normally" were also able to achieve more attitude change, although the content of the speeches was identical. What was normal dress in 1959 might not be normal in 1980 for college students, but the point is that these seemingly extraneous factors can affect the perceptions receivers have of sources. Miller and Hewgill[32] found that an excessive number of nonfluencies in speech affected the persuasive response that could be obtained. Burgoon and Saine report that personal appearance could affect the receivers' ratings of communicators.[33]

What sources say is extremely important, but how they say it, and how they behave while saying it do dramatically affect the receiver's perceptions of the source, thus influencing the extent of attitude change the receiver is likely to experience.

7. The credibility that people have can be affected by the people with whom they associate. If a potential audience sees a source as being associated with individuals who themselves possess high credibility, it is probable that some of that credibility will rub off on the source. Even the perceived credibility of the person introducing a persuasive speaker can affect the image of the speaker. In that way sources who are not well known can make use of a number of "sponsorship" techniques to increase their own influence.

McCrosky and Dunham[34] found that if a teacher remained in the room when an experiment was being conducted, the presence of the teacher influenced the ways in which the class responded to the experimenter. Harvey[35] also found that the credibility of the persuasive communicator is influenced by the audience's attitudes toward the person introducing the speaker. Thus, the relatively unknown source may enhance his influence by the individuals he invites to share the situation with him.

In a similar fashion, negative credibility may accrue if the source is introduced by, or associated with, an individual who possesses negative credibility. In 1971, the Gallup Polls showed President Richard Nixon had lost some of his

support from the conservat[...] party when he sponsored t[...] People's Republic of China [...] tions. Even though his ass[...] munists was public and di[...] may have been enough to [...] credibility.

8. Most of the research [...] most of the suggestions offe[...] nicator thus far, seem desig[...] one-way persuasive situa[...] however, affects people wh[...] together to achieve a goal. If [...] reach agreement with a [...] Council on marijuana refo[...] will be affected by his cre[...] ceive it and he will be affected by your credibility as he perceives it. Good, viable agreements may not result if the perceived credibility differences are too great between the two individuals. One party or the other would have to give up too much. Working together is essential to achieving many goals, but when people perceive too many differences between the parties, results are not likely to be easily achieved.

9. Self-persuasion may be a useful way of enhancing the credibility of a source. If I can get you to espouse a position I am advocating, you ought to become more favorable toward *me* as well as more favorable toward the topic. The attitude change that occured as a result of your playing devil's advocate may well rub off onto me as the source. We should note, however, that this can work in reverse. If I am unsuccessful in getting you to engage in self-persuasion, it is possible that you may think less of me, that is, I may lose some credibility as a result of my failure to get you to perform.

SUMMARY

We do not know all there is to know about the effects a source may have on the acceptance or rejection of a persuasive message. Some studies

suggest that there may be few such effects with certain topics. For instance, the topic itself is so important, that the nature of the source becomes less important, and the source thus becomes less influential. For most persuasive communication situations, however, sources who are perceived as having either high-positive or high-negative source credibility *can* make a difference in the attitude change of a receiver or group of receivers.

Each of the studies we have examined bears out the conclusion that source credibility is important. Regardless of whether it is called ethos, source credibility, status differential, opinion leadership, charisma, or power, the conclusion seems inescapable—who you are can influence how your messages are received.

FOOTNOTES

1. W. R. Roberts, "Rhetorica," in W. D. Ross, ed., *The Works of Aristotle*, vol. 2 (New York: Oxford University Press), p. 7.
2. F. S. Haiman, "The Effects of Ethos in Public Speaking," *Speech Monographs*, vol. 16 (1949), p. 192.
3. C. I. Hovland and W. Weiss, "The Influence of Source Credibility on Communication Effectiveness," *Public Opinion Quarterly*, 16 (1961), pp. 635–50.
4. C. I. Hovland, I. L. Janis and H. H. Kelley, *Communication and Persuasion* (New Haven, Conn.: Yale University Press, 1953), pp. 19–53.
5. K. E. Andersen, "An Experimental Study of the Interaction of Artistic and Non-Artistic Ethos in Persuasion," (Ph.D. dissertation, University of Wisonsin, 1961).
6. J. C. McCroskey, *An Introduction to Rhetorical Communication* (Englewood Cliffs, N. J.: Prentice–Hall, 1968), pp. 60–61.
7. D. Markham, "The Dimensions of Source Credibility of Television Newscasters," *Journal of Communication*, vol. 18 (1968), pp. 57–64.
8. D. K. Berlo, J. B. Lemert and R. J. Mertz, "Dimensions for Evaluating the Acceptability of Message Sources" (Research Monograph, Department of Communication, Michigan State University, 1966).
9. C. Osgood, P. Tannenbaum and G. Suci, *The Measurement of Meaning* (Urbana, Illinois: University of Illinois Press, 1957).
10. J. C. McCroskey, T. Jensen, and C. Valencia, "Measurement of the Credibility of Peers and Spouses," paper presented at the International Communication Association Convention, Montreal, 1973.
11. cf. R. F. Applbaum and K. W. Anatol, "The Factor Structure of Source Credibility as a Function of the Speaking Situation," *Speech Monographs*, vol. 39, no. 3 August, 1972, pp. 216–22, and G. Cronkhite and J. Liska, "A Critique of Factor Analytic Approaches to the Study of Credibility," *Communication Monographs*, vol. 43, no. 2. June, 1976, pp. 91–107.
12. J. Burgoon, "Ideal Source Credibility: A Reexamination of Source Credibility Measurement," *Central States Speech Journal*, vol. 27, 1976, pp. 200–206.
13. E. Katz and P. F. Lazersfeld, *Personal Influence* (New York: Free Press of Glencoe, 1955).
14. J. Gould and W. L. Kolb, eds., *A Dictionary of the Social Sciences* (New York: Free Press of Glencoe, Inc., 1965), s.v. "charisma."
15. R. M. Emerson, "Power-Dependence Relations," *American Sociological Review*, vol. 27, 1962, pp. 31–41.
16. W. D. Jacobson, *Power and Interpersonal Relations* (Belmont, Calif.: Wadsworth Publishing Co., 1972).
17. G. R. Miller and M. Burgoon, *New Techniques of Persuasion* (New York: Harper and Row Publishers, 1973), pp. 45–101.
18. I. L. Janis and L. Mann, "Effectiveness of Emotional Role-Playing in Modifying Smoking Habits and Attitudes," *Journal of Experimental Research in Personality*, vol. 1 (1965), pp. 84–90.
19. I. L. Janis and B. T. King, "The Influence of Role Playing on Opinion Change," *Journal of Abnormal and Social Psychology*, vol. 49 (1954), pp. 211–18.
20. G. R. Miller, "Counterattitudinal Advocacy: A Current Appraisal," in C. D. Mortensen and K. K. Sereno, eds., *Advances in Communication Research* (New York: Harper and Row, 1972).
21. I. L. Janis and J. B. Gilmore, "The Influence of Incentive Conditions on the Success of Role Playing In Modifying Attitudes," *Journal of Personality and Social Psychology*, vol. 1 (1966), pp. 17–27.
22. A. C. Elms and I. L. Janis, "Counter Norm Attitude Induced by Consonant Versus Dissonant Conditions of Role Playing," *Journal of Experimental Research in Personality*, vol. 1 (1965), pp. 50–60.

23. L. Festinger and J. M. Carlsmith, "Cognitive Consequences of Forced Compliance," *Journal of Abnormal and Social Psychology*, 1959, vol. 58, pp. 203–210.
24. Miller and Burgeoon, pp. 72–74.
25. R. L. Baron, "Attitude Change through Discrepant Actions: A Functional Analysis," in A. G. Greenwald, T. C. Brock annd T. M. Ostrom, eds., *Psychological Foundations of Attitudes, (New York: Academic Press, 1968), pp. 297–326.*
26. H. C. Kelman, R. M. Baron, J. P. Sheposh, J. S. Lubalin, J. M. Dabbs and E. Johnson, *Studies in Attitude Discrepant Behavior*, (Unpublished manuscript, Department of Psychology, Harvard University, 1969).
27. B. S. Greenberg and G. R. Miller, "The Effects of Low-Credible Sources on Message Acceptance," *Speech Monographs*, vol. 33 (1966), pp. 135–36.
28. E. M. Rogers and D. K. Bhowmik, "Homophily–Heterophily: Relational Concepts for Communication Research," Paper presented at the Association for Education in Journalism, Berkeley, California, August, 1969.

29. M. Rokeach and L. Mezie, "Race and Shared Belief as Factors in Social Choice," *Science*, vol. 151 (January 1960), pp. 167–72.
30. R. D. Brooks and T. M. Scheidel, "Speech as Process: A Case Study," *Speech Monographs*, vol. 35 (1968), pp. 1–7.
31. E. P. Bettinghaus, "The Operation of Congruity."
32. G. R. Miller, and M. Hewgill, "The Effect of Variations in Nonfluency on Audience Ratings of Cource Cedibility," *Quarterly Journal of Speech*, vol. 50 (1964), pp. 36–44.
33. J. Burgoon and T. Saine, *The Unspoken Dialogue: An Introduction to Nonverbal Communication*, (Boston: Houghton Mifflin Co., 1978), pp. 185–87.
34. J. C. McCroskey and R. E. Dunham, "Ethos: A Confounding Element in Communication Research," *Speech Monographs*, vol. 32 (1966), pp. 456–463.
35. I. G. Harvey, "An Experimental Study of the Influence of the Ethos of the Introducer as it Affects the Ethos and the Persuasiveness of the Speaker," (Ph.D. dissertation, University of Michigan, 1968).

SIX

THE PERSUASIVE MESSAGE: USING CODE SYSTEMS EFFECTIVELY

Persuasive communication requires both a communicator and a receiver. The various characteristics of source and receiver as they affect and may be affected by persuasive communication have already been discussed. As our discussion of source and receiver characteristics proceeded, it should have been clear that many of the conclusions we suggested, many of the principles cited, were highly dependent on the nature of the *message* being transmitted. If the message had been presented in another fashion, the conclusions we drew might have been somewhat different. The next two chapters are concerned with messages, their content, meaning, language, structure and construction.

Persuasive communicators always start with an idea. The idea may be related to politics, religion, science, human relations, ecology, war, advertising, or any other areas in which people see the need for change. Typically, communicators have some idea of the ways in which they wish a receiver or group of receivers to behave. A source may wish them to sign a petition for tax reform, vote for a new sewer system, buy a new product, change their attitudes toward dormitory regulations, or join in a march for welfare reform. The idea may be of vast importance in the affairs of mankind, or of little importance to anyone other than the source, but the idea, whatever it may be, is imprisoned within the mind of the communicator until it can be expressed in the form of a message to be transmitted to a receiver.

The only way that ideas can be acquired by receivers is through the creation and production of a message by a source and the subsequent perception of that message by a receiver. Messages may appear as sound waves produced by the larynx, ink marks on paper, a series of facial expressions, arrows cut in the bark of a tree, or pictures produced by the brush of a Chinese scholar. Messages are composed of *symbols*, and serve as stimuli to receivers, stimuli which have *meanings* for people, and which can elicit particular responses from them.

Before discussing some of the ways in which the persuasive communicator can use symbols more effectively, two topics need to be covered. First we need to look at some of the ways in which man categorizes symbols into larger structures called *code systems*. And second, we need to look briefly at the ways in which receivers develop *meanings* for the elements in any code system.

CODE SYSTEMS

Communication is dependent upon the development and use of sets of symbols which have shared meanings for sources and receivers. We sometimes fail to appreciate just how many assumptions we have to make about our receivers when we engage in even simple persuasive communication. Imagine a situation in which Jim Marshall approaches a receiver, shakes his hand, and then delivers the following message:

> John, I'm really glad to see you. I have been really worried about the extent of hunger and poverty around the world. I think that one of the main reasons for these problems is overpopulation. The only way we will ever be able to solve the population problem is through a government program of family planning and legalized abortion. I need your signature on this petition to show our senator how important an issue this is, and to urge him to vote more funds to solve the world's population problems.

Some of the assumptions Jim Marshall has made are easy to point out. He assumes that the receiver understands the sounds that he is making, and that the receiver understands them in the same way as does the source. He assumes that the receiver has some of the same

concerns he does about poverty and hunger, and is, therefore, willing to listen to him. He also assumes that the receiver knows how to write his own name, and that he knows what effect a petition might have. Other assumptions that the source makes are less easy to identify. He assumes that John will know what is meant when he shakes hands with him, and that he will not feel that he is being attacked. He further assumes that the receiver knows his own name, that the receiver has attitudes toward the source, and that these attitudes are friendly ones. If the source looks serious during the interaction, he also assumes that the receiver has shared meaning for that and other facial expressions.

The point we are making, of course, is that when Jim Marshall talks to John, the communication situation is dependent on the use of a number of different *code systems*. The code systems are used by them to show their intentions to one another, and to elicit responses from one another. We say that we have a code system when *there is a group of symbols and a set of rules for combining those symbols into larger units*. English is a code system. It has a set of symbols and a set of rules for combining the symbols into larger units that are meaningful to a set of receivers. The basic elements in English are words, transmitted either as sounds or as marks on paper. Each symbol has meaning to the individuals sharing the code system. The set of rules for combining words into larger structures is called grammar or syntax. This set of rules has to be understood by all users of the code system. Otherwise, a source could produce sentences such as "John, you see glad really I'm to." We do not produce such combinations of symbols because sources and receivers have an understood set of rules for the combination of symbols into larger structures.

In the example with which we began, mention is made of at least two code systems. One system is English; the other is represented by the initial handshake between source and receiver. It is a *nonverbal code system*, and may be more important in some persuasive communication situations than the verbal code system. In the example we have been using, we indicated that there was an initial handshake between source and receiver. It is a *nonverbal code system*, and may be more important in some persuasive communication situations than the verbal code system. In the example we have been using, we indicated that there was an initial handshake, but there were undoubtedly other nonverbal messages such as the facial expressions used by both parties, the vocal inflections used by the source, his gestures, his dress, the way in which he stood, and the kind of physical surroundings he selected for delivery of his message.

Nonverbal code systems have the same overall characteristics as verbal systems. They have elements and symbols with shared meanings. Thus, in our society, the handshake has a meaning of friendliness and is used as a greeting. Facial expressions—frowns, smiles, grimaces—come to have meanings for receivers, and form part of the general code system. Nonverbal code systems also have rules for the combination of elements. Frowning eyebrows are not combined with an upturned mouth when the individual wants to show displeasure.

Perhaps the major difference between the verbal and the nonverbal code systems as they are used in our society lies in the nature of the information gained from them. The verbal code seems better suited to the expression of cognitive things, such as the expression of an idea. We tell our receivers about the world of ideas, concepts, beliefs, and values through the verbal code system. The nonverbal system of gestures expresses emotions and feelings. Nonverbal communication tells us *about the communicator*, and not necessarily about the ideas being espoused. Receivers gain information about the persuasive situation through both the verbal and nonverbal bands, but the nature of the information gained is somewhat different.

Most of the formal education that people receive is devoted to an analysis of and practice in the verbal code system. English courses, speech courses, writing courses, and foreign language courses emphasize the verbal code systems our societies have developed. Most persuasive communicators have an understanding of the basic nature of the verbal system, and interested more in improving their skills than in acquiring a basic understanding about verbal code systems.

We all use nonverbal code systems, but most of us receive very little information about them through the formal education system. In part, this neglect stems from the fact that there were few attempts at studying nonverbal systems until relatively recently. The picture is changing, and changing rapidly. Many colleges and universities now have courses in nonverbal communication. The past ten years has seen a virtual explosion in the number and variety of research studies concerned with nonverbal communication. A steady stream of books has poured from the pens of scholars all over the world. We can, of course, cover only a small amount of the research literature relating to nonverbal communication. Our concentration will be on those ideas, concepts and studies that seem most directly related to persuasive communication. The reader who wishes to get a clearer picture of the nonverbal literature is referred to Burgoon and Saine's *The Unspoken Dialogue: An Introduction to Nonverbal Communication*,[1] and Knapp's excellent review of literature *Nonverbal Communication in Human Interaction*.[2]

Below, we examine gestural code systems and some of the important paralinguistic code systems that may accompany verbal communication. Then, we turn our attention to the development of meaning, a problem associated with both verbal and nonverbal systems.

GESTURAL CODES

All of us use gestures to accompany our speech. We point, smile, shrug our shoulders, turn one way or the other, or shake our fist at someone. These are part of the gestural or nonverbal behavioral acts that all cultures have. How should we classify such behavior? There are a number of attempts, ranging from Birdwhistell's[3] system which almost makes a muscle by muscle examination of an individuals gestures, to some 19th century elocutionary attempts at tying certain gestures to particular words in the language. A most useful analysis is provided by Ekman and Friesen[4] who suggest that our gestures can be divided into five categories:

1. *Emblems*. These are gestures which can be translated directly into the verbal code system. The elaborate sign language of the deaf in an example of a set of emblems. When the television producer draws his fingers across his neck in a chopping motion, he is using an emblem to tell a performer that his time is up. The raised hand with forefinger and middle finger separated into a V sign is another emblem. Today, it signifies peace, although during World War II it meant victory. Emblems may accompany a verbal message or be used alone.

2. *Illustrators*. These are body movements or other nonverbal acts which accompany speech. The gesture of holding the two hands apart when telling someone about the size of a just-caught fish is an example of an illustrator. Movements emphasizing a word, pointing to an object when talking about the object, or indicating some action are all illustrators.

3. *Affect displays*. These are the bodily motions which indicate the state of our emotions. Frowns, smiles, grins, hand motions all may be used to illustrate our affective states. Affect displays may accompany the use of verbal codes, or they may be used apart from the verbal code system. There may be a high degree of variance between individuals in their use of affect displays, but all of us use such nonverbal clues to indicate to others how we feel.

4. *Regulators*. These are gestures and facial movements which help to control the flow of communication in an interaction situation. They are used by the source and receiver to indicate the way in which the conversation is to continue, or to change the nature of the conversation. Such gestures include head nods, certain hand movements, and eye movements. They may tell the speaker that receivers are interested, that they want further information or want the speaker to repeat, and so on. Used by the source, they may indicate to the receiver that the source is nearly done, that the speaker wants to elaborate on a point, that the source wants to continue speaking after finishing a point, and so forth. Regulators may accompany similar verbal cues, or seemingly may not be tied to verbal messages.

5. *Adaptors*. Adaptors are the more personal, idiosyncratic movements that specific individuals develop, and which become part of the individual's personality and general communication pattern. One man may rub his hands together whenever he is about to ask a question, another his chin whenever he is nervous or excited. Adaptors do not carry general meaning in the same way that an emblem does. We have to get to know the individual before adaptive behavior will carry any meaning for us. Sources may be quite unaware of their own adaptive behavior, but may well learn to read the adaptors of receivers.

Adaptors are important to persuasive communication in two ways. They indicate to the source how a receiver may be responding to the message. They also indicate how the source may feel about the message.

Each of these five categories applies to the gestural or body language that people use when they communicate. Harrison[5] in his very useful book *Beyond Words*, says that each of these categories is part of the *performance codes* that people use. Performance codes are the gestures or movements of the body that people use to convey their meanings. Harrison points out, however, that if we want to make a complete analysis of nonverbal codes, we need to go beyond performance codes. A second category includes the *artifactual codes*, which involve the use of objects to produce meaning for a receiver. Artifactual codes include the use of such things as clothing, glasses, military insignia, objects on a desk and art. Artifactual codes may indicate the status of an individual, the direction in which an automobile is supposed to travel, the wealth a person has, or the state of health a person enjoys. These meanings are produced not with gestures, but with things.

The third category of code system includes the *spatio-temporal codes*. These codes elicit meaning through the use of space and time. For example, the physical distance two people maintain between each other may indicate the level of intimacy they enjoy. The amount of time an executive keeps a subordinate waiting in the outer office may indicate the status differential between the two people.

The final class of nonverbal code system includes the *mediatory codes*. These are the differences between messages in the same medium produced by such variables as different arrangements or different orders of presentation. For example, imagine that two photographers are shooting the same scene of a fire. One photographer might want to use a wide angle lens to emphasize how extensive the fire is, while the other photographer might use a telephoto lens to focus closely on the activities of a fireman working at the blaze. This would be an example of the use of a mediatory code.

We shall be primarily concerned in the last half of this chapter with the use of the five types of performance codes. Our focus on that aspect of nonverbal communication should not let us forget that there are other types of nonverbal codes which all of us use in our daily communication activities.

PARALINGUISTIC CODES

Most of our study of verbal code systems is concentrated on words and syntax. Thus, we learn that words hold denotative meanings, and that there are ways in which words can be constructed into sentences and paragraphs. All of us realize, however, that the same word, referring to the same object or event, can be said in many different ways. If we are talking about Women's Lib, we can use these two words sneeringly, encouragingly, depreciatingly, humorously, or sadly, all depending on the tone of voice used. The study of those nonverbal cues which surround the verbal code system is called *paralinguistics*. Unlike linguistics, which has been an object of scholarly study for many centuries, paralinguistics has been on the scene for only a few decades. Yet, for persuasion, paralinguistics may prove to be a more important area of study than the study of the purely verbal elements of a message. Trager[6] suggested that the study of paralinguistics involved at least two major elements:

1. *Voice qualities*. These include such things as speech rate, rhythm pattern, pitch of voice, precision of articulation, and control of utterances by the lips, tongue, and other articulators. Such voice qualities do seem to convey meaning as they accompany words and statements. The high pressure salesman who spits out his message at a very rapid rate conveys a sense of importance and urgency because of that rate. Thus, rate becomes a paralinguistic characteristic of the message.

2. *Vocalizations*. These include a number of sounds that do not have specific meanings, but which can indicate emotions when they accompany verbal messages. *Vocal characterizers* such as swallowing, coughing, heavy breathing, sneezing, yawning, and sighing, may indicate, for instance, that the individual has a cold, is

tired, or has just finished heavy exercise. When they accompany spoken messages, such vocal characterizers may indicate importance, nervousness of the speaker, or other emotional states of the speaker or listerner. *Vocal segregates* are interjections such as "um," "uh," "uh-uh," or "ah" placed in the message. They may signal the source to continue, or to stop for a question, or they may tell the listener that the source has more to say, or is almost finished. By using *vocal qualifiers* we indicate intensity in a message by speaking loudly or softly, indicate emotion by using extremely high pitch, or convey importance by speaking slowly and very precisely.

In addition to the paralinguistic elements suggested by Trager, other writers have suggested that other message elements such as pauses, vocal stress, speech errors, repetitions, and certain pitch patterns can be added to the paralinguistic code system. Most important for our purpose is the recognition that while paralinguistics exists outside of the verbal system with which we are most familiar, it can perhaps in some instances effect a successful outcome to a persuasive communication situation where words alone would have had little effect.

There are a number of different ways that nonverbal behavior can be used with verbal behavior to produce different persuasive effects. Some of the most important uses are discussed below:

1. *Repetition*. In many messages, the source can use a nonverbal behavior together with a verbal message in such a way that the verbal message is repeated. A teacher tells Suzy, "You did a very nice job on that assignment, Suzy," and the teacher smiles as she says it. The smile serves as a repetition of the verbal message, and thus enhances the effect of the message. It is, in essence, getting two messages for the price of one.

2. *Complementation*. Nonverbal behavior may add to a verbal message. Suzy may tell her mother, "I'm really sorry that I broke that vase, Mother." But Suzy will add to that message by the downcast face, drooped shoulders, and clenched hands. The nonverbal behaviors tell the receiver just how sorry Suzy really is.

3. *Contradiction*. In many situations, people say one thing, but their nonverbal behaviors are saying something else. The verbal message is contradicted by the nonverbal message. If Suzy said, "I'm really sorry I broke that vase, Mother," and stands with her feet apart, her hands on her hips, and with tightly clenched lips, Suzy's mother is receiving two contradictory messages. The verbal message may say, "I'm sorry," but the nonverbal message says, "I'm not sorry at all." Such contradictory messages may frequently account for the failure of persuasion.

4. *Emphasis*. We all use nonverbal cues to emphasize our verbal messages. We underline in a written message. We raise our voice in an oral situation; the orator pounds the table when the most important points are raised. We can greatly enhance persuasion by the way in which we use nonverbal cues for emphasis.

5. *Regulation*. Nonverbal cues will serve along with verbal cues to regulate the flow of communication in an interaction situation. A speaker finishes a point, and then turns to look at someone else. The turn is a cue to the next person that it is now time for someone else to speak, and the specific look suggests just whose turn it is. In another situation, a speaker may finish a verbal message, and then turn away, or look down. That tells the receiver that a reply is neither expected nor wanted. Nonverbal cues thus serve to regulate the flow of communication.

In the remainder of this chapter, we shall be most concerned with the ways in which persuasion is affected by gestural and paralinguistic codes. We should, however, mention the potential importance of certain situational factors which are also nonverbal in nature. The placement of furniture, the dress of the source, the lighting of the communication site, the type or lack of background music, the weather outside, or the background noise level may all have an important bearing on the eventual outcome of persuasion. It is difficult to predict exactly the outcome or importance of any given situational factor, therefore, we cannot deal as precisely with such variables as we might like.

All persuasive messages are made by selecting elements from some code system shared by the source and the receiver, using the rules of that code system to structure those elements according to the source's intentions, and then transmitting the message to the receiver. The messages may be entirely verbal, entirely nonverbal, or, more likely, a combination of both verbal and nonverbal elements. Thus any account of message elements which does not consider both verbal and nonverbal code systems is going to be incomplete.

DEVELOPING MEANING

For centuries scholars have been interested in attempting to explain just how a baby, born without language, can within a very few years acquire the ability to use an elaborate code system with competence and fluency. For some, the use of language was held to be a gift of God and further explanations were unnecessary. For others, language was imagined to be a result of an imitation of nature and the sounds of nature. Today, we know that code systems are *learned*, and learned according to many of the same principles we discussed in Chapter 2. When we say that a language or a code system has been learned, we mean that a set of meanings has been acquired for the elements and rules of the system. A brief discussion of what meaning is, and how it is acquired is essential.

Any discussion of the acquisition of language must begin with the birth of the child. When Karen Child is born, her eyesight is rela-

tively poor and it usually does not develop fully until she is several weeks or months old. Karen's hearing, however, is fully developed at birth, and she is immediately able to assimilate the sounds that are made around her. Despite the lack of development in eyesight, and in certain portions of the nervous system, and despite the lack of growth in the muscle systems of the newborn child, Eric Lenneberg[7] points out that each human being has the biological capacity to develop language. Contrary to many popular beliefs, the process of developing language does not start when the baby is a year old and first says "Ma Ma." The process begins when the child first begins to hear sounds and first sees things in the surrounding environment.

When Karen is first born, she cries when she is hungry or wet or simply uncomfortable. The sounds she makes, and the gestures she makes are impossible to distinguish from those of almost any other baby. We cannot tell whether Karen is living in an English home, a German home, or a Spanish home. It takes only a few short months, however, for us to be able to easily identify Karen as the product of a particular home and a particular culture. She is able to notice people, objects, and events around her, and respond to them. She knows her own parents and her sisters and brothers. She may respond favorably to them, but begin crying when strangers try to pick her up. The sounds she makes become more and more like the sounds made by her parents and family. Karen will begin to babble, that is, to imitate some of the sounds around her, and to repeat them over and over again. The basis for language is established long before the babbling stage occurs, but not until this stage is reached is Karen ready to learn to speak as her parents do.

Noam Chomsky has suggested that children have some built in mechanisms that help control the way in which they will acquire language.[8] If each of us had to learn every aspect of language at the same slow rate that it takes us to learn to swim or to ride a bicycle, we could never develop the rich code system that the average individual possesses. Chomsky suggests that there is a "grammar" of baby talk that enables children to express certain fundamental language relationships, such as, subject and predicate, noun and verb, or possession even before they have been exposed to formal learning of grammatical rules, or even if they are never so exposed. This capacity, possessed by all normal children, helps explain Karen's behavior as she responds to the world around her.

As Karen matures in terms of her reactions to the sounds she makes, she also matures in her ability to respond to the objects she encounters. Her first cries are relatively simple, and it is difficult to make distinctions between the cries. Later, she can respond with a whole series of distinct sounds that are not language, but are clearly the forerunners of language. It is at this point that language can begin. Figure 6.1 illustrates the process of acquiring *meaning* for a sound. Imagine that Karen is handed a bright, shiny ball for the first time. She will have a number of possible responses to the object, she may smile, kick her feet, smell, squeeze or put her arms around the ball. The chances are that when the ball is handed to Karen, her mother will say, "ball." If Karen is handed the ball several times, and each time her mother says, "ball," the process of association will take place.

If Karen's mother then walks into the room, and says, "Ball, Karen," the probability is that Karen will respond to that series of sounds in much the same fashion as she responds to the ball being handed to her. The sound "ball" becomes part of what the child is responding to, and through processes of contiguity and generalization, the time will come when Karen will respond to the sound alone *with many of the same responses that she made to the object*. Karen may smile, kick her feet, or even reach out with her hands as if to grasp the ball. At this point, an onlooker might be likely to remark, "The baby knows what the word means."

If we look carefully at Karen's behavior, we notice that Karen does not behave in exactly the same way toward the word as she does toward the object. She may make *some* of the same responses, but not *all* of the same responses. What has happened to all of the responses that were made toward the object? Charles Osgood suggests that they have become *detached* from the overt responses and are now made internally.[9] This process of acquiring a meaning for a sound is what Figure 6.1 illustrates. Obviously, the responses that are detached are those that the baby finds she does not have to make or are those that are difficult to make. If Karen does not have to kick her feet to make an adequate response to the sound

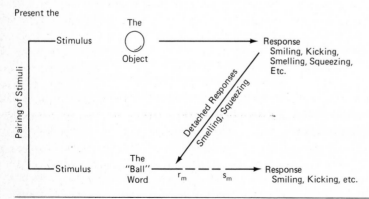

Figure 6.1   *How Meaning Is Learned*

"ball," then we predict that that response will eventually become internalized and dropped as an overt response. As time goes on and the child hears the word "ball" many times, her responses to the word will come to resemble her responses to the object less and less. Most of her responses will have become detached and internalized.

We have discussed the process of acquiring meaning in some detail, because the process, as described, indicates that at least two types of meaning are learned. The first is *denotative* meaning, or that meaning which serves as a link between word and referent. Denotative meaning is sometimes referred to as "dictionary meaning," since it indicates the references that a language community has for a particular word. Persuasive communicators usually make the inference that their receivers will use the same denotative meanings for words as they themselves do, but a look at the illustration with which we begin this chapter may demonstrate the perils of making that assumption. What do you mean by the term "overpopulation"? For one person, overpopulation may mean more people than we have at the present time. For another, it may mean having as many people per square mile as India does. To still another, it may mean having too many poor people, and not enough middle-class people. Or look at the possible meanings in the phrase "government program of family planning." This could refer to a law forbidding more than one child, to a voluntary sterlization program, or to a series of government-sponsored clinics. The words are the same, but because meanings are learned, even denotative meanings may differ from person to person. Thus, we shall have to look at problems in using language in terms of denotation in the text of this chapter.

The second type of meaning acquired is *connotative* meaning. This is the meaning associated with the attitudes that people develop toward words. Karen's experiences with the bright, shiny ball have been pleasant. We expect her to have developed positive attitudes about that particular object. If, on the other hand, we had not handed her the ball, but had thrown it at her each time, we might expect her attitudes to be highly negative. In either case, our theory suggests that Karen will develop connotative meanings to her experiences with the object. Osgood stresses the point that these detached responses are still made internally, and serve to *mediate* or control the individual's external behavior. As Figure 6.1 indicates, a set of internal mediating responses (r_m's) are created, which in turn are responsible for a set of internal stimuli (s_m's), and these internal stimuli help to determine the kinds of external reactions that the individual will make when perceiving a word. The internal responses and stimuli elicited by a word can be used to index the connotative meanings that people attribute to words.

Connotative meaning becomes important to persuasion because such meanings are more highly variable than are denotative meanings, and cannot be easily predicted. If we chose two children, placed one child in a very loving home, and the other in a home where the mother and father periodically indulged in child beating, just what kind of connotative meanings would those children develop? Both children might have the same denotative meanings for the words "mother" and "father," but we would certainly expect different connotative meanings to develop. Furthermore, we would expect the children to react differently to a persuasive message that suggested that the child do something "because your mother and father think it best."

Many examples can be used to illustrate how important connotative meanings are to the process of persuasive communication. Most people will have similar denotative meanings for the term "legalized abortion," but connotative meanings differ widely for various individuals. For some, legalized abortion has a favorable connotation, for others, it is more closely associated with murder. In our next section, we shall look at ways of measuring connotative meaning, and at ways of making the most effective use of the knowledge that people develop connotative meanings along with denotative meanings.

Our discussion has emphasized the meanings that people acquire for the basic elements in any code system, be they words or gestures. There is an additional type of meaning that needs to be mentioned: This is the meaning that is acquired through structuring elements into larger sequences, such as phrases, sentences, or paragraphs. We refer to this third type as *structural meaning* or *syntactic meaning*. To illustrate, look at two sentences: "John killed Jim;" and "Jim killed John." Both sentences contain exactly the same words. The connotative and denotative meanings for the individual words in both sentences are the same when taken separately, but most of us would agree that the sentences have a different meaning. The police would arrest a different person, and the undertaker would bury a different person. The differences in meaning arise from differences in the structure of the sentences.

Does it make a difference if we say, "I am worried about the hunger and poverty that the newspapers have been reporting," or, "I am worried about the newspaper reports of hunger and poverty around the world."? In the first case, concentration seems to be on the hunger and poverty, in the second, on the newspaper reports. One statement might well prove to be more persuasive than the other.

We cannot help developing meanings towards the stimuli we encounter. Whether we are talking about the verbal code system, or about nonverbal code systems, meaning becomes an important part of our consideration of persuasive messages.

The discussion of the development of meaning may be concluded by pointing out several implications of importance for the persuasive communicator:

1. People *learn* the meanings they associate with words and gestures.
2. People will use similar meanings, either de-

notative or connotative, only to the extent that their learning experiences have been similar. When meanings are different, they can be made similar only through the application of learning principles.

3. Because meanings are learned. it is incorrect to say that meanings are in words or gestures. Words or gestures serve only as the stimuli to elicit meaning responses. The meanings are in the people, not in the words or gestures.

4. Because meanings serve to mediate responses, they may serve as reinforcers of behavior and can be used as such by the persuasive communicator. Thus, the meanings that receivers possess will help determine perceptions of the world, the messages attended to, and the responses that are made.

We have now looked briefly at code systems, both verbal and nonverbal, and examined ways in which people acquire meaning. From this information, we can start to develop a strategy for using code systems effectively in persuasive communication situations.

USING CODE SYSTEMS EFFECTIVELY

Messages are composed of complex sets of stimuli. When receivers are exposed to a speech from a persuasive communicator, they hear words, vocal inflections, and any other sounds that may accompany the speech. They see the gestures made by the speaker, and notice the way in which the speech takes place, react to the messages, notice the reactions of people around them, and place all of these stimuli in a context that eventually enables them to each make a meaningful response to the message.

The elements of any persuasive message interact with one another. The receiver may focus on one element or another in a speech, but the focus is dependent on the ways in which other elements may affect perceptions. It is therefore difficult to take apart a persuasive message and concentrate on any one aspect. But if we are going to help sources improve their speaking and writing, we must look at variables independently and attempt to make assessments of the role they play in effective persuasion. We shall discuss those variables relating to message organization in the next chapter. Below, we look at problems in denotation, connotation, and the effective use of nonverbal code systems.

Problems in Denotation

We engage in persuasion to affect changes in the people around us. Whether we are engaging in traditional persuasive situations, acting as a source in attempting to change the behavior of some receiver, or engaging in interaction to reach some consensus on a problem, we persuade with intent. One of the major barriers to successful persuasion comes with a failure to elicit a response from another individual equivalent to the one intended. In other words, the receiver may not have the same meaning for the term used in a message as did the source. At least three variables can be cited which may contribute to the failure to secure similar responses to the same word or phrase.

1. *Abstractness.* S. I. Hayakawa,[10] and other general semanticists point to abstract language as a problem in communication. The more ab-

stract a term is, the less likely it is to elicit similar meanings from a group of receivers. Look at Figure 6.2. The terms on the left are relatively specific in meaning. There can be differences in meaning between receivers even with relatively concrete terms, but the probability is that the range of meanings will be narrower with concrete terms than with abstract terms. Most people will have approximately the same meaning for the term "book," although one individual may be thinking of a paperback while another thinks of a hardcover book. Nevertheless, the differences in meaning are not likely to be serious. If the communicator refers to a "teaching aid," however, the receiver may be thinking of a book, film, a picture, or even a teacher. The more abstract the term, the more necessary careful definition becomes.

2. *Technological terms.* As society grows in size and complexity, the nature of the experiences to which individuals are exposed can result in wide differences in meaning. As our country grows in technological complexity, there will be a tendency for words to move from the ordinary language to elicit specialized meanings as for the scientist or engineer. Similarly, words that were part of a technological vocabulary sometimes become part of the common language, but with slightly different meanings.

3. *Euphemisms.* One of the major problems in language use has arisen from the attempts by

Less Abstract	More Abstract	
Cat	Feline	Figure 6.2
Mother	Relative	*Word Pairs*
Cow	Cattle	
Bees	Insects	
Teacher	Educator	
Book	Teaching Aid	
Contraception	Family Planning	
Littering	Polluting	
War	Border Adjustment	

speakers and writers to make language pleasant to receivers. This results in the use of euphemisms that do not have precise meaning, and that produce wide variation in response.

During the Viet Nam war, the term "waste" was frequently substituted for the term "kill" by soldiers. To say, "We wasted them," rather than, "We killed them," is a clear example of a euphemism. It simply sounded better to soldiers. In similar fashion, we might expect different reactions from the use of the phrase "jailing of criminal suspects," than from the term "detention before trial." The denotative meanings may be exactly the same, but the connotative meanings are different, and we expect different persuasive effects. The euphemism may have value in many persuasive situations. There are audiences that would react more favorably to the use of a euphemism than to a blunter term, but the persuasive communicator must be able to make an analysis of the audience before composing the speech, or denotative meanings are likely to be confusing for the audience.

Each of these three problems relates to the variations in meaning which are elicited for the same word. As time passes, there are always changes in meaning for the elements of any code system. Different areas of the country tend to develop new terms or acquire new meanings for old terms. The advent of any new technology brings new words into the language and existing words are given new meanings by the users of the new technology. Teenagers use words amongst themselves, give the words new meanings, and the new meanings spread to the rest of the population. These changes in the language we use are natural. History suggests that our language is always in a state of change, but that the changes are usually slow enough so that all members of a society who are living at any one point in time will be able to engage in at least basic communication activities, even though there may be specialized areas that remain known only to subsets of the population.

Language change is normal, but it poses a serious problem for the persuasive communicator. Once the communicator has selected a topic, and cast it into a preliminary message, the problem of deciding whether there are terms or propositions that will need clarification must be faced. If there is a high probability that the terms will be misunderstood, the communicator must use one or more of the following methods to increase the probability that the use of the term will elicit the desired response.

1. *Relearning*. For those words or concepts that have a specific object, person, or event as a referent, the receiver can be led through a relearning process. The source can use scale models, visual aids, or other nonverbal clues to assist in demonstrating a complicated process, and even pointing to an object.

The same principles govern definition through relearning as govern the learning process the receiver went through to acquire the original meaning for the word. The word must be associated with the object or event. Repetition may be necessary in case of a difficult concept. All definition involves the application of learning principles, but many persuasive communicators tend to forget that complex language usage may require careful application of learning principles if the receiver is to acquire the intended meaning of a term or concept.

2. *Classification*. In one of the most frequently used types of definition, a source places an unfamiliar term or phrase within the category of other similar objects and then specifies the term's position within this category. For example, the phrase "clearcutting" might be defined as " a method of lumbering where all the trees in an area are cut down, not just selected trees." The source has placed the term "clearcutting" as one member of a class called "lumbering," and then specified just how clearcutting differs from other kinds of lumbering. In another example of the use of classification, the source might define the term "Bennie" as "one example of a drug used

to stimulate the nervous system." Audience members might know the term "Bennie," but might not know what other drugs the term is associated with.

3. *Negation*. A variation of definition by classification has been termed *definition by negation*. The procedure is for the source to define a term by telling the receiver what is *not* being referred to. For example, a source may refer to "drug users" in talking to a college audience. That term could cover many different activities. The source may attempt to define the term by telling the audience, "I am not talking about the use of marijuana, alcohol, tobacco, or legitimate prescription drugs, but only about "hard" drugs such as heroin or LSD." The source has defined the term by eliminating some possible interpretations from the meanings that are to be elicited.

4. *Operational definition*. Classificatory definitions have served persuasive speakers very well, but the problems they have created by suggesting the possible existence of a referent when none exists, have led some modern philosophers of science to suggest the usefulness of the *operational definition*. Here, the communicator specifies a set of operations, which, if performed, will identify the term being defined. For example, the term "socialized medicine" might be defined operationally as "payment of all medical bills by an agency of the federal government."

A number of other terms have been used as equivalent to the term "operational definition." These other terms which the reader might encounter include coordinating definitions, correspondence rules, epistemic correlations, and rules of interpretation. There are slight technical differences between these terms, but their intent is to help specify meanings by providing the receiver with a relationship between the term and a set of observable operations or behaviors.

The operational definition is one of the most useful tools the persuasive speaker or writer has available. Many of the terms in political discussions, religious arguments, social situations, and similar persuasive situations are ones that refer to complex behaviors. The communicator can help clarify meanings for such terms by specifying the steps an individual would have to go through to identify the concept as it is being used in the specific situation. As terms become more and more abstract, the difficulties of providing an operational definition increase. Let the reader try his hand at terms such as "technological insufficiency," "education," "socially deprived," or "racial discrimination." The operational definition is an important tool for the persuasive speaker or writer, but it is difficult to use when terms become abstract.

A problem in denotation occurs whenever the use of a term by a persuasive communicator fails to elicit a desired meaning on the part of a receiver. Most of these problems are caused by the fact that a source and receiver may have learned a different meaning for a particular term. To put the source and receiver on the same track, definition or relearning may be necessary.

Each of the types of definition cited is designed to provide assistance to a source in eliciting a desired response, but we cannot use the entire message to define terms. If we did, we would have no time for argument in favor of a particular persuasive intent. The careful examination of a message may show a source where a simpler word can be used, or a more familiar one, and the necessity for a definition eliminated. Such an analysis ahead of time may reduce the complexity of a message, provide more time for argument and appeal, and make the message far more effective in eliciting desired denotations.

PROBLEMS IN CONNOTATION

We have defined connotative meanings as the internal meanings people develop as they acquire various code systems. There are denotative and connotative components to every word, every phrase, every gesture. Before we can look at some of the problems which arise in persuasion because of connotative components of a code system, a brief look at the measurement of connotative meaning will be useful.

Measuring Connotative Meaning

Individuals encounter many objects, events, and persons in their environment and learn the words associated with them. If their encounters are pleasant and favorable, the connotative meanings associated with the objects, events or persons will also be favorable. If encounters are not rewarded or are painful, the connotative meanings that are built up will be negative and unfavorable. The result is that the individual has *evaluated* the world around him and that evaluation determines to some extent how he will behave toward the words he hears and reads.

Charles Osgood and his associates have suggested useful ways of measuring connotative meanings.[11] The problem in making such a measurement is that connotative meanings are internal, and do not lend themselves to the same type of analysis as do denotative meanings. Osgood suggests the use of the *semantic differential* scaling technique to measure the intensity of reaction individuals have toward words and concepts.

When you ask people about the feelings they have toward words, the answers are frequently given in terms of *descriptive adjectives* of varying kinds. For example, ask a man what he thinks about "government," and he may answer with terms such as "strong," "weak," "necessary," and "bureaucratic." Osgood assembled a large number of pairs of polar adjectives, such as pleasant–unpleasant, smooth–rough, active–passive, low–high, good–bad, clean–dirty and happy–sad. Each polar adjective is placed at the end of a seven-point scale, and individuals are asked to indicate how they feel about particular concepts. An illustration (Figure 6.3) indicates

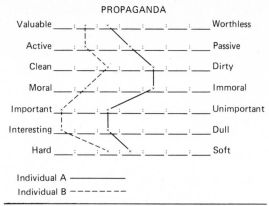

Figure 6.3   *Differences in Connotative Meaning*

how two listeners might rate the same concept. The illustration also indicates the differences in connotative meaning that can arise between two individuals as a result of different experiences.

If a large number of people make responses to a number of concepts and the results are then subjected to a factor analysis, three major dimensions tend to emerge. These are called the dimensions of connotative meaning.

The first dimension is a general *evaluative* one, in which the scales express the degree of favorableness a person feels toward the word. Scales connected with the *evaluative dimension* include good–bad, valuable–worthless, fair–unfair, honest–dishonest, and so on. The second dimension is an *activity dimension*, which expresses the perceptions of a receiver toward the amount of movement or activity in an object or event. Activity scales include active–passive, fast–slow, vibrant–still, dynamic–static, and varied–repetitive. The third has been termed the *potency dimension*, which represents the feelings of strength and weakness that are perceived by an individual. Potency scales include serious–humorous, potent–impotent, strong–weak, heavy–light, and hard–soft.

These dimensions of connotative meaning seem to be stable for a number of concepts and even for a number of different languages (Kumata,[12] Suci,[13] Triandis and Osgood,[14]

Osgood, Ware, and Morris[15]). This stability does not mean that people have the same connotative meanings for words, but simply that they tend to use the same dimensions with which to judge words. I may feel that "roast pork" is a concept that ought to be judged as highly favorable, and a Moslem friend may feel that the same concept ought to be judged as highly unfavorable. We are, however, using the same dimension of evaluation to make our judgment.

It is interesting to note that the semantic differential scaling technique uses the same approach to identifying connotative meaning as was used to identify the dimensions of credibility. Equally interesting is the fact that the three dimensions of credibility discussed earlier seem to be parallel to those of connotation. Safety, competence, and dynamism seem to be very similar to evaluation, activity, and potency. People apparently judge others in much the same fashion as they judge words.

We are well aware that the average persuasive communicator will not have a chance to administer a semantic differential to a potential audience in most situations. There will be times when the results of prior research will be available and can be utilized, but this is not the usual situation. Why spend time on an examination of a technique that is not easily available? We argue that an understanding of the bases on which connotative meanings can be analyzed will enable anyone, either source or receiver, to look at natural languages and make predictions as to potential effects. In the sections below, we illustrate some of the ways in which the connotative dimensions of language can be used more effectively.

Emotional Language

One of the problems facing persuasive communicators is the decision to use words that may elicit highly affective responses from an audience. In many situations this question places the communicator in the position of being asked to choose between a conventional referent evoking only neutral responses and a referent evoking highly intense reactions on the part of an audience. In many situations this question places the communicator in the position of being asked to choose between a conventional referent evoking only neutral responses and a referent evoking highly intense reactions on the part of an audience. This is the process of using *metaphor*. It is reflected in many persuasive situations:

1. Draft laws are legalizing *murder*.
2. Passing this bill means the *rape* of our woodlands.
3. Federal aid to education is another way of *trampling* states' rights to death.
4. Legalized gambling is legalized *sin*.

What effect does the use of metaphor have on the effects of persuasion? Bowers[16] reports on a study in which all ideologically loaded words were removed from a series of speeches and then systematically replaced with words having varying degrees of emotional content. Receivers were exposed to the speeches, and they reacted to the emotional terms within the context of the speech. Bowers' conclusion was that ". . . a metaphor nearly always communicates a stronger attitude than does a conventional expression." He goes on to suggest, however, that to conclude that metaphor usage will be effective in attitude change is not to conclude that such emotional language usage will necessarily be in a direction desired by the source. For the receiver who holds relatively moderate views about the topic, a message that uses very extreme language is likely to have a kind of boomerang effect. Attitudes may be changed less with such an extreme message than with a more moderate one.

Highly emotional language in a message directed toward an audience that is already inclined to side with the source may serve to strengthen those attitudes, but receivers may tend to react negatively toward the use of extremely emotional, highly intense language. This conclusion, like all such generalizations, needs some explanation. Clearly, there are people who respond favorably to the use of highly emotional language, and its use in certain situations is justified. Members of certain evangelical churches, certain types of club situations, football teams at half-time, and student bodies during a pep rally both use and expect that highly emotional language will be used. But many of us would find it just a bit embarrassing if a teacher in the classroom used the same type of language, or the President of the United States used highly emotional language in addressing the country. For some reason, we expect persuasion in many situations to be "cool," and the use of highly charged language does not meet with favorable responses.

Let us look at some examples of the differences between moderate language and intense language. In Figure 6.4 we make comparisons between words which have approximately the same denotative meaning, but which differ in the connotative meanings they elicit. The first word is the more moderate of the pair, while the second is more likely to invoke intense reactions.

Emotional language produces differential responses from receivers. The occasional use of a highly emotional term may simply serve to heighten a receiver's attention to a message. The use of many terms carrying high emotional content, and the accompanying of that language with emphasis through the nonverbal code system, may have a large part to play in determining a receiver's responses. We must point out that the use of highly emotional language does not always result in the changes desired by a source. There are many receivers who react negatively to what they perceive as an overuse of emotional language, and they may reject the message. The implication of using emotional language must be interpreted by the communicator in terms of the initial attitudes held by an audience, and the effects that may be desired.

Enhancing Attitudes Through Language

Sometimes, the topic that the communicator is interested in is difficult to make interesting or important to the receiver. A discussion of parasites, or foreign affairs, or new teaching methods may be extremely important, but it may be difficult for the source to select euphemisms or words which can enhance a desired attitude. After all, there are many topics that do not readily lend themselves to the development of intense metaphor or of euphemism. Yet those topics may become very important to the persuasive communicator. How can the communicator tell the receiver about the importance of a particular topic? In English, we normally use *adjectives* of varying intensity to emphasize the message we send. A consideration of the role

Moderate	Intense	Figure 6.4
Government ownership	Socialism	*Word Intensity*
Confused	Insane	*Comparison*
Provocative	Sexy	
Thin	Skinny	
Trusting	Gullible	
Investigation	Probe	
Unattractive	Revolting	
Inebriated	Drunk	
Marijuana user	Pothead	

adjectives play in enhancing attitudes will be helpful to the communicator.

A series of sentences is presented in Figure 6.5. The first member of each pair has no descriptive adjectives, or ones which appear to be attitudinally neutral. The second has been changed by adding adjectives which might enhance the attitude the communicator wishes to obtain.

Some readers may not agree that they are more affected by the second sentence in each pair, but the effect of the additions and changes made is intended to change the overall connotative meaning for each sentence. An advertiser would expect to have a more favorable response to the second message in each pair than to the first.

Note that the intended denotative meaning of each pair is the same. Both forms point to the same event or proposal in physical reality. The importance of using descriptive adjectives for the communicator is that they intensify the message, and can perhaps help insure a more favorable reception for the message.

A related problem to the use of adjectives for the enhancement of meaning arises when a new word is coined. Every year in the United States, new products appear on the market. Frequently, they receive names that have not existed in the language before. In other cases, an old word is used to name the new product.

If a manufacturer is to be successful in selling products, messages must be presented that will allow a receiver to acquire meanings for the product. People ordinarily do not buy products which have no meaning for them. In addition to the problem of getting receivers to develop a denotative meaning for a new product, there is also the problem of getting receivers to develop favorable connotative meanings for the product name, since people do not typically buy products about which they have negative attitudes.

Marketing of new products is not the only important situation which involves the development or enhancement of meaning. The Peace Corps worker who wishes to introduce a new idea or concept into a village in a developing country faces the same problem. So does the politician who wishes to get a bill passed that would raise taxes, change a zoning requirement, or provide for a new state building. If people do not have a name for it, or if they have unfavorable connotations, the persuasive communicator must use language to help solve the problem.

Werner and Kaplan[17] report an interesting study in which nonsense words were placed within meaningful contexts, and groups of children were asked to report on what they thought the nonsense syllables meant. Their reports showed that the context was largely responsible for the attitudes which were developed.

---

a. An apple a day keeps the doctor away.
b. A tasty apple a day keeps the doctor away.
c. The new state income tax bill is unconstitutional.
d. The nefarious new state income tax bill is unfair and completely unconstitutional.
e. The new plastic product resembling leather will soon be available to shoe manufacturers.
f. The fabulous new plastic product which out-leathers leather will soon replace all other products used in the manufacture of superior-quality shoes.
g. Syrian jet fighters overflew Israeli Army positions in the Golan Heights yesterday.
h. Communist-made Syrian jet fighters intruded into legally held Israeli air space when they overflew defensive Army positions in the Golan Heights.
i. Legalizing abortion will help control population growth.
j. Giving women their legal right to control of their own bodies to decide whether they want to bear a child will also help curb runaway population growth.

Figure 6.5
Using Descriptive Adjectives

Dodge[18] did a study in which subjects were presented with a realistic story about a fictitious tribe, the Meblu, in which the word "Meblu" was placed in association with adjectives characteristic of the three dimensions of connotative meaning. Again, the results suggested that the connotative meanings acquired by the subjects for the word "Meblu" had the same characteristics as the adjectives that had been used to describe them. Even more interesting, in one part of the study the intensity of the adjectives was varied, that is, the Meblu were called the "friendly" Meblu in one version, and the "very friendly" Meblu in another. Dodge's results showed that the use of the more intense signs produced greater change in the post test situation.

The results of these studies suggest that the persuasive communicator can enhance a topic through the judicious use of adjectives carrying intense connotative meanings. A term which is connotatively neutral can acquire favorable or unfavorable attitudes as a result of the evaluative adjectives which are placed in association with it. Enhancing attitudes is a frequent problem for the persuasive communicator, but an analysis of connotation may assist.

Combining Words for Persuasive Effect

Most of the language that a persuasive communicator uses in a message contains words that already have both connotative and denotative meanings for the members of an audience. Messages about education, medicine, abortion, juvenile delinquency, gambling, drug usage or racial discrimination are messages for which the average receiver already has some meaning. Can the connotative meanings a receiver holds be changed substantially? How should a source proceed if changes in connotation are desired?

Howes and Osgood[19] and Bettinghaus[20] have reported studies indicating that evaluative meanings are affected by the adjectives used to describe a noun. We might expect this to be the

case, but their results suggest that the communicator can predict rather precisely the direction the shift will take after the presentation of a message.

Basically, the methodology in both studies involved measuring evaluative meaning toward a series of nouns, such as "secretary," "student," "doctor," "spider," "wrestler," and "nurse." They also measured evaluative meaning toward a similar set of descriptive adjectives, such as "wonderful," "horrible," "shy," "gregarious," "sincere," and "miserable." Then the words were presented a second time to the subjects in word pairs such as "horrible doctor," "sincere spider," "miserable student," "wonderful doctor," "turbulent wrestler," and similar pairs. The results in both the Howes and Osgood study and in the Bettinghaus study showed that the adjectives did affect the way in which judgments were made. Significant predictions could be made by taking the original meaning for both words and applying a *congruity* or *consistency* theory prediction to obtain an estimate of the direction and amount of the connotative shift that the subject would make. For example, if the evaluative meaning for "spider" was negative, and for "wonderful" was highly positive, we can predict that when a subject is asked to rate "wonderful spider," he will show a rating lower than that of "wonderful," and higher than that of "spider." Similar results were obtained for the majority of combinations tested.

In a second phase, Bettinghaus tested the hypothesis that the results would be persistent, that is, the results of seeing the pair of words together would rub off on the subject. So three days after presenting the pairs of words, the subjects were asked to rate the noun alone. Again, the hypothesis was supported. Imagine that one group had originally judged the combination "wonderful doctor," and another group had judged the concept "horrible doctor." Three days later, both groups rate "doctor" alone. The group originally rating "wonderful doctor" rated the noun alone more favorably than did the group who had rated the combination "horrible doctor."

These studies indicate that words do have an effect on the way in which language is perceived. The motion picture referred to as "stupendous" or "mystifying" will acquire some of the characteristics of the adjective used to describe it. The studies also indicate that even when a word has a connotation already attached to it, the appropriate use of language may change that connotation. Choosing the appropriate adjectives to adequately describe a set of phenomena, or characterize a word becomes one of the primary tasks of the communicator.

There are a number of problems that arise from the necessity of having to use qualifying adjectives or adjectives having high emotional content. Most of these problems revolve around the different reactions of receivers to emotional language. For example, McEwen and Greenberg[21] did a study which suggested that credibility was affected by the use of intense language. Speakers using highly intense language were perceived as more credible than those who did not. The same study, however, was unable to conclude that speakers using highly intense language were also more effective in persuasion. Clearly, other factors than simply the use of emotional language must play a part. Burgoon and Stewart[22] suggest that there may be a sex difference. Male communicators were more effective than female communicators when using high intensity language. Miller and Lobe[23] suggest that the nature of the receiver's involvement is related to the use of intense language. Audiences that are neutral to a topic are more influenced by highly opinionated language, while audiences where the members are already involved are less likely to be influenced.

How should we interpret these findings? Perhaps the simplest explanation is given by Burgoon and Ruffner[24] when they point to the influence of expectations about language on the subsequent behavior of receivers. These expectations are the language *norms* of a society, and

individuals who attempt to break the norms may lose credibility and influence as a communicator. In our society we "expect" females to use less intense language than males do. When a female communicator does use highly intense language, there may be a violation of expectations for an audience member which could lead to the rejection of the source and her message. There is evidence that the stereotypes we have about men and women in our society are changing, but clearly, there are still some sex role differences associated with persuasive communication, and it is important to take these into account.

Problems in connotation, like problems in denotation, revolve around the different internal meanings that receivers develop for words. When sources can make an assessment of the kinds of variation in meaning that are likely to be encountered in any persuasive communication situation, it may be possible to use language which will assist in obtaining desired changes in attitude and behavior.

PROBLEMS IN USING NONVERBAL CODE SYSTEMS

An old proverb suggests that, "What you do may speak more loudly than what you say." In this saying lies the basis for many of the problems that arise when the nonverbal code system is considered. Our facial expressions, our bodily movements during a speech, the gestures we use, the vocal inflections we employ to emphasize particular words, our manner of dress, and even the physical surroundings of the communication situation may either enhance or detract from the persuasive message. Obviously, the persuasive communicator would hope that these nonverbal elements can be used to enhance the message being delivered. Three types of problems seem appropriate for discussion: using the nonverbal code system to help achieve credibility, using paralinguistic elements to enhance the message, and avoiding conflicts between the verbal and the nonverbal code systems.

Nonverbal Code Systems and Credibility

We have already discussed some of the elements making up source credibility, and discussed ways in which the source might improve credibility with an audience. One important element of credibility is the trust or liking that a receiver places in the source. Several studies by Albert Mehrabian[25] suggest that a source can elicit various degrees of liking by the manner in which facial expressions, postures, and gestures are used.

Mehrabian gives the following formula for the "total liking" of a receiver for a source:

Total liking = percent verbal liking + 38 percent vocal liking + 55 percent facial liking.[26]

The impact of facial expression is more important than either the words the speaker is using, or the vocal characteristis being imparted to those words. In any situation in which the facial expresssion does not seem to square with what the speaker is saying, Mehrabian suggests the facial expressions will dominate, and thus, help to determine the impact of the total message. For example, we have all known speakers who continually frowned when speaking, even though they were not delivering a serious message. This is inconsistent behavior, and the source can expect to lose credibility as a result.

We may believe that the nonverbal cues we emit do not play an important part in the way in which receivers judge us, but most of us have mannerisms which seem to be able to be detected by receivers. Nerbonne[27] found that subjects listening to a telephone message were able to accurately distinguish between males and females, blacks and whites, among 20–30 years old, and 60–70 years olds. The listeners were further able to make accurate distinctions between individuals with less than a high school education, high school graduates and college graduates, and among speakers from various parts of the country. Harms[28] found that listeners were able to make a accurate judgments of the social class or status of speakers on the basis of their voices alone. To the extent that social class and status are related to credibility, they may be determined in part by the vocal characteristics of sources.

Hair length and dress style have received more attention in the popular press than perhaps they deserve. Yet the fact is that these are nonverbal symbols to which people react. If a man is speaking to a middle-class audience, and his hair extends well below his neck line, and his dress is anything other than a suit and tie, it may make little difference what he says. His audience will have judged his trustworthiness in terms of the nonverbal cues he emits, and the message may go unattended. Even the way a receiver looks at a source can affect credibility, and thus persuasion. High credible sources tend to have more eye contact directed toward them than sources possessing lower credibility.[29]

We have already mentioned the importance of *expectations* in using language effectively. In similar fashion, every receiver or group of receivers has a *set of expectations* about the nonverbal cues which a source emits. When the set of cues corresponds to the expectations of the receiver, credibility is enhanced. When there is a conflict between the expectations and the cues, credibility will suffer, and so will the persuasive effectiveness of the communicator.

THE PARALINGUISTIC CODE

Earlier we defined the paralinguistic code as those vocal elements which are attached by speakers to the words they use. Figure 6.6 illustrates the changes in meaning that come when different words in a statement are emphasized.[30]

a. *I* am selling the car to John.
   The emphasis is on the speaker's act, not on someone else.
b. I am *selling* the car to John.
   The car is being sold, not given away.
c. I am selling the *car* to John.
   Only the car is being sold, nothing else.
d. I am selling the car to *John*.
   The car is only for John, not Jim or Sally.

Figure 6.6
*The Infuence of
Vocal Inflection*

In each of these examples, the verbal elements remain the same, but the total meaning of the message may change drastically depending on which words are being emphasized.

Other vocal characteristics may enhance or detract from the message. Opubor[31] found that receivers have connotative meanings for loudness and rate of speech, even when the message is delivered in a foreign language. Mehrabian[32] found that the tone of the speech was mainly responsible for the inferences which the receiver made about the attitude of the communicator. He suggested that ". . . when the attitude communicated in content contradicted the attitude communicated by negative tone, the total message was judged as communicating negative attitude." A man may say, "I believe in Women's Lib," but the tone in which he delivers the statement may tell the receiver more accurately that he does not.

The impression that the speaker makes simply in terms of speaking style may well lead to the credibility the speaker has. Pearce and Brommel and Pearce and Conklin suggest that a speaker who has a conversational style of delivery, that is, calm and measured rather than intense and strident, will have higher credibility.[33] Sources who have extremely high pitched voices tend to be less credible than those with deeper pitched voices.[34]

Understanding the paralinguistic code is important for the persuasive communicator. Each of the elements which makes up that code has meaning for receivers in a particular language community. Some of the elements have specific denotative meanings within a language community. The rising inflection at the end of a statement signaling a question is an example of an element carrying denotative meaning. But many elements have primarily connotative meanings. Many of the *vocal segregates*, for example, will carry negative connotations. The "uhs" and "ahs" and "yuh knows" that a speaker unconsciously sprinkles through a speech, may rub many receivers the wrong way. Their reactions to the message may depend not at all on what the speaker says, but on the extraneous vocal segregates used.

The advice that we can give to persuasive communicators and receivers of persuasive messages is clear. Do not listen only to the words themselves. Listen also to how the source delivers the message. Does the source seem bored with the whole idea? What are the vocal infections really saying to the receiver? If you are a source, listen to your own words. Do you come across as someone who knows the topic and sounds like it? Or do you come across as hesitant and unsure of yourself? It is the paralinguistic elements that carry that portion of the message.

CONFLICTS BETWEEN THE VERBAL AND NONVERBAL CODE SYSTEMS

It may be impossible to completely predict the effect of the nonverbal elements of a speech on an audience, but the persuasive communicator can enhance the effect of a message by careful practice to make sure that the nonverbal elements of the message correlate with the verbal elements.

In Chapter 2, we noted the importance of cognitive consistency as a theoretical approach to explaining inconsistencies in perceptions. That same theory may help to explain what happens when a receiver perceives an inconsistency between the verbal statements of an individual and his nonverbal behavior.

We have all been in situations when one individual referred to another as "stupid!" or "you slob!" or "idiot!" Such words might provoke a fight, but when they are accompanied by a smile, they usually do not. We have two conflicting stimuli but, as Mehrabian indicates, the facial expression is more important than the verbal expression, and the balanced position is resolved in favor of the smile. As a result, the receiver does not think about punching the source in the nose, but treats the message as a friendly joke.

In the situation described above, source and receiver usually know each other. It would be more difficult to utter such an epithet to a total stranger, even if accompanied by a smile. Most persuasive communication situations occur between sources and receivers who are not well acquainted with each other. Inconsistencies between the verbal band and the nonverbal band become more important in the total effect of the message. Imagine a situation where a president is saying to a nationwide audience, "The latest threats of the Soviet Union seem to be just talk. I urge you all not to get unduly excited about them." At the same time, the camera focuses on the president's hands, and we see him nervously twisting them. The chances are that an audience is going to be highly influenced by the nonverbal cues, and fail to respect his plea for calm.

One historical incident points up the importance of verbal-nonverbal conflicts. In 1960, the two contenders for the presidency were John F. Kennedy and Richard M. Nixon. They engaged in a series of nationwide debates to one of the largest audiences of the time. Before the first debate, the opinion polls had Nixon ahead slightly. After the conclusion of the debate, the polls showed that Kennedy had edged in front, and he remained in front for the remainder of the campaign. Social scientists point to the importance of nonverbal behavior on Nixon's part during the debates as a possible cause for his loss. Those people who did not see the debate on television, but heard it on the radio or read it in *The New York Times* were inclined to think that Nixon had "won."[35] Those who saw it on television, however, felt that Kennedy had a clear edge. Some of the nonverbal cues that seemed to enter into the situations were the differences in dress between the two candidates, and the fact that Nixon appeared to need a shave, was perspiring and nervous, and sat tensely in his chair while waiting to speak. Kennedy, on the other hand, was seen as calm, confident, and poised during the debate. The nonverbal code elements that Nixon emitted did not seem to fit with his words, and the viewer judged him accordingly.

One can imagine all kinds of incongrous situations where the conflict between the verbal and nonverbal band may result in a lack of success for the communicator: the speaker arguing in favor of capitalism, while wearing a set of overalls, or the speaker arguing in favor of socialism, while his clothes suggest a man of extreme wealth. I once had a debate judge who criticized a member of the team for lack of eye contact with the judge. All the while the criticism was being delivered, the judge was staring at the ceiling. Needless to say, the individual being criticized did not take the criticism with great seriousness.

The examples we have cited are clear, but they do not emphasize the potentially serious effects that conflicts between the verbal and nonverbal code systems can sometimes produce. The boy who hears his mother say that, "Stealing is bad," but also sees his mother take money from his father's wallet, may be in a conflict situation. In similar fashion, the child who hears a parent say, "Don't fight, children," but also sees that that same parent hasn't moved from an easy chair to break up a fight also may be in a conflict situation. The chances are that after a period of time observing and listening to conflicting messages, the child will fail to be persuaded by any verbal messages unless the nonverbal code that accompanies the message is congruent with the verbal message. Persuasion is not likely to be enhanced by the use of messages in which there are conflicts between the verbal and nonverbal code systems.

We have briefly discussed some of the problems involved with denotation, connotation, and the use of the nonverbal code system. Messages are total entities. Communicators cannot pay attention only to possible denotation problems, or spend time only in an examination of descriptive adjectives. Effective persuasion demands careful consideration of all language elements.

SUMMARY

In this chapter, we have concentrated on the ways in which code systems can be used to build successful messages. The elements of any code system, either verbal or nonverbal, have meanings for each receiver who shares the code system. These meanings may be denotative or referential, connotative or evaluative in nature, or arise from the ways in which the elements are structured. Any element will have both connotative and denotative meanings. All meanings are learned, and all meanings are in people, not in the elements themselves.

For successful persuasive communication, the source must be able to predict what meanings will be elicited from a receiver when a term is used in a message. We may have problems in predicting either the denotative or the connotative aspects of meaning, and we must consider the role that nonverbal code systems will play in eliciting a successful response from a receiver being exposed to a persuasive message.

FOOTNOTES

1. J. Burgoon and T. Saine, *The Unspoken Dialogue: An Introduction to Nonverbal Communication*, (Boston: Houghton Mifflin Co. 1978).
2. M. L. Knapp, *Nonverbal Communication in Human Interaction*, 2nd Edition, (New York: Holt, Rinehart and Winston, 1978).
3. R. L. Birdwhistell, *Kinesics and Context*, (Philadelphia: University of Pennsylvania Press, 1970).
4. P. Ekman and W. Friesen, "The Repertoire of Nonverbal Behavior: Categories, Origins, Usage, and Coding," *Semiotica*, vol. 1 (1969), pp. 49–98.
5. R. P. Harrison, *Beyond Words: An Introduction to Nonverbal Communication*, (Englewood Cliffs, N.J.: Prentice–Hall, 1974).
6. G. L. Trager, "Paralanguage: A First Approximation, *Studies in Linguistics*, vol. 13 (1958), pp. 1–12.
7. E. H. Lenneberg, *Biological Foundations of Language*, (New York: John Wiley and Sons, 1967).
8. Noam Chomsky, *Aspects of the Theory of Syntax*, (Cambridge, Mass.: M.I.T. Press, 1965).
9. C. Osgood, *Method and Theory in Experimental Psychology*, (New York: Oxford University Press, 1953), pp. 680–727.
10. S. I. Hayakawa, *Language in Thought and Action*, (New York: Harcourt, Brace & World, 1964).
11. C. Osgood, P. Tannenbaum and G. Suci, *The Measurement of Meaning*, (Urbana, Ill.: University of Illinois Press, 1957). See also *Semantic Differential Technique*, J. Snider and C. Osgood, eds., (Chicago: Aldine Publishing Co. 1969).
12. H. Kumata, "A Factor Analytic Investigation of

the Generality of Semantic Structures across Two Selected Cultures," (Ph.D. dissertation, University of Illinois, 1957).

13. G. J. Suci, "A Comparison of Semantic Structures in American Southwest Culture Groups," *Journal of Abnormal and Social Psychology*, vol. 61 (1960), pp. 25–30.

14. H. C. Triandis and C.E. Osgood, "A Comparative Factorial Analysis of Semantic Structures in Monolingual Greek and American College Students," *Journal of Abnormal and Social Psychology*, vol. 57 (1958), pp. 187–96.

15. C. E. Osgood, R. E. Ware and C. Morris, "Analysis of the Connotative Meanings of a Variety of Human Values as Expressed by American College Students," *Journal of Abnormal and Social Psychology*, vol. 62 (1961), pp. 62–73.

16. J. W. Bowers, "Some Correlates of Language Intensity," *Quarterly Journal of Speech*, vol. 50 (1964), pp. 415–20.

17. H. Werner and E. Kaplan, "Development of Word Meaning Through Verbal Context: An Experimental Study," *Journal of Psychology*, vol. 29 (1950), p. 251.

18. J. S. Dodge, "A Quantitative Investigation of the Relation between Meaning Development and Context," (Ph.D. dissertation, University of Illinois, 1955).

19. D. Howes and C. E. Osgood, "On the Combination of Associative Probabilities in Linguistic Context," *American Journal of Psychology*, vol. 67 (1954), pp. 241–58.

20. E. Bettinghaus, "Cognitive Balance and the Development of Meaning," *Journal of Communication*, vol. 13 (1963), pp. 94–105.

21. W. J. McEwen and B. S. Greenberg, "The Effects of Message Intensity on Receiver Evaluation of Source, Message and Topic," *Journal of Communication*, vol. 13 (1963), pp. 94–105.

22. M. Burgoon and D. Stewart, "Empirical Investigations of Language Intensity: I. The Effects of Sex of Source, Receiver, and Language Intensity of Attitude Change," *Human Communication Research*, 1 (1975), pp. 244–248.

23. G. R. Miller and J. Lobe, "Opinionated Language, Open-and Closed-Mindedness and Re-

sponses to Persuasive Communications," *Journal of Communication*, 17 (1967), pp. 333–41.

24. M. Burgoon and M. Ruffner, *Human Communication* (New York: Holt, Rinehart and Winston, 1978), pp. 417–19.

25. A. Mehrabian and S. E. Ferris, "Inference of Attitudes from Non-Verbal Communication in Two Channels," *Journal of Consulting Psychology*, vol. 31 (1967) pp. 248–52. See also A. Mehrabian and M. Wiener, "Decoding of Inconsistent Communications," *Journal of Personality and Social Psychology*, vol. 6 (1967), pp. 109–114.

26. A. Mehrabian, *Silent Messages*, (Belmont, Calif.: Wadsworth Publishing Co., 1971), p. 43.

27. G. P. Nerbonne, "The Identification of Speaker Characteristics on the Basis of Aural Cues," (Ph.D. dissertation, Michigan State University, 1967).

29. A Mehrabian, "Significance of Posture and Position in the Communication of Attitude and Status Relationships," *Psychological Bulletin*, vol. 71, (1969), p. 365.

30. This example was adapted from M. Knapp, *Nonverbal Communication in Human Interaction*, 2nd Edition (New York: Holt, Rinehart, and Winston, 1978), p. 323.

31. A. Opubor, " 'Vocal' Communication: The Effects of Rate (Speed) and Intensity (Loudness) on Response Messages," (Ph.D. dissertation, Michigan State University, 1969).

32. A. Mehrabian and M. Wiener, "Decoding of Inconsistent Communications."

33. W. B. Pearce and B. J. Brommel, "Vocalic Communication in Persuasion," *Quarterly Journal of Speech*, vol. 58, (1972), pp. 298–306; W. B. Pearce and F. Conklin, "Nonverbal Vocalic Communication and Perception of a Speaker," *Speech Monographs*, vol. 38, (1971), pp. 235–41.

34. D. W. Addington, "The Effect of Vocal Variations on Ratings of Source Credibility," *Speech Monographs*, vol. 38, (1971), pp. 242–47.

35. D. Krech, R. Crutchfield and E. Ballachey, *Individual in Society*, (New York: McGraw–Hill, 1962), p. 235. Also R. Harrison, personal communication.

SEVEN

STRUCTURING MESSAGES AND APPEALS

The basic units of any persuasive message are the ideas that communicators bring to the situation. In order for communication to occur, the communicator must cast ideas into a code system and then transmit the coded elements so that they will be received by a listener or reader. It has already been noted that ideas can be expressed with different words from the same language code, that the use of different modifiers can drastically change a receiver's impression of the message, and that nonverbal code elements can enhance or detract from the reception of an intended message. Messages, however, do not exist as single words or gestures. Messages are created from the placement of single words into larger language units (sentences, paragraphs, sections, and chapters). Each message could have many different structures, depending on where a particular sentence is placed, or how a chapter is organized. Are there more effective and less effective ways of organizing messages? Do some types of message structure have greater impact on receivers than others? Our first concern in this chapter will be to examine various ways of organizing messages, and to make recommendations for more effective message organization.

In addition to the problem of choosing an effective structure for the message, the persuasive communicator also has the problem of maximizing the effectiveness of the *appeals* that are used in the message so that receivers will agree with the message. Should the source appeal to receivers beliefs in their own rationality? Or should the source try to scare receivers into agreeing with the message? Are there other appeals which would be effective with an audience? Our second concern in this chapter is to examine the effectiveness of various types of appeals.

MESSAGE ORGANIZATION

There is ample evidence to support the statement that *some* kind of organization is essential in a speech or an article. To have no organization at all would mean that words would appear completely at random. Paragraph 2. is an example of what happens when the message presented in paragraph 1. has all organization stripped from it:

1. It is correct to say that all meanings are found in people, that they are learned, and that they are personal. However, if we could not abstract some uniformity in meaning, some public dimensions of meanings, and if we could not code these into some system, we could not communicate.[1]
2. Personal say we they public that is of meanings communicate we we in to code some all meanings into uniformity if meaning people some not however abstract dimensions are that learned it not correct could meanings say these system that they could if to are found and in are.

Our example, of course, is unrealistic. In any practical situation, one would never find a message arranged in completely random fashion. There are a number of studies which compare organized messages with disorganized messages in terms of their relative effectiveness. Petrie[2] examined a series of speech studies. He concluded that the evidence was inconclusive; some studies showed that organized messages produced more retention of the speech materials, while others concluded that organization made no significant difference in retention. In an earlier review of the literature, Beighley looked at written messages rather than oral messages.[3] He found clear evidence that comprehension is greater for organized than for disorganized structures in written messages.

In specific studies, the effect of organization on both retention and on attitude change has been examined. Thompson[4] found that individuals listening to an organized message retained more of the material, but that organization did not seem to affect the amount of attitude change. Darnell,[5] on the other hand, using a written message, found that it took a great deal of disorganization before retention was affected, but that even minimal amounts of disorganization affected attitude change toward the message. The Darnell results were confirmed by Sencer[6] who manipulated the number of grammatical errors in a message, and found that adding grammatical errors did not seem to affect learning, but adversely affected attitude change.

Although some of the studies seem to show inconclusive results, there are no studies indicating that presentation of a disorganized message is more effective than presentation of an organized one. If some organization is preferable to no organization, the next question is whether there are any patterns or arrangements more effective than others? Is it possible to set up any guidelines about the kind of organizational patterns that *might* be acceptable in persuasive communication situations? One principle frequently mentioned is that of *familiarity*. Receivers expect sources to use certain relatively familiar patterns of organization. When the speaker or writer severely violates this basic expectation, it is predictable that the result may not be as persuasive. There are a number of organizational patterns that have been used with success in many communication situations:

1. *Space pattern* In this pattern, the source organizes material in terms of geography or space. For example, in talking about the necessity for further increases in the efforts of the federal government in helping solve our polution problems, the communicator might make an outline dividing the topic into sections that would cover the major areas in the United States. Such basic outline might have five major sections:

    I. Problems in the Eastern States
    II. Problems in the Midwestern States

III. Problems in the Southern States
IV. Problems in the Far West
 V. Problems in Alaska and Hawaii

In each section of the message, the source would then proceed to discuss some of the specific problems associated with each area, and how federal effort might help alleviate the problem. Our example is simple, but the same plan can be used for far more extensive sets of materials. Audiences do find this type of organization to be familiar, and the communicator will seldom violate expectations with a space outline.

2. *Time order* In this familiar pattern, the persuasive communicator outlines a sequence of events leading up to the problem as an historical background against which the proposed solution is set. An editorial writer, arguing for the development of a mass transportation system as a way of alleviating the energy crisis, might organize materials as:

 I. The use of multipassenger vehicles—trolleys and buses—in the nineteenth and twentieth century.
 II. The development of the automobile in the twentieth century.
 III. The decline of mass transportation between 1945 and 1978.
 IV. The necessity for redevelopment of mass transportation.

A time order is useful when some problem has a clear history, and when some attention to that history may provide a useful way of organizing a topic. A caution should be issued to the source who plans to use this particular organizational pattern. There is some danger that the source will get so wrapped up in the history, that the persuasive message will fail to be received by the audience. The time order, and the use of an historical approach is a convenience, and should not be the major thrust of the speech. All a time order does is to suggest that when a problem has a history, some attention to that history may provide a useful organizational pattern.

3. *Deductive order* The deductive pattern of organization is one of two types of so-called logical patterns frequently used. In this organization, the communicator proceeds from a set of general statements to more specific materials or suggestions. In practice, the writer of an editorial might outline a number of areas on which general agreement is expected. Then the message is concluded by calling for some action that seems to follow logically from the earlier agreements. For example, imagine that we want to argue for increased economic aid to a group of underdeveloped countries in Africa. We might begin by pointing out the economic strength Japan and West Germany have regained since World War II. We could note the increased manufacturing power of France and Italy in the last thirty years. Then we would point out that the growth of economic strength could be a direct result of the foreign aid program of the United States which poured money into those countries. In the final section, we would proceed to the specific persuasive point we want to make, and suggest that increased economic aid to African nations ought to have the same effect on them as it did in Europe.

Note that in a deductive arrangement, the communicator engages in persuasion at each step of the way. The source has to get audience agreement on each of the major statements before asking for agreement on the final statement. The use of a deductive arrangement is based on the assumption that by agreeing to a series of more general statements, the receiver will find it easy to agree to a more specific proposition as the concluding statement. In order for this chain of reasoning to be effective, the source must be careful to show the relationship between the general cases or statements that appear in this message, and the specific final proposition.

4. *Inductive order* An inductive arrangement attempts to let the reader or listener "reason

with" the communicator. The communicator presents a number of specific examples and waits until the end of the message before drawing a conclusion. The following sentence outline illustrates an inductive arrangement:

 I. Pittfield has a public swimming pool and a low juvenile delinquency rate.
 II. Omio has a new pool, and their juvenile delinquency rate has dropped drastically.
 III. Sunfield had two people killed in drag-racing accidents, built a new pool, and has had few problems since.
 IV. Therefore, if New Berlin were to build a pool, it could also reduce its delinquency problems.

This example represents an inductive pattern of organization, with an *explicit* drawing of the conclusion. At times, the communicator will give the audience a number of examples, but will allow the audience to draw the conclusion for themselves. This can be referred to as *implicit* conclusion drawing. For example, a political speaker may refer to the poor record the incumbent has generated, but never say the incumbent should be turned out of office. Obviously, there is a danger in using an implicit conclusion. The audience will probably draw a conclusion, but may *not* draw the conclusion intended by the speaker. In the case of the political speaker, the audience may decide not to vote for the incumbent, but may also decide not to vote for the person making the speech but for a third party. A conclusion was drawn, but not the one intended. The best advice to the communicator is to use the implicit method of organization only in those situations where the conclusion to be drawn is completely obvious to the audience. In most cases, the inductive or indirect organizational pattern should involve an explicit drawing of the conclusion.

5. *Psychological organization* Monroe and Ehninger suggest that organization be based on what they term the "motivated sequence," as a succession of steps that would lead the listener

down the same path that he might psychologically be expected to go by himself.[7] He suggested five steps to such an outline:

 I. Attention
 II. Need
 III. Satisfaction
 IV. Visualization
 V. Action

The effectiveness of the psychological pattern in persuasion has never received systematic testing in a research situation. This pattern, however, would seem a particularly appropriate one for the persuasive communicator to use in many situations. For example, imagine that the speaker wishes to convince an audience of the necessity for a program of legalized abortion. In the attention step, the source might point to the tremendous increase in population that the world is experiencing. In the need step, the speaker points out that current family planning efforts are failing to have any effect on reducing population. In the satisfaction step, the speaker might point out that legalizing abortion would have a positive effect on a reduction of population as it has had in Japan. In the visualization step, the communicator outlines exactly how the plan would work. And, finally, the speaker will outline exactly what actions the audience might take to bring legalized abortion into effect as a national policy.

The example we have used allows us to look more closely at each of the steps in this pattern, and to specify exactly what the source does for each step. The *attention* step is designed to get the audience to be willing to listen to the message. Here, the communicator presents any materials that would serve to make the receiver aware of the problem and become interested in the problem. After all, just why should I be interested in listening to a speech on overpopulation? Unless the speaker does something that makes me interested, it is likely that I will simply turn off whatever the speaker is saying.

In the *need* step, the source presents any materials that will demonstrate exactly why there is a problem, and why we need to do something about the problem. There are many topics about which people can speak. Persuasion occurs every day, and most of us are bombarded with persuasive messages. Unless a source can tell us why this is an important problem, and just why we should do something about the problem, there is little reason for a receiver to be very much concerned.

The *satisfaction* step is the point in the message where the communicator tells the receiver that a proposed solution will work. In the example we have used, the speaker points to the results that were obtained when the solution was used in another country. The speaker could also have used statistics from research studies or from small trials here in the United States. The argument behind this type of reasoning is that audiences are not inclined to be persuaded about a potential solution unless they can see that the plan might work. Obviously, one of the best ways of making that demonstration is by showing that a similar plan has worked elsewhere.

The *visualization* step is the point in the message where the source tells the audience exactly how the plan would work. This might be done by simply suggesting that a law be passed, or it might require the presentation of a very elaborate plan of work. If the source does not go through this step, the audience is being asked to accept a proposal with no indication of exactly how the proposal would work.

Finally, the *action* step tells the audience exactly what the speaker wants them to do. It may be to vote for a piece of legislation. It may be to write their congressman. But the action step gives the audience member something to do. Perhaps this step is one of the most important additions to persuasion that Alan Monroe contributed. Speakers and writers for centuries have made suggestions to their audiences. Monroe was one of the first to recognize that the action step be an integral part of almost every successful persuasive speech.

There have been other organizational patterns based on the ways in which receivers are supposed to attack problems. Such patterns, like Monroe's "motivated sequence" can prove extremely useful to the persuasive communicator.

6. *Problem–solution order* This is another popular and familiar type of organization. The communicator first details the nature of the problem, and then proceeds to discuss the steps that ought to be taken to solve the problem. An outline for a message organized in this fashion might be as follows:

I. We have had a number of riots in our community.
II. These riots are apparently located in areas where most individuals have low incomes and few opportunities for normal recreational activities.
III. When teenagers and young adults cannot participate in ordinary recreational activities, they are likely to make trouble.
IV. Perhaps we can solve some of our problems by passing a bond issue for a new park and a new swimming pool within the low-income area of the city, with free access for all residents.

Again, the problem–solution pattern of organization is one used frequently in persuasive communication, since many persuasive speeches suggest changes in attitude or action based on the existence of a specific problem.

7. *The Toulmin pattern* A pattern of message organization that is increasingly popular is based on an analysis of the way in which people actually make decisions. Stephen Toulmin, a British philosopher, suggested in his book *The Uses of Argument*,[8] that people make decisions in everyday life based on a fairly limited number of argumentative patterns. Since his initial formulation, several people have extended his work into more elaborate schemes of argumentative analysis and message organization (cf. Ehninger

and Brockriede,[9] Windes and Hastings,[10] and Bettinghaus[11]). In this section, we present only a simple organizational pattern appropriate to persuasion in order to illustrate this very useful approach.

Figure 7.1 presents the Toulmin pattern in a basic form, and utilizes only three of the six elements that Toulmin describes. By *evidence*, we mean any data, observations, personal opinions, case histories, or other materials that are relevant to the issue under consideration. The *claim* is the statement that the communicator wishes people to believe, or the action that is desired. And the *warrant* is the linking statement between evidence and claim. It is a statement showing the reasoning—why people ought to accept the source's conclusions. In the very simple argument below, each of these elements is present:

> Inflation in the United States has risen to the double digit level. (*evidence*) We must cut government spending by thirty billion dollars a year, (*claim*) because deficit financing at the federal level is responsible for inflation. (*warrant*)

Obviously, one could take these three simple statements and expand them into a lengthy speech by adding more evidence, expanding the claim into a specific plan, and adding support for the warrant so that the connection between the claim and evidence has become clear.

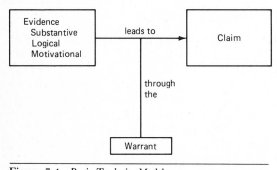

Figure 7.1. *Basic Toulmin Model*

Toulmin would argue that his patterns of argument are valuable because they represent the way in which people actually think. We change our beliefs because someone asks us to, and in the asking give both evidence and a reason for the change.

One of the advantages of the Toulmin method of message organization is that it allows even very complex arguments to be analyzed and placed into an effective message form.

Figure 7.2 illustrates a more complex message, and one which makes use of all six of the elements that Toulmin identified. The more complex model presented in Figure 7.2 introduces three additional elements that need definition. By a *qualifier*, we normally mean the use of some adjective that softens or modifies the claim. In the sample we used, we could add a qualifier to the claim by saying, "We must cut government spending by *approximately* 30 billion dollars a year." Adding a qualifier may make it easier for a receiver to accept the claim. A *reservation to the claim* simply sets out any limitations that the source wishes to place on the claim. It sets the conditions under which the claim should or should not be accepted. Using the same example, we could add a reservation to the claim by rewriting as, "We must cut government spending by approximately 30 billion dollars a year, unless we find that Russia has drastically increased the size of their defense budget." By adding the last clause, the source suggests that there may be conditions that would make it impossible to accept the claim. Finally, the element *support for the warrant* adds materials that adds further justification for the use of the warrant in linking evidence and claim. Again, using our example of inflation, the phrase ". . . since federal deficits allow too much money to be put into circulation," would be support for the warrant. Warrants can be supported by historical data, or statistical materials, or analogies from other situations. Support for the warrant helps to strengthen the warrant, and make it more believable.

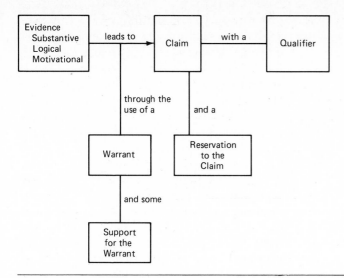

Figure 7.2. *A Complex Model*

Below, is a more elaborate version of the simple argument with which we began:

Inflation in the United States has risen to the double digit level. (*evidence*) Our balance of payments deficit will reach almost thirty million dollars this year. (*evidence*) The price of gold has risen to the highest level in history. (*evidence*) Because of these facts, we must cut government spending by thirty billion dollars a year, (*claim*) unless we find that Russia has drastically increased the size of their defense budget and that we would then fall behind in our defense preparations. (*reservation to the claim*) Such a cut is necessary because deficit financing at the federal level allows too much money to be put into circulation (*support for warrant*) and those deficits are responsible for inflation. (*warrant*)

This message looks more complicated, but it consists of just the six elements that Toulmin identifies. You can take this message and diagram it in exactly the same form as is illustrated in Figure 7.2. Furthermore, the source could expand this short message into a much longer speech either by using a series of similar arguments, or by adding even more evidence in support of the claim.

The examples we have used have been short messages, but the various kinds of patterns of organization that the Toulmin model allows can easily be adapted to much longer messages. It is a very flexible system, related to various formal types of logical analysis frames, yet based firmly on the psychological behavior of people making critical decisions.

These are some of the standard ways of organizing the main points of any persuasive message. In addition to the main points, the speaker or writer will need to include supporting materials or evidence. Our concern here has been primarily with methods of organizing the ideas constituting the major portion of the message the speaker wishes to transmit.

In ignoring the organization of the total message, we have made the assumption that the speaker will be familiar with this type of organization. The basic ideas in a message will ordinarily form the "body" or main section of a formal message, with the rest of the message consisting of an introduction to the speech, possibly a thesis sentence, and a conclusion or summary at the end of the message. A number of sources are available for more complete discussions of organization, and the reader is referred to several of these.[12]

Although there is little conclusive evidence of a scientific nature regarding the relative effectiveness of any of the patterns of organization discussed above, there is no justification in concluding that there is no research relating to message organization. There is, but the research available has not directly tested the patterns discussed. Instead, a number of questions that relate to several kinds of arrangements have been studied. These include: Where should the longest or the best arrangements be placed within the persuasive message? Are people affected by the use of logical structures or patterns? Should persuasive messages present both sides of an issue or only the side that the source advocates? In discussing these questions below, the point must be emphasized that these questions may affect almost all the patterns we have already mentioned.

ORDER EFFECTS

Most messages will have more than one piece of evidence to support a given conclusion and more than one section in the entire speech. The communicator faces a decision regarding the placement of these materials. Some elements will be regarded as more persuasive than others, some sections will be longer than others. Is it more persuasive to place the most important materials at the beginning of the message, in the middle, or should the most important materials come at the end of the message? Questions like this revolve around the strategy of message element placement.

One line of message strategy research deals with the order that the most important elements in the message should occupy. The re-

search model that is frequently employed presents messages having the same topic, but differing arrangements, to comparable audiences, and then sees which audience has the most response. The assumption is that if the messages all use the same topic, and if the audiences are actually comparable, any differences in response among the audiences must be due to the different types of order that the messages utilize. A *climax order* places the most important materials last; an *anticlimax order* arranges the most important materials first; and a *pyramidal order* places the most important materials in the middle of the message, with less important materials both first and last. The researcher has demonstrated a *primacy* effect if the material placed first in the message has the greatest effect. It is a *recency* effect if the element positioned last in the message has the most effect.

Lund,[13] Jersild,[14] and Knower[15] have all reported studies which support a primacy effect. These very early studies, however, used two complete messages and varied the order of presentation. In later studies, more conflicting results were obtained. Hovland and his associates have completed an entire series of studies on the effect of order on attitude change.[16] Their results, in general, do not show a primacy effect. In one of their studies,[17] only one of the three groups tested showed a primacy effect, while two showed slight recency effects. These studies all used written communication.

Studies in which the messages were delivered orally are not a great deal more illuminating. The study with the most complete design and analysis is by Gulley and Berlo,[18] who used organizational patterns of climax, anticlimax, and pyramidal structures in a series of persuasive speeches. Their results suggested that either climax or anticlimax orders are preferable to pyramidal orders. The data from their study show that the climax order was consistently slightly more effective than anticlimax order, but since the differences between the two forms were not statistically significant, we are really not justified in using the difference to support a recency hypothesis.

Conclusions about simple order effects are difficult to make when the results of various studies seem to confirm several hypotheses. Clearly, however, the studies show no support for the placement of an important piece of material in the middle of a message. In choosing between climax or anticlimax order, the evidence seems to show a slight preference for a placement in final position. This conclusion, however, makes the assumption that order is the only factor that is in operation.

Rosnow and Robinson, however, argue that simple order effects are not always the most important factors operating in any communication situation.[19] After reviewing some of the many studies in this area, they suggest that controversial topics, very interesting topics, materials that are very familiar to the receiver and issues that are seen as less important to the receiver are likely to be subject to a primacy effect. Where these factors are involved, we would argue for an anticlimax arrangement to the speech. In contrast, uninteresting topics, issues that are unfamiliar to the receiver, and issues that are seen as very important are more likely to produce a recency effect. In these cases, we argue for a climax arrangement as being the most effective.

The use of contradictory information is also a variable associated with the strategy we use in presenting information to a receiver. When contradictory information was presented in the same message and by the same communicator, the material first presented tended to be the major influencing factor in attitude change.[20] This study is important because it indicates some of the conditions under which a researcher might conclude that a primacy effect was responsible, even though the effect was actually due to some factor other than order. Thus, the nature of the material to be presented in the persuasive message, the prior condition of the receiver's attitudinal system, the relevance of the material to the listener or reader, and the state of attention arousal of the receiver are all important in deciding placement of the material.

Message strategies associated with order may be important to many persuasive communication situations. The effects that may be linked to order are clearly not dramatic in nature, but when two communicators are both attempting to convince an audience, it could well be that the source with the best organization will be the most effective.

ONE-SIDED VERSUS TWO-SIDED MESSAGES

For almost all persuasive communication situations, there are those in opposition as well as those in favor of a proposed change. Also, there are arguments that can be used to support either side of a proposition. Should Rockport build a new swimming pool? One person decides that the answer is yes, because it will help control juvenile delinquency. Another says no, because it will raise taxes. Should there be a national law forcing open housing on all cities and states? One person argues in favor of open housing because it will help promote equality of opportunity for all. Another argues against it because it would destroy an individual's right to sell to any person. Most communicators have reached their own position after hearing at least some materials on both sides of the proposition. When people begin to communicate their ideas to others in the hope of getting agreement with the positions they advocate, decisions must be made about the nature of the message. Should communicators mention materials from the other side? Or should the materials and arguments be confined to those that support their own position?

In communication research, the question of one-sided or two-sided messages has been investigated in two ways. Both are closely related to the patterns of organization. In one series of studies, materials presenting the other side of a question are introduced along with materials from the side supporting the thesis of the message. This results in a comparison of one-sided versus two-sided message presentations. The first study was carried out during World War II by Hovland, Lumsdaine, and Sheffield.[21] They used two messages supporting the United States in the war against Japan. One message was a straight presentation of materials arguing for the proposition with no mention of the possibility of materials existing in support of the other side. The other set presented one side but made specific mention of arguments from the other side. The two-sided presentation stressed only the side on which most of the material had been presented.

The study concluded that the one-sided presentation was more persuasive but only for men with lower educational attainment. For men with at least some high school education the two-sided presentation was more effective. The one-sided presentation was also slightly more effective for men who had originally been in favor of the view expressed in the materials, apparently serving as a reinforcing stimulus in this case.

A second method of attack comes from studies by Thistlethwaite and Kamenetzky[22] and Thistlethwaite, Kamenetzky, and Schmidt.[23] They talk of refutation of opposing arguments rather than simple mention of opposing arguments. In their studies, the speeches containing refutation of opposing arguments consisted of a main argument with elaborate supporting materials, then a mention of an opposing argument, and finally a denial of the opposing argument. In one study, the denial of the opposing argument took the form of the simple statement that the opposing argument was not true. In others, the denial was elaborated into a complete refutation.

The results of these studies are inconclusive. The authors concluded that the speeches with a mention and refutation of opposing arguments had the effect of actually strengthening opposing attitudes. They suggest that listeners apparently discounted the speeches with refutation as "phony" attempts to seem impartial.

Other attempts to deal with the problem of message sidedness come in studies by Hilyard[24] and by Bettinghaus and Baseheart.[25] Both studies were interested in looking at sidedness in messages which opposed a position as well as in messages which supported a position. Hilyard found that one-sided, pro-messages produced significantly more attitude change than did the one-sided, con-messages. He suggests that the receivers may have been less informed than those receiving the pro-messages.

Bettinghaus and Baseheart utilized approximately the same design as Hilyard, but introduced a commitment variable. They found that commitment did produce an interaction with the sidedness variable, again demonstrating the importance of variables other than sidedness to persuasion. Their investigation failed, however, to find support for the generalization from prior research that two-sided messages were more effective in changing attitudes for the more highly-educated individuals.

One factor that is extremely important in attempting to make a decision about whether to include opposing materials in a message is the extent to which the opposing side has been mentioned in the mass media. Hovland, Lumsdaine, and Sheffield conducted their study during the middle of World War II. No television existed and any information that did reach the population as a whole was rather carefully controlled. Furthermore, the educational level of the population was significantly lower than it is today. If there is a strong chance that the audience members will either have information about the opposing sides, or if there is a strong chance that they will become aware of opposing arguments, then a two-sided message should be presented.[26] To do otherwise is to run the risk that audience members will later find out about the opposing side, and reject the communicator because no mention of it was made.

The studies considering the effect of message sidedness all suggest that this variable tends to interact with a set of other variables. Commitment, level of education, and prior information level all interact with message sidedness. The research to date can be summarized by saying:

1. Two-sided messages seem to be preferable for audiences with higher educational levels, although the obtained differences are not supported in all studies.
2. Two-sided messages seem to be preferable when the audience initially disagrees with the communicator's position.
3. Two-sided messages seem to be preferable when there is a possibility that the audience will be exposed to messages opposing the source's position.
4. One-sided messages are more effective when the receiver is already in agreement with the source, *provided* that the receiver is not likely to be exposed to later opposing messages.
5. Prior attitude and commitment may interact with sidedness, tending to cover up the potential effects of message sidedness.

Considering all the problems that a source might have in attempting to deliver a one-sided message, perhaps the best advice is to be willing to acknowledge to your audience that there *are* opposing arguments. A church evangelical meeting, or a meeting of a political party are among the few situations where a one-sided message might be effective.

LOGICAL ARRANGEMENT IN MESSAGES

Inductive and deductive patterns of organization have already been discussed. Presumably, receivers ought to respond to logical patterns, recognize their validity, and be more influenced by messages that are organized in either inductive or deductive arrangements. The research evidence, however, indicates that logical arrangement, or the use of formal logical structures within messages as proof units, is not necessarily persuasive.

In a very early study, Knower's[27] results suggest that original commitment to the topic is a

far more important variable than is the organizational pattern into which messages are cast.

Classic syllogisms such as the following have been used in a number of studies to test the effectiveness of logic upon judgments.

> All men are mortal.
> Socrates is a man.
> Therefore, Socrates is mortal.

Lefford[28] showed that when people are asked to judge the validity of syllogisms, the mistakes they make are likely to be in the direction of the bias they hold toward the concluding statement of the syllogism.

The Lefford results seem to hold up even when the subjects are given training in how to judge syllogisms. Bettinghaus and Swinney[29] asked a group of students to indicate their attitudes about a set of thirty statements relating to current events and student affairs. They then received training in how to judge the validity of syllogistic structures. One week later, they were again asked to judge the validity of a set of syllogisms which used the thirty statements as concluding statements. Training helped, but when the students made mistakes, they were almost always in the direction of the students' biases. In fact, almost 20 percent more mistakes were made when the subject agreed with the conclusion of an invalid syllogism or disagreed with the conclusion of a valid syllogism than when the subject's bias did not conflict with the conclusion.

Feather[30] shows that the tendency to accept or reject the conclusions of formal syllogisms is related positively to the strength of attitude a receiver has toward a conclusion. Bettinghaus, Miller, and Steinfatt,[31] in a recent study show that there is more attitude change when the syllogism is attributed to a positive source than when it is attributed to a negative source. In a subsequent study, Steinfatt, Miller and Bettinghaus[32] suggested that the more complex the syllogistic arrangement was, the more errors were people likely to make in judging validity. The error rate seems more dependent on complexity than on prior belief, but having logical arguments did not prove to be a positive benefit.

Why, then, do we tell communicators that having logical arrangement of messages is beneficial? It is a simplistic answer to say that logic does not make a difference. There is some merit in having the *appearance of logic* in a persuasive message, even if there is little merit in actually making sure that the materials are arranged in such a way as to ascertain their validity. In an unpublished and limited study, I attempted to test this hypothesis. Two audiences listened to a persuasive speech. For one audience, each argument was introduced by, "Isn't it only logical that . . .," while the other audience heard exactly the same speech except that it contained no cues to indicate that the speaker thought the speech was logical. The results showed a small but significant difference in favor of the speech having its arguments labeled as logical. What seemed to be operating was a feeling by audience members that "logic" ought to be a desirable thing. It is very doubtful, however, that many communicators have the training or the inclination to produce speeches or messages which include arguments arranged according to a strict logical pattern which would be valid in the logician's sense. There is evidence, however, which indicates that communicators would exercise good judgment if their messages and the arguments within the messages are made to *appear* logical, even if they cannot be easily tested.

It is not the intention of this book to endorse message organization which is unclear nor to recommend the use of evidence that the communicator knows or suspects is false. Beyond every immediate communication situation there are other situations with which the source may have to deal. The communicator who deliberately misleads an audience and wins a temporary victory may well lose when other information becomes available. The historian frequently argues that in the long run, the truth will come out. If the historian is correct, the

communicator is best advised to communicate for permanent, not temporary success.

EFFECTIVE MESSAGE STRATEGIES

Much of the early research on persuasive messages concentrated on the ways in which a message might be effectively structured. Useful as that research has been in helping speakers and writers organize messages, Miller and Burgoon argue that we must recognize the fact that there has been little discussion of message strategies that might be used by a communicator to induce compliance in a persuasive communication situation.[33] Below, we discuss two such techniques which deal with the question of the size of an initial request to a receiver.

The first technique has been termed the "foot-in-the-door" technique. In essence, it suggests that the persuasive communicator make an initial request of the receiver that is very small. The assumption is that this first request is so reasonable that no one will refuse. Then the first request is followed by larger and larger requests until the communicator has achieved complete success. As an example, imagine that you want Mr. Buck to donate enough money to your university to enable the institution to build a new library. The foot-in-the-door strategy would suggest that you first ask Mr. Buck to join the alumni association. Then you ask him for some money for an athletic scholarship. You continue making requests for funds which are reasonable until Mr. Buck is accustomed to being approached for funds. Finally, you make the pitch for the very large sum of money necessary to build the new library.

There are a number of studies that support the effectiveness of the foot-in-the-door technique.[34] The major assumption underlying use of this strategy is that people behave in accordance with past behavior. If Mr. Buck does comply with the first request, the probability is strong that he will comply with later requests, even though they are more demanding.

The second strategy has been termed the "door-in-the-face" technique. It is almost the opposite technique from the foot-in-the-door strategy. In following this second strategy, the communicator presents a first message which makes a huge demand, so large that it is sure to be rejected. Once rejected, the communicator follows with a second request which is much more reasonable, and is, in fact, what was desired all along. The assumption is that having indignantly rejected the first request, the receiver will feel some pressure to comply with the second request.

If we look again at the case of Mr. Buck, suppose that what we really want is for Mr. Buck to be willing to lead a fund drive to get the funds for a new library. Our first request of him is to donate all the money that is necessary. This request is turned down, but we then follow it with a request that he be willing to head the committee that will collect the money. Following on the heels of a request for a large sum of money, Mr. Buck may sigh with relief and quickly agree to head the committee.

As was true with the foot-in-the-door technique, there is significant research supporting the door-in-the-face strategy.[35] This research comes from some of the literature on reciprocation as well as that concerned with negotiation. As yet, however, we do not have research which suggests exactly which technique might be used in a particular situation.

Both techniques are supported by the research literature. Both techniques are appropriate to a number of persuasive communication situations. The reader wishing a fuller discussion of these strategies is referred to the recent article by Burgoon and Bettinghaus.[36]

MESSAGE APPEALS

After persuasive communicators determine what their goals are and the effects they wish to achieve, they must locate the materials that will support their position and then plan a tentative outline. But we cannot stop there. Persuasion demands that communicators find appropriate *appeals* to add to the message. In the best of all possible worlds, one might expect a source to simply present a set of statistics or some data, and then expect the audience to draw the desired conclusion from the data. Everything we have said about the way in which human beings behave, however, suggests that we do not live in the best of all possible worlds. People *are* affected by the presentation of data, but they are even more affected by *appeals*. We may appeal to either biological or learned motives, but persuasion is improved when appeals are used that can be made relevant to the frames of reference that people have. Are receivers stirred by appeals to their emotions? Or is it better to suggest that their teeth will drop out if they do not brush with a particular tooth paste? Will receivers be motivated to respond by suggestions that the country will be better off if Candidate X is elected? Or ought we appeal to an individual's personal desire for money and suggest that Candidate X will help the receiver get a better job? These, and other questions, lead to the research studies in this section.

Fear Appeals

More research has been done on the effectiveness of fear appeals than on any other type of appeal. Examples of fear appeals might include: "Stop smoking, because smokers get lung cancer;" or "Prepare a fallout shelter in your home to protect you in case of nuclear war." Essentially, the message built around a series of fear appeals tries to frighten the individual into thinking a certain way or into acting a certain way.

One of the earliest studies in fear appeals is that by Janis and Feshback.[37] They used groups of high school students and the topic of tooth decay. Some groups received high-fear messages, while others received low-fear messages. Their results indicated that the *lower* levels of fear were more effective in changing attitudes toward tooth brushing. They suggested in the conclusion to the study that high levels of fear appeal seemed to produce an avoidance reaction, which negated the effects of the persuasive materials. The implication is that high fear appeals produce high anxiety, and as a consequence, receivers paid little attention to the content of the messages, and a lot of attention to their own state of anxiety.

For many years, the advice given persuasive communicators followed the Janis and Feshback findings, and sources were advised to use low levels of fear appeal to help insure attitude change. Other studies have made us modify that advice. Hewgill and Miller[38] worked with materials relating to civil defense, specifically the building of home fallout shelters. They found that the level of fear appeals used varied with the credibility of the communicator. When highly credible sources were used, high levels of fear appeals could also be successfully used. When the source was not highly credible, however, low-fear appeals were more successful.

Hewgill and Miller also found that the success of fear appeals depended on the perceived relevance of the topic to a receiver. For example, they found that using fear appeals to try to get people to build a fallout shelter worked better with younger people with children. Obviously, people without children had less concern for their own safety than did those who had the responsibility of providing for others. Other organizations have used this approach with some success. They will tell you to go to the doctor for a checkup because you owe it to your family. Colburn[39] found that the level of fear appeal used depends at least in part on the importance of the topic. When the receiver was faced with a topic which he considered to be extremely important to him, high-fear appeals were effective. As the importance of the topic to the receiver declined, the success of high-fear

appeals also declined. One might suggest that what happened in the Colburn study was that when the topic was less important, the receiver was able to "step back" and reject the persuasive materials which were supported by a set of high-fear appeals. When the topic became extremely important to the receivers, they were not able to detach themselves, and consequently reacted to the appeals. Goldstein[40] looked at the relationship between the level of fear used in persuasive messages and the personality types of the receivers. He suggested that receivers could be divided into "copers" and "avoiders." Copers could recognize their personal involvement in aggressive statements, while avoiders would read the same statements and find no personal implications in them. Goldstein reports that copers were responsive to much higher levels of fear than were avoiders. In real life, there are a number of cases in which fear appeals were highly successful. In the People's Temple case, for example, The Reverend Jim Jones, leader of the group, apparently used fear appeals in order to tighten his grip on his followers. He threatened them with physical harm, made them write and sign notes threatening the life of the President, and then threatened to send the notes if the person tried to escape. He was so successful in using external threats as a weapon that most of his followers were apparently willing to commit suicide rather than resist his commands. How could this happen? Certainly psychologists and psychiatrists will offer many elaborate explanations, but an examination of the nature of the appeals and the situation may help us to understand. For most of the Temple members, Jim Jones was a very highly credible source. He had, by all accounts, a high degree of charisma to his followers. Why did high levels of fear appeals work? First, we should point to the high credibility he possessed. The research suggests that high fear appeals are effective for sources who are highly credible. Second, there was no counter information in the system. He could tell his followers that they would be killed if they attempted to escape, but there was no one to tell the same people that they wouldn't be killed. Finally, the topic was extremely important to his followers. Most of them were relatively uneducated; many were life-long "losers." To be told that they *did* amount to something, to be given positions of responsibility, to have an optimistic (although simplistic) religion presented to them, was highly persuasive. This case is an excellent example in real life of a situation in which all of the variables affecting the use of fear appeals came together and were completely successful.

Obviously, additional studies are needed on this topic, but our research does suggest that when communicators know little about their audience, they are better advised not to use high levels of fear appeal. On the other hand, if communicators do know something about the perceived importance of the topic to the receiver, or know something about the credibility ascribed to themselves, or knows something about the personalities of the audience, much higher levels of fear appeal might prove to be effective.

Emotional Appeals

We have already made brief mention of emotional appeals while discussing logical arrangement. One can talk about "logical" arrangement versus "nonlogical" arrangement, and define the second type as "emotional" arrangement. The speech may be cast into any of the organizational patterns we have discussed, using statements or language which would appeal to a receiver's emotions. Such statements might include name calling, appeals to sentiment, unsupported generalizations, and other examples of language which appeal primarily to affects.

Hartmann[41] distributed two kinds of leaflets prior to an election. Both called for the election of a Socialist party slate. One leaflet was labeled an "emotional" leaflet, while the other was labeled "rational." Although the differences in voting behavior he obtained were not large, he concluded that the emotional political appeal was a better vote-getting message than the rational message.

Lewan and Stotland[42] provide us with another piece of data regarding the efficiency of emotional appeals. Their study presented an emotional appeal under two conditions. One audience received a prior neutral fact sheet before reading an emotional appeal. The second audience merely read the emotional appeal. Their results showed that the group receiving some prior information changed their attitudes less than did the group reading the emotional message without the benefit of having the neutral fact sheet.

This latter study suggests some cautions to the persuasive communicator. When audience members are informed about the topic to be discussed, when they already have a well-formed frame of reference, the effect of an emotional appeal may be expected to be less than when the topic is a new one, and the audience is reacting with no structured base of prior information.

One of the central problems with advising persuasive communicators to either use or not use emotional appeals comes with the question of whether receivers are able to recognize when an emotional appeal is being used. In a study by Ruechelle,[43] the conclusion was that receivers cannot easily tell whether an appeal was an emotional appeal or a logical appeal. This conclusion makes sense when we consider the studies cited about the recognition and judgment of logical appeals. When people agree with the conclusion, they are likely to feel that the appeal is a logical appeal, and when they disagree, they feel that the appeal is emotional.

Practitioners of persuasive communication have long advocated the use of emotional language in persuasive situations. They do so on the grounds that emtions are aroused and changes will occur if the communicator can relate ideas, topics, statements, and suggestions to the needs and desires of the receiver. Even though we do not have clear experimental evidence, the following may be some ways of arousing the affect dimension of human behavior:

1. *The use of highly affective language to describe particular situations* For example, the communicator could use the statement, "The X Steel Company has been dumping its mining wastes into Lake Superior for thirty-five years." The communicator could also make the same statement by saying, "The irresponsible X Steel Company has been criminally polluting the clear, blue waters of Lake Superior with its poisonous mining wastes for thirty-five years." The factual content of both statements is the same, but the second is designed to appeal to a set of potential emotional responses on the part of the audience.

2. *The association of proposed ideas with other either popular or unpopular ideas* Persuasive communicators are frequently faced with attempting to get an audience to accept or reject some idea that is not well known. If the source can associate this less well-known idea with one that is well known, and arouse strong emotions, some of the emotions are likely to rub off onto the new idea. For example, in Michigan, in 1970, massive school bussing was proposed as a way of reducing racial segregation in school systems. Some of those in favor of bussing attempted to link the opponents of bussing to the Ku Klux Klan, an organization which presumably would arouse negative emotions. Thus, the implication seemed to be, "If you are against bussing, you are in favor of the Klan." In any strict, logical approach to the subject of school bussing, the Ku Klux Klan might not necessarily be seen as in any way related to the subject, but rationality has little to do with the responses of receivers to emotional ideas and words.

3. *The association of ideas with visual or other nonverbal elements that might arouse emotions* This is a technique that is very frequently used. The message might be simply, "Donate to the Red Cross," but the communicator presents the message by attaching it to pictures of children on crutches, buildings being blown up, children sitting starving among ruins, or a fireman bending over a drowning victim. Again, the attempt is to use emotion-producing stimuli to carry a persuasive message.

4. *The display of nonverbal emotional cues by the communicator* This seems obvious, but it isn't always so. Many of us have listened to a man speaking on a highly emotional topic, but watching him, one might have gotten the impression that he was not at all affected by his topic. If the facial, body, and vocal characteristics of the speaker do not conform to the language he is using, or the nature of the message he is delivering, the audience cannot be expected to react to that same message. Speakers must display at least some of the same emotion they expect to engender in a receiver.

Rewards as Appeals

How effective can a communicator be who makes promises to the audience if they agree to the message? In Chapter 2, we discussed the importance of reinforcement to the process through which attitudes are learned and modified. In this section, we shall discuss the use of rewards as motivating devices. It would seem reasonable that a message promising receivers something they need or want will be more successful than a message that does not make such promises. It also seems reasonable that a message promising *more* of some reward will be more successful than one promising *less* of some reward. Thus we expect more change from a promise of twenty dollars than from a promise of one dollar.

Everett Rogers[44] points to the influence of

monetary rewards on the rate of voluntary vasectomy as a method of family planning in several Asian countries. His general conclusion is that the more money offered, the greater the rate of adoption. In interpersonal situations, similar results have been obtained.

There are few studies which deal with the case of other types rewards in persuasive communication situations. Undoubtedly, as Andersen[45] suggests, this is because of the difficulty of adequately operationalizing the variable. Despite the lack of specific research evidence, the use of messages which appeal to, or offer the receiver personal gains can be effective. Why should an audience in Kansas City be concerned about pollution problems in St. Louis? If a source can point out how control of pollution in St. Louis would benefit Kansas City residents, the audience is more likely to accept the message. Why should the United States engage in massive programs of foreign economic assistance? If the communicator can show that the standard of living for all Americans will be raised if the rest of the world is economically healthy, an audience may be more likely to accept the argument. Why should a man vote for taxes to benefit schools which are not in his area? If we can show some personal gain to the man through lowered taxes for welfare, he may be more inclined to vote favorably.

In each of these examples, communicators may use different patterns of organization for the ideas and basic materials, but somewhere in the message, each communicator will include statements promising some reward, some personal gain for the receiver who accepts the message.

Motivational Appeals

In one sense, all the types of appeal we have discussed so far are motivational appeals, but there is also a class of learned motives. Many textbooks on public speaking or persuasion will suggest that the speaker appeal to the receiver's sense of fair play, or to patriotism, humanity, religion, values, or any one of the many motives for action that seem to affect people. The few studies that have attempted to look at the value of appealing to learned motives, however, have reported very inconclusive results. It seems that these motives are highly dependent on the specific individual. For one woman in an audience, patriotism might be an extremely important motive and she will react favorably to an appeal based on patriotism. For another, patriotism is not a motivating force, and the individual either does not react, or reacts negatively. In either case, the net result is to show little overall effect of the appeal.

One can hardly disagree with the proposition that learned motives are responsible for much of our behavior, but the range of individual differences is so large that the communicator cannot depend on securing results by the use of such appeals. The communicator must know the receiver. If we know that a particular individual or small group of individuals has a highly developed sense of fair play, a message appealing to that sense is likely to be effective. In the absence of such knowledge, however, such appeals are likely to prove ineffective.

Message appeals are an integral part of the overall strategy which the persuasive communicator must use in planning a message. After selecting a pattern of organization to fit the particular topic and casting the materials into that pattern the communicator must plan the nature of the persuasive appeals to be used. A series of fear appeals, appeals to a particular learned motive, attempts to arouse an emotional response, or offers of some reward may be selected. One of the differences between the message planned solely to transmit information, and the message designed to persuade, is the use of appeals.

SUMMARY

This chapter has been concerned with message organization and message appeals. In making a list of conclusions, caution must be exercised against hasty acceptance of these conclusions as principles to be treated as inviolate laws of human behavior; much scientific study is still needed in this area.

1. There are a number of patterns of organization that seem to be widely used and are thus probably least disturbing to receivers.
2. There seem to be order effects operating in the receipt of persuasive messages, but the choice between climax and anticlimax order must be made after consideration of prior attitudes and the previous commitment of the receiver.
3. Two-sided messages probably are more effective than one-sided messages in the communication situations which the average communicator will encounter, but if the audience is already committed to the communicator's position, strengthening that commitment is best done with a one-sided message.
4. The use of message appeals is extremely important to persuasive success, although the use of such appeals is highly dependent upon prior attitudes and frames of reference of the receiver.

FOOTNOTES

1. D. K. Berlo, *The Process of Communication*, (New York: Holt, Rinehart and Winston, 1960), p. 190.
2. C. Petrie, "Informative Speaking: A Summary and Bibliography of Related Research," *Speech Monographs*, vol. 30 (1963), pp. 79–91.
3. K. C. Beighley, "A Summary of Experimental Studies Dealing with the Effect of Organization and Skill of Speakers on Comprehension," *Journal of Communication*, vol. 2 (1952), pp. 58–65.
4. E. Thompson, "An Experimental Investigation of the Relative Effectiveness of Organizational Structure in Oral Communication," *Southern Speech Journal*, vol. 26 (1960), pp. 59–69.
5. D. Darnell, "The Relation Between Sentence Order and Comprehension," *Speech Monographs*, vol. 30 (1963), pp. 97–100.
6. R. Sencer, "The Investigation of the Effects of Incorrect Grammar on Attitude and Comprehension in Written English Messages," (Ph.D. dissertation, Michigan State University, 1965.)
7. A. H. Monroe and D. Ehninger, *Principles of Speech Communication*, 7th brief ed., (Glenview, Ill.: Scott, Foresman and Co., 1975), pp. 243–65.
8. S. Toulmin, *The Uses of Argument*, (New York: Cambridge University Press, 1958).
9. D. Ehninger and W. Brockriede, *Decision by Debate*, (New York: Dodd, Mead and Co., 1963).
10. R. Windes and A. Hastings, *Argumentation and Advocacy*, (New York: Random House, 1965).
11. E. Bettinghaus, *The Nature of Proof*, (New York: Bobbs-Merrill, 1972), pp. 123–41.
12. Cf. D. Bryant and K. Wallace, *Fundamentals of Public Speaking*, 5th ed. (Englewood Cliffs, N.J.: Prentice-Hall, 1976); M. Burgoon and M. Ruffner, *Human Communication*, (New York: Holt, Rinehart and Winston, 1978); D. Ehinger and W. Brockriede, *Decision by Debate*, (New York: Dodd, Mead & Co., 1963).
13. F. H. Lund, "The Psychology of Belief: IV. The Law of Primacy in Persuasion," *Journal of Abnormal and Social Psychology*, vol. 20 (1925), pp. 183–91.
14. A. Jersild, "Modes of Emphasis in Public Speaking," *Journal of Applied Psychology*, vol. 12 (1928), pp. 611–20.
15. F. H. Knower, "Experimental Studies of Changes in Attitude: A Study of the Effect of Printed Argument on Changes in Attitude," *Journal of Abnormal and Social Psychology*, vol. 30 (1936), pp. 522–32.
16. Carl I. Hovland, *et al.*, *The Order of Presentation in Persuasion*, (New Haven: Yale University Press, 1957).
17. C. I. Hovland, *et al.*, *The Order of Presentation*, p. 130.
18. H. E. Gulley and D. K. Berlo, "Effects of Inter-

cellular and Intracellular Speech Structure on Attitude Change and Learning," *Speech Monographs*, vol. 23 (1956), pp. 288–97.

19. R. L. Rosnow and E. J. Robinson, *Experiments in Persuasion*, (New York: Academic Press, 1967), pp. 99–104.

20. C. I. Hovland, *et al.*, *The Order of Presentation*, p. 122.

21. C. I. Hovland, A. A. Lumsdaine and F. D. Sheffield, *Experiments in Mass Communication: Studies in Social Psychology in World War II*, vol. 3, (Princeton, N.J.: Princeton University Press, 1949), pp. 201–27.

22. D. L. Thistlethwaite and J. Kamenetzky, "Attitude Change through Refutation and Elaboration of Audience Counterarguments," *Journal of Abnormal and Social Psychology*, vol. 51 (1955), pp. 3–12.

23. D. L. Thistlewaite, J. Kamenetzky, and H. Schmidt, "Factors Influencing Attitude Change through Refutative Communications," *Speech Monographs*, vol. 23 (1956), pp. 14–25.

24. D. Hilyard, "One-sided versus Two-sided Messages: An Experiment in Counterconditioning," (Ph.D. dissertation, Michigan State University, 1965).

25. E. Bettinghaus and J. R. Baseheart, "Some Specific Factors Affecting Attitude Change," *The Journal of Communication*, vol. 19 (1969), pp. 227–38.

26. J. R. Weston, "Argumentative Message Structure and Message Sidedness and Prior Familiarity as Predictors of Source Credibility," (Ph.D. dissertation, Michigan State University, 1967).

27. F. H. Knower, "Experimental Studies of Changes in Attitudes: I. A Study of the Effect of Oral Argument," *Journal of Social Psychology*, vol. 6 (1935), pp. 315–47.

28. A. Lefford, "The Influence of Emotional Subject Matter on Logical Reasoning," *Journal of General Psychology*, vol. 34 (1946), pp. 127–51.

29. E. Bettinghaus and J. Swinney, (Unpublished study, 1968).

30. N. T. Feather, "Acceptance and Rejection of Arguments in Relation to Attitude Strength, Critical Ability and Intolerance of Inconsistency," *Journal of Abnormal and Social Psychology*, vol. 59 (1964), pp. 127–37.

31. E. Bettinghaus, G. R. Miller and T. Steinfatt, "Source Evaluation, Syllogistic Content, and Judgment of Logical Validity by High- and Low-Dogmatic Persons," *Journal of Personality and Social Psychology*, vol. 16 (1970), pp. 238–44.

32. T. Steinfatt, G. R. Miller, and E. Bettinghaus, "The Concept of Logical Ambiguity and Judgments of Syllogistic Validity," *Speech Monographs*, vol. 41 (1974), pp. 317–28.

33. G. R. Miller and M. Burgoon, "Persuasion Research: Review and Commentary," in B. D. Ruben ed., *Communication Yearbook II.* (New Brunswick, N.J.: International Communication Association, 1978), pp. 29–48.

34. Cf. J. L. Freedman and S. C. Fraser, "Compliance Without Pressure: The Foot-in-the-door Technique," *Journal of Personality and Social Psychology*, vol. 4, no. 2, (1966), pp. 195–202; P. Pliner, H. Hart, J. Kohl, and D. Saarl, "Compliance without Pressure: Some Further Data on the Foot-in-the-door Technique," *Journal of Experimental Social Psychology*, vol. 10, (1974), pp. 17–22; M. Snyder and M. R. Cunningham, "To Comply or Not Comply: Testing the Self-perception Explanation of the 'Foot-in-the-Door' Phenomenon," *Journal of Personality and Social Psychology*, vol. 31, no. 1, (1975), pp. 64–67.

35. Cf. J. M. Chertkoff and M. Conley, "Opening Offer and Frequency of Concession as Bargaining Strategies," *Journal of Personality and Social Psychology*, vol. 7, (1967), pp. 185–93; R. B. Cialdini et al., "Reciprocal Concessions Procedure for Inducing Compliance: The Door in the Face Technique," *Journal of Personality and Social Psychology*, vol. 31, (1975), pp. 205–15.

36. M. Burgoon and E. P. Bettinghaus, "Persuasive Message Strategies," in M. Roloff and G. R. Miller, eds., *Persuasion: New Directions in Theory and Research*, vol. 8, (Beverly Hills, Calif.: Sage Publications, forthcoming).

37. I. Janis and S. Feshback, "Effects of Fear-arousing Communications," *Journal of Abnormal and Social Psychology*, vol. 47 (1953), pp. 78–92.

38. M. Hewgill and G. R. Miller, "Source Credibility and Response to Fear-arousing Communications," *Speech Monographs*, vol. 32 (1965), pp. 95–101.

39. C. Colburn, "An Experimental Study of the Relationship between Fear Appeal and Topic Importance in Persuasion," (Ph.D. dissertation, University of Indiana, 1967).

40. M. Goldstein, "The Relationship between Coping and Avoiding Behavior and Response to Fear Arousing Propaganda," *Journal of Abnormal and Social Psychology*, vol. 59 (1959), p. 252.

41. G. Hartmann, "A Field Experiment on the Comparative Effectiveness of 'Emotional' and 'Rational' Political Leaflets in Determining Election Results," *Journal of Abnormal and Social Psychology*, vol. 31 (1936), pp. 99–114.

42. P. C. Lewan, and E. Stotland, "The Effects of Prior Information on Susceptibility to an Emo-

tional Appeal," *Journal of Abnormal and Social Psychology*, vol. 62 (1961), pp. 450–53.

43. R. C. Ruechelle, "An Experimental Study of Audience Recognition of Emotional and Intellectual Appeals in Persuasion," *Speech Monographs*, 25 (1958), p. 58.

44. E. Rogers, "Incentives in the Diffusion of Family Planning Innovations," *Studies in Family Planning*, vol. 2, no. 12 (December 1971), pp. 241–48.

45. K. Anderson, *Persuasion: Theory and Practice*, (Boston: Allyn & Bacon, 1971), p. 61.

EIGHT

USING COMMUNICATION CHANNELS EFFECTIVELY

We have now looked at sources and receivers of persuasive communication. We have torn apart persuasive messages, and tried to see just what kind of messages will be the most important. But what about the *channels* that must be used if any message is to reach a receiver? Should we write the message down, and send it in a letter to the receiver? Ought we pay the money to get an advertisement placed on television? Or should we just concentrate on getting the receiver in a room where we can communicate face-to-face? These and similar questions are related to the kinds of communication channels that sources can use, and are the subject matter of this chapter.

We do not know when writing was invented. We do know, however, that even after mankind could make written records, writing affected the lives of only a small percentage of the world's people. In excavations made in the earliest cities we have yet found, thousands of clay tablets recorded the commerce of the city, but the tablets could be read by only a few. The clerk held an honorable position, but so did the soldier, the farmer, or the shopkeeper. Even in those earliest excavations, however, we find persuasive messages. One king sent a tablet to another monarch, telling how many battles he had won, how many men he had killed, and how much wealth he possessed. These messages are our earliest examples of the attempt to establish credibility.

The invention of printing helped make it possible for a single written message to reach many receivers and thus increased the potential effectiveness of those few individuals who could pay for reproduction and marketing of their messages. In theory, the invention of printing should have made it possible for the poorest peasant to be able to know what the richest nobelman could know. In fact, it was likely that neither the peasant nor the nobleman could read. The nobleman, however, was still ahead, because he could buy the services of people who did know how to read. Today, the written word is available cheaply, and available to almost all of the world's population. If the intent, however, is to reach as many people as possible in any country, the written word is not the most effective method. Millions of people in the United States are illiterate, and the number is even higher in many other countries of the world. Even in those countries that do have a high literacy rate, the written message is not the most effective or efficient method of reaching the masses, although it may be very effective in reaching certain target audiences.

It was not until the invention of radio that a technology existed which could reach literally everyone in the world with a single message. The use of radio began slightly over sixty years ago, and it marked the beginning of the communications revolution, and coincidentally the beginning of a major change in persuasive communication. During the depression of the 1930s, a writer on persuasive communication might have been justified in restricting the discussion to platform speaking before relatively large audiences, because that was the best way to reach the largest number of people in the United States. Thus we had the whistlestop political campaigns with short messages delivered to audiences from the back of a train. Even by that time, however, the electronic media had become important, and many Americans were influenced by President Franklin Roosevelt's "Fireside Chats."

During World War II, radio became the most important link between the war and the homefront. No longer did we have to wait for messages to travel by boats and then appear in a newspaper. No longer did we have to submit to the vagaries of the telegraph. Edward R.

Murrow came into our homes every night direct from London. We bought millions of war bonds when Kate Smith asked us to give to the war effort.[1] That war bond drive was perhaps the first attempt in all recorded history to persuade an entire nation's populace to purchase a product. Its success spawned many successors in the more than three decades since Kate Smith made her appeal.

Today, the communications revolution continues unabated. The development of mass marketing techniques for books, magazines and newspapers; the spread of telephones, radio, television, and movies; the developments in film techniques, sound recording and transmission facilities; the advent of video tape and the home video recorder; the use of cable to link homes in a community, satellite-based programs, and computer aided transmissions have made us forever forget the days when a man could expect to influence or be influenced by only those few people with whom he could interact personally. In many cities, cable television provides an opportunity for the average citizen to walk in off the street and send a message to any other citizens that might happen to be watching.

When I was writing the first edition of this book during 1966 and 1967, the promise of television was clearly on the world's horizon, and had arrived for most North Americans, but radio was still the predominant medium for most of the rest of the world. Radio was effective. A persuasive communicator using a newspaper in Latin America could expect to reach only a small proportion of the population. Through radio, that communicator could expect to reach people living in some of the most distant places on earth. Natives living in villages within remote areas of Latin America and Africa knew about the death of President John F. Kennedy almost as rapidly as did the millions of Americans who glued themselves to radios and television sets for that long weekend.

In writing this third edition, the perspective

must again be changed. Television is sweeping the world in the same way as radio did during the fifties and sixties. More people have seen Mohammed Ali fight, and have watched the Muppets, than ever listened to the voice of President Roosevelt. Politicians still make personal appearances, but they win elections only when they can make effective television appearances. In 1978, a news report on television identified a town in the Southwestern part of the United States that did not have television. That was news, and the gap was quickly filled by an entrepreneur who ran a microwave relay into the area so that the townspeople would not "suffer."

The persuasive communicator *must* take channels into account in planning strategy. For many people, the use of a particular channel of communication may be a more important factor in determining whether there will be changes than the actual message being sent or the speaker sending the message. A number of questions are of interest to the persuasive communicator. Are single channels of communication more effective than multiple channels? Under what circumstances is face-to-face communication more effective than communication making use of one of the mass media of communication? A third question we shall be concerned with is the relative role played in our society by mass media and by face-to-face contact? In each of these areas, there is current research which can be linked to our analysis of persuasive communication. Finally, we shall look at persuasive strategies which the persuasive communicator ought to consider when planning messages.

MULTIPLE COMMUNICATION CHANNELS

Imagine that you are interested in controlling the pollution produced by a local cement plant. You have been granted a period of time by the city council to present your arguments. What should you do in that period of time? The following are only a few of the possible methods you might consider:

1. A straight persuasive speech to the council members.
2. A speech augmented by slides taken of the smoke pouring from the smoke stack of the plant.
3. A speech augmented with short movie scenes of some of the conditions produced by emissions from the plant.
4. A movie with a sound track that would tell the whole story.
5. A speech augmented with charts, diagrams, or models of the plant and surrounding areas showing the effect of the emissions on the surrounding area.
6. A series of tape-recorded interviews with people in the neighborhood of the plant who have been affected by the emissions from the plant.

Some of the methods suggested depend largely on being able to *see* the major elements of the message while others depend on the receiver's *hearing*. Still others represent a mixture of visual channels and aural channels, that is, the use of *multiple channels* of communication. For many years, practioners of communication have urged the use of multiple channels as being far more effective than a single channel. Are they right? Should we immerse an audience in messages for the ear at the same time we send visual messages? Before considering some of the research in this area, we need to pay some attention to the physiological apparatus that every person uses to process information.

When a child is born, its hearing is well developed, although it may take several months for eyesight to develop fully. Long before the child is a year old, however, extensive use will be made of a number of different mechanisms to gain knowledge of the world. We term these physiological mechanisms the *senses*, and it is only through their use that any of us can know the world around us. The most important senses are vision, hearing, touch, kinesthesia, taste, smell, and the vestibular sense. Of these, vision and hearing are by far the most important for communication. Touch, taste and smell can play a role in communication, and in persuasive communication, but the amount of information we receive through the use of those senses is minute in proportion to that received by the eyes and ears.

Since people gain all the information they have for making decisions through the senses, it seems reasonable to suggest that the communicator make use of as many senses as possible when transmitting a message. It is this feeling about vision and hearing that produces admonitions in textbooks on audiovisual education and public speaking to use multiple channels of communication. These admonitions include suggestions such as, "Make it clear, use the eye as well as the ear." "Do not merely tell the receiver, show a picture at the same time." It is better to have a movie than just a speech." "It is better to have the speaker present than to have a tape-recorded message from the source." These principles suggest that the straight speech is a less effective method of communication, and any combination of vision and sound must be ranked as superior to either sight alone, as in a written article, or sound alone, as in a taped presentation. In general, whenever the persuasive message might be viewed as *highly redundant* or *difficult*, multiple channels are likely to be of some value. Some of the specific types of situations are discussed below:

1. Is the material very complex? Imagine that we wish to argue against a new sewer project on the grounds that it may destroy a natural watershed. The charts and data that would have to be used in this situation are likely to be complex, and not easily understood. But if the source presents an oral explanation along with the visual material, the entire message may be more effective than if just a single channel is used.

2. Is the material likely to be unfamiliar to a receiver? Imagine that the source wishes to use an aerial photograph to illustrate a point. Most receivers would find an aerial photograph quite unfamiliar, and most receivers would have difficulty in identifying objects on the photograph. The use of an oral explanation will help the receiver in understanding the visual presentation.

3. Is the receiver going to be interested in the message? One of the most frequently used ways of attracting attention to a message is by the use of a colorful, multiple media presentation. A display of flashing lights together with a loudspeaker will attract more attention than either the lights alone or the loudspeaker alone. One study suggests that the use of brightly colored backgrounds in serial learning tasks seems to improve learning.[2] The author also points out, however, that the backgrounds may have produced their effects at the expense of information lost from an auditory signal played at the same time. In other words, while the use of multiple channels did enhance interest, there was some loss in information. The best advice that we can give to a persuasive communicator is to suggest that the use of a multiple channel to arouse interest is helpful, but that caution should be exercised to insure that the receiver is also acquiring the intended message.

4. Is the message a very long one? Receivers have difficulty in attending to long messages, and the best advice we give any communicator is, "Keep it short." There are some topics, however, that simply cannot be covered in a short, simple message. Convincing someone to buy life insurance is not always done in a short, five-minute speech. Multiple channels may be helpful in keeping the interest and attention of an audience when long messages are to be presented. Receivers seem to grow fatigued with the presentation of materials through a single channel for long periods of time. The addition of other channels, or the switching of sense mo-

dalities during a long message may be helpful in reducing this fatigue effect. We should note that there may be cultural differences as to how long is too long. A speech by Fidel Castro running over two hours would certainly produce sleepy people and boos from an audience in the United States. Accounts from Cuba suggest that that length of time is not considered too long by a Cuban audience. The point, however, is that long messages can be broken up by a careful use of multiple channels.

5. Is the material highly repetitious? Advertisers frequently have the problem of transmitting a fairly simple message such as "Buy Brand X Beer," to potential customers. If the advertiser simply repeated that statement over and over again in an advertisement, the chances are that any reader or listener would quickly become bored, and might even refuse to buy the product on the grounds that the company is insulting the intelligence of its potential buyers. Using multiple channels in such situations may help prevent a simple message from being perceived as boring by an audience. The message can be repeated over the air with a voice, shown with pictures, repeated in writing, and a number of channel variations will help fix the message for the receiver and yet avoid boredom.

The examples we have used to illustrate the conclusion that deciding whether or not to use multiple channels for a message is not always simple. The communicator must consider the nature of the situation and the type of materials to be presented before deciding on the presentation to be used. In most cases, using multiple channels to transmit a message will enhance the source's chances of obtaining a desired response. On the other hand, there are situations thay may be best served through the use of a single channel, and many others where it just does not make a difference.

There is one communication decision usually placed under the heading of multiple channels that deserves special mention. Many persuasive communicators are faced with the decision of whether to write a message in an article, editorial or letter form, or deliver that same message in a face-to-face situation. The discussion thus far in this chapter has been concerned with the use of multiple channels in which the visual mode is going to be used to present charts, graphs, line drawings, or pictures to enhance an oral presentation. The question of the relative effectiveness of written versus oral materials, in situations where the communicator has a choice to make, deserves special attention, because the decision-making process that the source must use is applicable to many other communication situations.

Imagine that a company has proposed rezoning a tract of land in order to build a new manufacturing plant. A number of people living adjacent to the proposed plant site object to the proposal, because they feel that it will increase pollution and traffic problems, and decrease the value of their own property. What should they do to prevent the plant from being built? Rezoning is the responsibility of the city council. Should they write letters to the editor? Should they ask for time before the city council? What will be the most effective tactic to use? Imagine that you are one of the affected citizens, faced with a choice of things that you might do to get the plant turned down by the city council. In order to make a decision, you ought to ask yourself several questions.

1. How difficult is the material that the communicator has to present? Many studies suggest that written communication is better than oral communication for difficult materials. This makes sense, since the reader can set an individual pace, whereas the listener, when listening, is forced to go at the rate of the speaker. Furthermore, the reader can read and reread, while the listener must grasp the message the first time. On the other hand, the communicator who writes a message for the newspaper or who writes a letter to a member of the city council has no chance of obtaining

any immediate feedback about the success of the letter. In fact, the source frequently cannot even find out whether a message has been read or not. In a face-to-face situation, the communicator has at least some idea that the message is being listened to. The risk is between being sure that one is attended to, although perhaps not understood, and having some confidence that one is understood, even though one is not sure that the message has been read.

2. What are the language skills of the receiver? In the United States less than six percent of the population is considered functionally illiterate, and thus unable to read at a high enough level to make use of written materials in everyday life. But for every individual who cannot read at all, many more cannot read at a level that would make persuasive written communication an effective form. Although such individuals can read, reading is hard work for them, and written messages are avoided in favor of oral messages. For such individuals—and they may constitute a majority of the adult population of the United States, although not the most influential portion of the population—spoken messages are the only realistic message form. In the specific example we have used, however, it is likely that one could expect all members of a city council to be able to read any written messages that might be sent. Since such individuals are generally representative of their communities, some estimate of their ability to understand the message can be made by examining the demographic characteristics of the community.

3. What sized audience needs to be reached? As audience size increases, spoken communication in the face-to-face situation becomes more expensive and less effective. In our example, if the real audience is only the few members of the city council, spoken communication in face-to-face situations is undoubtedly the most effective way to proceed. City council members, however, frequently make their decisions only after finding out how their constituencies feel about a situation. Thus it may be necessary to

persuade a large segment of the population of the community *before* approaching members of the city council. In that case, the persuasive communicator might adopt a strategy of writing letters to the newspaper or asking for editorial space, in order to convince the large body of voters that cannot be reached in face-to-face situations. Following that effort, the city council members could be approached with face-to-face messages that would have maximum impact.

4. How important is the credibility of the persuasive communicator? City council members are political beings. They are far more likely to respond to a source that has high source credibility than to one who does not stand out from the crowd. It takes a master craftsman to make a written message seem associated with a particular source. Oral communication, on the other hand, may bear the stamp of the person delivering the message in an unmistakable fashion. Pick up the newspaper and read all of the editorials and the letters to the editor. Do you get any clear pictures of the people writing the messages? It is very difficult to make an estimate about source credibility from a written message. When a person appears before us, however, we can make far more accurate estimates as to the person's credibility, and thus their believability.

5. How much money does the persuasive communicator have to spend? It may seem strange to consider the cost, but the choice of message strategies may hinge on the amount of money that the source has to spend on the message. Preparing high quality visual aids for a persuasive message takes both time and money. If you are going to appear before the city council to make a presentation in opposition to zoning, it may cost several hundred dollars to collect data, and prepare slides, films, charts or graphs in order to show the problems that the proposed plant would cause. If it is necessary to have materials printed for distribution to citizens in the community, the cost can run quickly to several thousands of dollars. In

contrast, driving down to a city council meeting and asking to appear in the public comment section of the meeting will cost the source some time, but the number of dollars that need to be spent will be relatively small. Even if the personal appearance is not as effective in reaching the required audience, it might be the best choice for a source in terms of the available funds.

Making a decision between an oral message and a written one is not easy. The best advice that can be given the persuasive communicator is to attempt to determine what kind of message needs to be delivered to an audience, and then to begin to ask the kind of questions we have discussed in this section. Similarly, there are no easy answers to questions dealing with multiple channels such as, "Should I use illustrations in my presentation?", "Should I write out the message?", or "Can I afford movies to illustrate the message?" It *is* possible to improve the chance of success by thinking through some of the problems involved whenever a message is transferred from the idea stage to the presentation stage.

INTERPOSED COMMUNICATION

Before examining the use of the mass media in persuasive communication, it will be useful to discuss some of the ways in which the mass media differ from face-to-face communication. After all, one might conclude that watching an individual speak to a large audience from a distance seventy-five feet away might not be very different from watching that same individual on television. The late Paul Deutschmann described all communication situations which did not involve face-to-face communication as "interposed communication situations."[3] Something has been place between the source and receiver. It may be space, or time, or a physical barrier of some type. We label most of the methods we use to communicate in interposed

communication situations as the "mass media." Strictly speaking, there may be interposed communication in interpersonal communication situations as well. For example, if I call to someone in the next room, I am in an interposed situation. We have, however, tended to make a major distinction between face-to-face communication and communication by means of the mass media, that is, radio, television, newspapers, books, magazines and movies. A number of studies have attempted to isolate differences between messages delivered in face-to-face situations and those in interposed situations.

During the 1930s and 1940s there were a number of studies comparing face-to-face lectures and speeches with the same material presented over radio, or over a speaker setup, or with printed messages.[4] The studies tended to show few, if any, significant differences in learning effects between any of the messages, but there were significant differences in the effect on attitudes and opinions between the various methods. In most studies, the greater differences in attitude change were in the face-to-face situation.

These early studies did not use television as one of the experimental variables. If we are interested solely in the variable of interposition, however, television is an excellent medium. A live speaker situation is not directly comparable with radio, since the nonverbal band has been eliminated from the experimental situation. With television, this objection is eliminated. While one group of receivers views the live presentation of the lecture, another group may view it simultaneously in the interposed form of closed-circuit television. Differences found between the two groups ought to be the result of having or not having the speaker physically present. There have been a number of studies done in which face-to-face presentation of materials has been compared to television presentation of the same materials. Almost all of these studies have been made in instructional situations, where the primary interest was on the acquisition of information rather than on opinion or attitude change.

In general, television is just as effective a teaching medium as the lecturer operating in the classroom. When information acquisition alone is considered, there is a decade or more of studies to show that there are few significant differences between materials taught over television and materials taught in the more familiar classroom situation. Moreover, for medical students, for instance, the television camera can teach more students with better shots than was formerly possible when the student had to watch an operation from an amphitheater located above the operating table. There are, however, a few studies showing that face-to-face communication in the classroom produces better test scores on objective materials than are produced when the material is presented over television.

Learning effects have been mentioned because persuasive communication demands that something be learned in many situations. Since we are primarily concerned with attitude change or with direct action changes, however, it is also important to consider the effect of interposed situations on these types of changes. The findings are not as clear-cut as in the case of learning effects. Janes[5] reports that college students are divided in their attitudes toward television as a potential classroom medium. He studied students over a three-year period in different classes as they were exposed to televised instruction in a general science course. There were high variations in attitude toward the course, not over the several times the course was offered, but at different times within any one offering of the course. Some students thought the televised classes were wonderful because they could watch them in comfort in their dormitories. Others complained about poor viewing conditions and the impersonality of the televised presentations. In general, the results showed a high rate of individual variation in attitude toward the medium.

The students in Janes' study grew up when television was in its infancy, and when it was still a novelty in many homes. Furthermore, during the early 1950s, when Janes' subjects were just beginning to enter the elementary school system, there were very few educational shows available. The college-aged students of that time had little experience in learning through television. Today, the situation is quite different. Almost every home in the United States has a television set, and in most of these homes, the set is a color set. Before ever attending a school, most children have been exposed to educational television through "Sesame Street," "The Electric Company," "Captain Kangaroo," or the "Big Blue Marble." Schools at all levels utilize television or television sets with videotape sets as primary teaching tools, along with computer assisted instruction, movies, slides, and other types of audio-visual materials. There is clear evidence that children learn from television, even when those children are not forced to watch television.[6] Other studies suggest that there are simply no differences between learning from television and learning from face-to-face instruction.[7]

If it is the case that people no longer learn differently from this interposed medium of communication, then perhaps we can tell the persuasive communicator that it no longer makes any difference as to what channel is used, and that the communicator is free to use whichever is available. Unfortunately, that is not the case. Wilbur Schramm, while summing up the research using the mass media, points to the problem that the persuasive communicator has:

> Students learn from *any* medium, in school or out, whether they intend to or not, whether it is intended or not that they should learn (as millions of parents will testify), providing that the content of the medium leads them to pay attention to it. Many teachers argue that learning from media is not the problem; it is hard to prevent a student *from* learning from media, and the real problem is to get him to learn what he is *intended* to learn.[8]

Schramm's conclusion pinpoints the central problem for the persuasive communicator. It is difficult, if not impossible to *control* the behavior of a receiver when there is an interposed communication situation. The man sitting in his living room may turn off the television set when a program ceases to interest him. He may switch it to another channel, or go to the kitchen for a beer just when the communicator's most important point is to be made.

Because persuasion cannot be expected to be successful if the receiver does not attend to the message, face-to-face contact becomes more important in situations outside of the classroom or laboratory. When a source faces Councilwoman Jane Black and asks for her support on a rezoning ordinance, it is fairly difficult for her to say, "No." Councilwoman Black does not wish to offend someone who is there in person, and who may be an important supporter on other issues. It is easier to say a mental "No!" to the politician on television who asks for our support, because we know that the source has no way of checking on whether we are impressed with the message or not. Katz and Lazarsfeld examined the changes over several months of 800 women in their food-buying habits, fashion preferences, and personal opinions about current events. They found, for those opinion changes in which the source of the change could be identified, that personal influence from friends, relatives, and others was more effective than the messages received from any of the mass media.[9]

In the free market place of ideas, face-to-face communication appears more effective than any of the forms of interposed communication. If you, as a source, are interested in getting people in your community to sign a petition to prevent rezoning for a new plant, you are better off conducting a door-to-door campaign than attempting to use a television campaign where people are asked to come to your house and sign the petition. Television can be used to help make people aware of the petition-signing drive, but television messages must be followed

up with face-to-face persuasive efforts if there are to be maximum benefits.[10]

Because we know that there are few, if any differences in audience reactions to a message delivered via a television set in the classroom, and the same message delivered in a face-to-face setting, we can also conclude that the primary variable of interest to the persuasive communicator is the variable of *control*. It is easier for the source to command attention when in face-to-face contact with the receiver. It is easier to utilize feedback and make modifications in a message in a face-to-face situation. On the other hand, it is unfair to conclude that the mass media cannot be used for any persuasive messages. They have one advantage over face-to-face communication that makes it imperative that we carefully consider their use. We can reach far more people with the same expenditure of time and energy using the mass media than we can when forced to work in person. This central advantage of the mass media has to be considered, and is the topic of the next section of this chapter.

THE MASS MEDIA IN SOCIETY

The Communications Revolution began to gather a full head of steam with the spread of television following World War II. As we enter into the decade of the 1980s, the status of that revolution is demonstrated in just a few figures. There are over 10,000 paid-circulation magazines in the United States, and countless other printed publications issued by corporations and government agencies that are designed for special audiences. Only 1 percent of the homes in the United States do *not* have a radio, and more than half of the homes have more than one radio set. In the short quarter of a century since the first television stations were licensed in the United States, the number of homes with television sets has grown to now include almost every home in the country. Less than 3 percent of the homes in the country do not have a television set, and the majority of these who do have color sets. In the average home, the set is watched over six hours a day. The newspaper has not suffered as a result of the more glamorous media. There is a daily newspaper sold for every three people in the United States, and 90 percent of all adults read a daily newspaper.[11]

From the standpoint of a persuasive communicator, the availability of the mass media can be seen as a problem as well as an advantage. Fifteen years ago, the average community had a single television station, and the citizen watched that station, or none at all. With the advent of cable television, the citizen in that community may have available a choice of all three major networks, as well as independent stations, and several educational stations. First run movies as well as major sporting events are available in the home. Many cable systems provide channels for public use by the city council, the school board, and even for average citizen participation. Daily and weekly newspapers carry more advertising, and therefore there is a larger amount of space that can be devoted to news, editorials, and other community affairs. The opportunity for an average citizen, in most communities, to be able to get a letter printed in the local newspaper is greater than it was thirty years ago.

With the increasing availability of the mass media, the persuasive communicator ought to have some idea of the role played by the mass media in our society. We would agree with those scholars who argue that the mass media have essentially four major functions in any society:

1. To serve as conveyors of information to the population.
2. To serve as a means of socializing the population in terms of attitudes, values and behavior.
3. To provide entertainment for the members of the culture.
4. To serve as a forum for those advocating social change.

The last of these functions is most clearly related to persuasion, but each of the four has elements that are important to the persuasive communicator. Each deserves separate consideration.

Information Transmission

In their role as conveyors of information to the public, the mass media serve to keep people informed about current events and happenings around the world. Typically, this function is carried out by media personnel who observe and then report on any situations which are *available* to reporters and which are considered *important* enough to justify either time on the air or space in a newspaper. We have underlined the words "available" and "important" because they illustrate both the strength of the media as well as the weaknesses.

In a perfect information system, all events would be considered and would be rated for their importance to the maximum number of people in the society. The system would transmit as much information as possible, and transmit it in relation to its rated importance to the members of the society. We do not have a perfect information system. The media personnel, that is, the reporters and news gatherers cannot possibly consider or even find out about all the millions of events that occur each day in the United States. Furthermore, there are no adequate methods of determining what is important and what is not important in any absolute sense. I may consider something to be extremely important to me, while it might make no difference to you whether you learn about that item of news or not.

We do not have a perfect information system. What we do have is a system in which the people who work in the media serve as "gatekeepers" for the rest of the society. They determine which events are to be reported and which are not. They determine how important an event is, and thus how much space or time it deserves. In countries where the press is either controlled by the government or is a government monopoly, the decision as to what news will be used and how it will be reported is, of course, subject to the policies of that government. In some countries, news about opposition parties is not allowed in the media. In other countries, stories about government corruption are banned. In the United States, the media are part of the private enterprise system, owned and operated by individuals who are interest in making a profit on their enterprise. There is government control through the Federal Communications Commission over radio and television, and over newspaper advertising by the Federal Trade Commission, but that control is supposed to be exercised to achieve fairness in newshandling, and not to ban certain types of news. The result is that the business decisions associated with the news media are made by business executives, while the actual content of the news is normally determined by reporters and editors using criteria only indirectly related to the business decisions.

What are some of the criteria used to determine what will be transmitted via the mass media and what will not? We have already stated that the persuasive communicator must inform the receiver about some condition or event before suggesting any changes. In the rezoning example we used in this chapter, for example, if no one knows that rezoning has been requested, it will be very difficult for a source to muster any public opinion against the rezoning. The criteria we suggest below may help the persuasive communicator to decide just what events important to a cause are most likely to be disseminated through the mass media.[12]

1. *Magnitude*   The bigger the event, the more likely it is to be reported. If an event affects many people, or if a large sum of money is involved, the event is more likely to be reported and diffused. For example, many murders occur in the United States each year. Most of them are reported in the local media, but are not likely to be reported beyond a local newspaper. If, however, someone murders more than one person, the news magnitude goes up,

and it is far more likely to be reported beyond the local level.

2. *Significance*   The impact that a problem or an event will have on people is a strong determiner of how likely it is to be viewed as news. The passage of a new tax law that will affect large numbers of people is an example of a significant event. In contrast, passage of a resolution of congratulation to an athletic team from the state is likely to receive little play in the media.

3. *Conflict*   Any events that cause or could cause conflict between people have a high likelihood of being reported. War news has traditionally had a place of major importance in the news media, even when there is little relation between the conflict and the receivers of the news. For example, in 1979, when the government of Cambodia was ousted in a civil war supported by Vietnamese troops, the news received major treatment in American news media, even though that war did not really directly affect the United States. In similar fashion, if the event in which the persuasive communicator is interested can be cast as a potential conflict between people, it has a higher probability of being reported.

4. *Proximity*   How close the event occurred to a particular community is an important determiner of whether the story is going to receive any attention. It is possible that a rezoning issue in East Lansing, Michigan will receive press coverage in the local newspaper or even on the local television news broadcast. It is doubtful that that story would receive any coverage in the Detroit or Ann Arbor, Michigan papers.

5. *Timeliness*   Newspapers are published every day or every week. Normally, a radio station broadcasts news every hour, and a television station broadcasts news twice every day. The closer to the time the story is received, the more likely it is to be used. The news media

want to be "first." If an event is several days old, the chances are that it will already have received some attention in another news source, and thus have lost its timeliness for other media. This factor is one frequently forgotten by people who want to get the newspapers to carry some event. If a wedding was a week ago, it has lost most of its news value. If a meeting took place two weeks ago, it has little news value.

6. *Prominence* The better known people are, the greater the chance of having their activities reported. The President of the United States has almost every activity reported. The Senator from the state in which the newspaper is located (but probably not the Senator from a neighboring state) is given news coverage very frequently. The wealthiest person in the community is given a lot of coverage. In some cases, the persuasive communicator can obtain news coverage by linking a campaign to someone who is very prominent, and therefore likely to be covered.

7. *Unusualness* The news media tend to cover that which is unusual. If an event is very unlikely to occur, it will be covered. Thus we have the stories that are trivial in all other respects, but that they are complete oddities. The "World's Largest Tomato," or "Woman Is Reunited with Cousin Lost for Fifty Years," are examples of stories selected as the result of applying this criterion. In some cases, the persuasive communicator can make use of this criterion to get coverage of an event that might otherwise not be covered.

The criteria we suggest are seldom written down, but they are among the most frequently used by a local newspaper or television station in selecting information for transmission. In persuasion, we are usually interested in making sure that our audience is aware of certain events, events that have caused us to want some changes made or some actions taken. If we have a product to sell, or want someone elected to public office, we can try to obtain public awareness through advertisements. If funds are limited, however, or if our cause is related to public concerns, some information about the ways in which news is selected in the United States may be of considerable value.

Socialization

In almost any society, the important elements of the culture and what the culture holds to be of value are transmitted to all citizens via the mass media. This is termed the "socializing" function of the mass media. Obviously, the mass media are not the only institutions in the society that have a socializing role to play. Families serve a role in the process, as do churches, schools, and governments. As societies have grown more complex, however, the mass media have become more and more important in the transmission of societal attitudes and values.

If one thinks just a bit about the questions of socialization, it becomes easy to see the process taking place in our newspapers and magazines, and over our radio and television sets. The United States is a European culture. We have few oriental music programs, or oriental dramas. In our comics, the "bad men" always lose in the end, although they are sometimes made to appear more interesting than the forces of law and order. The media tend to glamorize the activities of certain types of people, and to give little attention to others. The film star is sure to be covered, while the salesman will get little coverage. Our media treatment of minorities and women tends to reflect the values we hold toward members of those groups.

We do not wish to argue about whether the media should or should not exercise a socializing effect on our society. The fact remains that they *do* play a powerful role in helping to establish the attitudes and values that people hold. What is more important for our current discussion is whether this function of the mass media can be utilized by the persuasive communicator. In any society, the mass media tend to reflect the attitudes and values of the great mass of that society. Stories selected for their news value also tend to reflect those attitudes and values. If the persuasive communicator has a goal which can be identified with prevailing norms of the society, it is easier to receive favorable news coverage.

An example will help illustrate this notion. In the United States, we tend to favor the small businessman, or the consumer over the supposed strengths of the large corporation. If the source can identify a plan as one which will benefit the "little guy," the message is more likely to get printed. In the rezoning example, we used in this chapter, it may be possible for the disagreement between the residents and the company wanting to build a plant to be portrayed as a battle of the people against the big, uncaring corporation. It is quite possible that presenting the disagreement in such a light will make it easier to obtain more media coverage, and more favorable media coverage, than if the disagreement is not given such a slant.

The mass media do serve as a socializing influence in the society. From "Sesame Street" to "Saturday Night Live," materials appear in the media that tend to reflect the attitudes and values of the society. The persuasive communicator who can make a message correspond to those attitudes and values will find it easier to obtain media coverage than if the message seems to attack normative values.

Entertainment

It is certainly no secret that one of the major functions of the mass media in our society is to entertain. For television, the entertainment function is a primary one, and large sums of money are spent in trying to find out exactly what will be entertaining to the largest number of people at any hour of the day or any week of the year. The same criteria apply to radio, although the pressures are somewhat different, since there are more stations, and appeals can be made to a more limited audience on any specific channel. Many magazines are based on an entertainment function and are successful only to the extent that they succeed in appealing to their audience as entertainment. Newspapers obviously do not have entertainment as a central function, but many of their features, such as the comics, are designed to serve an entertainment function.

The persuasive communicator, of course, is usually interested in topics that are not necessarily oriented to entertainment. Furthermore, to the extent that the media are being used for pure entertainment, they cannot be used for education, for information dissemination, or for persuasion. This suggests that a communicator's strategy ought to be to:

1. Utilize those media which do not have a central entertainment function. Newspapers and news magazines may have some entertainment functions, but their primary purpose is not entertainment. Therefore, one can expect that people who read these types of mass media are far more likely to be willing to expose themselves to persuasive messages than those who typically use the mass media only for their entertainment function.

2. Approach audiences who are using the mass media for entertainment in indirect ways, for example, through advertisements. The politician does this during election time, in buying space to tell the electorate about qualifications. A wise politician will pay for as much prime time space as possible, because the largest number of people will be watching the media during those hours.

3. Try tying a cause to an individual associated with the entertainment function. One of the best examples we have of this strategy is the use of comedians Jerry Lewis and Danny Thomas. Both gained their reputation as entertainers, but both have long been associated with charitable causes, and have raised huge sums of money through their persuasive efforts. This strategy works even at the local level,

where local media personnel may carry considerable credibility and may be willing to ally themselves with the communicator's cause. We will discuss this strategy in more detail when considering social action in the final chapter of this book.

4. Attempt to tie a persuasive message to specific entertainment events. It has sometimes been said that the American public prefers their education in small doses, and made as palatable as possible. Persuasive messages can frequently be considered as medicine, necessary, but successfully administered only if disguised with a sugar coating. Religious programs frequently use entertaining music during the major portion of the alloted time, while the religious message is given a much shorter space. Some radio stations have switched to a format where very short news programs, that is of five minutes duration, are aired three or four times an hour, rather than for a longer period once an hour. It is sometimes possible to convince local theatre associations or local sports associations to tie themselves to your cause, so long as the cause does not become more important than the entertainment.

The mass media do serve an entertainment function, but the persuasive communicator can frequently use that function in order to serve a persuasive goal. Think of yourself as a television station owner, who must use entertainment to be able to sell time on the station. Without the entertainment, the owner would have no viewers, and the people buying time would not be selling ideas and products.

Forum

If we think of the primary purpose of *any* communication channel, the forum function of the mass media becomes clear. A channel is used to carry a message from one person to another. By using face-to-face communication we could theoretically eventually reach everyone in the United States, but the spread of our message would be slow, so slow that some people would probably have died before the last person heard the messages. If, on the other hand, we use radio, or television, or newspapers, we can reach almost every person in the entire country within a matter of hours. The mass media, then, serve as a means by which the major ideas, problems, and issues in a society can be aired and discussed, solutions proposed, and decisions made and disseminated. That function of the mass media works in the United States as a whole as well as in smaller divisions such as states, cities, towns and villages.

In an ideal society, one might expect the mass media to serve as the means by which all controversial positions are identified and discussed in detail by those concerned, and where the knowledge arrived at serves as the basis for decisions within the society. Ours is not an ideal society. The central problem is that there is far more information to be transmitted than there is space in the average newspaper; the electronic media can carry even less information. After considering the huge volume of news that comes into a single Wisconsin newspaper, Cutlip points out that only a small percentage of the information received can possibly be printed.[13] This means that some ideas will not come to the societies' attention. Some persuasive messages will never see the light of day. Only a few of the letters to the editor will be printed. As we can see, the mass media *can* serve as a forum for ideas, but not for *all* ideas, not for *all* proposals, and not for *all* potential persuasive messages.

As a result of these limitations the media tend to serve an *agenda setting* function for dialogue in the society. Those ideas, events, and proposals that receive high play in the media tend to be the ones that the public reacts to, and the ones that become discussed and eventually acted upon. The task of the persuasive communicator, therefore, is to first work at getting on that agenda. This has to be done before there can be any expectation that the media can help transmit persuasive messages.

How does one go about "getting on the agenda"? Obviously, if the persuasive communicator is interested in a topic that affects many people, the media may be easily persuaded to include the topic. For example, many people wanted the United States to get out of Viet Nam during the early 1970s. It wasn't necessary to first convince an editor that the topic deserved space. In fact, getting space became a problem for those opposed to the war. Most problems, however, are not of the magnitude that the Viet Nam war was. Consider the problem of the rezoning issue that we discussed earlier in this chapter. How can the persuasive communicator make sure that the public is aware of the problem, has important information about the problem, and is ready to listen to persuasive messages about the topic?

Before looking at some strategies for gaining access to the mass media, we should understand that there is no *right* of access to the media in our society. Newspapers are privately owned, and they usually do exercise a public responsibility by opening their pages to many different viewpoints, but there is no law compelling them to do so. Radio and television stations are licensed by the Federal Communications Commission to serve the public interest, but there is nothing in that licensure that *requires* a station to give time to any individual person. What this means is that the persuasive communicator must be able to make a particular cause seem newsworthy or important enough so that the media will give space or time to the issue. Below are a few suggestions to help in accomplishing that task:

1. *Form a committee* If the communicator can speak for a committee of people interested in a particular topic, it raises the probability that the media will pay attention. A committee has more weight than a single individual.

2. *Issue a press release* Newspapers just hate the person who calls up and says, "I have something that I want you to put in the paper." They have to take time to take down all the de-

tails of the story, and then take further time to write the story. If a story is really newsworthy, calling it in will work, but if the story is borderline in terms of newsworthiness, calling it in is likely to prove a failure. On the other hand, there are almost always "holes" in a paper or on a radio or television news broadcast that need to be filled. An editor is likely to reach for a recent news release when that occurs.

3. *Appear before a public body* The media tend to cover the meetings of local city councils, school boards, planning commissions and other public bodies. At most such meetings, there is a time for comments from the public. The persuasive communicator who uses that time to make a short, reasoned statement is likely to be covered by whatever reporter is present. Furthermore, the communicator who also has a written summary of the remarks available is even more likely to see those remarks in a subsequent story.

4. *Tie the event to someone important* We have already commented that people of prominence are more likely to receive media coverage than the average citizen. If the persuasive communicator can find some way of involving someone of real prominence, even if only peripherally, it raises the probability that the event will receive media attention.

5. *Write a letter* Newspapers can print only a few letters each day, but there is a good chance that a very well-written letter calling attention to a situation that the paper may have overlooked will be chosen for the editorial page. Editors tend to get very few *well-written* letters, and will certainly prefer those over the mass of mail that comes in. Other excellent outlets are television stations. Many television stations have a short editorial space on the evening news and will offer that space to local citizens who write in and make a case.

6. *Call in to a talk show* One of the most popular radio formats is the one where the radio host takes calls from listeners who have things they want to discuss. These shows do enjoy a large listening audience, and it is quite

possible that a question raised during one of these sessions will help the source succeed in transmitting a concern to the intended audience.

The mass media *can* be used even by the average citizen. It does take effort, but it can be done. Very few citizens ever go to the trouble of trying to do any of the things we have suggested above. Unless a persuasive communicator has tried some of these methods and still failed, it is unfair to lay the blame on the media for not being responsive to the people. Whether it is in the forum function, or in the information function, the mass media in our society play a major role in determining the outcomes of persuasive campaigns.

THE INFLUENCE OF THE MEDIA

In 1949, Star and Hughes collected the data that led to the formation of the hypothesis which has been called the "two-stage flow" of mass media influence.[14] They were interested in the effects of a six-week campaign in Cincinnati to improve attitudes toward the United Nations. Materials were presented on radio, in newspapers, and through other mass media outlets. Measurements were taken very shortly after the campaign was over, and the results showed that relatively little attitude change seemed to have occurred. If final conclusions had been made at that time, they would have been that the mass media campaign had been a failure. But the authors made a second measurement some weeks after the first. In this delayed post-test the results were quite different. Considerable attitude change had taken place in favor of the United Nations. The campaign was over. Information from the mass media could not have reached the public in any great quantity.

Star and Hughes hypothesized that after the presentation of materials through mass media channels had been made, people in the city turned for confirming evidence to a set of *opinion leaders* and that through interpersonal contact with these opinion leaders, attitudinal changes were finally made.

An extremely simplified version of the original two-stage flow hypothesis is that a communicator has an idea and makes use of the mass media to transmit the idea in a persuasive message to the population of a city or area. All of the people, or at least most of the people, may be exposed to the message, but attitude change after this initial presentation takes place for only a few. Some of the individuals who *are* affected by the message when it is initially presented through the mass media become opinion leaders and proceed to engage in personal persuasive contact with others. If the opinion leaders are successful in their efforts, then, after some time has passed, the message first presented through the media may affect the entire audience, and measurably significant changes will have occurred.

The two-stage flow hypothesis was first fully formulated by Lazarsfeld, Berelson, and Gaudet in *The People's Choice*, a report of an election campaign.[15] Since then, a number of other studies have been performed specifically attempting to test the two-stage flow theory. The studies cover a wide range of topics and audiences. Merton studied the communication patterns and personal influence patterns in Rovere, New Jersey.[16] Katz and Lazarsfeld[17] made a landmark study in Decatur, Illinois of the ways in which decisions were made by individuals about marketing, fashions, movie going, and public affairs. They confirmed the central notion that there are a small number of individuals who serve as opinion leaders in each of these areas of decision making. Berelson, Lazarsfeld, and McPhee[18] studied voting habits in Elmira, New York. Coleman, Katz, and Menzel[19] reported on the diffusion of a new drug among the physicians in a community, and Troldahl and VanDam[20] reported on information-seeking behavior among people in Detroit.

The two-stage flow hypothesis has been criticized by a number of researchers as being oversimplified.[21] The process of influence is not, they say, a simple two-step process where a single group of opinion givers listens to the media and then feeds their opinions to a less enlightened group of passive receivers. Instead, there seem to be many opinion givers, operating at several levels. Opinion leaders have their own opinion leaders. There are different opinion leaders for each topic and group. An individual serving as an opinion leader for one group may not serve the same function in another group. Furthermore, opinion leaders are themselves influenced by other influentials, so that a more accurate portrayal would seem to involve a multi-step process.

A major criticism of the original two-stage flow hypothesis is that it tends to underestimate the amount of direct influence of the media. Chaffee suggests that direct influence from the media is the rule, and not the exception.[22] Many people become aware of a problem directly through the mass media, and then turn to opinion givers for confirmation of the message, or for further discussion of the message.

Despite the criticism of the two-stage flow hypothesis, no one disputes that there are opinion leaders in the society, and that these individuals have an important role to play in the dissemination of ideas and information. Those people who do serve as opinion givers seem to have a few characteristics that set them apart from the larger mass of receivers:

1. Opinion leaders tend to be greater consumers of the mass media than those who consult the leaders for information. They listen more, read more, and view more television than their followers. Troldahl and VanDam suggest that individuals can be separated into essentially two groups in terms of their mass media usage.[23] One group consists of individuals with relatively high mass media usage and also high interpersonal contacts. They ask for informa-

tion, and they give information. The ranks of the opinion leaders are filled from this set of individuals, and individuals shift from leader to follower status depending on the particular topic under discussion. The second group consists of individuals who are essentially inactive. They do not make extensive use of the mass media, nor do they make many interpersonal contacts. This study is helpful because it separates the active receivers from the inactive receivers, and makes it easier to see the information receiving characteristics of those who act as opinion leaders.

2. Opinion leaders are centers within a communication net. They are consulted more frequently for information, and they frequently consult the other members of their groups. In other words, there is a constant interactive process going on through which people give and receive information. A diagram of the process might appear as in Figure 8.1. Mr. A. is clearly an opinion leader. He is talked to by many people, and he talks to many people. Note that Mr. A is the opinion leader for that one group. In another group, Mr. A may seek the advice of another opinion leader, as shown in his relationship with Mr. B. In the Decatur study, there was clear evidence that the flow of information was not always a two-stage process.[24] The authors identified several chains leading from one opinion leader to another, and they pointed out that it may be necessary to trace back through several opinion leaders before finding the primary source of information as it came from the mass media.

3. Opinion leaders themselves are affected more by face-to-face communication than by the media. It is certainly the case that opinion leaders are heavy users of the media and decisions are made on the basis of this contact with the media. But the persuasive communicator cannot expect to place a message on television or an advertisement in the newspaper and then sit back to wait for results. The opinion leader is affected more by people than by the media.

People are affected by their exposure to any

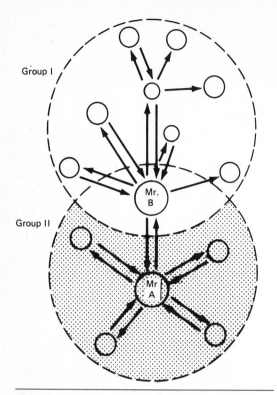

Figure 8.1 *Opinion Leaders in Two Groups. Mr. A is an opinion leader for Group I, while Mr. B is an opinion leader for Group II.*

of the media of mass communication. Communicators cannot bombard a receiver with messages from all sides or every message will fail to make an impression. The mass media have a powerful influence on our society. They serve as a reinforcer of attitudes and opinions, as a determiner of the way in which we view the world around us, and as an important force in shaping behavior. Like many other variables in communication, however, these effects are not simple. At times, interpersonal face-to-face situations will counteract the influence of the mass media; at other times, a message from the mass media will cancel out a message from an interpersonal source. At still other times, the media and interpersonal sources will act to-

gether to provide a powerful stimulus to attitude change and eventual social action.

Before summarizing our chapter on the mass media channels available to the persuasive communicator, we should give some advice to that communicator wishing to plan a persuasive campaign. Below are some questions that the source ought to ask regarding the use of the mass media as a channel for persuasive messages:

1. Does the communicator merely want to draw the *attention* of an audience to a problem that will be dealt with later in a more extensive manner? The mass media can serve very effectively as an attention getting, agenda setting method of reaching an audience.

2. Does the intended audience hold strong or weak attitudes about the proposed topic? The mass media alone may serve to change weakly held attitudes, particularly in the absence of opposing sources, but the mass media alone are not particularly effective in changing attitudes which are deeply rooted or intensely held.

3. Are receivers in favor of or opposed to the topic being communicated? The mass media are more effective in strengthening attitudes than in changing attitudes. Face-to-face communication may be necessary if strong negative attitudes are held toward a topic.

4. Is there a necessity for personal commitment to a behavior on the part of a receiver? For example, if a persuasive communicator needs to have the personal commitment of a receiver so that the receiver will follow through on a promise, the mass media are a poor channel. Commitment is more easily secured through personal contact.

5. How much money does the source have to work with? Television, on any large scale, costs money, money in very large amounts. A senatorial campaign in a large state might cost more than 2 million dollars for television time alone. A one-minute spot during the Super Bowl Game may cost over 300 thousand dol-

lars. Personal, face-to-face communication will reach far fewer people than will television or any of the other mass media, but its cost is in terms of the source's time and energy, and thus affordable.

6. Who are the receivers? Many times, a persuasive communicator examines a problem and concludes that all the citizens of a community need to be contacted. A more careful analysis may show that the eventual decision will be made by only a few influentials in the community, and that a face-to-face campaign will be far more effective. When only a few must be reached, personal contact may be the most effective method to use. When the audience is very large, the mass media may have to be used, even if the message will not be as effective with each receiver.

Questions like these must be asked and answered by the communicator who wishes to make a decision between a face-to-face presentation of his material and a presentation in which something is interposed between the source and his receiver.

SUMMARY

Communication channels can be viewed by a source in a number of different ways. It is useful first to examine the basic mechanisms which we use to acquire information from the world around us, our eyes and our ears. This examination will assist the persuasive communicator in deciding which is the best channel to use to transmit a particular message. A decision regarding whether the communicator should utilize face-to-face communication or one of the less personal channels, will depend on the source's intentions, the nature and size of the audience to be reached, and the type of message to be transmitted.

The mass media are very important channels of communication. They allow the persuasive communicator to reach audiences otherwise unavailable, but the source must be aware that the mass media are not a panacea for all problems in reaching an audience. Persuasive communication and mass media may depend on a combined use of interpersonal communication and mass communication. The persuasive communicator can maximize efforts by using the mass media to gain attention and to educate, while using face-to-face communication to reach those influentials most important to the persuasive effort.

FOOTNOTES

1. R. K. Merton, Mass Persuasion: *The Social Psychology of a War Bond Drive*, (Harper and Brothers, New York, 1946).
2. R. N. W. Travers, "The Transmission of Information to Human Receivers," *AV Communication Review*, vol. 12 (Winter 1964), pp. 373–85.
3. P. Deutschmann, "The Sign-Situation Classification of Human Communication," *Journal of Communication*, vol. 7 (Summer 1957), pp. 63–73.
4. Cf., F. R. Knower, "Experimental Studies of Changes in Attitudes I: A Study of the Effect of Oral Argument on Changes of Attitude," *Journal of Abnormal and Social Psychology*, vol. 6 (1935), pp. 315–47; H. Cantril and G. Allport, *The Psychology of Radio*, (New York: Harper & Row, 1935).
5. R. W. James, "Pre-existing Attitudes of College Students to Instructional Television," *AV Communication Review*, vol. 12 (Fall 1964), pp. 325–36.
6. S. Ball and G. Bogatz, *The First Year of Sesame Street: An Evaluation*. (Princeton: Educational Testing Service, 1971).

7. Useful summaries of this literature have been made by G. C. Chu and W. Schramm. *Learning from Television*, (Washington: National Association of Broadcasters, 1967), and R. Dubin and R. A. Hedley, *The Medium May be Related to the Message: College Instruction by TV*. (Eugene, Ore.: University of Oregon Press, 1969).

8. W. Schramm, *Big Media, Little Media: Tools and Technologies for Instruction*, (Beverly Hills: Sage Publications, 1977), p. 267.

9. E. Katz and P. F. Lazarsfeld, *Personal Influence: The Part Played by People in the Flow of Mass Communications*, (New York: The Free Press of Glencoe, 1955).

10. Denis McQuail, *Towards a Sociology of Mass Communications*, (New York: Macmillan Co., 1969), pp. 44–49.

11. S. H. Chaffee and M. J. Petrick, *Using the Mass Media: Communication Problems in American Society*, (New York: McGraw-Hill, 1975), pp. 18–19.

12. *Ibid.*, pp. 34–35.

13. S. Cutlip, "Content and Flow of AP News— From Trunk to TTS to Reader," *Journalism Quarterly*, (Fall 1954), pp. 434–46.

14. S. Star and H. Hughes, "Report of an Educational Campaign: The Cincinnati Plan for the United Nations," *American Journal of Sociology*, vol. 55 (1950), pp. 389–400.

15. P. Lazarsfeld, B. Berelson and H. Gaudet, *The People's Choice*, (New York: Columbia University Press, 1948).

16. R. Merton, *Social Theory and Social Structure*, (New York: The Free Press of Glencoe, 1949).

17. E. Katz and P. Lazarsfeld, *Personal Influence*.

18. B. Berelson, P. Lazarsfeld and W. McPhee, *Voting: A Study of Opinion Formation in a Presidential Campaign*, (Chicago: University of Chicago Press, 1954).

19. J. Coleman, E. Katz and H. Menzel, *Doctors and New Drugs*, (New York: The Free Press of Glencoe, 1968).

20. V. Troldahl and R. VanDam, "Face-to-face Communication about Major Topics in the News," *Public Opinion Quarterly*, vol. 29 (Winter 1965–66), pp. 626–34.

21. J. P. Robinson, "Mass Communication and Information Diffusion," in F. G. Kline and P. J. Tichenor, eds., *Current Perspectives in Mass Communication Research*, (Beverly Hills: Sage Publications, 1972), pp. 71–94.

22. S. H. Chaffee, "The Interpersonal Context of Mass Communication," in F.·G. Kline and P. J. Tichenor, eds., *Current Perspectives in Mass Communication Research*, (Beverly Hills: Sage Publications, 1972), p. 107.

23. V. Troldahl and R. VanDam, "Face-to-face Communication," pp. 632–34.

24. P. Lazarsfeld and R. Merton, "Mass Communication, Popular Taste and Organized Social Action," in L. Bryson, ed., *The Communication of Ideas*, (New York: Harper and Row, 1948).

NINE

PERSUASION AND THE GROUP

Persuasion always involves message transactions between people. Our analysis of persuasive communication situations in previous chapters has involved a consideration of the intent of source and receiver, the characteristics of the people in the situation, the nature of the channel of communication, and the kind of messages being sent. Most of the research we have examined makes the implicit assumption that only a single source and a single receiver are involved in the situation. Thus the research model does not typically take into account any influences that might be present because there are more than two people listening to a speech or discussing a problem. We have looked at the ways in which group memberships affect receiver responses, but this chapter will examine the ways in which the physical presence of other people affects the behavior of receivers. When communication takes place in a *public* setting, rather than a *private* setting, factors operate to change the predictions that are made about the success of a message.

The study of people in groups has become a highly complex, highly sophisticated task for the social scientist. One may study decision making in small groups, task performance, group satisfaction, leadership variables, and literally hundreds of other topics. We cannot adequately concern ourselves with *all* of the group variables and be able to do justice to any of them. Our approach, therefore, is to look only at those group variables that seem to have high relevance to persuasive communication and which have been studied in depth. In particular, this chapter excludes persuasion as it might occur within a formal organization such as a company or a government department. That important topic will be discussed in the next chapter, but here we shall be concerned with those group situations in which organizational structure is not also a primary variable.

Many persuasive communication situations do involve only a source and a receiver. A message may be sent over radio, and reach a person driving to work alone in a car. Or you may be able to talk alone to your girl friend about attending a particular party. If you are like most persuasive communicators, however, the majority of your efforts will be in situations involving groups of interested receivers in a community. Are you interested in getting a paper recycling system set up in your community? You alone cannot do the job. Do you want to set up a beer party? The chances are that the person on the other end of the telephone line is not alone. Or do you want to sell yourself as a candidate for political office? The television advertisement you buy may reach the voters as they sit alone in their living rooms, but it is far more likely that they will be watching television with wives, husbands, children or friends.

The fact that groups of people are gathered together to listen to a message does make a difference in the effects that a message might have. If John Leader advocates a march on the administration building to protest dormitory regulations, he may be more successful if he makes his speech to a group of 200 students gathered together. The presence of other receivers in this situation tends to release inhibitions and produce behavior that would not occur under other circumstances. The snake oil salesman in the Old West used to pay a few shills to stand in the audience and rush up to buy his product. He knew that this activity on the part of supposed members of the audience would affect other members and perhaps produce sales where sales would not otherwise result. The modern politician who asks for endorsements of his position from prominent actors and athletes is attempting the same thing.

For most situations where persuasive communication is directed toward an audience of individuals, different predictions should be made because there are other people involved. The presence of more than one receiver in a communication situation may help to facilitate certain behavior and aid in inhibiting other kinds of behavior. In this chapter, we shall be concerned with an examination of some of the factors contributing to behavior in group situations.

There are many definitions of the term "group." One definition distinguishes between a *collectivity* and a *group* on the basis of the amount of interaction taking place. The college classroom with 600 students listening to a lecture, is a good example of a collectivity. After the lecture begins, there is normally very little interaction between the students in the classroom. Everyone is (presumably) concentrating on what the professor has to say, and paying little attention to the behavior of the other students in the room. The commuter train (except for the club car) is another example of a collectivity, as is the reading room of a large library. A *collectivity* is a gathering of individuals in which little or no formal interaction between the individuals takes place.

A *group*, on the other hand, is a gathering of individuals where significant amounts of interaction take place. A dormitory bull session, a meeting of the city council, a university board of trustees, a bridge club, and a citizens' meeting to protest higher taxes are examples of groups. A group, for our purpose in this chapter, is a gathering of individuals in which members are interacting with some regularity. That interaction may be of a verbal nature, or a nonverbal nature, or with elements of both. The interaction may involve each member of the group approximately equally, or it may be confined to a relatively small number of group members. The distinction we make between a group and a collectivity is not the distinction used by all researchers,[1] but is a necessary one for our future discussions.

The distinction between a collectivity and a

group is necessary in discussing persuasion because of the differences in the predictions we might make about the two situations. In a group, everyone in the group has the chance to communicate, to influence and to be influenced. Group communication processes normally involve a series of interpersonal interactions between the people in the group, and thus many of the group properties we will discuss in this chapter are applicable. In a collectivity, on the other hand, there may be influence from the other members present, but the situation is far more likely to be influenced by intrapersonal factors than by group factors. Communication in a situation such as a lecture, or a graduation address is more a one-way situation than it is a group communication situation, even though more than two people are involved.

The literature relating to collectivities and to groups is extensive. The behavioral scientist who wishes to read every article concerned only with small groups (groups that have up to nine members), would have to read well over twenty-five hundred different research studies. Not all of these studies involve either communication or persuasive communication variables. Areas of interest to the behavioral scientist alone, such as group formation, problem-solving strategies, and the relation between individual motives and group goals, are not discussed in this chapter. We shall be concerned with the effect on persuaison of two kinds of variables: factors relating to physical characteristics that different groups possess and variables relating to psychological characteristics of groups.

PHYSICAL PROPERTIES OF GROUPS

Groups vary physically in many was that can become important in persuasive communication situations. The size of the group may make a difference. The physical arrangement of a group, the way in which communication flows in the group, the presence or absence of a leader, and the potential for feedback are all important to the possible effects of a persuasive message. These are *physical* properties that groups possess. The communicator can sometimes manipulate these properties in order to obtain a climate that is optimal for the message. At other times, the communicator may be faced with a group whose properties are fixed, and the message must be adjusted to the group. In order to make decisions, the persuasive communicator must have some idea of how the physical properties of group affect, and are affected by, persuasive communication.

Group Size

Much persuasion occurs in face-to-face situations in which the source must conduct a give-and-take session with receivers. The most obvious effect of an increase in group size is to decrease the amount of time any person in the group has for interaction with the source or for interaction with other groups members. Thus, as a group's size increases, any effects of persuasion that might be caused simply by the amount of personal communication from a source will be diminished. Futhermore, as the number of different people increases, the potential number of positions on an issue will also increase. This can mean that a compromise position may be reached by the group which does not represent the views of any one member of the group.

Studies by Hare[2] and by Slater[3] indicate that as group size increases, member satisfaction decreases. Slater's groups seemed to prefer five members as the optimum size when they were working on a solution to a human relations problem. Both of these studies were concerned with task-oriented groups, that is, groups not passively listening to a source but actively dealing with various problems. These, and similar studies suggest that when the persuasive task is the defense of a proposed solution or the proposal of an alternative solution, a small-group situation in which considerable interaction is possible produces a higher degree of group satisfaction. In fact, Pervin argues that satisfaction is always the result of the interaction of an individual with a particular situation, and a given task.[4] The amount of group satisfaction may turn out to be an important factor in the acceptance of any message upon which the group finally agrees. Groups in which the members become individually dissatisfied with their participation are not as likely to be willing to change attitudes and behavior as a result of messages presented within the group. It can also be argued that as the controversial nature of the topic increases, the necessity to keep a group of receivers satisfied also increases, and thus smaller groups of receivers are more desirable.

In some persuasive communication situations the source will be faced with opposition, opposition that is also engaged in persuasion. Sometimes these are formal groups that will give equal time to all sides. In most situations, however, the source will have to get a message across in spite of an opposing member. As the size of the group increases, however, the total amount of communication per unit of time does not increase to a significant degree. Instead, the relative amount of participation by each member of the group decreases. Thus, any individual member of the group may be involved less and less as the group gets larger and larger.[5] In such a situation, a source is faced with several alternatives. It may possible to increase the *quality* of a message, so that it stands out from the background of all other messages, and people will pay more attention to it. This is the method followed by an advertiser who hopes that the advertisement for a company's product can be made more distinctive than that for any other product.

A second method that frequently works is to divide the group into smaller groups. Sometimes it is possible to have subgroups working on a topic, thus increasing the time proponents

of a measure will have available to them to advocate a particular stand. Sometimes, it is even possible to structure the small subgroups in such a way that much of the opposition is concentrated in a single group, while the support is distributed among several groups.

A recommendation sometimes made is for the persuasive communicator to attempt to be appointed as the leader of a group, thus obtaining more time and prestige with the group members. The prestige factor is clearly important in very large groups, where the leader may be able to control the agenda, and have a prominent place on that agenda. In smaller informal groups, the leader of the group doesn't necessarily have that same set of advantages. In smaller groups, there is a greater expectation that the amount of time available will be shared, and the individual attempting to dominate such a group may encounter hostility.

Studies by Bales and Borgatta[6] of communication behavior in groups ranging from two to seven members, provide at least some tentative hypotheses for the persuasive communicator to consider. Their conclusions suggest that smaller groups inhibit overt disagreements and expressions of dissatisfaction from group members more than do larger groups. The persuasive communicator who leaves a small group feeling that there is agreement in the group may be misled because of the reluctance of the group to engage in active disagreements. On the other hand, it would also seem to follow that the communicator will have more trouble in controlling larger groups in which dissatisfactions are more openly expressed.

The Bales and Borgatta findings also suggest that when people communicate in extremely small groups they are reluctant to express negative feelings about the other members of the group. Larger groups tend to have subgroups, and these subgroups provide *support* for diverse opinions, and, therefore, support for more open expressions of dissatisfaction. For example, if I am a source talking to a group of five people, it may be that one man doesn't agree with me. He says nothing, however, because he may think that everyone else agrees with me. If I am talking to a group of twenty-five people, however, there may be several who do not agree with me. Those individuals may form a subgroup, and thus feel less constrained about openly disagreeing with me, since they receive support from other members of the subgroup.

Thus far, our discussion has been limited to groups of two to nine members and to groups in which there is ample opportunity for interaction with the communicator. As groups become even larger than nine members, several things happen. First, the probability that there will be a formal leader increases. When there are twenty people in a room, bedlam will result unless there is someone charged with the responsibility of conducting the session. When there is a leader, social power (the ability to achieve compliance from group members) tends to accrue to that leader. In such a situation, it becomes imperative that the outside communicator, or the individual group member work with the leader in the presentation of messages. In many situations, the presence of a formal leader other than the persuasive communicator may reduce the work that the communicator has to do. Rather than concentrating on reaching every member of a group, it may be enough to persuade the formal leader, and then to depend on that leader to do the persuading with the rest of the group, or at least to smooth the way for access to the rest of the group. We must note, however, that when a persuasive communicator shares a message with a group leader, there is a distinct risk of having the message distorted by the group leader, as well as having much of the credit for any persuasive success be given to the leader and not to the originator of the idea. Thus, there are advantages and disadvantages in approaching larger groups where there is a leader already designated.

Second, larger groups are more likely to have cliques and splinter groups. In smaller groups, social pressures operate to prevent cliques and splinter groups that deviate from the beliefs of the majority. In larger groups, the pressures to prevent deviance are harder to apply, and deviant groups are more likely to form. For the persuasive communicator, the danger is that the probability of overt, organized opposition to a message will increase. The increase may not occur because of any fault in the message, but merely because a large group has permitted the formation of a splinter group in opposition to any policy advocated by the leadership. It should be noted, however, that the clique or splinter group may also serve as a wedge into a group that would normally oppose the communicator's message. The persuasive source may be able to use the splinter group to gain entry to the larger group. If the splinter group can be convinced of the desirability of some goal, it may carry the message to the larger group despite the opposition of the formal leaders of the group.

Finally, as groups become very large, the entire mode of group operation changes, and the presentation of messages to the group will change. That is true in all persuasive situations, whether the goal is an eventual change in attitude or in behavior. Typically, large groups develop *rules* for monitoring the flow of communication within the group. These may be extremely formal sets of rules, such as the rules developed by legislatures and formal organizations. Perhaps the best known example of such rules are those codified in Robert's *Rules of Order*.[7] Even in less formal groups, rules of conduct will develop. Students learn in the first grade to raise their hand when they want to talk. The formality of the rules is almost always directly proportional to the number of people involved. An instructor can conduct a class for college students with complete freedom on the part of the student to ask questions, interrupt, and make comments when there are 5 or 10 members of the class. When there are 25, such freedom becomes more difficult, and when the group size reaches 100, the constraints on both the teacher and the student force changes in the way in which materials are prepared, in the way in which they are presented, and in the amount of interaction that any one class member may have with fellow students or with the instructor. In general, the mode of presentation becomes more formal.

Another example of this point might be useful. If you are a candidate running for public office in a small town, it ought to be possible to get your message across in an informal situation. A series of "coffees" for the candidate allows quite informal interaction, where the candidate can make a position clear, and people can ask questions about the views the candidate holds. If a community has more than twenty-five thousand people candidates cannot reach all of the voters through these informal groups. They must supplement such informal gatherings by using the mass media.

Again, we should note that there are both advantages and disadvantages to the formality attached to large groups. The disadvantages lie in the lower satisfaction levels found in such large audiences and in the difficulties of gaining entry to large groups. But there are some advantages for the persuasive communicator who does gain an audience with a large group. Usually, the source will have more time to present a message, and will not have to face severe questioning by other group members. There may be opposition, but the opposition will have the same time constraints, and the merits of the proposal can be argued equally.

Thomas and Fink[8] have reviewed a number of studies in the small-group area concerned with group size. They suggest that group size has a significant effect on both individual and group performance, on the nature and kind of interaction that will occur, on the type of group organization that will emerge, and on several psychological variables. The persuasive communicator must be concerned with all of these factors in planning for the presentation of messages to groups of receivers.

Spatial Arrangement

An Figure 9.1 shows how the variable of spatial arrangement might operate in a persuasive communication situation. When people are seated so that interaction between each member is as easy as interaction with the communicator, as in type B, the nature of the communication in the group will obviously be different from the communication occurring when people are seated so as to reduce communication between group members and increase communication with the speaker, as in Type A.

We can specify some of the differences that might obtain under these conditions, and the reader can undoubtedly make additional hypotheses about differences between the two situations. In the situation illustrated in type A, the communicator will have maximum control over communication in the group. Messages will tend to originate with the source, and flow to the receivers. It is difficult for private conversations to take place between the receivers. In the type B situation, the source will have much less control over the receivers. Two receivers can sit and talk to one another, with relatively little risk that the source can control their discussion. In type A, the source can monopolize the communication more effectively than in B. On the other hand, in A, the source will find it far more difficult to obtain feedback from the members of the group. The situation is so formal that receivers may be reluctant to volunteer comments to the source. In B, feedback is much easier to obtain; the situation is less formal. In B, however, individual Z sitting at the other end of the diamond may be able to exercise as much control over the group as the source. If Z is in opposition to the source, the spatial arrangement may prevent success on the part of the communicator. There are other conclusions that can be drawn from an analysis of these two spatial arrangements, but the point should be clear: space may be an extremely important variable in persuasive success.

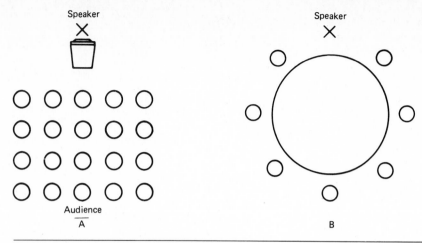

Figure 9.1 *Two Types of Interaction Situations*

The best-known study of the effects of organization patterns on group performance is that by Harold J. Leavitt.[9] Figure 9.2 illustrates the four types of spatial arrangements with which he was concerned. With the circle type of arrangement, each member could talk to any other member. In the wheel arrangement, the members forming the spokes could not communicate with each other, but only with the person in the center. In the chain, or V, arrangement, individual A could communicate only with B who could communicate only with C, and so on. In the Y type, however, A and B could communicate with C, who could work with D, who could communicate with E. Leavitt was interested both in group satisfaction and group productivity. The major interest we have in this study lies with the group satisfaction variable, since it may be directly related to persuasion. Leavitt found that the circle arrangement seemed to produce the greatest amount of group satisfaction. On the other hand, the wheel pattern was the most effective pattern when the variable was productivity. It is easy to see what happened in the Leavitt studies. In the circle arrangement, everyone

was allowed to talk to everyone else. The members of the group did talk to everyone else to set up the production system. That took time, and the extra time cause productivity to fall off. In the wheel arrangement, no extra time was needed, because the person in the middle simply issued orders, and did not worry about whether other members of the group agreed or were satisfied with the arrangement. Other research studies have tended to support the Leavitt findings, but offer more detail about predictions of morale level for other kinds of communication situations.[10]

Perhaps the most important finding in these studies as far as persuasion is concerned is related to the concept of "centrality." Centrality is the relationship of the individual to communication receiving and sending. Individual A, in Leavitt's wheel arrangement (Figure 9.2), is more central than any of the other group members, while in the circle arrangement, all groups members are equally central to the group. Centrality, therefore, is concerned with the amount of communication *control* an individual can exercise over other members of the group. Control obviously depends on whether an individ-

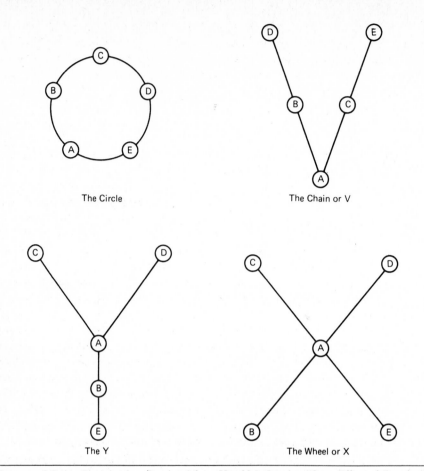

The Circle

The Chain or V

The Y

The Wheel or X

Figure 9.2 *Patterns of Group Organization. Reprinted from Harold J. Leavitt, "Some Effects of Certain Communication Patterns on Group Performance,"* Journal of Abnormal and Social Psychology, *vol. 46 (1951, with permission of the author and the American Psychological Association.*

ual is dependent on others for the ability to communicate, or is independent of others. The more control, the more independent an individual is, and thus the higher the centrality of the individual. The research shows that the more central an individual is, the higher the satisfaction with the group.

The Leavitt findings suggest that member satisfaction can be raised by allowing more interaction to take place within the group. An individual statisfied with membership in a group ought to be more susceptible to persuasion from another member of the group. There is no direct test of this hypothesis, and when we discuss the variable of cohesiveness, we shall see that there is another explanation for this particular situation. The conclusion that member satisfaction is related to susceptibility to persuasion must be modified to note that as more and more members are encourage to participate in the work of the group, the nature of the decision reached by the group may deviate more and more from the expectations of the persuasive communicator. Furthermore, as the flow of communication is opened to all, the probability also increases that the communicator will face opposing factions who will openly communicate their dissatisfactions and their alternate solutions to other members. Freedom of discussion is thus a two-edged sword, and thought must be given to the possible effects of increased interaction.

The patterns of spatial arrangement and communication flow studied by Leavitt and those additional patterns reported in a review by Glanzer and Glaser[11] are for small groups of five to seven. There are no studies of the most satisfactory spatial arrangements of group members in situations involving very large groups. Given that the intent of all persuasive communicators is to effect some change in the attitudes, emotions or behavior of a receiver or set of receivers, perhaps the best advice we can offer the source is that an arrangement in which the source has the ability to direct the flow of communication ought to be more effective than one in which there is the opportunity for cliques to form, for private discussions to start, or for leadership to be shifted to someone else in the room. It is certainly true that when members are allowed free interaction with everyone else in the group, more satisfacation with the situation and with any decision ought to result. But the danger is that with increased interaction, the communicator may lose control over the group, and the idea which satisfies the group may not represent the persuasive communicators ideas, but some modification of those ideas. Thus, an arrangement such as illustrated in B of Figure 9.1 with people sitting in a large circle, might not be as satisfactory as the other arrangement in a A of Figure 9.1, with receivers facing the source. Hare and Bales[12] have done some preliminary work which indicates that cliques will form and leadership will vary as a function of seating position. Spatial arrangement, then, is an important part of the communicator's concern in planning for persuasive communication.

Many times, a persuasive communicator will not have an opportunity to exercise any control over the spatial arrangements that will exist in a prospective situation. There are times, however, when the communicator can come into a room ahead of time, and ask that the podium be shifted, or that the chairs be arranged in a different fashion. When such control is possible, persuasion may be facilitated by asking some questions ahead of time:

1. Is the group going to be too large to handle in an informal manner? If the group gets much beyond twenty, the communicator must be in a position to control the kinds of interaction taking place in the group, or the message may not get across. Thus, a formal arrangement with the communicator facing the audience and the audience seated in such a way as to discourage interaction between audience members (as in A of Figure 9.1) may be advised.

2. Will there be opposition to the communicator's proposals? Some spatial arrangements facilitate the development of cliques among group members and should be avoided. Any arrangement in which members can easily communicate with each other rather than focus their attention on the communicator raises the probability that opposition cliques will be formed.

3. How difficult to understand will the message be? For some materials successful persuasion will depend on the receivers' understanding the material very well. This may mean that they will have to ask questions of the source. Individuals sitting in the front of a classroom tend to ask a disproportionate number of the questions. The communicator who concludes that since only the people sitting in the front row ask questions, everyone else understands the message, is probably making an error.

4. What is the communicator's specific intent? If the primary intent is simply to raise interest in some idea, an arrangement that inhibits question asking may be desirable. The

source can then make a presentation, but is not force to dilute interest by answering a lot of detailed questions about the idea. In such a situation, a large auditorium, where the communicator stands on a raised platform, using a microphone, is an arrangement in which question asking is difficult. If, however, a communicator is interested in actually persuading an audience to make changes in their behavior, it may be necessary to engage in significant amounts of interaction before the receivers are persuaded, and an arrangement that facilitates interaction may be desirable.

5. What kind of an atmosphere is more desirable for the topic under discussion? Receivers become accustomed to receiving messages in particular situations, and arrangements that violate their expectations are likely to be less effective. For example, receivers might be somewhat disturbed at the use of a church for a political speech. The use of a small informal seating arrangement to deliver a formal speech might be similarly disturbing to those who expect a more informal style with an informal spatial arrangement. The communicator must plan ahead of time to provide a spatial arrangement conducive to obtaining the types of effects desired.

These questions suggest that spatial arrangement is a variable that cannot be separated from group size in the consideration of the situation. The interaction of various factors will be evident in several of the remaining variables we shall consider.

Feedback

The success of many persuasive messages cannot be predicted in advance. Sources may not be able to find out much about the audience, and thus audience analyses are necessarily hasty and incomplete. In other situations, the communicator may present a message to a group and have to leave the situation without obtaining information as to the possible recep-

tion of the message. This happens when there is no *feedback* to the source to enable a check on the reception of the message. By feedback we mean *any information that the source gains from receivers about the probable reception of the message*. A nodding of the head may tell a communicator that the receiver is following and understands what is being said. A slight frown may be interpreted as doubt or disagreement on the part of the receiver, and a source might stop, change the message slightly, ask a question, or take other action to make sure that a receiver understands and agrees with the message. Thus, smiles, frowns, attention, inattention, questions, comments, shuffling of the feet and gestures are all examples of behaviors that can be used as feedback by a source.

Feedback can be either *immediate* or *delayed*. In face-to-face situations communicators ordinarily make use of as much immediate feedback as can be obtained from the audience. During the presentation of a message, the source may use feedback to make changes in the message, trying to improve its acceptability to an audience. After the message has been presented, a source tries to obtain delayed feedback by asking audience members how the speech went, by checking on the later behavior of the group, or by asking outside observers about the presentation.

In interposed situations, however, immediate feedback cannot be obtained. When the message is presented on television, or radio, or in a newspaper, the communicator cannot ask questions of the receivers nor observe their behavior. Sources must develop delayed feedback methods in order to help prepare for future messages. Questionnaires may be sent to receivers after the message has been transmitted. A portion of the audience may be sampled, as is done with Neilson ratings on national television shows. Friends may be asked to make comments about the message. None of these methods is as effective as actually being able to meet with a group and interact with them over a period of time. When a group meets in the absence of the communicator, feedback attempts cannot be as effective as in the face-to-face situation.

Ideally, communicators should be able to structure the communication situation to allow for feedback during the presentation of a message. The small, face-to-face group setting is an ideal one in which to obtain and use feedback. Unless the source makes arrangements ahead of time, however, even the small group situation is one in which feedback may be absent. The group sitting around the table (as in A of Figure 9.1), where the communicator can see everyone clearly and can ask and answer questions freely, is an example of a physical setting in which there are many opportunities for feedback. The formal lecture hall, on the other hand, is normally not designed to make the obtaining of feedback easy for either the speaker or the audience. The lights generally shine into the speaker's eyes so that it is virtually impossible to observe the reactions of the audience or to respond to raised hands by persons wanting to ask questions. As a result, the speaker may feel that the speech was a success, while the audience remains unchanged.

Leavitt and Mueller[13] have done a number of studies in which various types of feedback were tested for their efficiency in aiding learning and in reducing frustrations within the group. Their general conclusions are that feedback increases accuracy and results in greater source and receiver confidence in what they are doing. They suggest that the problem with feedback is a question of *time*. In order to use feedback properly, the communicator must allow for adequate time for questions and answers. This may drastically alter the amount of time required by a given communication situation.

Feedback is related both to group size and to spatial arrangement. The larger the size of the group, the more difficult it is to make sure that everyone in the group has responded appropriately to the source's message. The more scattered a group is, or the less able it is to interact with the communicator, the lower the quality of feedback available to the communicator.

Feedback is an important variable with which the communicator must be concerned. Decisions made about feedback may structure the entire presentation. Some of the questions that will help in structuring a group in order to utilize maximum feedback include:

1. What is the intent of the communicator? If the intent is primarily to arouse emotions or to attract attention to an issue, there is less need for high quality feedback than if the intent is to change the overt mode of behavior of the group members.

2. What kind of receivers will be involved? Where the communicator faces a friendly audience and the intent is to reinforce already-existing attitudes, there is small need for elaborate feedback systems. On the other hand, when the audience is hostile and the intent of the communicator is to achieve a drastic change in attitudes or behavior, the communicator needs to have elaborate feedback mechanisms built into the situation.

3. Will there be opposing communicators operating within the situation? When there is opposition, the necessity for feedback increases. Without feedback, it is difficult to make judgments about the effect that opposing arguments have had on a group of receivers or about the strength of the attitude change that the opposition might have been able to generate.

4. Will there be an opportunity for additional contact with the group? One way of helping to overcome a lack of feedback opportunity is through repetition of the message to the same group. If the group did not understand the message the first time, a repetition may help to clarify points which were confusing. This is the principle used in advertising and political campaigns in which the sponsor or the candidate cannot be sure that any message was received on its first presentation.

5. How similar are the participants in the group? Earlier, we suggested that communica-

tion is easier when the source and the receiver have similar characteristics and backgrounds. Communication is far more difficult when the participants have vastly different educational backgrounds, different occupations, different religions, or belong to different racial groups. The problem of communicating with people different from ourselves is closely tied to the ability to use feedback. If we get to know another person very well, we usually get better and better at interpreting the cues that the person uses as feedback. We learn that Mary's frown doesn't mean dislike, but concentration, that Mike's doodling is not a sign of disinterest, but of nervousness. When we are very different from other people in the group, and have had little contact with them, we must plan for longer periods of interaction so that we can learn how to interpret the feedback they are giving us.

One other factor must be mentioned about feedback. In most group situations, both sources and receivers are observing each other. We often forget that we are giving off cues to the receivers as much as they are giving off cues to us. If a source delivers a message in a completely deadpan fashion, whey should there be any expectation that the receiver will act excited about the message? If a source frowns while delivering an important point, do we not expect the receiver to interpret the frown as the source would interpret the same behavior on the part of a receiver? Persuasion in group settings is seldom a one-way street, although sources frequently behave as if it were. What you do as a source will be utilized as feedback by your receivers, and their behavior may be influenced as much by those nonverbal cues as by the contents of the message you send.

The opportunity or lack of opportunity to obtain feedback may be extremely important to the eventual success of any persuasive message. Arranging the conditions under which feedback can be secured from a group, however, is largely a concern with the physical arrangement of the group. Some arrangements lend themselves to adequate feedback, others do not. The communicator should take care in planning the situation to obtain the type of situation that will best fit the objective.

Emerging Leaders

Groups meeting over long periods of time with relative frequency are very likely to have a leader. Groups which come together for short periods of time, which have no social structure, or in which no social structure has developed, are likely to have no designated or discernible leader. The next chapter will be concerned with those groups in which there is formal organization, in which a leader has arisen or has been designated. This section, however, will look briefly at the role of the persuasive communicator in those groups in which there is no discernible leader.

The persuasive communicator is likely to face many groups in which no apparent leaders have emerged. The group coming together for a dormitory "bull session," the neighborhood "coffee klatch," the informal political meeting, the meeting of individuals in a student union building, are all examples of situations in which leaders may not be easy to identify. The audience of parents meeting with an individual proposing a school bond issue, the teenage night club, or the country club luncheon are other examples.

Social psychologists tell us that in any group which has been together for any length of time, leadership will emerge. It may be a shifting leadership, there may be more than one leader, people in the group may not always agree on who the leader is, but there *will* be individuals who exercise leadership functions. This suggests that many groups will have *emerging leaders*, that is, individuals who exercise leadership functions but have not been designated or recognized as formal leaders. The persuasive communicator improves chances of success by being identified as an emerging leader or by prior interaction with a potential leader.

The importance of locating an emerging leader within a small group lies in the boost that might be given to a persuasive message because of the leaders support, and in the diminished probability of success if a leader emerges who opposes the goal of the persuasive communicator. Furthermore, since emerging leaders have the best chance of becoming permanent, formal leaders, an early convert to the communicator's position may become an even greater asset at a later time. Thus sources who are going to be working with groups should spend time to locate leaders and emergent leaders and to direct communication carefully to them in the hope of adding influential supporters.

It is easy to say, "Look for an emerging leader," but what do we look for? How can we identify those people who will eventually become the leaders in small group settings? One way of going about the task is to look at the functions that leaders perform in informal groups. If we can identify individuals who perform some of the functions discussed below, we can also predict that such individuals are likely to become leaders in the group, and have influence with the group. Our list is not complete. Burgoon, Heston and McCroskey[14] provide a rather complete list of leadership functions. We list only those that seem to have distinct relevance to the types of informal groups we have been discussing. Additional functions will be discussed in the next chapter when we look at formal organizations.

1. *Initiation* Leaders tend to speak more than other people in the group. New ideas come from leaders more than from other members
of the group. Thus we can look for people in our groups who are verbal, always beginning a conversation, throwing out new ideas or buttonholing different members of the group.

Such an individual is likely to either be a leader, or to be in the process of getting accepted as a leader.

2. *Oranizational efforts* Informal groups usually do not exist for very long without some structure. They may begin as entities with an informal structure, but their continued existence usually depends on eventually having some formal type of organization. Emerging leaders are usually involved in attempts to formalize the group structure. This may mean attempting to get the group to set an agenda, or proposing systematic meetings, or suggesting tasks the group could do. The point is that individuals who try to get groups to organize themselves are likely to be emerging leaders.

3. *Integration efforts* One of the major problems with informal groups is that they tend to break up as easily as they form. If people are relatively happy with their experiences in the group, however, they tend to want to continue with the group. Emerging leaders frequently attempt to create the kind of conditions that will make group members want to stay in the group. If you find people in the group talking about being satisfied, trying to resolve conflicts among group members, or trying to set up pleasant experiences, it is likely that those individuals will be group leaders in the future.

4. *Information management* One of the more important characteristics of the group leader is the amount of communication transmitted relative to the rest of the group members. In general, leaders speak more often, issue more statements, have fewer questions than others, interrupt more frequently, and try to manage the nature of the communication that flows between members of the group. A potential leader may often be spotted by the attempts made to manage information to the group.

5. *Gatekeeping function* In a small group situation, someone has to manage the way communication is handled. Not everyone can speak at the same time, although when a group has just formed it may seem as if everyone is speaking

at once. Eventually, someone will suggest rules (usually informal in nature) to straighten out the maintenance of communication within the group. Eventually, if the group ever becomes a formal, stable group, someone will arise as a leader to function as a manager of information within the group. Potential leaders may frequently be spotted by their beginning attempts to get a group to work together.

These are some of the functions that leaders perform in informal groups, and we are helped in identifying emerging leaders by looking at what is happening within any group. In addition to locating emerging leaders in groups which the communicator approaches with a message, we should also note that there will be groups formed that do not have even an emerging leader. In such situations, the persuasive communicator may find it possible to take the leadership role within the group. In order to do so successfully, sources should note what leaders do, and then determine whether they can perform some or all of those functions for the group. Obviously, when such an opportunity does arise, sources are in a position to dramatically increase their chances of success. Leaders can control the communication environment to a far greater degree than nonleaders in a group, and they can increase the probability of persuasive success through their own endeavors.

Group size, spatial arrangement, feedback, and leadership are all physical variables that communicators can identify without questioning members of the group. Sources need to be observant, and it may require time in message preparation or additional time in actual communication, but these variables can be identified and planned for in preparing a message.

PSYCHOLOGICAL VARIABLES

Some group properties cannot be directly observed. They must be inferred from the behav-

ior of the group. The behavioral scientist who is interested in studying communication in group situations has developed a number of ways of studying these psychological variables. One may simply ask the group members a number of questions about how they feel while in the group situations. That allows, for example, the scientist to make estimates about the satisfaction level of the group. Or the scientist may set up a series of standards based on the performance of other groups and thus be able to rate succeeding groups against the standards. Experimental situations may be used to make inferences about the behavior of the group as a result of the conditions imposed. All of the psychological characteristics we shall talk about can be distinguished from physical variables in that the former are not directly observable properties. They must be inferred.

One may ask why the persuasive communicator ought to be interested in psychological properties of groups. A central reason is that persuasion is a process, a complex process, which occurs over a period of time. If we find, for example, that satisfaction in a particular group is positively related to the acceptance of any ideas which might be presented to the group, then we would advise the persuasive communicator to look closely at this variable in planning a message to the group. As we shall see, each of the variables examined in this section may affect persuasive success, and thus, may require careful planning on the part of the communicator.

Group Satisfaction

An individual's level of satisfaction may help determine receptivity to persuasive messages. If an individual is dissatisfied with a particular policy, the persuasive speech which promises to change the policy may find a highly receptive listener. On the other hand, the individual who is satisfied with current policy may prove to be difficult to change through persuasion.

When we look at *group satisfaction*, a similar

kind of analysis can be made. The group which has come together because of some set of dissatisfactions with policies may be receptive to persuasion that suggests changes in those policies. If the group task, however, is one that requires close cooperation among members of the group, a high level of satisfaction will be necessary in the group if the communicator is to succeed in getting the group to work together.

Group satisfaction is a unitary concept, determined by asking individuals who are engaged in group activities about their satisfaction levels. From these individual ratings, a group score is composed. This means that there may be several members who are highly satisfied with the group and its activities, while there may be others who are extremely dissatisfied with the group. In this case a total score would show that the group is only minimally satisfied or minimally dissatisfied, although individual members fall at one end of the scale or the other. In such a situation, the persuasive communicator should concentrate attention on the satisfied members in the hope that they, at least, will be receptive. An alternative strategy might be to work on the dissatisfied members of the group, in the hope that they will accept any ideas that might make their group membership more satisfying to them.

It is of interest to find out how the persuasive communicator can work with a group to achieve the highest amount of satisfaction within it and can thus enhance the probability of success for any persuasive message transmitted to the group. The variable frequently advanced as the most important is *centrality*, which has been defined as a measure of closeness of the individual in the group to the center of activity.[15] In experimental studies, centrality has been identified by asking individuals how they felt about working with a particular group and by then determining which individuals within a network had the lowest satisfaction levels. In the Leavitt studies, for example, the wheel design proved to have the lowest *group* satisfaction ratings, although the individual oc-

cupying the center of the wheel had the highest ratings of any individual in any of the spatial arrangements with which Leavitt was concerned.[16] The four people on the fringes of the group felt that they had little control over the operation of the group and that they received little information about the way in which the group was operating. In the kind of simple task-oriented situations that Leavitt was studying, the role of individuals on the periphery was merely to supply answers to questions about their performance, and they were able to observe little about the way in which the rest of the members worked.

It is important to note that satisfaction is not necessarily related to productivity. The wheel arrangement is an effective organization for short run productivity, but one might expect that in the long run the organization would tend to become less productive, since the dissatisfied individuals would tend to pull out of the group. It is also important to note that group satisfaction cannot be determined by questioning ourselves, if we happen to be a member of the group, and particularly so if we happen to be a leader in the group. Leaders tend to judge the satisfaction of others by their own satisfaction, so this method is very likely to be inaccurate. It is true in this case, as is true with most of the psychological variables, that group satisfaction can be determined only by asking group members how they feel.

The persuasive communicator will never encounter a group arranged in exactly the same manner as the artificial groups studied by Leavitt, but every group will have individuals who are more central to the group than others. Imagine, for example the individual who belongs to a student government organization, or to a sailing club, a ski club, a political action group, or any other relatively loosely formed group. It is almost invariably the case that the actual work of the association is done by a handful of people. They hold all the offices in the group, have the most communication about the group, are the ones who really decide policy, and would be reported as the most central to the group. Other members are not as central. They belong, they share in some of the activities, but they are on the fringes of all the action. The persuasive communicator, in working with a group, has a delicate balancing act to perform. Communicators cannot afford to antagonize individuals who have central roles within the group and who may be leaders or emerging leaders for the group, yet all the rest of the group members must be made to feel that they too are extremely important to the communicator. Thus, an evaluation of satisfaction within the group cannot depend on the verbal reports from group leaders alone, but must also include reports from members who do not occupy central positions in the group. Only in this way can the persuasive communicator be assured that the group as a whole has a high satisfaction level.

Cohesiveness

Cohesiveness can be defined as the attractiveness of the group to its members. Experimentally, cohesiveness is measured by asking group members whether they wish to continue to work with the group. Then groups are ranked on a scale ranging from highly cohesive to less cohesive, based on the desire of their members to remain with the group.[17] In a highly cohesive group all or almost all members are eager to continue working with it, while in a less cohesive group, members do not wish to continue.

Cohesiveness has proved to be an extremely useful variable in small-group research. There are few studies directly measuring the effectiveness of persuasion transmitted to high and low cohesive groups, but the effects can be inferred from what is known about other kinds of situations. Our discussion of the relevance of cohesiveness to persuasion must take the form of a set of hypotheses that are untested, but inferrable from other research.

1. The persuasive communicator will find that groups with high cohesiveness will tend to have fewer deviant members who might oppose the group's decisions. Highly cohesive groups tend to place pressures on all individuals in the group to conform, and so deviant members are either rejected or they conform to group behavior. When the persuasive communicator is the sole deviant member in a highly cohesive group, or is opposed by the majority of the group, the probability of success is reduced. On the other hand, when the source of a persuasive message is expressing an idea with which the majority of the group seems to agree, the agreement may quickly extend to the entire group, because there will be extreme pressure on all members of the group to conform to the desires of the majority.

Political parties are an excellent example of this situation. At the primary stage, there may be many candidates, each vying for a victory in the primary. The party seems torn into many fragments. But after the primary, when one candidate has won a victory, the remaining party members close ranks, and "bury the hatchet." The group is basically cohesive, and although disagreements may occur, the members would rather belong to the group than leave the group. One of the marks of immature organizations, such as some student political groups, is that they are not cohesive. When a splinter group develops, there is no basic cohesiveness, and the splinter group is just as likely to break away from the main group to start a new organization as it is to remain.

2. In general, groups which are more cohesive are more likely to be influenced by persuasion. There are more pressures to be uniform in a highly cohesive group than in a less cohesive group. Thus, when the group becomes the recipient of persuasive communication, there are more pressures to do something about the message. When there are outside pressures for acceptance of the message, they apparently tend to produce more influence.[18]

3. Communication within highly cohesive groups is of a different nature than it is within less cohesive groups. There tends to be a larger total amount of communication in highly cohesive groups, and the communication is more equally divided among group members. Thus, the persuasive communicator is likely to find more willingness to discuss a set of proposals in a highly cohesive group. This willingness raises the probability of achieving understanding of the message through increased communication and, as a result, of obtaining more attitude change in favor of the message.

4. In groups where a message might appear to be a threat or might imply hostility toward the group, the highly cohesive group receivers are more likely to reject the message than members of a low cohesive group.[19] In the frequent persuasive situation where the communicator wishes to persuade a group of individuals to take some action that they might find distasteful, or difficult, or unpleasant, the probability that the communicator will be successful is lower for the high cohesive group than for the low cohesive group. Members in highly cohesive groups tend to offer support to one another and thus, tend to reject threatening messages as a group. In less cohesive groups, there is less communication and less support for group action.

Examples of this phenomenon abound. The Amish or Mennonite groups in our society have traditionally been very cohesive. When threatened by outside forces attempting to persuade them to a different way of life, they draw together and support each other in their rejection of incoming messages. Similar behavior is found in some of the communes that have been set up in the United States. In such situations, it may be the best strategy to wait until internal forces lower the amount of cohesion within the group, and to work through deviant members to achieve a particular aim. As these deviant members are reached, and as they change their attitudes, the probability that other deviant members can be reached increases, and the persuasive communicator thus raises the probability that members will accept the message.

5. Another approach to utilizing the cohesiveness variable is to regard it as an opportunity that a persuasive communicator may have to increase cohesiveness in a group and, thus, produce immunization against opposing messages. To be able to accomplish this, the source must be aware of some of the factors contributing to an increase in cohesiveness. These factors include:

a. The personal attractiveness of the members of the group to one another
b. The attractiveness of the message which they receive
c. The perceived prestige of the group itself.[20]

In a message to a group, the persuasive source can enhance each of the variables and in doing so, help to produce a group that can withstand opposing arguments.

Again, there are several examples of groups that have been able to withstand tremendous pressures because of their high cohesiveness. The Irish Republican Army is one such example. Some religious groups, such as the Black Muslims and the Pentecostals, also have the highly cohesive nature that enables them to maintain their beliefs in spite of constant pressure. You may not be working with such extreme groups, but any group can be improved in terms of cohesiveness so that the communicator will have more assurance that its members will not be subject to change in the face of opposing arguments.

Cohesiveness is an important variable. It is more difficult to obtain cohesiveness with large groups than with small, more difficult to obtain cohesiveness in heterogeneous groups than homogeneous groups, more difficult with informal social groups than with formal organizations, and more difficult to induce high cohesiveness with unpleasant messages than with pleasant ones. Nevertheless, persuasive communicators must frequently try to obtain high cohesiveness in the groups with which they are working in order to raise the probability that the changes they are interested in producing will be permanent ones.

Conformity Pressures

Sometimes, a group situation can be used to make individuals *conform* to a desired behavior, even though they may have some feelings that what they are doing is not correct. Before considering the experimental literature in this area, we should examine Kelman's view of the three process of *compliance*, *identification*, and *internalization*.[21]

For Kelman, *compliance* is achieved when an individual behaves in a particular fashion at the request of another in order to get a favorable reaction in return. In other words, I do what you want me to do because I hope that you will then do what I want you to do. The process of *identification* occurs when an individual behaves in a particular fashion in order to be perceived as similar to the individual making the request. Thus, I do what you want me to do because I want to seem similar to you. The process of *internalization* involves behavior changes which occur because the receiver really believes in the behavior being adopted. Thus, I do what you ask only because I have come to feel that it is the best thing for me to do.

On first examination, it would seem that the best goal would be to have receivers change their attitudes and behavior as a result of *internalizing* the message. This would indicate that they had made changes because they really had come to believe in the message. There is a risk to setting internalization as the persuasive communicator's only goal. When a receiver does finally internalize some idea or piece of information, that acceptance may trigger changes in many other beliefs associated with the adopted belief. From our discussion of con-

sistency theories we know that associated beliefs will tend to be internally self-consistent. If a change occurs in one belief, changes in others may have to occur in order for the entire set to remain self-consistent. It may be the case that when the persuasive communicator makes a change in one belief, there will have to be such major changes in other beliefs that other persuasive goals may not be met. Thus, an analysis of the potential effects of internalization indicates that there are sometimes risks that have to determined before automatically assuming that internalization is the best way to proceed.

Just as there may be risk associated with the use of internalization, both *compliance* and *identification* may have risks associated with their use as well. Let us consider an illustrative example of compliance and identification, and then identify both the strengths and attendant risks. Imagine that I persuade a rock-ribbed Republican neighbor to vote for a Democratic candidate, not because of a strong belief in the Democratic party or in the candidate, but simply because the neighbor admires me and does not wish to disappoint me. The neighbor has identified with me, and complied with my request. From one standpoint, we can argue that, "A vote is a vote," in these circumstances, whether the neighbor has really internalized the choice or not. One could furthermore argue that having performed a new behavior, and having found no bad consequences, the probability of eventually internalizing the new behavior is increased. Both of these arguments could be advanced in support of compliance.

There are, however, some arguments against this goal. For instance, how are we to *know* that the neighbor actually did vote for the Democratic candidate. There is no way of checking whether the vote was appropriately made unless we set up some type of surveillance on the inside of the voting booth. That, of course, is both illegal and impractical. Yet surveillance may be a requirement if we are to be assured that a receiver did comply. The risk of a receiver not complying is always present, and presents a serious threat to the utility of the compliance process.

A second question arises over the identification process. Remember that identification is the situation in which people comply with a message because they want to seem similar to the persuasive communicator sending the message. Obviously, this can be very flattering to a source. But what happens if the receiver takes the recommended action and finds it to be unrewarding? In all likelihood the eventual rejection of the persuasive communicator. The source will lose credibility, and future messages may not be accepted by that receiver.

It is possible to get people to conform with a persuasive request, but as we discuss conformity pressures in more detail, we must keep in mind that there are risks as well as benefits associated with the process.

Conformity pressures occur in group settings, and provide a way of getting people to comply with a request without internalizing the behavior or attitude change. A simple example of conformity pressures is given in the classic study by Asch.[22] Subjects were shown a standard card on which there was a short line. Then the subject was shown a comparison card on which three lines were printed. One of the three matched the standard card line, and the subject had to tell which line it was. Figure 9.3 is an example of the kind of task Asch set for his subjects. His method consisted of calling in five people, having them sit down, and explaining that he wished them to judge the length of the lines. He would add that in order to facilitate the recording of their answers, he would call upon them in turn. The real aim of test was not to see whether people could judge the length of the lines. Instead, in each group of five people, there was only one naive subject. The other four were confederates of the experimenter. On certain test items, the confederates would give the wrong answer by prearrangement. The naive subject was called

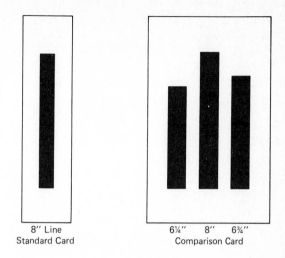

8″ Line
Standard Card

6¼″   8″   6¾″
Comparison Card

Figure 9.3 *A Typical Conformity-Pressure Stimulus Task*

upon last, and the study was designed to see whether he would answer according to his own convictions or conform to what he thought the rest of the group believed the right answer to be.

The results of Asch's study, and similar ones by Crutchfield,[23] indicate that approximately one third of all subjects will conform, that is, give an answer they think is probably wrong. Subjects who did conform reported they distrusted their own judgments or that they longed to agree with the majority. Even those who did *not* conform reported that they felt varying pressures to do so. These results have been repeated with varying tasks, different kinds of subjects, and different numbers of naive and nonnaive subjects. The overall results of all these studies indicate that a fairly high percentage of individuals, averaging approximately 33 percent over many studies, will conform under some conditions. This finding is of obvious interest to the persuasive communicator. Our interest in the finding can be further detailed by considering some of the specific studies and relating them to the transmission of persuasive messages.

1. Individuals can be pressured into yielding on opinion statements such as those in a persuasive message, as well as on objective judgments.[24] For example, in private, a group of military officers all disagreed with the statement, "I doubt that I would make a good leader." When placed in a situation in which they were led to believe that all the other officers in the group agreed with the statement, 37 percent of the officers indicated that they now agreed with the statement that they would not make a good leader. This is obviously an extreme statement for an army officer, and one might expect even greater conformity with statements which are less central to their belief systems.

The evidence that Crutchfield collected suggested that there may be personality differences between those individuals who yield to conformity pressures and those who do not. Individuals who are less secure, more authoritarian, or more dogmatic might be expected to yield more often than others.

The findings of Asch and Crutchfied suggest that persuasive communicators might be able to successfully use conformity pressures when they are able to analyze the group ahead of time, find people in the group who are already in favor of the issue and who are willing to express agreement after the message is delivered.

One practical step which persuasive communicators can sometimes take when working with a group is to "load" the audience, that is to have a number of supporters come to a meeting where there might be opposition. The verbal support of these individuals may be enough to sway other individuals in the group who are undecided as to their beliefs and attitudes. The communicator will wish to consider the obvious ethical questions concerned with deliberately "loading" an audience.

There are many practical examples of the use of the "loading" technique in situations involving closely divided issues. Political caucuses considering the merits of two candidates will jockey to get many people in favor of a particular candidate to speak first, in the hope that the apparent swell of opinion will convince those receivers who are sitting on the fence. Legislative committees will sometimes do the same thing. The committee chairman will schedule all the witnesses supporting the side that the chairman supports first, and relegate all others to a short space at the end of the day, hopefully long after the reporters have had to leave the hearing.

2. The percentage of individuals yielding to conformity pressures is far greater on difficult judgment items than it is on easy judgment items. In the Asch situation, if the difference between the standard line and the other test lines is made very large, few individuals will yield. Many persuasive situations involve judgments that are admittedly difficult to make, and persuasive speakers can perhaps steer all of the group to their way of thinking by obtaining the cooperation of some members of the group. In addition, when there is a greater chance that the decision could go either way, the proportion of conforming answers rises. Many persuasive situations involve attempts at attitudes which might not be strongly held, and thus, will be more susceptible to pressures from others in the group.

3. In the laboratory situation, the conformity effect seems largely to disappear if there are any differences of opinion expressed. In those situations, the naive subject is really going against what he believes to be the case. So if one other member of the group disagrees with the rest of the group, the naive subject is happy to express agreement with the minority member, even though all the rest of the group supports the other side. In persuasion situations outside of the laboratory, communicators who wish to make use of conformity pressures must attempt to ascertain whether there will be opposition or dissent before receivers are asked to agree with the message. If there are such

opposing voices from members of the group, predictions of success based on conformity pressures may be invalid.

Obviously, the communicator cannot ordinarily use force to control what other people are going to do, but it may be possible to use group size or the spatial arrangement of the group to isolate those individuals who might express some opposition, thereby minimizing the possibility of opposing speakers.

4. Conformity pressures, like the compliance process they are related to, do not necessarily produce lasting results. In private sessions after the experiments, many of the yielders expressed doubts about what they said in the group and tended to return to their own private judgments. In persuasion, some messages are intended for temporary effects, while in other situations, the communicator will want the effect to remain for a longer time. In the latter case, the original yielding position must be supplemented by additional communication in order to insure that the individual will continue to agree with the position taken in the group situation.

5. It is not actually necessary to have a group meet in a face-to-face situation for conformity pressures to operate. Crutchfield placed the subjects in a booth alone and then, utilizing a light system, purported to feed them information about the judgments of other people sitting in surrounding booths. Actually, all subjects got the same message. This suggests that the conformity pressure variable could be made to operate in a situation in which the members of a group received written communication or in which the persuasive communicator visited each individual in turn and reported on the feelings of the rest of the group. A similar situation to this one is termed the "bandwagon technique" in which the communicator tells an audience that "everyone" believes a particular idea or is participating in a particular activity. The communicator attempts to make the audience feel that almost all other people already believe what the source is attempting to get this group to believe.

Although this technique has been used successfully on many different occasions, there is an obvious danger to the communicator. If members of a group get together and talk about the message, they may find out that each of them has been led to believe that the other already believes the message. The technique, when used, must be employed with extreme caution and preferably in situations where the majority *does* tend to believe the message.

Conformity pressures *can* be used to raise the probability that a message will be acted upon favorably. As Kelman has pointed out, however, conformity pressures operate at varying levels, with varying degrees of commitment to the response made. A decision made in private will not be adhered to nearly as strongly as one made in public. One made when a receiver believes that everyone agrees with the communicator will be held more strongly than one made when there has been some opposition expressed. Despite these limitations, conformity pressures do tend to make members of a group arrive at uniform beliefs. Deviant members who wish to continue as members of the group are under real pressure to conform.

Norms

The development of *norms* within a group of people is well illustrated by classic experiments conducted by Sherif.[25] If an individual is placed in a dark room and asked to look steadily at a pinpoint of light shown against a wall, the light will eventually appear to move. This phenomenon is a natural, physiological event, and it has been termed *apparent* movement, or the *auto-kinetic effect*. Sherif used this physiological reaction to demonstrate a psychological variable, the formation of a *norm*. He put several people in a room and then asked them to decide as a group how far the light seemed to move.

His results, and the results of similar studies, suggested that individuals at first answered with a fairly wide range of guesses as to how far they saw the light move. Eventually, however, the group began to narrow down its range of estimates to vary more closely around one point. There were still differences expressed, but those differences were relatively small.

The reader may wonder how the Sherif study could be in any way related to persuasion. In many persuasive communication situations the source requests that a group change their behavior in certain ways. The group discusses the problem and eventually takes a position regarding the request from the communicator. In subsequent situations, the same group will continue to take much the same position. They will develop a common standard of judgment, or *norm* of behavior, with respect to the message and to all other messages like it. This type of behavior is similar to the standards, or norms, that the groups developed in the Sherif situation.

A formal definition of a norm is that it is *a uniformity of behavior produced and maintained by group pressures.* Norms are not produced by overt, physical pressures, but rather behavior is regulated covertly, without the application of direct power. There are many examples of the development of norms. In factories, norms of production are developed over time. A man coming into a factory for the first time may attempt to produce in excess of the norm developed by the rest of the group. He soon experiences social pressures, frequently unstated, which aim at slowing him down to the pace of the group. People won't talk to him, drink coffee with him, or ride home with him. When he finally does begin operating within the range of production allowed by the norm, the pressures ease, and he finds himself to be one of the group. He is being rewarded for following the norms of the group, and can be expected to being enforcing those norms with other new people when they enter the factory.

Many other examples of norms exist in on-going groups. The college freshman entering a dormitory situation may find that a norm exists for Friday night parties. He will be met with strong social pressures if he attempts to study on Friday night. Today, many groups oppose long hair for men. The student, who has grown a fine head of hair in response to the freeedom of a college campus, may find that when he takes a summer job on a construction gang, there is strong social pressure on him to conform to the norm developed by the rest of the group. Norms will vary from area to area, and from group to group, but one of the characteristics of groups is that they tend to develop norms.

Festinger suggests that group norms arise in two ways which are important to the persuasive communicator.[26] First, many people are somewhat unsure about the beliefs they hold. They frequently turn to the groups to which they belong in order to obtain assurance about their beliefs. A college student may turn to the "bull session" in the dormitory to explore with others persuasive messages that may have been received. People who are not sure of their religious beliefs may join and participate in groups which will assist them in deciding that a particular set of beliefs is correct.

Festinger goes on to say that norms will also develop in informal groups to insure the survival of the group. When an informal group emerges, and there are threats to its existence either from inside or outside the group, the group may develop a set of norms that will help to insure its survival. A social group, for example, may agree to make a contribution to some charity, and to hold a dance every year to raise the money. Without the agreement to hold the dance, the group might well break up, since there might be little else holding it together. Giving the group a purposeful norm helps to insure that the group will stay together.

Persuasive communicators increase the probability of success when they know what the norms of the group are and can apply them in constructing and presenting messages. For example, when there is a norm relating to the clothes worn in a particular group, deviation from the group norm is not likely to help the communicator's position. There may be beliefs the group members hold in which they have full confidence. Unless adherence to the belief is actively antithetic to the source's position, arguing against the belief is likely to result in rejection of the entire message.

There are three major applications of group norms for persuasive communication situations. Sometimes, communicators are interested in *developing norms* within newly formed groups. At other times, persuasive communicators may be interested in helping to *maintain norms* when they are threatened from outside the group. And finally, communicators may be interested in *changing norms* for groups. These three applications deserve elaboration.

1. *Norm formation* Groups of individuals meeting for the first time do not have a set of norms unique to them. Their behavior is determined by prior associations, not by their membership in the new group. The uniformities of behavior which the group will eventually develop will be formed by close association over a long period of time. Whenever a norm is formed, stimuli and responses to those stimuli by each member of the group are involved. For example, if one man makes a statement regarding some behavior he wishes the group to adopt, he can anticipate that others in the group will also make statements suggesting behavior slightly different. The chances of the audience taking the step he recommends will be increased if he can show that the step will be rewarding to the group. If, over a period of time, the communicator can show the group that his suggestions are satisfying, he will have the opportunity of having his ideas adopted as the norm for the group.

In attempting to develop a norm in a newly formed group, communicators must take the chance of having the final norm be slightly different from that which they may have advocated. The literature on norm formation shows that the end product is almost always a compromise position of the initial positions advanced by the various members of the group. Persuasive communicators can improve the chances of having a final position be close to their own if they can obtain the cooperation of some group members early in the process in helping to apply pressures to other group members. Hopefully, cooperation can be secured from group leaders, who are likely to have the greatest leeway in following norms.

Communicators must also take positions that are not likely to be immediately perceived by audiences as representing an extreme position. The experimental studies of norm formation show that advocating an extreme position with a newly formed group may place the communicator in the position of being a deviant member of the group. If the rest of the group indeed perceives him as deviant, even a retreat to neutrality will not help the communicator regain his influence. The student who has gained a poor reputation may reform, but the group will be the last to see it. It is certainly the case that a source has a better chance of succeeding in establishing a "way out" position when working with a group which is just forming, and has not developed strong norms, than when attempting to work with an already formed group. Even so, the probabilities are not good in either case. Groups tend toward the mean of the behaviors of the members, not toward the extremes.

2. *Norm maintenance* For every communicator who is suggesting changes in behavior, there will be another communicator who is working to maintain the present situation. In persuasion research and group research, the position of the first individual has been carefully examined. Few studies, however, have looked at that individual who is concerned with maintaining a set of group norms, not changing them. Yet persuasive communicators frequently find themselves in groups where they represent the majority, normative position. How do such sources operate to maintain those

norms in the face of attempts to change the group?

Norms exist because members of a group find them rewarding. If communicators wish to perpetuate a particular type of behavior in a group, they will need to make reference to the desirable aspects of continuing to do what has been tried and proven over a period of time. In some cases, suggestions by a source of new behavior will be related to behavior discussed when the norm was first established. An individual who wishes to maintain the status quo may point out that the group had already, at one time in the past, rejected the position which the source is suggesting.

In every group, the majority of group members are going to be more interested in maintaining group norms than in changing them. That is, after all, what group norms imply. Sources will have to use those majority members of the group, particularly the leaders of the group, to help in the maintenance of norms. In such cases, the messages sent by the source might suggest that changes in behavior will result in the disintegration of the group, or in an influx of undesirable members wishing to join the group.

We should note that the normal trend of any group is toward the *status quo*, that is, toward the maintenance of a given set of norms. Change in a group is accomplished only slowly. Therefore, the odds favor the persuasive communicator who is faced with the task of attempting to maintain a set of beliefs or behaviors in a group over the source who is attempting to change beliefs or behaviors.

3. *Changing norms* Once a group has developed a set of norms, the norms will be maintained unless the group finds them no longer rewarding or unless a more satisfactory mode of behavior can be substituted. In factories, suggestions from management regarding new work procedures may result in walkouts in protest over the proposed new rules. It may be that management has designed the new rules for the advantage and comfort of the workers. Still they are rejected The motivating factor is fear that the new procedures might result in a loss of jobs, or simply a fear of change—a change in well-established norms. New procedures result in new norms, and the establishment of new norms by outsiders is strongly resisted. New procedures suggested by people who are already well-established with the group, however, may be accepted and may result in behavioral changes. People who know each other and trust each other are far more likely to be able to make changes in a group, because they are trusted by the group. If persuasive communicators are not members of a group, they may be able to accomplish their goal by turning to insiders and convincing them to deliver the message.

Norms are maintained at different levels within groups. They tend to be maintained more strongly in a group which feels itself under attack. Small religious groups, not associated with larger mainstream groups, frequently develop very strong norms, and resist any attempts by outsiders to suggest change to the group. Even on a societal level, whenever there is an era of suspicion and fear, such as the McCarthy era of the early 1950s, the tendency to maintain norms is heightened. Communicators must recognize this tendency in preparing messages designed to change norms. A fear appeal will be of little use in this situation. Far better would be messages suggesting that the proposed behavior will strengthen the group, not weaken it.

Norms are maintained more jealously for behavior which the group regards as significant than for those which they regard as peripheral to the group. The communicator who advocates change in group behavior should point out that this change is not one that will disturb the basic operations of the group, but that it will even enhance those operations. Messages which emphasize that a change is merely a logical extension of previous beliefs or practices have a better chance of resulting in changed norms than do messages advocating drastic changes.

Finally, norms are maintained unequally among group members. There will frequently be a central core of individuals advocating strict adherence to a set of beliefs or behaviors and a group of individuals who follow the norms but do not really believe them to be extremely important. It is this latter group that can sometimes be utilized by a communicator to change a norm. If they can be convinced that a particular uniformity of behavior is not important and that some other type of behavior is more desirable, the power of the group's central core may be broken.

Open housing in the United States is an example of this situation. A norm of behavior among real estate dealers, certain bankers, and many individuals has been responsible for maintaining many segregated housing areas. When housing integration has taken place, it has frequently been because a new real estate firm is established in an area and the members of that firm are not under strong pressure to behave like the older firms in the area. There will be some pressure on them to engage in practices designed to maintain segregation, but if the members of the firm resist and do sell to minority persons, others are far more likely to break the norm and follow suit. The point is that new behavior in this situation occurred because people peripheral to a group found it rewarding.

Norms are an extremely important group variable. They explain much of the behavior that people in groups exhibit. They are not always deterimental to the communicator's purposes. Sometimes, the norms of a group can be used to advance the goals of a persuasive communicator, and to successfully maintain certain types of behavior or successfully change other norms through persuasion. Regardless of the ways in which norms can be effectively utilized in communication, we should remember that norms tend to limit the degree of change possible in a group. They must be taken into account in determining how much change is likely to be possible.

We have discussed norms in terms of the effect they may have on the outcome of a persuasive situation. More importantly, however, norms may serve the persuasive communicator as an indicator of the possible reaction of a group member toward the message. If the message threatens to violate the norms of behavior according to which the individual operates, the message and the communicator may well be rejected. Norms are a predictor of the possible success or failure of the persuasive communicator, and must be taken into account when working within a group situation.

Equilibrium

The last psychological variable we shall discuss in this chapter is the pressure from within the group to maintain a balanced situation. This variable may seem similar to the norm concept, but it has been explained and applied somewhat differently. Groups are composed of people who have many different characteristics. If it is to be an enduring group, rather than a temporary one, the common factor holding the group together is each individual's desire to belong to the group. The group, however, is subject to many pressures, pressures to maintain task efficiency, to change members' positions, to maintain socio-emotional stability, to adopt new ideas, and so forth. The equilibrium notion states that the pressures on the group will always tend to result in movement of the group toward states of balance, or equilibrium. Thus, the concept is closely related to the consistency hypotheses we discussed in an earlier chapter.

The differences between congruity and group equilibrium is the difference between what happens to an individual and what happens to a number of individuals. The equilibrium concept suggests that if a persuasive communicator introduces a message into a group, any changes in the group will be minimal, but that there will be some changes. Any pressures on the group will be absorbed as much as possible by the members and counterbalanced against whatever pressures there are in order to maintain an earlier position. It suggests to the communicator that if large changes are the intent, constant communication will be necessary, and constant pressures on the group will be of help in producing real changes.

The equilibrium notion imagines groups to be somewhat like a bowl of Jello. Push a spoon down on the Jello, and it takes on a different shape. But remove the spoon, and the Jello returns to its original shape. In order to make a permanent change in the shape of the Jello, you have to remove some of the contents of the bowl, or add something to the bowl, or provide for a differently shaped container for the contents of the bowl. In similar fashion, the equilibrium notion suggests that groups also change only when there is pressure from the outside, and that the group will return to an original set of behaviors unless the pressure is kept constant.

The equilibrium notion might suggest to the reader that groups are permanent entities, relatively monolithic in nature, and always tending toward a central position. This is not a fair position. Groups are more likely to break up after a period of time than they are to stay together. Ask yourself: of the groups you now belong to, how many did you belong to even five years ago? The chances are that the number will be very small. You change, and as you change you either change the groups to which you belong or leave them.

The equilibrium notion implies that groups do not change rapidly. They do not change except when under pressure to do so. Individuals within the group may change drastically but if their changed behavior is maintained for any period of time, they are rejected and tend to leave the group. Thus, persuasion must be planned in terms of many messages, not one. The stronger the group, the more important the subject, and the more resistance there is to the topic, the longer will the communicator have to work in order to reach the persuasive goals that have been set.

There are several interesting situations that can arise in the life of a group during which persuasive communication may play an important part:

1. When a group is just in the process of being formed, it tends to be relatively unstable. The relationships among the people in the group have not been established, and it is somewhat easier to steer the group in one direction or the other. Note, however, that the group will tend toward equilibrium, even when it has just been formed. Thus messages which promise to stabilize the group should be well-received at this point and acted upon favorably. A group which does not have a tight bond tends to seize upon messages which promise more stability for the group. The direction that the group will take, and the behaviors that the group will find acceptable are also easier to control when the group is just forming.

2. After a group has been in existence for a period of time, and has found a position of equilibrium, the group tends to shut out any information that might disturb that balance point. This phenomenon is similar to the cognitive dissonance situation we discussed earlier, where an individual, after just having made a decision, was unreceptive to messages persuading change. Thus, we will find a group unreceptive to persuasive messages asking for change if the group is at a point in its life where equilibrium has been reached. Something will have to happen to the equilibrium for there to be a willingness to accept new information.

3. After informal groups have existed for a long period of time, the bonds between members of the group tend to grow weak, even though the group is in a state of equilibrium. For example, after a bridge club has existed for several years, the members tend to grow a bit bored with the group. It isn't that the group is unstable, but rather that the group has had little reinforcement for the conditions that brought it together in the first place. At this point in the life of a group, things are ripe for

change. The persuasive communicator who is able to suggest the addition of new members or new ideas to the group, has an excellent chance of moving the group on to new behaviors, and thus to a new equilibrium point.

The equilibrium notion is one deserving of considerable thought on the part of the persua-sive communicator. An analysis of the group is essential to discover what stage the group is in, and thus what kind of messages the group will respond to. Such as analysis may prevent fail-ure on the part of the communicator, and en-hance the potential success of a message.

SUMMARY

When people come together and interact, they form groups. Groups of receivers behave differ-ently toward persuasive messages than do single receivers. The persuasive communicator must take into account some of the important factors in group situations in planning messages, in arranging the communication situ-ation and in predicting the success the messages are likely to have on the members of the group.

We have considered two different kinds of variables that are characteristic of groups and important to the persuasive communicator. Physical factors include group size, spatial arrangement, feedback mechanisms, and the presence or absence of leadership within the group. The source may have the opportunity to manipulate these variables in planning messages, or may have to adapt the messages to the type of group to be faced.

Psychological factors important to persua-sion include group satisfaction, cohesiveness, conformity pressures, norms, and group equi-librium. These are variables which are inferred from the behavior of group members. They are variables which can either aid or inhibit the communicator in planning a persuasive cam-paign. They must be taken into account when the communicator is obliged to work within the confines of a group situation.

FOOTNOTES

1. For a discussion of some of the problems which arise in defining a *group*, see G. C. Homans, *The Human Group*, (New York: Harcourt, Brace & World, Inc., 1950); and J. W. Thibaut and H. H. Kelley, *The Social Psychology of Groups*, (New York: John Wiley & Sons, 1959).
2. A. P. Hare, "Interaction and Consensus in Dif-ferent Sized Groups," *American Sociological Re-view*, vol. 17 (1952), pp. 261–267.
3. P. E. Slater, "Contrasting Correlates of Group Size," *Sociometry*, vol. 21 (1958), pp. 129–39.
4. L. A. Pervin, "Performance and Satisfaction as a Function of Individual-Environment Fit," in N. S. Endler and D. Magnusson, eds., *Interactional Psychology and Personality*, (Washington, D.C.: Hemisphere Publishing Corp., 1976), pp. 73–74.
5. R. F. Bales, *Personality and Interpersonal Behavior*, (New York: Holt, Rinehart and Winston, 1970), pp. 467–70.
6. R. F. Bales and E. F. Borgatta, "Size of Group as a Factor in the Interaction Profile," in A. P. Hare, E. G. Borgatta and R. F. Bales, eds., *Small Groups: Studies in Social Interaction*, (New York: Alfred A. Knopf, 1965), pp. 495–512.
7. H. M. Robert, *Robert's Rules of Order Revised*, (New York: Scott, Foresman and Company, 1951).
8. E. J. Thomas And C. F. Fink, "Effects of Group Size," in A. P. Hare, E. F. Borgatta and R. F. Bales, eds., *Small Groups: Studies in Social Interac-tion*, (New York: Alfred A. Knopf, 1965), pp. 525–36.
9. H. J. Leavitt, "Some Effects of Certain Commu-

nications Patterns on Group Performance," *Journal of Abnormal and Social Psychology*, vol. 46 (1951), pp. 38–50.

10. For a discussion of these studies, see R. T. Golembiewski, *The Small Group: An Analysis of Research Concepts and Operations*, (Chicago: University of Chicago Press, 1962), pp. 93–97.

11. M. Glanzer and R. Glaser, "Techniques for the Study of Group Structure and Behavior: Empirical Studies of the Effects of Structure in Small Groups," in A. P. Hare, E. F. Borgatta and R. F. Bales, eds., *Small Groups: Studies in Social Interaction*, (New York: Alfred A. Knopf, 1965), pp. 400–26.

12. A. P. Hare and R. F. Bales, "Seating Position and Small Group Interaction," in A. P. Hare, E. F. Borgatta and R. F. Bales, eds., *Small Groups: Studies in Social Interaction*, (New York: Alfred A. Knopf, 1965), pp. 427–33.

13. H. J. Leavitt and R. A. H. Mueller, "Some Effects of Feedback on Communication," *Human Relations*, vol. 4 (1951), pp. 401–10.

14. M. Burgoon, J. Heston and J. McCroskey, *Small Group Communication: A Functional Approach*, (New York: Holt, Rinehart and Winston, 1974), pp. 147–48.

15. Glanzer and Glaser, "Study of Group Structure," p. 417.

16. Leavitt, "Effects of Feedback," pp. 38–50.

17. D. Cartwright, "The Nature of Group Cohesiveness," in D. Cartwright and A. Zander, eds. *Group Dynamics*, (New York: Harper and Row, 1968), pp. 182–91.

18. Golembiewski, *The Small Group*, p. 165.

19. K. Back, "Influence through Social Communication," *Journal of Abnormal and Social Psychology*, vol. 46 (1951), pp. 9–23.

20. Golembiewski, *The Small Group*, p. 157.

21. For a simplified discussion of Kelman's basic postulation, see G. R. Miller, *An Introduction to Speech Communication*, (New York: Bobbs-Merrill Co., 1972), pp. 65–75. Readers who wish to examine Kelman's notions in depth are referred to H. Kelman, "Processes of Opinion Change," *Public Opinion Quarterly*, 25 (Spring 1961).

22. S. Asch, "Effects of Group Pressure upon the Modification and Distortion of Judgment," in H. Guetzkow, ed., *Groups, Leadership, and Men*, (Pittsburgh, Pa. Carnegie Press, 1951).

23. For typical studies by Crutchfield, see R. S. Crutchfield, "Conformity and Character," *American Psychologist*, vol. 10 (1955), pp. 191–98, and "Personal and Situational Factors in Conformity to Group Pressures," *Acta Psychologica*, vol. 15 (1959), pp. 386–88.

24. R. S. Crutchfield, "The Measurement of Individual Differences in Conformity to Group Opinion among Officer Personnel," (Institute of Personality Assessment and Research, University of California at Berkeley, *Research Bulletin*, 1954).

25. M. Sherif, "A Study of Some Social Factors in Perception," *Archives of Psychology*, no. 7, 1935.

26. L. Festinger, "Informal Social Communication," *Psychological Review*, 57 (1957) pp. 271–82.

TEN

PERSUASION IN THE FORMAL ORGANIZATION

Informal organizations are important to all of us. We move in and out of social groups, recreational groups, or problem solving groups many times a year. But the informal groups we belong to are not nearly as important, not nearly as influential, as the *formal organizations* to which we belong or with which we come in contact. Each of us belongs to a number of formal organizations. We work for a company, belong to a church, attend a university, work with a political party, are a member of a credit union, live in a fraternity, or are a member of the Army Reserve. Of how many other formal organizations are you a member? If you try making a list, you may be surprised at the number of formal organizations to which you belong. The number of formal organizations to which we belong, however, is dwarfed by the number of organizations that affect our daily lives even though we are not members. The grocery store, the drug store, the local television station, General Motors, the Internal Revenue Service, the local police department, a hospital, the Republican Party, and the local school board are just a few of the formal organizations that may have a direct influence on the quality of our lives. This chapter analyzes formal organizations, their nature and structure, and discusses some of the tactics that persuasive communicators must use when working with such organizations.

One of the first questions we must ask is how formal organizations come to be? When groups of people associate over long periods of time, when they develop specific goals that justify their existence, when leaders emerge and are recognized as leaders, we must stop using the term "informal group." Instead, we say that those individuals have become organized into a *social system. Social systems arise when individuals find that they need the help of others in oder to attain their own personal goals.* In our cities, people are dependent on others for their food, their shelter, their schooling, and indeed for almost every facet of their daily lives. The farmer may be less dependent on the presence of others, but the American farmer today cannot farm without the help of those who supply him with equipment, seed, feed, and so forth. The dependence of one individual on another or on many others is one of the prime reasons for the existence of social systems.

Some social systems "just happen to form" and are relatively informal in nature and temporary in duration. There may be one specific goal, and when that goal is reached, the organization is disbanded. The large group of people who banded together in 1972 to collect money for starving people in Bangladesh is an excellent example of a temporary social system. When their goal was reached, they disbanded. Other social systems, however, are enduring, hierarchical structures, with specific goals, expectations, rules and choices. Such enduring social systems become the "formal organizations" that are to be the focus of this chapter. General Motors was not formed to produce cars for a single year, and then disbanded. Michigan State University does not exist to educate only those students who enter in the fall of 1980. The Internal Revenue Service does not collect taxes for just a single year and then disband. Each of these are formal organizations, social structures with goals, different tasks for members of the organization, different communication patterns, and different relationships with other organizations.

Formal organizations come into existence when a specific need emerges from the larger society. The original goal of such organizations tends to be in accord with the needs, beliefs, and expectations of some segment of the society at the time of formation. When Henry Ford brought out the Model T, society cheered at his attempt to provide the masses with effective. low-cost transportation. When Proctor and Gamble brought out the detergent Tide, house-

wives quickly replaced their soap with the new product because it was a more effective cleansing agent.

In the case of Ford Motor Company and Proctor and Gamble, a small organization became a very large one because the product was successful. In other cases, a single person may have an idea that is accepted, and a small business is eventually developed into a major organization. Such is the case with Kentucky Fried Chicken, where a single individual developed a product that eventually required the attention of a huge formal organization. In still other cases, an original idea produced an organization that eventually developed into a larger organization with far different kinds of goals. A good example is ITT, a group starting out with telephone and telegraph interests, but which now has holdings in many different kinds of industries.

When conditions change, and the needs of people change, the institution that does not change, or does not change rapidly enough, becomes a target for the change agent—the persuasive communicator. In this chapter, we shall consider two main kinds of situations. Some of us already belong to organizations we feel need to be changed. We are *insiders*, but not particularly happy with what we see. We feel that we, and our ideas are not being accepted, and want to induce change in the institution. A second type of situation involves communicators who find that an organization is standing in the way of achieving some goal. They are *outsiders*, who want the formal organization to change in some way. There are some differences between the persuasive tactics that insiders and outsiders will use in attempting to effect change in the organization. Common to both situations, however, is the necessity of understanding those variables that seem to facilitate or inhibit the flow of communication through the organization. It is impossible to study every one of the formal organizations persuasive communicators may wish to affect with their messages. Nevertheless, certain variables can be abstracted from all organizations, whether social, military, corporate, educational, or governmental, and can be discussed in terms of their importance to persuasive communication.

Three major sets of variables are of importance to the persuasive communicator. First, we shall examine the *basic functions* of all organizations, and relate those functions to the task of the communicator. Second, we shall look closely at some of the *basic communication concepts* as they apply to formal organizations. And finally, we shall examine *organizational expectations* relating to persuasion as they occur in formal organizations. For each of these three major sets of variables, we shall look at the role of the persuasive communicator in attempting organizational change.

ORGANIZATIONAL FUNCTIONS

Formal organizations do not just "happen" to come into being. Firestone Tires, Texas Instruments, The Department of Agriculture and Michigan State University were formed with a specific purpose in mind. The initial purpose may have been to manufacture some product, to perform some service, or to serve the needs of a group of people. Once the organization has been formed, there is a tendency for the organization to take actions to continue operating. Some of the efforts that were originally placed into producing a product are now placed into efforts to keep the organization alive. In times when the organization is faced with a rapidly changing society, the members of the organization will also devote considerable time and attention to trying to develop new products, or new ideas.

The differences we find between organizations suggests that it might be useful to look at the *functions* of formal organizations as a way of coming to a better understanding of the way in which communication works in an organization. Jacob[1] reviewed a number of attempts to describe the functions of organizations. She

eventually decided that there were five major categories that scholars used: work, maintenance, motivation, integration and innovation. The last three categories are all related to the socio-emotional climate of organizations, and many of the communication patterns necessary to perform these functions are the same. For that reason, Farace, Monge and Russell[2] prefer to discuss only innovation as the central socio-emotional function for formal organizations. We have chosen to examine the three major organizational functions of *productivity*, *maintenance*, and *innovation*. Each of these three is closely related to persuasive communication, and an understanding of these organizational functions will assist the source in the preparation of messages.

The *productivity function* is present in every organization, although the strength of that goal may vary from organization to organization. The Ford Motor Company produces automobiles, and it sets standards regarding the number, quality, design and profits to be expected from this goal. Much of the communication within the organization is directed toward the attainment of that goal. The University of Illinois has as one of its productivity goals the graduation of students with bachelor's degrees. Although the University has other functions as well, much of the communication within the university will be directed to making sure that students are recruited, educated and eventually graduated. The Internal Revenue Service has a productivity goal of collecting taxes, and much of their communication and organizational efforts will be devoted to achieving this goal.

It is easy to isolate the goals of formal organizations such as manufacturers, universities and governmental organizations. It is somewhat harder in the case of organizations that do not produce a "hard" product such as cars, taxes, and graduates. What is the productivity goal of a city council? What about a regional planning group? Such organizations might respond by talking about the improvement of the city or policy-making for a region, but it is more difficult to ascertain just what the productivity goals of such formal organizations are. Making that analysis is important for the persuasive communicator, as we shall see when we look at organizational goals as they relate to persuasive communication.

The *maintenance function* is a characteristic of formal organizations helping to distinguish them
from temporary organizations. A maintenance goal is the desire to do whatever it takes to continue the existence of the organization. General Electric produces many products, but it attempts to operate in such a way as to guarantee that it will continue to operate for many years. It sets up safeguards against members of the organization doing anything which might result in the elimination of the organization. General Motors could, possibly, produce twice as many cars per year as it does, by operating around the clock, and hiring more workers. It cannot sell that many cars, however, and it would soon go out of business. A balance must be maintained between the productivity goals and the maintenance goals in order to insure the survival of the organization.

Maintenance goals are frequently so powerful that they will cause productivity goals to be changed. For example, the March of Dimes collected money for many years to aid in the fight against polio. Its money was spent in research and in aiding the victims of the disease. Finally it was successful. The Salk vaccine was developed, and polio became almost a thing of the past. If the eradication of the disease had been the organization's only goal, the March of Dimes organization might have been expected to disband. Of course, this is not what happened. Over the years the people associated with the organization had developed maintenance goals, which resulted in a wide network of paid members and many unpaid volunteers who felt a loyalty to the organization. When the eradication of polio seemed to be only a few months away, the production goals of the organization were changed, and the eradication of

all childhood birth defects became the new production goal. This goal is so broad that no one associated with the organization need ever fear that a position will be in jeopardy, and the organization may exist for generations to come. In this case, the maintenance goal was so strong that it dictated what the productivity was to be.

The *innovation function* is closely related to both the productivity and maintenance functions. Productivity functions concentrate on the actual work of the organization. Maintenance functions attempt to make sure that the people working in the organization are satisfied enough with their jobs so that they don't quit and thus lower productivity. The innovation function looks to the future. In essence, it is a recognition that the world is always changing, and that formal organizations must also be able and willing to change. Some organizations set up a Research and Development section that is given the task of finding new products or improving old products so that the company may be constantly ahead of its competitors. It is easy to see just how important the innovation function is by looking at the computer industry. If a company had entered the computer industry in 1960, it would have manufactured and sold computers that occupied entire rooms, and required expensive heating, electrical and air conditioning equipment. Today, computers of equivalent function can be kept nicely on one corner of a desk. If a company had not engaged in innovation, it would have very quickly gone out of business.

It might seem at first that the maintenance function and the innovation function are one and the same. Careful analysis, however, shows some important differences between the two functions. An organization that gives the innovation goal extremely high priority may have trouble maintaining an employee force. Such an organization is likely to place strong emphasis on new ideas, on hiring new people, and on turning out those members of the organization who do not seem to be coming up with new ideas or products. The organization runs the risk of collapsing because when so many people are lost stability is threatened. An organization that places high value on the maintenance goal is likely to have a very stable work force, one where workers like each other, socialize with each other, and one where promotions are almost always made from inside, and where few new people are added. Such an organization is usually quite stable over time, but may not necessarily be counted on for a lot of brilliant new ideas.

All organizations, then, have a set of functions or goals that help in distinguishing them from other formal organizations. In the formal organizations with which we shall be concerned, the three major sets of goals, that is, productivity goals, maintenance goals, and innovation goals, can be ranked for each organization. The rankings help in determining just how successful persuasion is likely to be in different situations within the organization. The rankings of goals in terms of importance within the organization at any given time is a function of:

1. The individual presently within the organization
2. The ways in which the organization makes decisions
3. The pressures on the organization from outside agencies and groups

Goals are changed when new members are added or when members leave the organization. Normally, such changes in goal rankings are minimal, since the new people are most likely to be quite similar to individuals already in the organization. They are simply absorbed. This is why it is so disappointing to the communicator who joins an organization, and finds that efforts for change do not seem to have much effect. There may be a "critical mass" of new individuals necessary in order for meaningful change to occur.

Organizational decision-making processes also help determine the amount of change that is

possible. For example, in some large corporations, subunits are given the freedom to make operating decisions. It is logical to expect that in such an organization separate sections will have developed different ideas about what the goals of the organization are and the relative importance of any productivity or maintenance goal. It may be easier to introduce change in such an organization than in one where control is exercised strongly from the top, and the relative importance of particular goals remains approximately the same for the entire organization. A large university is frequently an example of such an organization, where many of the most important curricular decisions are made at the level of the department, and the larger university serves primarily to set overall policy for the units. Many large newspaper chains operate with maximum flexibility at the local level, and give each of the local newspapers complete freedom to set editorial policy. If the persuasive communicator did not know that such a degree of local autonomy existed, the temptation would be great to try to work from the top down, while a more successful strategy might be to work at the local level until a number of the local units have been convinced. Thus, knowledge about the ways in which decision making is done within any particular organization becomes important to the persuasive communicator who wishes to introduce change.

Finally, the problems or pressures from outside help determine the ways in which any set of goals will be ranked. For example, General Motors ranks very high the production of an automobile that can be sold at a big enough profit to satisfy the stockholders. Introducing safety devices or pollution control devices will be of much lesser importance, and, in fact, may be ignored until either an outside agency tells the corporation that without such devices it will not be allowed to sell any cars, or until the buying public demonstrates to the company through lack of sales that it will not buy cars that do not possess such devices. In either case, the change has been produced, not because

General Motors has independently changed its ranking of goals, but because the company has found it cannot achieve its productivity goal without making an adjustment. A similar example can be found in the school boards in any large city. Ten years ago the central goal of any school board was primarily to provide schools and teachers for those students who lived in the nearby community. Today, and for many years to come, school boards will face the problem of insuring an adequate racial balance within the various schools in a district. This additional problem was not one the school boards dreamed up themselves. The reranking of educational goals was forced on school boards by outside groups who were concerned because change did not come from within the organization. Thus, the problems that an organization is forced to face, help determine the goals set, and the relative importance of those goals.

There is a close relationship between persuasion and the goals an organization possesses. Just as persuasion that appeals to individual needs is more successful with an individual, so is persuasion that appeals to a highly ranked organizational goal. If you can show The Dow Chemical Company that ceasing to manufacture a particular product will result in increased profits, you have more chance of succeeding than with a message that says, "This move will decrease your profits, but it will be a desirable one in other respects." A corporation that has a strong profit motive is not likely to be persuaded by a message arguing for smaller profits. In similar fashion, a company that has a strong effort under way to innovate, will be more persuaded by a message promising a new wonderful product if certain steps are taken than will a company that is maintenance oriented. All organizations have productivity goals, maintenance goals and innovation goals, but each organization will differ in the value placed on each goal. We can improve our persuasive efforts by considering how some of the different goals might be used by the persuasive communicator.

1. Which are more important to the organization you are concerned with, productivity goals or maintenance goals? In some organizations, productivity is the central goal, and individuals who do not produce are dropped from the organization. In other types of organizations, maintenance becomes the primary goal. Having "one happy family" is more important than achieving the highest rate of production possible. Advocating a behavior requiring much additional effort in order to raise production in an organization rating maintenance goals higher than production goals is not likely to be really successful. Instead, the response might be, "Don't rock the boat." On the other hand, suggesting maintenance activities to organizations that are oriented to production or innovation may also produce the same types of rejection for similar reasons.

2. Are organizational goals made with broadly based participation, or are they primarily the province of a few individuals? The League of Women Voters of the United States sets a series of goals each year. In order to establish those goals, the entire membership of the organization participates in a consensus process until the final decision is reached. Presumably, there will be far higher commitment to goals reached through such a process, than when goals are dictated by a small board of directors. In corporate organizations, goals may be proposed by a managerial group and ratified by a board of governors. In government organizations, goals are actually defined in the legislation establishing an agency, and operational goals are then established by directors within the agency.

The point is that there are a number of different styles an organization can use in arriving at its goals, and these operating processes become important to the persuasive communicator. In an organization in which goals have been set by a small group of people, and imposed on the rest of the organization, one might expect to find some success through communication directed to the remainder of the organization. This tactic has frequently been used by union organizers in approaching "family owned" corporations, in which a small group of family owners and managers set policy with no involvement of the rest of the corporation.

3. How much division of opinion regarding organizational goals exists within the organization? Organizational goals are not determined by a flip of the coin, nor are they usually set completely by outside agencies. They are determined by the people that compose the organization and the people who are served by the organization. Almost always, there will be some differences of opinion among the people who are in the organization or affected by the organization. When the organization is large and complex, not all of its members are equally committed to its goals. The persuasive communicator may find that it is easier to recruit adherents to a proposed change from those people who are not fully committed to the organization's stated goals.

4. What are the specific problems and pressures facing the organization? Any message that proposes to provide solutions for an organization's problems is going to be received with far more attention than one that merely promises to add to its problems. For example, if a school board currently faced with the necessity of coming up with a solution to racial imbalance is suddenly presented with a proposal to provide more music activities within the school district, we ought not to be surprised if that message fails to receive due consideration. No matter how much merit there may be in the proposal, or what problem the message proposes to attack, the board is all too likely to say, "Thank you for your interesting presentation," and then shelve all consideration of it until it solves what it believes to be its primary problem.

An organization that sees itself as under strong external pressures frequently is very difficult to change. The organization draws into itself, and refuses to pay attention to any messages that do not remove the pressures the organization feels. If a competitor is pressing strongly on an automobile company, for example, the company may refuse to listen to any advice on how to improve next year's cars. The organizaton *will*, however, be receptive to messages that promise to remove the pressures from the competitor. Finding what problems face a formal organization may be of distinct help in planning a persuasive message.

5. How does the communicator's intent relate to previous goals held by the organization? Most universities devote their attention to teaching, research, and service to the community. The goals of the organization are stated in terms of these three areas of concentration. But service has normally been defined in terms of assistance in research and planning to various agencies. Conducting an action program, such as running a birth control clinic, is a step that will be attacked on the grounds that it goes beyond the goals the university espouses. Suggesting that the clinic is being established in order to study the best way in which to organize birth control clinics may well result in acceptance of the proposal, since research is of high value to the university. The general rule is that new goals are seldom adopted if they represent a change felt to be far beyond goals and values currently held. Another way of looking at this question is to say that organizations seldom make sweeping changes. Persuasive communicators will increase their chances of success if proposed changes are presented as small extensions of established goals, or even better, if they appear to support an already established goal.

6. What is the reward structure of the organization? The ways in which an organization rewards the members of the organization is a strong indicator of the value placed on certain organizational goals. Thus the persuasive communicator who can tie an idea to that reward structure may strongly help influence the decision. Organizations that place a great deal of emphasis on merit increases, for example, tend to be organizations that also place high value on

productivity and innovation. Organizations that tend to give across-the-board raises to everyone, making no distinctions based on performance, tend to be maintenance oriented. The communicator who knows the organizational goals, can sometimes design messages to further those goals. For example, the source might suggest in the message that taking the proposed action will mean increased profits to be shared by all the members of the organization. Or the suggestion might be made that the proposed change will benefit the most effective sections in the organization.

7. How successful has the organization been in the past? Past accomplishments are frequently mentioned in a persuasive message and are interpreted in terms of organizational goals. The organization that has had a number of failures can be asked to look at those failures as evidence that they need new policies. The organization that has been very successful can be told that their very success makes it important to adopt the new policy so that the success will continue.

8. Finally, how do similar organizations operate? The spirit of competition is strong among many formal organizations. So also is the fear that another agency or organization might take part of the market or a portion of the task. The organization with strong maintenance goals is always fearful that something or someone will operate in such a way as to threaten the life of the organization. In such situations, the persuasive communicator can sometimes play off one organization against another, by introducing a change in one that the other has to adapt to, or even by suggesting that there might be such a threat from outside. If one automobile company can be persuaded to emphasize safety, it enhances the probability that another company can be induced to do the same thing.

This section has been concerned with the functions or goals of formal organizations and the relation of those goals to the intentions of persuasive communicators. The three functions

we discussed, productivity, maintenance and innovation are not, of course, the only functions that take place within a formal organization. They are, however, perhaps the three most important functions performed by any organization. Different organizations place varying importance on each of these goals. The communicator must understand the values placed on organizational goals by people within the organization in order to be successful in attempts to effect change in the organization.

ORGANIZATIONAL COMMUNICATION CONCEPTS

Organizations are formed in order to fulfill some perceived need within the society. Once a formal organization has been established varying patterns of communication will be adopted to achieve the goals. Formal organizations are composed of people, and people communicate with each other in order to achieve their goals. Farace, Monge and Russell[3] point to four major kinds of communication concepts as relating to the goals of formal organizations. The four concepts include:

1. Communication flexibility
2. The directionality of message flow
3. The initiation of messages within the organization
4. The amount of communication within the organization

Each of these concepts is also related to the potential success of persuasive communication within the organization, and deserves separate discussion.

Communication Flexibility

Every formal organization develops rules or norms for controlling the ways in which communication is allowed to flow within the organization. In some organizations, communication is initiated at the top of the organization, and flows down to the lowest level workers. Communication through other than those very formal channels is discouraged. Other organizations are far less formal, and communication is encouraged across the organization as well as up and down the organization. Such an organization tends to be far more flexible, and oriented more toward maintenance or innovation goals than toward productivity goals. We can distinguish between these two organizations on the basis of the degree of *flexibility* the organizations exhibit in their communication patterns. The organization with very strict rules, and limited communication patterns thus shows minimal flexibility, while the organization with many informal channels of communication and few restrictions will have high flexibility.[4]

It is not our task to suggest that either low flexibility or high flexibility is the more desirable state for an organization. The kind of flexibility the organization develops depends largely on the nature of the goals the organization has, the reward patterns that develop within the organization, and the authority structure the organization has developed. For example, in Figure 10.1 we see a set of communication patterns within an organization that has minimum flexibility. Reports flow up the organization on demand from the top, and orders flow down the organization. The communication pattern is inflexible, quite formal in nature, and follows the hierarchical arrangement of the positions within the organization. Figure 10.2 shows the same organization, but now there is a far more flexible set of rules governing communication within the organization. In Figure 10.2, the people at the same level in the organization, but in different divisions are encouraged to share information with their counterparts. The organization will have far more flexibility than the one depicted in Figure 10.1. Note that the organization depicted in Figure 10.2 is still not maximally flexible because communication between lower level workers in separate divisions does not occur.

There seems to be a tendency for any organ-

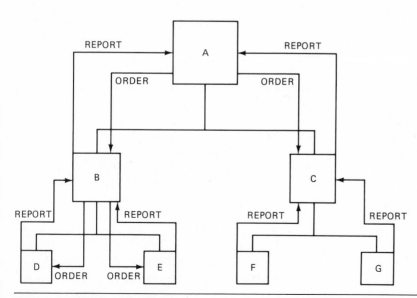

Figure 10.1 *Minimal Flexibility*

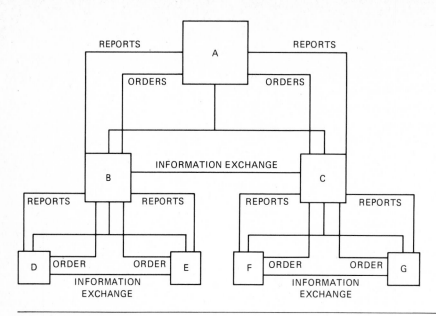

Figure 10.2 *High Flexibility*

ization to attempt to develop maximum flexibility. If the formal rules of the organization do not allow for flexibility, as in the case depicted in Figure 10.1, it is likely that an *informal* pattern of communication will develop, informal communication that seems to cut across the formal channels established by the organization. A secretary will learn about a new proposal before her boss finds out. The janitor will be knowledgeable about information supposedly known only at higher levels. Figure 10.3 shows the presence of a grapevine in a formal organization. Information passes to varying levels of the organization and across the organization in ways which do not correspond to the formal authority structure.

The presence of informal communication networks means that the persuasive communicator cannot depend solely on an analysis of the authority structure or of the formal rules of an organization to know something about the pattern of communication prevailing in an organization. An analysis must also be made of the possible informal networks that exist within the organization. This is easier if the individual is an insider in the organization. If the persuasive communicator is outside the organization, it may be necessary to develop contacts within the group at various levels in order to see what is happening.

Most organizations will develop both formal and informal networks of communication. An assessment of the flexibility of communication within any organization must also include an analysis of the informal channels in operation within the organization. A look at several kinds of organizational characteristics will help the persuasive communicator in making predictions about the success of a message.

1. Organizations which exhibit high degrees of flexibility or which have well-developed grapevines tend to have high levels of knowledge among members. Such flexibility allows for the transmission of information to every member of an organization, rather than only to

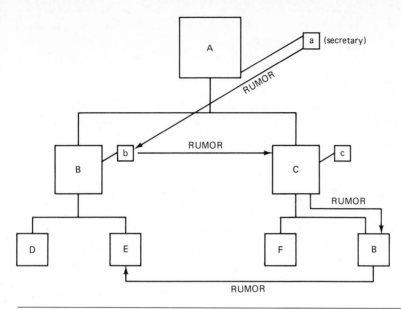

Figure 10.3 *An Informal Network*

those people in authority positions. The communicator can often use such channels to avoid material being buried at any given level. There are two disadvantages in working with such an organization. First, there are times when a persuasive communicator might not want information to reach all members of the organization, and that is difficult to prevent when there is high flexibility. Second, the opportunities for distortion of the message are greater when there is a strong grapevine operating. Because the message has not been authorized for transmission, the people who obtain and pass it along are frequently not accurate in transmitting the message.

2. Grapevines can frequently be used to sound out the members of an organization. Frequently, individuals in positions of authority will leak information into an informal network as a test. If there seems to be general acceptance of an idea, the message is then placed within the formal system and passed on as policy. If the message provokes significant objec-

tions while it is in the informal network, the individual releasing the information can deny making the proposal, and thus, avoid losing credibility or authority. Sometimes, the communicator can reach an individual who is not willing to commit to a proposal, but is willing to leak the proposal.

We should note that this suggestion of "floating a trial balloon" works best in those organizations in which there is a grapevine. In those situations where there is very high flexibility, the trial balloon idea does not always work. When everyone in the organization has easy access to everyone else, it is easy to check on the accuracy of any new idea with other people in the organization.

3. Organizational flexibility is closely related to the accuracy with which a message is received within an organization. An organization which has high flexibility is one that encourages feedback, and individuals within the organization are thus able to check the accuracy of any persuasive messages that have been

transmitted within the organization. On the other hand, an organization which has relatively low formal flexibility, but a well-developed grapevine may have a tendency to distort any persuasive messages transmitted within the organization. Feedback is more difficult when a grapevine is being used, since checking accuracy is not sanctioned in any official manner. Furthermore, in the formal channel, the message may be written down, thus serving as a check on any possible distortion. The informal channel is more likely to make use of oral communication, and thus increase the possibility that a message will be distorted as it passes from person to person. This is a disadvantage because a persuasive message placed by an outside communicator into a channel may become completely distorted and yet the source will have no opportunity to correct the message.

4. There are few checks on the operation of compliance in an informal channel. When a message ordering some action, or even suggesting some action, is transmitted within a formal network, the individual occupying a higher position has the power to urge compliance on those in lower positions. For the message that passes through the informal network, however, no such compliance mechanism is present. The message will have to succeed or fail on its own merits.

We should note that compliance is also difficult to secure in a highly flexible organization. Such organizations typically encourage communication between members of the organization, and when debate, argument, or suggestions are encouraged, compliance is harder to secure. Persuasion has to depend more on the merits of the issue, and less on the position of the source, or the social power the source might possess.

5. Flexibility may be controlled within an organization, and an organization can help to determine over time just how much flexibility it is likely to have. There is no way to determine just how a grapevine is likely to be organized or how it will operate. For example, there may be a grapevine composed of all members of the organization who attend the same church, or who went to school together, or who are in the same car pool. An individual who is in one informal net as a member of a car pool may be in another as a member of the company bowling team. One network may overlap with another solely as a result of this one individual. Predicting exactly who will be in a particular network is difficult, and this may result in the failure of a message to pass through the network. Most organizations include both formal and informal networks. Which can be used with the most effectiveness is a decision that the communicator will make after careful analysis of the situation.

Communication flexibility is an important characteristic of any formal organization. It is closely related to accuracy of information transmission within the organization, and to organizational goals. Formal organizations develop rules and norms regarding information transmission within the hierarchy, and frequently develop informal channels that bypass the formal communication networks.

Direction of Communication

Organizations develop characteristic methods of communicating within the hierarchical levels composing the corporation, agency, or social club. In some organizations, communication between sections of the same agency or corporation is not encouraged. Managers are told to report to their superiors, and when the messages have reached the top of the organization, they are then relayed down to the appropriate section. This is an example of strong *vertical* communication—the transfer of information between successively higher levels of authority. Such an organization will exhibit relatively little *horizontal* communication, that is, the transfer of information between units on the same level. In organizations that have strong vertical patterns, one section will know little about the work of another section. In such a situation, the communicator enhances the chances of effecting changes by being able to place the message as close as possible to the top, since it will then have less chance of being distorted. Information introduced into a communication channel at any level *may* reach the top, but the probability is considerably lower than the probability that messages put in at the top will reach individuals at the lower levels. Many corporations are organized in this fashion, while governmental agencies tend to be organized in such a way that a great deal of horizontal communication occurs.

In other organizations, information and ideas are received at the top, and orders are issued from the top. Members of the organization in lower positions do not ordinarily have much to say about the operation of the group. Such a communication pattern is typically found in a family-owned-and-operated corporation or in a firm that depends on the inventions of its president for its very existence. It might also be found in certain social clubs having essentially a strong-man type of leadership. Such an organization can be thought of as one with heavy downward communication. The role of the persuasive communicator in this situation is obvious. Messages that are not directed to the person at the top or at people very near the top are not likely to succeed.

A third type of communication pattern is one in which there is a great deal of communication across the organization. Every project is checked with all divisions and sections before it is introduced as practice. These organizations can be extremely frustrating to an individual wishing to introduce change. Using horizontal communication patterns takes time, time in large chunks. In one university, a course proposal typically took five years from the time a professor had the initial idea until it was finally adopted and taught. Every possible governing and administrative body in the institution had

to examine the proposed course, making suggestions and comments, before the course was finally approved. The professor initially proposing the course might very well feel that suggesting innovations was hardly worthwhile, since ideas might become out of date by the time they were finally adopted. Such organizations make very few errors in judgment, but they also make very few changes in their policies and behavior.

Sometimes, it is possible to cut across channels in such an organization, but the communicator who does so may run the risk of achieving a temporary gain and losing any further advantages. Organizations with this type of communication pattern tend to react negatively to attempts to cut across channels, and subsequent proposals are likely to be buried in the bureaucracy. Thus, the persuasive communicator must normally expect to take the time required for such an organization to process and make decisions about a proposal, frustrating as this process can sometimes be.

A final type of communication pattern is one in which there is considerable autonomy among various sections, with communication to the top for information purposes only. Many partnership organizations follow this organizational pattern. Here, the major problem the communicator faces is in finding the right section of the organization to which to make an initial appeal. If there is some success with one section of the organization, it may be that the rest of the organization will respond with little further effort needed on the part of the source.

Our discussion, of course, has used examples illustrating the importance of directionality which are fairly simple. In reality, most organizations have more balanced directional communication patterns than the defining examples we have cited. There is generally communication across the organization, as well as communication from both the bottom and the top. Nevertheless, organizations do tend to favor one kind of pattern over others, and a careful analysis of the type of communication pattern being primarily used is necessary if success is to be assured.

Initiation of Communication

We have already discussed the directional flow of information within organizations. Now we can also consider the way in which messages are initiated within the organization. Organizations differ with respect to the place from which messages typically start, and this variable can become important to the persuasive communicator.

In many organizations, all messages emanate from the top and flow to the bottom. There will be a request for information sent to lower levels, and when the information has been supplied, the response will eventually take the form of orders sent to those same people. In such organizations, both the requests for information and the eventual actions emanating from that information originate at the top. The evidence suggests that the best estimate of how much an individual engages in communication is the individual's status within the organization. Higher status people communicate more, and are better informed about the affairs of the organization.[5]

Obviously, persuasive communicators will have considerable difficulty in reaching such organizations. It may be necessary to convince the person occupying the highest position in the organization in order for messages to be welcome within the organization. This tends to take away certain lines of argument from the persuasive communicator. It is difficult to argue for a course of action that will benefit the entire organization, since top down organizations are less concerned with the total membership of the organization than they are with the people at the top. Another difficulty in reaching people in an organization where messages are initiated by those at the top, is that there is typically a considerable degree of isolation of that individual. It is hard to get to such people in order to deliver persuasive messages.

In contrast to the organization where all messages tend to originate from a single source, other formal organizations encourage communication from all levels of the organization. If people at the lowest operating level of the organization have questions, problems, or suggestions, they are encouraged to voice them to anyone in the organization. If people have ideas, they are encouraged to submit the ideas to higher levels. There are, of course, requests for information from higher levels in the organization and orders sent from higher levels. But the more open organization will encourage people to send information that may not have been specifically requested, and will encourage people to suggest modifications to orders that have been issued.

It is generally easier for the persuasive communicator to work in an organization where communication is encouraged from all members of the organization. Persuasive messages can be legitimately fed into the system by any person in the organization. If the persuasive communicator is already an insider, there is little problem in initiating a message to the other members of the organization. If the communicator is an outsider, it is necessary to convince only a single person within the organization to begin sending the message. This is a sharp contrast to the organization where only a single person is empowered to initiate messages.

We have discussed the initiation of messages as if there were only two types of formal organizations with respect to this variable. Our descriptions are of extremes, and probably describe nonexistent organizations. Most formal organizations will tend to fall either toward the side where messages are originated primarily from a small set of top level officers, or will be of the type where more people are encouraged to initiate messages. There are few, if any, organizations in which every member of the organization is given equal freedom to initiate messages. Similarly, there are few, if any, organizations in which only a single person is allowed to initiate communication. The variable *is* an important one for persuasive communicators to consider, because of the differences in approaching organizations which vary along this dimension of organizational communication.

Amount of Communication

Some organizations are oriented to the production of goods. Ford Motor Company has as its primary goal the production of automobiles, and one will expect any communication that flows within that organization to be limited to that which is necessary to produce automobiles and to maintain the organization. In contrast, the Rand Corporation has communication as one of its major products, in that it is engaged primarily in research studies. That corporation will produce far more communication during an equivalent period of time than will the Ford Motor Company. Thus, one can talk about the amount of communication that is being processed in an organization.

Farace, Monge and Russell[6] note that it is possible to distinguish between organizations on the basis of the proportion of time and resources specifically budgeted for communication activities versus those budgeted for actual manufacture of goods. To arrive at such a figure, we must look at all of the communication activities of an organization, such as the paperwork processed, meetings held, memos produced, and the frequency with which people talk to one another during work hours. Such an examination will allow us to characterize communication as ranging from high amounts of communication to low amounts of communication being processed by the organization.

Why should the persuasive communicator be interested in the amount of communication that is being processed by the organization? There are several reasons. In organizations that process heavy loads of communication, the addition of one more message may have little effect. The one persuasive message, may, among all of the other messages being processed in the organization, not be noticed at all. In contrast, a per-

suasive message sent to or emanating from an organization which does not have a heavy communication load may stand out, and be reacted to more strongly.

Our first reason suggests that persuasive communication may be more effective in organizations which do not have a heavy communication load. This has to be tempered somewhat by the fact that some organizations do not have adequate mechanisms for processing information. In a plant which is engaged in manufacturing, and where the primary goal of the organization is productivity, there may be few ways of legitimately introducing persuasive messages. Organizations which do not have a heavy communication load sometimes do not have ways of handling messages which suggest change, and the message may be rejected before it can reach the members of the organization. Such organizations are frequently not receptive to any messages other than those that promise increases in productivity.

Organizations which engage in large amounts of communication processing as a primary function are frequently used to making careful evaluations of persuasive materials. They frequently must make decisions between competing products, competing research projects, and competing ideas. The persuasive communicator who wishes to introduce change or new ideas into such an organization may find it difficult. The organization may have elaborate procedures of making evaluations of proposals, or may have rules controlling the flow of communication through the organization. In contrast, while it may be difficult to get a message into an organization that does not have much of a communication load, the message may have far greater impact once it has been introduced.

The amount of communication, along with communication flexibility, the directionality of message flow within the organization, and the source of communication within the organization are important variables for the persuasive communicator to consider. A successful communication strategy will depend on being able to make an analysis of the organization in terms of these four communication concepts, and then on planning the tactics to use in approaching the organization.

ORGANIZATIONAL EXPECTATIONS

Every formal organization develops a set of expectations about the way in which its members ought to behave, about the ways in which new information is sought, and about the ways in which decisions ought to be made within the organization. In this section we shall look first at some of the ways in which organizations control the ways in which information is sought and processed, and then examine some of the characteristic ways in which organizations attempt to solve the problems that arise in attempting to reach the goals of the organization.

Information Seeking

Every organization must develop ways of processing the information and the messages it receives. Even if the organization does not have a large amount of information to process, there are still going to be some rules and norms for handling information. For many organizations, of course, one of the primary goals of the organization is to handle information. Such organizations become very complex and develop elaborate rules. The federal government provides an excellent example of the complexity that can develop within an organization in the processing of new messages, persuasive or otherwise. Imagine that you wish to suggest a change in a current government policy. You write a letter to the agency concerned. The letter is likely to be read by a clerk who then routes it to the section of the agency where he or she thinks it belongs. Then another clerk will dispatch the letter to an individual in that section charged with answering letters from the public. If you are lucky at that point, you will receive a polite letter thanking you for your

concern and either giving a reason why your suggestion cannot be adopted or assuring you that it will be given careful consideration. It is necessary to include the phrase, "if you are lucky," because the letter may still not have reached the right section of the agency, or even the right agency, and the entire process may have to be repeated. Even if you have reached the right section, the message will have been read by three or four people, none of whom are likely to have any real decision-making powers within the organization.

If you had picked a large corporation, the results might be much the same. These examples suggest that many organizations do not actively seek information from outside, and certainly do not seek it from unsolicited sources. Organizations tend to react to new information or to persuasive messages in ways that entail minimum effort for the organization. The people who have the power to effect change seldom are exposed to messages advocating change.

These examples do not mean that individual persuasive efforts will never have any effect in getting behavioral changes adopted in large formal organizations. They simply mean that the probabilities of success must be increased through imaginative efforts on the part of the communicator. What can a persuader do to increase the probability that a message will have some impact on a formal organization. Several steps can be suggested:

1. Can the name of a specific individual in charge of a relevant section be secured? In large organizations, messages addressed simply to "Company X" are not likely to get to an individual who could handle the problem. If the name of a particular individual can be secured, the probability of success or at least attention can be raised.

2. Can an individual be found within the organization who is willing to carry messages and support the communicator? A letter from the outside or a telephone call may carry little weight with decision makers in an organization.

If the persuasive communicator is able to find and convince some present member of the organization that a particular persuasive intent is desirable, the probabilities are increased that attention will be paid to the message. Note, however, that the selection of an insider is important. If the individual selected has little status, the communicator might be worse off.

3. Who is the persuasive communicator? It may not be fair that one source will have more weight with an organizaton than will another, but that is the way it is, as our earlier discussion of credibility suggested. In approaching a corporation or a government agency with a proposal, the person who is writing the letter, making the telephone call, or talking to a member of the organization, does make a difference. It may well be that the first step will be to convince a credible communicator to carry a message.

4. How many people are supporting the proposed move? A single individual may have a large effect on an organization, but this is the exception and not the rule. More frequently, suggestions by the average individual are taken very lightly. When more than one individual makes the same suggestion, the establishment tends to wake up. This does not mean that great attention is paid to form letters or to petitions. Most congressmen and government agency officials say that they do pay close attention to carefully worded and individualistic letters, but they do not respond favorably or even pay attention to form letters or petitions signed with many names. Collecting names for a petition is easy to do, regardless of the subject. What this means is that the communicator who wishes to get through to an organization must be able to coordinate the efforts of many people, yet appear to have those individuals acting independently. This is not easy, but it has been done in past campaigns.

5. What does the message have to offer to the organization? This question is related both to organizational goals and to organizational expectations. What it suggests is that organizations treat messages differently. Messages that offer nothing to the organization, either in helping it attain its goals, or in correcting deficiencies, are not nearly as successful as those that purport to offer such help.

Formal organizations have many of the same characteristics that individuals do. This is not surprising, since they are comprised of individuals. Why *should* they change their procedures? Why should they attempt to install expensive devices to control pollution? Why should they donate money to the Community Chest? If the persuasive communicator cannot show an organization just how the proposals will help the organization, the information-processing channels of the organization are likely to reject the message.

These five questions are all related to the expectations organizations develop, expectations regarding the ways in which information will be received and processed by the organization. Formal organizations develop such procedures in order to protect the integrity of the organization and in order to handle large amounts of information more effectively. If the organization expected every member, every worker to read or listen to all of the information it received, the chances are that the organization would spend all of its time reading and listening while working little. For this reason, it sets up a series of expectations and procedures to handle information, and then translates those expectations into a set of operating procedures within the organization. Those procedures must be understood by the communicator if there is to be any hope of the message reaching the relevant people.

Decision Making and Persuasion

Many different ways exist for an organization to make decisions. Typically, organizations will adopt a method which fits the personalities of the members of the organization, which is in accordance with the goals of the organization, and which fits the communication characteristics of the organization. In this section, we shall examine three general approaches to problem solving in formal organizations: avoidance of uncertainty; conflict resolution; and decision through personal power.

Avoidance of Uncertainty

Avoiding uncertainty is a method of organizational choice that resembles dissonance reduction for the individual, and is equally important. There are many points of similarity between the two concepts. Most organizations today face uncertain futures. A government agency does not know whether Congress is going to continue its operation or, if so, at what level the operation will be continued. A corporation does not know whether its products will be declared unsafe and banned from the market, whether it will have the same overseas markets it had last year, or whether it will be attacked for polluting the environment with a product that seemed safe a year ago. The school board is uncertain about whether citizens will pass a bond issue, whether it will have to invest in a large fleet of buses, or even whether it can predict the number of students it will have. In the face of these uncertainties, many organizations opt for a decision-making style that attempts to avoid uncertainties. There are a number of characteristic ways in which organizations can do this, and each way suggests certain strategies the change agent can use to attain a persuasive goal:

1. Organizations evolve *short-run*, decision-making methods that are used in place of longer-run methods. Uncertainties grow larger as the time span of consideration grows longer. If an organization has to make "five-year plans," the uncertainties inherent in such a period of time are quite large. Thus, the organization places its strongest emphasis on solving

those problems that seem immediate. Thus the persuasive communicator wishing to achieve change must appeal to short-run problems if the decision-making apparatus of the organization is to be able to respond to the message.

2. Formal organizations develop *traditions* that attempt to avoid all new decisions. When the organization can point to a tradition and say, "We have always done it this way," the possibilities for the introduction of uncertainty are reduced. In essence, this method avoids the decision that might arouse uncertainties as to the adequacy and acceptability of the decision. If the organization can point to a tradition or a set of rules of conduct as an excuse for failing to open discussion on a topic likely to raise the uncertainty level, the necessity for making decisions is reduced, and the organization will feel more comfortable.

Many organizations develop elaborate sets of standard operating procedures that attempt to take care of all possible problems. Other organizations develop methods by which all possible conflicts can be referred to a negotiating committee.

There are benefits in working with organizations that attempt to reduce all uncertainties: some decision is going to be made about every persuasive message that is received. Having unanswered messages raises the uncertainty level. But it also suggests that the decisions about messages are likely to be negative, because positive reactions to persuasive messages mean that there will be changes of some sort, and change tends to mean uncertainty.

3. Formal organizations attempt to protect the entire organization from uncertainty by *shifting potentially disturbing proposals* to a small section of the organization. Thus, the corporation has its planning committee, and the city council establishes a planning commission. These smaller groups protect the larger group from being exposed to potentially disturbing communication. A controversial proposal can be buried in a planning group for years and years, until the necessity for its introduction

has long passed, or until it can be modified in ways that might be more acceptable.

The best persuasive tactic in this type of organization is to put pressure on the planning committee or the program development committee to release and approve the proposal. If this does not work, the communicator must almost always fall back on attempting to have the details of the proposal made public through the rest of the organization, and hope that public opinion will eventually force the proposal out of the planning group. The danger here, and it is a real one, is that the planning group, in feeling threatened, will release the proposal with a negative recommendation.

A decision model based on the reduction of uncertainty suggests that a communicator who can place suggestions within the context of an organization's traditions or rules will have a better chance of succeeding than one who has to buck a set of established rules. Most organizations include a method for the disposing of communications that come into the organization.

Conflict Resolution

Organizations typically have a general set of goals to which every member of the organization subscribes at least nominally. Each section of the organization, however, will have a set of private goals that are unique to it, and each member of the organization will also have a set of unique personal goals. Inevitably, many of these goals will be conflicting. Sales divisions are always pushing for more salesmen. Production units want to have more technicians to produce higher quality products. The fiscal department wants to hold down the number of workers at all levels in order to cut costs. Individuals want to have higher wages and more responsibility while top management wants to retain its power, keep salaries down, and profits up. These different individual and departmental goals can produce conflicts.

When conflict resolution is used as the method to make decisions, the attempt will be to resolve as many of the conflicts between individuals and sections as possible. This procedure usually results in very small gains for everybody, and large gains for nobody. Personnel departments are awarded some additional control over hiring people, but production supervisors are given more control over setting quality standards. Any proposal that is made to the organization is evaluated in terms of the amount of conflict that it might cause within the organization. Proposals are likely to be avoided if they might result in conflicts. In other words, the decisions and choices an organization makes are made against a background of conflict avoidance and resolution.

What does this method of organizational choice mean for the persuasive communicator? Persuasive messages are deliberately designed to induce change—changes in attitudes, perceptions, emotions, and actions—and change is likely to cause conflict within an organization. When an organization is highly dependent on conflict resolution as a generalized method of solving problems, persuasive messages must have something for everyone. Large gains will be difficult to achieve, and the message that promises to introduce the smallest changes with the least amount of conflict is likely to be the more successful.

Although the persuasive communicator cannot expect success with a message that seems to imply the introduction of conflict into the organization, the message that promises to reesolve conflict may be a highly successful one. This has caused the development of tactics in which a highly threatening message is transmitted to the organization, and then the real message, one that promises to resolve the problem and avoid the threatened conflict is sent. Such tactics have proved very successful in a number of situations.

Conflict may be introduced by any message relating to an existing frame of reference. When a message impinges on a current practice or becomes particularly relevant to an individual or subgroup of individuals within the organization, the probability of conflict increases. This suggests that one strategy of persuasive communication is to avoid questions of winning and losing. Changing the frame of reference so that it does not seem relevant to any one individual or group of individuals may result in an increased probability of success for the message.

It should be noted at this point that organizations do not advertise the way in which they make decisions. The communicator has to study the organization in order to determine how it makes its decisions. For example, in many government organizations, any proposal has to pass through an entire echelon of officials before it can be adopted. Each official seeing the proposal has to "sign off" on that proposal. If any one person has suggestions, they are added, and then the proposal goes back down the chain of organization while everybody "signs off" on each of the changes. The final result is not likely to produce much conflict. Neither is it likely to represent a large stride forward. This is decision through conflict resolution, and such organizations present problems to the persuasive communicator.

Decision through Personal Power

Some organizations vest all final decision-making power in a single man at the top. The individual may own the organization, or may be given the power by a board of governors. Such organizations are both easy and difficult to approach. If it is possible to get to the man at the top, the decision can be made without further reference to any one else. However, such individuals usually protect themselves from all outside influence, and the communicator will be traveling from underling to underling, each listening, but promising nothing. If any one feels that the proposal has merit, he will pass the message along, but if any one of the underlings feels that the proposal is not worthy of further consideration, he usually has the power

to kill it, even though he doesn't have the power to pass favorably on it.

What is particularly frustrating is that it may be difficult to find out that decisions are actually made at the top. Each subordinate listens and talks as if he had power. In the end, he simply asks the communicator to talk to one more individual. In spite of this pattern, several suggestions can be made about dealing with an organization which concentrates power at the top:

1. Attempt to apply outside pressure on the organization. It is quite frequently the case that the top man in such an organization is a member of several community groups. It may be possible to get action started in such a group to approach the man directly, and influence him from the outside, when he is not able to be influenced from the inside.

2. Start action within the organization at a number of different levels. Even though a single person holds final decision-making power an analysis of such decisions would suggest that his decisions do not tend to go against the majority of the other employees. If some pressure can be placed at various levels of the organization, the chances are enhanced that action can be taken.

3. Begin a mass action campaign. Organizations in which power is concentrated at the top are particularly susceptible to such campaigns. In an organization where power is distributed at various levels, the mass campaign tends to have its effects blunted through the necessity of contacting many individuals. In one where the "heat" can be placed on a single individual, such campaigns have had much better success.

4. Approach the organization through a member of the controlling board. All corporations that issue public stock, most universities, and even many privately held corporations have a board of trustees or a board of directors who set broad policy for the organization and oversee the "top man". It may be possible to gain entry to the organization by persuading a mem-

ber of the board and using that as an entry to the rest of the organization.

Regardless of the methods used, such organizations are not easy for the persuasive communicator to reach. The main advantage to tackling such an organization is that when a decision if finally reached, the communicator is usually assured the change will actually be made, and will not be blunted by additions and changes made to the proposal by various subordinates.

This section has studied the formal organization in much the same way we study an individual. Many of the same concepts seem applicable to both. Organizations can be described in terms of their goals, their expectations, and the way they make decisions. Every organization develops characteristic ways of reacting to these variables, and the persuasive communicator must carefully analyze these variables to attain a goal.

The warning mentioned earlier should be repeated. Organizations may be viewed as individuals, and viewed profitably in this way, but they are not individuals. The establishment *is* composed of individuals, individuals who differ in their own goals, expectations, and decision-making processes. What this indicates is that an organization is far more variable than is an individual, and predictions about the probable behavior of an organization cannot be made at a level of confidence as high as those made for an individual.

SUMMARY

Much persuasion has to be carried out within formal organizations. Our nation is composed of many different groups: government groups at the federal, state and local level; corporations ranging from giants such as General Motors to the small restaurant around the corner; educational organizations; service organizations; and many, many more. All of these formal organizations are groups of people that may affect persuasion and be affected by it.

If persuasive communicators are going to be successful, they must be able to work within and with formal organizations. They have to reach such organizations, either as insiders or as outsiders with a message for the members of the group.

Many factors affect the receptivity that the persuasive communicator might expect to find for any message. The goals the organization has established are important factors in the way in which the group will receive and act upon persuasive messages. The expectations that members of the organization have, and the ways in which decisions are made are all important to the kinds of messages that are produced and transmitted to the organization.

The structure of the organization, whether tightly or loosely organized, may make a difference in persuasion. The types of communication patterns, the characteristic ways in which information is received and processed by the organization may make a difference, as do the people who occupy positions within the organization. Persuasion may well depend on reaching an individual who has real power in the organization before actual change will occur.

FOOTNOTES

1. Martha A. Jacob, "The Structure and Functions of Internal Communication in Three Religious Communities," (Ph.D. dissertation, Michigan State University, 1972).

2. Richard V. Farace, Peter R. Monge, Hamish M. Russell, *Communicating and Organizing*, (Reading, Mass.: Addison-Wesley Publishing Co.), 1972, pp. 55–59.

3. *Ibid.*, p. 76.

4. Our analysis of the communication relationships and the structure of formal organizations owes much to the following sources: P. R. Monge, J. A. Edwards and K. K. Kirste, "The Determinants of Communication and Communication Struture in Large Organizations: A Review of Research," in B. D. Ruben, ed., *Communication Yearbook 2*, (New Brunswick, New Jersey: Transaction Books, 1978) pp. 311–31; A. C. Sanford, G. T. Hunt and H. J. Bracey, *Communication Behavior in Organizations*, (Columbus, Ohio: Charles E. Merrill Publishing Co., 1976), pp. 3–35; and R. M. Cyert and J. G. March, *A Behavioral Theory of the Firm*, (Englewood Cliffs, N.J.: Prentice-Hall, 1963).

5. R. V. Farace and M. Pacanowsky, "Organizational Communication Role, Hierarchal Level and Relative Status," paper presented to the Academy of Management Association, Seattle, Washington, 1974.

6. Farace, Monge, and Russell, *Communicating and Organizing*, pp. 97–125.

ELEVEN

SOCIAL ACTION

...d the 1970s was *change*. Societies around the world were rapidly ch... ...s we moved from an era dominated by the great colonial powers to an era of nationalism. If we had attempted to predict the 60s and 70s from the relatively safe and calm era of the 1930s or even the 1950s, the chances are that we would have missed most of the significant events of the two decades. Who would have predicted the Viet Nam war? Would anyone have argued for Watergate and its effects? What brave seer would have predicted a peace treaty between Egypt and Israel?

I do not think it any more possible to predict what changes will take place within our society during the 1980s than to have been able to make a prediction about the two decades just past. What is certain, however, is that there will be continual change in the political, social, economic, religious and educational institutions within society. Even a cursory analysis of history tells us that the one thing we can count on is that things are always changing. Sometimes the changes seem to occur slowly, as is typically the case in small, agrarian or tribal societies. Sometimes, the change occurs very rapidly, as was the case in the first few decades following the Industrial Revolution. Even during the "Dark Ages" social changes were occurring and each decade, each century can be differentiated from those preceding and following it.

It sometimes can seem as if changes in the world occur randomly. One can get the feeling that the average person is just being swept along, as if society does not involve people and people can do nothing to change their lives. This feeling—labeled *anomie*—can be placed in sharp contrast with our previous view of persuasion as a primary tool in assisting our desire to understand, control, and manipulate our world. If we look at specific instances of social change, however, we must agree that they *do* involve people— people working together, learning together and talking together.

The overthrow of the Shah of Iran in 1979 involved people working very closely together for many months. Passing a tax limitation proposal in California and Michigan took the efforts of several thousand people involved in direct efforts and the eventual agreement of several millions of people. Getting an open housing ordinance passed in Detroit involved people who became concerned and who expressed their concerns in a persuasive form to those in legislative power. Change may seem random, but it always involves the pushing and pulling, the moving forward and holding back of the people in our society. Engaging in the attempt to either change society or to preserve society is a characteristic of mankind that extends back to the times when our hominid ancestors walked the savannahs of Africa.

The United States has always been characterized by the extent to which people and groups engage in social action. Our society was founded on a successful attempt to bring about change. We have struggled and fought to preserve the right to make changes in our government and in our institutions. At any given time in a typical community in the United States, one group will be agitating for a new swimming pool, another group for increased taxes for schools, a third group for reducing taxes, and a fourth for increased opportunities for minority members of the community. Some people in the community may be working for an organized civic club, others for a student social club, still others for a corporation, or for a local political party. Sometimes, people work as individuals, at other times, they join with other members of the community. In each case, they are engaged in *social action, the process by which decisions are made and actions taken in communities, institutions, organizations and countries.*

When social change is examined closely, two characteristics are apparent. First, it is clear that not all social action campaigns are or can be successful. If one group is successful in getting a school millage proposal passed, another group may fail in getting a bond issue passed for a new stadium. Success in getting increased welfare payments may mean that better garbage collection may have to be postponed. Success in getting an increased number of minority students on a student governing board may mean that another group will fail in their attempt to cut student taxes. Simons points out that persuasion inevitably means conflict between ideas, people, and groups of people.[1] Conflict may be an inevitable product of social change and may always accompany the attempts of people to change the environment in which they live. Being successful in achieving some persuasive goal, then, may depend on the effectiveness of the way in which a campaign is organized and carried out. If every successful campaign means that another campaign will fail, the campaign with the better organization ought to have the best chance of succeeding.

A second characteristic of social change depends on the distinction between violent and peaceful change. It is possible to achieve social change by violent means. The history of war and bloodshed in our past illustrates that possibility all too well. But it is also possible to achieve social change through peaceful means. In that case, social action depends heavily on persuasion as the means by which social change can be achieved. Persuasion is involved at almost every step of the way, from the time when someone gets an idea for a change to the moment when that idea is placed into action by the rest of society. In this chapter, we shall not discuss the use of violence to achieve change. The reader will find it easy to locate materials detailing man's attempts to change the behavior of other men through violence. We concentrate our attentions on tactics of change that do not involve violence as a planned strategy of change. First, we shall look at some of the recent tactics that people have used to achieve change, and then we shall look at a model of social action that will assist the persuasive communicator in designing campaigns for change.

TACTICS FOR CHANGE

The past two decades have seen the full development of strategies for changing society. The methods we describe below are by no means new to the world. Most of them, in one form or another, have been around for hundreds of years. The Committees of Correspondence of the American Revolution are not much different from the opinion letter writing campaigns conducted by the John Birch Society or by those interested in abolishing abortion. The difference lies in the fact that we are now able to study many of these tactics, and to make assessments of their effectiveness. Some of the tactics have been highly successful. Others have produced no real changes. In this section, we shall analyze some of the methods used, and the results secured by those methods. The reader who wishes to obtain an analysis of various tactics is referred to Saul Alinsky's book *Rules for Radicals*[2] which presents a careful philosophical analysis of the success that varying groups have had in achieving change. Here, we look at some of the more common techniques, techniques that are not beyond the scope of the average persuasive communicator. These techniques include (a) opinion letter writing campaigns, (b) petition drives, (c) mass demonstrations or marches, (d) mass strikes, slowdown activities, or economic boycotts, and (e) mass movements involving minor violence such as riots. These activities are not mutually exclusive, and proponents of a social program may utilize several techniques. They deserve separate analysis.

Opinion Letter Writing Campaigns

Almost everyone has felt the urge to sit down and write a letter to an editor or congressman complaining about some item. In the past decade, several groups have organized mass letter writing campaigns in which each member of the organization was urged to write a letter to a congressman, or to a corporation president urging some action. Conservative groups, radical groups, business groups, community groups, and millions of individuals write letters urging the support of organizational policies.

What effect does writing a persuasive letter have on its receivers? John Bear[3] reports very mixed results regarding the effects of opinion letter writing. For example, the Pillsbury Company, makers of Funny Face powdered drink mixes originally had two flavors labeled "Chinese Cherry" and "Injun Orange." Letters to the company were apparently responsible for the company's changing the names to "Choo Choo Cherry" and "Jolly Olly Orange."

If we look at more serious questions, however, the success of mass letter writing campaigns is less assured. Bear examined forty-four separate letter writing campaigns conducted by the John Birch Society in the five years from 1960 to 1965. The Society suffered thirty-four total failures, eight partial successes, and two total successes. Of these ten successes, however, no more than five could have been influenced by the efforts of the Society. They just happened to be cases in which the letter writing campaign of the Society corresponded with changes which the organizations concerned had already decided to make. Thus, the Society was perhaps responsible for changes in only five of forty-four campaigns.

The problem for the communicator rests on being able to generate high-quality letters. The letters written by members of the John Birch Society were low-quality letters for their audiences. Each one was approximately the same. Each one contained many of the same phrases suggested by the Society publication. The recipients of such letters apparently do not pay much attention to them, regardless of the number. On the other hand, testimony from many politicians, senators, and congressmen would indicate that individual letters, containing the writer's own language and thoughts, can be of real importance in changing attitudes and votes on crucial issues.

It is, apparently, relatively easy for a persuasive communicator to generate a real flood of letters to people in key positions. It is not so easy to generate letters of high quality, original in nature, and stating the writer's opinions in words that are not echoed by every other writer. Without originality, the letters are not likely to be of much importance in changing the opinions or behavior of an individual or a corporation.

Petition Drives

One of the most popular persuasive techniques is that of the petition drive. Hardly a day goes by in the United States when someone is not out trying to collect signatures on a petition. Petitions can be loosely divided into two types. The first is the petition attempting to *influence* potential legislation or policies. For example, in the late 1960s many people and groups collected signatures denouncing the war in Vietnam. Others have collected signatures in favor of abortion reform, for or against busing, and many others. This type of petition is difficult to assess. In general, such petitions do not seem to have much effect. Some organizers have estimated that it would be possible to collect fifty thousand signatures favoring the boll weevil in a few days. In general, then, petitions which merely indicate that a group of people favor or do not favor a current policy seem to have relatively little effect, except on the people who work at collecting signatures.

The second type of petition drive is more important. This is the drive to collect signatures to place an item on the ballot of a state or community. This type of drive *can* materially affect behavior. Drives have been successful in reducing the income tax, defeating additional property taxes, recalling politicians, and placing abortion reform on the ballot. Here, the

persuasive communicator is working for a specific end. Success depends on whether the issue can legitimately be placed on a ballot, and whether the number of signatures collected is the right percentage. The communicator will need to carefully study the state and local laws. In some cases, 10 percent of the voters must sign, in others a larger percentage is required. There may be restrictions as to the wording of the petition, and restrictions on the number of signatures per page. In some states, laws prevent petitions on certain kinds of measures, and a petition drive would be a waste of time.

The petition drive has proven to be an extremely useful weapon in the persuasive communicator's arsenal of tactics. We must hasten to note, however, that it is typically only a first step. After signatures have been gathered in sufficient numbers, the group advocating a change will still be faced with the necessity of conducting a campaign to assure that an eventual ballot proposal will be successful. That subsequent campaign will involve persuasion in the same way that the original drive did, but it will be directed toward all of the voters of a state, not just toward the committed individuals who signed the petition.

Mass Demonstrations or Marches

The mass demonstration, or march, probably saw its finest day during the late 1960s. The nation saw marches on Washington for peace, marches on many state capitols, marches on college campuses, and mass demonstrations in many places. Such demonstrations and marches have probably served their purpose. They were undoubtedly successful in maintaining a constant spotlight on the war in Viet Nam. Although we have no way of adequately documenting the fact, they may also have been important in changing official policy toward the war (even though there was little change in the conduct of the war). They were an important weapon of the blacks in being able to secure advances in education and working conditions for black people. The public may have become tired of mass demonstrations and may no longer support such persuasive attempts.

The general public did support such marches as long as they were a fresh attempt to do something about our problems. When massive marches on Washington did not seem to result in demonstrable gains for the marchers, however, the public grew disillusioned, and no longer supported such tactics. I do not want to dismiss these tactics too lightly. It is quite possible that in isolated cases, when the cause is local in nature, bringing together a large number of people to support a particular cause may be successful. Nevertheless the evidence indicates that such tactics may not be the most successful way of tackling many of our current problems.

The experience with mass marches and demonstrations suggests that there may be a cyclical nature to the acceptance of particular tactics. The public becomes turned off to a method after it has been used too frequently. For example, the farmers who drove tractors to Washington during the winter of 1979 were greeted with jeers in the press and massive indifference by the rest of the population. The tactic probably rebounded against the farmers' interests. The same tactic, in another day and another place, might have been considered an effective and innovative way of bringing legitimate complaints to the attention of the public.

A look at Iran during the last part of 1978 and the first part of 1979 suggests that the mass demonstration may not have seen its last. There is no question that the demonstrations in Iran were largely responsible for the downfall of the government of the Shah of Iran, although many observers have commented that the seeds for that overthrow were laid years before in his treatment of the populace. It should also be noted that the reaction of the government to the marches was to crack down with violent reprisals. The history of such reprisal attempts suggests that they usually have the ef-

fect of turning neutrals on the issue against the governments, not against the demonstrators. It may be a hard way to make a point, but it may also be the only way.

There is one major benefit to be derived from the involvement of masses of people in a demonstration or march. Even if the march is not successful in achieving its immediate objective, the people involved in the march usually have been convinced as to the justice or merits of the cause. They may be individuals upon whom the communicator can call for further efforts. Their behavior shows that they have become committed to the cause, and are likely to vote, or to take further actions favoring the cause of the persuasive communicator.

The facts are, however, that the mass demonstration, once rather effective, has lost much of its effectiveness. It may be that the pendulum will swing once again, but as this volume is being written, such tactics seem to have lost much of their effectiveness.

Strikes, Slowdowns, and Boycotts

The strike is a time-honored method of persuasion in the United States. From the time of the great Pullman strike of 1898 through the Ford sitdown strikes of the 1930s, to the many strikes we experience today, striking has been an effective weapon. In general, it has been used to advance the economic status or improve the working conditions of workers in specific plants or industries. In similar fashion, the work slowdown, or the boycott of a particular industry or product has frequently been successful in changing the attitude of an industry or a particular corporation.

In general, strikes, slowdowns, and boycotts have been successful only when performed by the employees of a particular company, who have had the time and the motivation to carry on the strike until management is forced either to close the organization or to bargain effectively with the workers. There are only a few cases of community groups being able to successfully carry out such tactics. One notable example came with the great "Grape Boycott" of the late 1960s when millions of people refused to buy grapes until the grape growers in California acceded to union demands. There is no direct evidence that the boycott was actually responsible for the growers' recognizing the union, but they eventually did so, and the boycott may have been at least partly responsible.

Many people have tried to organize tax boycotts, in which they attempt to get large numbers of people to refuse to pay their taxes until a particular policy has been changed. In general, these attempts have been unsuccessful. Some important publicity has been gained, but very few people actually have refused to pay their taxes. Students at the University of Michigan organized a renters' strike in which they refused to pay their rent until the apartment owners made certain concessions. Again, some concessions were made, but the total effect of the renters' strike is difficult to determine.

The major problem with a strike or a boycott is that it takes so much time to be successful that both sides tend to lose interest. A strike in the automobile industry, for example, will not be felt immediately by the parties concerned. Unions do have strike funds, and the impact on the workers is somewhat cushioned. States have unemployment insurance, so that workers in industries affected by the strike have the impact lessened. The company has built up a stockpile of automobiles to be sold, and it is not dramatically affected for some period of time. Experience has proved that it is very difficult to make the pressures so great that either side will capitulate in a short period of time.

There is an exception to this rule. There are certain tasks that must be accomplished. The strike of a garbage handlers union, for example, is felt within the first week. Although most states and communities outlaw strikes by state and municipal employees, strikes do occur, and have been relatively successful. The secret, of course, is that the service being performed has to be one that is not easily replaced, and that is considered vital by the public.

Organization of a strike, slowdown, or boycott is difficult. It takes much organization to get large numbers of people to engage in such activities. The typical persuasive communicator cannot be advised to completely forget the strike as a tool, but certainly the road ahead is both difficult, and possibly nonproductive. If the communicator has an organization that can make a strike meaningful, it may be worthwile exploring this tactic. Ordinarily, however, only the well-organized labor organization can expect to carry out such a strategy successfully.

Mass Violence and Riots

The 1960s and 1970s saw many examples of this tactic, both in the United States and around the world. From the riots in Watts and Detroit and Iran, to individual bombings by the Weathermen, the Irish Republican Army and the Palestine Liberation Organization, news of persuasion by violence has swept across our newspapers, and flooded the television screen. What has been the effect of the tactics of violence? No one can argue that violence has had no effect. The riots in Watts alerted large segments of the population in the United States to the fact that blacks had a number of grievances. The Students for a Democratic Society helped bring the Viet Nam war to the consciousness of a generation of students. The Palestine Liberation Organization finally focused the attention of the world on a long festering problem.

In 1970, when I was working on the second edition of this book, I argued that violent tactics seem to have little long range effect. I suggested that the buildings burned in Detroit were still there, remaining as mute mementoes to violence. Now, ten years later, I am not as positive that violence may not result in long run changes. Most of the burned out buildings are gone, and Detroit has entered into a new era of growth. Did the riots have anything to do with today's Detroit? Would Detroit have changed without the riots? The Palestine Liberation Organization has been fighting Israel for ten years or more. It may seem that violence has produced nothing of benefit to the Palestinians. Yet today, there is a peace treaty between Egypt and Israel, and at least the promise of a change for the West Bank and Gaza Palestinians. That area is not as far along as is Detroit, but there *is* change. Did the PLO have nothing to do with that change? I doubt that anyone would wish to argue that they have not affected current events.

The tactics of violence make headlines and draw the attention of millions of people to conditions about which they knew nothing. They undoubtedly have resulted in changes being made in policy and actions. Alinsky suggests that violence does have its place, but that permanent change through violence is difficult to achieve in our society. Permanent change results from successful attempts at breaking down the establishment, not at making that establishment draw together for mutual protection. One of the major results of the violence of the 1960s and 1970s seems to have been the drawing together of many establishment organizations in a united front against the forces of radical change. That drawing together, however, has also been characterized by changes in the establishment. The vote for eighteen-year olds, the pressure for equality for women, the growth of affirmative action programs and the liberalization of abortion laws are all establishment responses to the pressures of the 1960s and 1970s.

I personally do not feel that violence should be considered a legitimate tactic until all other tactics have been tried and failed. I also feel that violence will not be an acceptable tactic in the United States for the next decade. When tensions in a society are very high, as was the case during Viet Nam, violence may have the effects we have noted, but the aftermath of violence may result in a repression and a retrench-

ment in society that negates much of the change that was seemingly introduced by the more violent actions. There are better ways, and hopefully, our analysis of social action will point us toward them.

Each of the methods we have enumerated has been used by persuasive communicators in attempts to induce change within formal organizations, that is, within the establishment. Each method has had its adherents and its detractors, it successes and its failures. The persuasive communicator who wishes to obtain long-run changes ought to examine very carefully the results of mass campaigns. Certain elements have proved very useful, but many elements of such campaigns have been useful for very short-run efforts, and have not resulted in even semipermanent effects.

A MODEL FOR SOCIAL ACTION

The study of social changes within large social systems has traditionally been the central concern of sociologists. In more recent times the work of a number of rural sociologists has led to the formation of some working models describing instigated social changes. This research tradition got its start because of the relative ease of following the development of new ideas within relatively isolated rural communities. Since then, other social scientists have become interested in social change, and the early models have been refined to fit social systems other than the rural community.

Social scientists such as Paul Miller,[4] Charles Loomis,[5] Harold Kaufman,[6] Charles Hoffer,[7] and Christopher Sower,[8] have all presented models attempting to delineate the stages of a successful social action campaign. Paul Miller, for example, analyzed community health campaigns and suggested that they seemed to require four stages in their development:

1. Recognition of some prior social situation

2. Some initial activity on the part of individuals
3. The beginning of organized sponsorship of the proposed campaign
4. The organization of the entire community toward the mobilization of resources.[9]

Other descriptions have been suggested on the basis of investigation of social action campaigns. Rogers and Shoemaker[10] suggest a model attempting to account for the adoption of new ideas in communities all over the world. Their model is concerned with the diffusion of innovation within social systems. Normally, a researcher develops a model after extensive study of a campaign or a number of campaigns. The adoption of new farming practices, the change in a governmental body, successful or unsuccessful attempts at controlling pollution, working for new hospital facilities, and reorganizing school districts have all been studied as examples of social action campaigns.

It is possible to examine the role that persuasion plays in the social action process by comparing the viewpoints taken in the several models describing the process. Our approach, however, will be to take a model which seems to have very general applicability and base our discussion almost exclusively on that model. The model we have chosen to present has been adapted from one first developed by George M. Beal and Joe M. Bohlen. It was first used in the *National Project on Agricultural Communication* training workshops on communication. Since its original publication in 1956, Beal has suggested a number of changes in the construct.[11] For our discussion, we have retained the general framework suggested by Beal and Bohlen, but made a number of modifications in order to generalize the model to more situations, and to place persuasion more clearly within the model. Before presenting the model, however, there are some cautions that must be expressed. We, therefore, take up some of the problems with our model before presenting the stages of the model itself.

Cautions about Social Action

It is always tempting to present the social action model as if it were a series of prescriptions, prescriptions like aspirin or penicillin. The physician prescribes a drug in the hope that its application will result in a cure for some problem that has arisen. The steps in social action can be made to sound much the same as a doctor's prescription. If you read only the steps in the social action process, you might get the impression that all you had to do was to follow these steps, and you could cure any of the ills of the world. But the social action model is not a prescription for a society's problems.

The social action model was developed by looking at a number of successful and unsuccessful campaigns to change society or to introduce new ideas and practices. Social scientists attempted to identify the stages that seemed to be present in successful campaigns, and then looked to see what had been left out of unsuccessful campaigns. If the task could be done perfectly, the final description of stages would indeed represent a guide for successful social action. The problem is that we have not been able to examine all possible social action campaigns. Thus, there are a number of problems which limit the generalizability of the results we report.

1. The stages suggested here do not always occur in the same sequence for all ideas, all communities, and all people. Thus, it is impossible, or at least unwise, to follow the suggested time sequence slavishly, with no thought of possible deviations. One stage may follow another in one situation, and precede it in a second situation.
2. All stages are not present in all cases. In some cases a stage may occur several times, or not at all, or be telescoped into another stage.
3. Stages may occur simultaneously or overlap to a great extent and make careful separation necessary.

4. Even if the process is carefully followed, there may be competing ideas and programs which have also been carefully designed and the competing idea may be adopted rather than the first.

In spite of the fact that these problems can be identified, and some caution is necessary in the acceptance of the social action construct, I feel that this model has a number of advantages which recommend it to the prospective persuasive communicator.

1. The model identifies the stages or functions which seem to be embodied in social action campaigns. The stages are identified in such a manner that the necessary segmentation of the time sequence is divided into parts which can be handled operationally by the communicator who wishes to set up a campaign for change.
2. Although there may be variations in the way in which the stages occur, the construct seems to include all relevant stages.
3. The construct has been tested in a number of different situations and thus represents a model that can be used as a generalization for many social problems. Furthermore, an attempt has been made to reconcile the construct with the results of other studies and with the models suggested by other sociologists.
4. The construct is functional in the sense that it has actually been used as a plan of action for successful social action campaigns. It is not merely a dream of some theoretician. It *is* possible for an individual who has an idea and who wishes to introduce some social change into a community to use the social action construct as a plan of action, modified, of course, by the particular conditions in that community.

There are advantages and disadvantages to any model of social change. The social action construct we offer may not be the only approach which can be used. We offer it as an aid to the communicator who must secure community cooperation in getting ideas across.

STAGES IN SOCIAL ACTION

Below, we take up the stages in social change that have been identified by a number of researchers. We first describe the function played by each stage in the process, and then examine the role that persuasive communication may play.

STAGE 1: THE PRIOR SOCIAL SITUATION

Some social action campaigns fail because those in a particular social change have forgotten to make a careful analysis of the prior social situation existing in the group or community. For example, consider the case of the group wishing to pass a bond issue for a new swimming pool. If there has recently been a successful attempt to pass a bond issue for a new civic center, it may be that the campaign for a pool will fail, not because it isn't needed, but because citizens are not interested in taking on a new tax burden. Similarly, consider the case of the student group that wants to introduce a new student government organization on campus. If there has recently been such a reorganization, the new proposal, no matter how meritorious, may fail until the student body has had an opportunity to ascertain the results of the recent changes.

All social change takes place within the framework of a whole series of prior decisions, messages, and actions that communities, groups, and organizations have made in past years and months. Some of those decisions are ones which might actually facilitate the adoption of a new idea, if the idea can be tied to a previous decision. Other prior decisions may hinder *any* changes for a period of time.

If we consider some of the more recent massive social changes, it is easy to see that there had to be a set of prior conditions that facilitated the change. In Uganda, in Nicarauga, and in Iran, the lot of the average person had not improved, although the countries had large increases in their revenues. The perception that the revenues were going to only a few privileged people led to the revolutionary movements in those countries. The addition of information about conditions in other countries further fed the fires that fomented revolution within the country. Revolutionary activities would probably not have occurred, however, if the prior conditions had not set the stage.

Not only were there economic and political events that shaped the prior social situation, but also communication events that played a role. Other people have made persuasive speeches about the situation. Other people have called attention to a problem. The communicator is wise to pay attention to the role that prior communication has played in any particular situation. If the communicator has made no analysis of prior communication and prior decisions, there can be no effective use of past experiences. Many of the most persuasive ideas and techniques that are incorporated into messages are drawn from prior events within a community. Recounting the automobile accidents at a corner over the past year may be enough to insure the placement of a stop sign at an intersection. Only an analysis of the prior social situation will allow the communicator to have the information necessary to avoid making serious errors in the presentation of ideas.

Early Greek philosophers suggested that one cannot step into the same river twice. People and communities do change over time. But an everchanging river does not mean that the bed of the river will not remain approximately the same, and an everchanging community does not mean that social changes are made without any foundation in past events. The opposite is true. All social changes rest on a matrix of prior

events that helps to determine the nature of the change and the speed with which it is eventually adopted.

STAGE 2: DEFINING THE UNDERLYING PROBLEM

The social situation at any given time may be seen as undesirable by many residents of a community or citizens of a state. Yet simply feeling that something is wrong is only the first step in attempting to provide a remedy. At some stage, for every social action situation in which someone seeks to induce some social change into a society, a problem situation is responsible for the suggested change. It is important to recognize precisely what the problem is, what the dimensions are, how it may be best defined, and the relationship between the underlying problem and the suggested solution.

Defining the problem is not always easy. Just what is the underlying problem that causes an extremely high rate of unemployment for black teenagers in Detroit? Is it racism on the part of the white community? Or is the problem caused by the lack of training of these youth, or by inflation, or the school system, or an economic recession? There may very likely be a number of different causes for the underlying problem, but if any solution is to be proposed, the different causes must be identified and clearly defined.

Frequently, groups, institutions, and communities cannot recognize their own problems. It may be necessary for someone from outside the particular social system to define the nature of the problem. Companies hire outside experts, groups bring in consultants, and communities invite government teams to inspect their operations and define the nature of the problems the community faces.

This stage in social action usually involves some definition of the nature of the problem, some indication of the seriousness of the problem for the group, some tentative selection of desired goals, and at least some decisions as to the appropriate lines of action to be taken. This does not mean that further changes will not be made as time goes on. This early recognition of a problem, however, is usually responsible for the suggestions advanced.

Clearly, not all problems will be defined in the same way for all groups within the community. Labor may see a problem as an economic one, to be solved with higher wages. For others, it may be defined in terms of a health problem, and for still others, as a problem in juvenile delinquency. The campaign organizer is going to be talking to a number of different groups within the community, and each group may need to receive a slightly different definition of the problem. Over time, the communicator may be trying and modifying, several definitions of the problem. A source will have to ascertain how various audiences might respond, and then attempt to define the problem in a variety of ways suitable to the various audiences.

It might seem to the average communicator that defining the problem is an unnecessary step; that if a need is recognized, the problem is automatically defined. Yet the history of social action campaigns is replete with situations in which some need was recognized, and actions taken before careful definition and analysis took place. Later, the need was still there, and the entire process had to be undertaken once again, by wiser communicators.

STAGE 3: Locating Relevant Groups and Institutions

For every problem that may be identified within a community, there will be some people who are directly affected by the problem, others who are less affected, and still others that seem not at all affected. Identifying the relevant groups within an institution or a society is an important element in eventually completing a successful persuasive campaign. For example, imagine that a proposal is made to place significant numbers of students on the faculty governing bodies of a university. Any university includes groups other than students and faculty. Cooks, janitors, technicians, physicians, bookkeepers, secretaries, and many others are also a part of the institution, but they are not likely to be directly affected by the proposed change. Messages designed for these individuals, important though they are in the total operation of the institution, are not as likely to be productive for this problem as are messages designed for the faculty and students.

A careful campaign will attempt to identify all the groups that will be affected by a proposed change, and the ways in which they might be affected must be outlined. If groups are overlooked, or by-passed, the communicator may find at a later stage that these same groups are in active opposition to the project. Care taken in the beginning of the campaign may prevent this later opposition, and help solidify the entire community behind the proposed change.

Stage 3 is not a stage in which much active persuasion is going on. It is primarily an information gathering phase in which the communicator prepares for the future. There may be some minor need for interpersonal persuasion while engaged in the process of locating relevant people and groups, but there will be little need to engage in mass persuasive efforts. The groups located in stage 3 are those that will eventually become the groups to which later persuasive efforts are going to be addressed.

In addition to locating relevant groups, the communicator must also be prepared to identify the ways in which the group is actually relevant to the overall problem. Each group will be relevant to the total problems, but also have its own special interests that must be recognized in future messages. Taking this stage seriously will improve the communicator's chances of success.

STAGE 4: USING INITIATING SETS

Very few social changes are begun and carried through to completion by a single individual. Generally, an idea must be accepted by many other people before the social change can be expected to take place. In looking at examples of induced social change, researchers have noted that the early period is characterized by the formation of a number of small groups of individuals who are in agreement with the aims of the proposed change and who can be used to contact other individuals and groups. These small groups have been called "initiating sets," and their role is to instigate communication with other relevant individuals.

Imagine that students on a college campus desire changes in the health service of the institution. There are very likely other groups, including local physicians, druggists, physical education teachers, and police groups, who would be interested in seeing improvements in the facilities. Certainly, all students will benefit. Certain special interest groups may have particular reasons to favor the proposed change, and their support may be extremely important in getting the proposal adopted.

There may be only a single group of people serving as an initiating set, or the proposal may impact on several groups of people who can be persuaded to serve as initiating sets. These groups may have different reasons for joining the first group, and there may be varying numbers within each group. In all likelihood, the original change agents, the individuals with whom the idea originated, will be part of one of the initiating groups. Each of these groups will offer *consultations, problem definition*, and *contact* functions to the campaign.

We have emphasized that few campaigns can be carried out by a single individual. The initiating sets are individuals who become convinced of the desirability of the proposed change. They help the persuasive communicator in further definition of the problem, in refining any proposed solution, and in being willing to "talk up" the project among their own friends and acquaintances. Without these individuals, it is doubtful that the communicator would be able to reach all of the necessary groups, or view the problem in such a way that it would meet the needs of the larger population.

The role of the persuasive communicator in the initiation stage is easy to see. Persuasive communication is necessary in order to reach the prospective members of the initiating sets. The source will have to contact members of the community who would be likely to support the idea and will have to engage in interpersonal attempts at convincing them of the value of the proposed changed. All of the principles discussed in the first chapters will be put to use in this task.

It is necessary to emphasize personal contact because forming the initiating set is so important that the change agent will wish to select set members carefully and to reach every member. In some situation, however, the change agent may not know who may be available, or which individuals should be contacted. In this rather common situation, the communicator will have to approach a number of community groups either through persuasive speeches made to members of the groups, or through written or televised messages designed to elicit support. The hope is that individuals from those groups will become interested in the proposal and can be formed into initiating sets. Obviously, the communicator will want to approach groups that seem relevant to the situation, since the chances of attracting interested members from relevant groups is high.

In situations involving broad social changes within a community, such as a change in governmental structure, or a change in tax structure, the initiating sets ought to include representatives from each of the major elements in the community. The sets ought to include individuals who have contact with influential members of the community. It is frequently the case that a particular community leader will listen more closely to one individual than another. The change agent must make a determined effort to secure the support of those individuals who do have access to particular leaders. Hopefully, the initiating sets will contain individuals who are themselves competent persuasive communicators. This will be helpful when initiating set members are to be used in contacting other community groups or leaders.

One might think that finding interested people to help solve social problems is easy, but evidence suggests that this task is usually one of the hardest ones. There may indeed be a number of people interested in a set of ideas, but moving those people from the interest stage to an involvement stage is not easy. Most people do not want to get involved until they see everyone else involved. Leaders in a community frequently do not want to get involved because they are afraid of losing credibility if the idea proves to be a poor one. Even if the idea is a good one, a persuasive communicator feel like someone crying in the wilderness while attempting to form initiating sets. Finding people interested in an idea or problem and involving them as members of an initiating set may involve considerable persuasion on the part of a source. Persuasive communicatiors might feel inclined to "go it alone." Experience suggests that that is usually impossible. There are only a few situations where a single person has been able to accomplish meaningful social change within a large social situation.

The initiating function in social action is an important one. There is one unavoidable danger. It is at the initiating stage that communication about the proposal first reaches people other than the original developer of the idea. The change agent must remember that other people have ideas, and it is very likely that changes will be suggested in the initial plans and ideas of the originator. In fact, in some social action programs there are so many additions and changes made to the original idea that the originator may wish that there were some way to become dissociated from the whole proposal. Suggestions, advice, new ideas, and changes are all important if initiating sets are to be successfully formed, but the change agent who wants to retain control of ideas will have to tread a delicate tightrope in order to avoid losing complete control of the campaign.

STAGE 5: USING THE POWER BASE

Within every community, within every organization, company, or institution, there are certain individuals who hold the reins of authority over new ideas. If they reject an idea, the probability is that the idea will fail. If they are willing to give their blessing to the proposal, the probability of acceptance by the rest of the community increases.

We can refer to these key people as *legitimizers* and their function is to improve or disapprove of proposals for social change. Paul Miller studied a group of these legitimizers in Lansing, Michigan.[12] There were forty members from a number of different groups, but they had many attributes in common. All of the forty tended to know that they were influential persons. The majority were over fifty years of age. They tended to belong to many different organizations, an average of over thirteen organizations each. The influential person either was active or had been active in each of the organizations, active in the sense that he was responsible for major policy decisions within the organization. Over 80 percent of the group of forty had attended college. Each of them held or had held a position in a company or a governmental body which could be described as having high prestige. The characteristics we have cited might change slightly from community to community, but these are the kinds of individuals who form the power base in a community.

The role of legitimizers is a peculiar one. They are seldom active in the early stages of a social action campaign. They do not make speeches in favor of the proposal. They do not write letters to the newspaper, and they frequently ask that their name not be associated with the new idea. They may not want to give a formal approval to a new proposal. Yet they can effectively block the adoption of a new idea by saying, "No" If legitimizers do come to agree that the proposal is a desirable one, the way may seem to be miraculously cleared for the future operations of the change agent.

The existence of a power base, of a set of legitimizers, depends on two kinds of people. The first type is the *formal* legitimizer. This is an individual with the legal or appointed power of decisionmaking. The mayor, chief of police, president of a university are all individuals who may be formal legitimizers. Their role is to examine new proposals and lend the weight of their office to their acceptance or rejection. For example, a group of students in one midwestern university town wanted to organize a fireworks display for a Fourth of July celebration. The proposal seemed to receive general acceptance from various city and university officials. When the plan was submitted to the chief of police, however, he said, "No." He pointed out the difficulties of controlling traffic and the possibility of fire. A proposal may die because of a single negative statement from a formal legitimizer with specialized authority within the group to be affected by a proposed idea.

The second type is the *informal* legitimizer. Informal legitimizers are very much like the opinion leaders we identified in Chapter 8. They may not hold any office that would give them control over a proposal, they might not even be extremely well known, but if such informal legitimizers are not consulted in some way and their acquiescence secured, the proposal is likely to fail. In a university, the President and other top officials are the formal legitimizers, but there may be a long-term faculty member who serves as an informal legitimizer. Without consultation and agreement from the faculty member, the proposal is likely to fail. In a school system, teachers and principals are the formal legitimizers, but there

may be a parent in the school district who exercises an informal role in approving or rejecting proposals.

Most of us understand the role of the formal power figure, since we have dealt with authority and authority figures since early childhood. The role of an informal legitimizer is somewhat harder to understand. The people serving in that role do seem to have some characteristics that will help the communicator in identification. They are likely to be the center of a communication net. They talk to many people, and many people talk to them. In a rural town in a neighboring state, I knew a man who served as an important informal legitimizer. He held no formal office within the town, but he was the president of a small bank, and in the course of business, almost everybody in the town had occasion to enter the bank and talk to him. Because of the amount of communication which flowed through him, he eventually became a legitimizer. Someone always checked out new ideas with him. In addition to being a central figure in a communication net, informal legitimizers tend to have high esteem. They may not be in a position that carries high prestige, but they have acquired high personal attractiveness. In many cases, such as in the Lansing group identified by Miller, the individuals may be people who have held formal authority positions in the past, and have left them to become informal advisors to an institution or group.

Regardless of whether we are talking about formal or informal authority figures, the process of legitimization is perhaps the most important in the entire social action process. Or, to put it another way, the legitimization stage can seldom be successfully bypassed. In recent years, many groups have sought to bypass the formal authority and take their message directly to "the people." At first, it may look as if such tactics have been successful. People do become interested in drastic social changes, but if you look at what happens after the people have been stirred up, too frequently it is the case that the actual program is worked out by the normal people in authority, and the end result is a bypassing of the change agent, not the authority figures. Thus changes are minimal, and made within the original groups and instituions. People interested in change must learn that legitimizers, both formal and informal, are where they are because they have their finger on the public pulse and are able to predict and act in ways the rest of the public will accept and emulate. We ignore the legitimization function, the power figures within an institution or society, at our peril.

Before we move on to the next stage, we should note that initiating set members may also be formal or informal legitimizers. This is not always the case since the functions are different. In situations where the social institutions involved in the proposed change are hierarchically arranged, some individuals within the organization may be members of an initiating set as well as being legitimizers whose formal approval is sought. This situation illustrates the difficulties of making clear distinctions between various parts of the social action process. We emphasize the *functions* that need to be performed, and these will always remain. When functions are translated into actions, however, the actions may involve more than one function. Legitimization is one of the most important functions in the social action process.

STAGE 6: GETTING THE WORD OUT TO EVERYONE IN THE SYSTEM

In order to induce social change within a community or institution, knowledge about the problem must move at some time from the stage of being known to only a small group or groups to a stage where the project becomes known to all the people who will be affected by it. This is particularly true in situations where there has to be an eventual vote on the proposal. This means that at some point, information about the proposal will have to be *diffused* to that portion of the population or group that

previously has not heard about it. Those groups of individuals who engage in diffusion of information can be referred to as *diffusion sets*. As in the case of initiating sets, there may be one or several diffusion sets.

Members of a diffusion set are characterized by:

1. The access they have to many people or groups of people
2. The abilities they have in persuading and transmitting information
3. The amount of time they have to engage in diffusion activities
4. The organizational abilities they possess that can be directed toward diffusion.

In a typical community, members of a diffusion set might include local ministers, newspapers and broadcast personnel, the secretary of the Chamber of Commerce, and officers in local civic organizations. On a college campus, diffusion set members might be members of the student government, staffers for the student newspaper, resident assistants for a dormitory, members from some of the fraternities and sororities, and faculty members belonging to the academic committees. Each of these individuals, by virtue of the position they hold and presumably by the skills that they have developed, may be qualified to become a member of a diffusion set. In the larger community, people who might be selected for the diffusion task include officers in professional associations, officers or important members of civic clubs, officers in labor unions, and similar individuals.

How can we know whether someone will be a valuable member of a diffusion set? People who are good at diffusion are those who see and talk to many other people, or those who have access to the mass media and can transmit messages in that fashion. Not all influential persons are good diffusion set members. The president of a large corporation, for example, may be an important legitimizer, but may be very protective of personal time, and may set up rules that prevent contact with many outsiders. Such individuals may have power, but may have neither the desire nor the abilities to communicate with large numbers of people. Within a community, almost every group will have people who can become valuable members of the various diffusion sets that will have to be formed. The task of the persuasive communicator is to identify such individuals, and then provide them with the information that is to be diffused.

The role of the persuasive communicator in the diffusion stage is analogous to the role in forming initiating sets. Diffusion set members are people who have agreed to the principles behind the proposed change, and are willing to talk to others about it. The change agent will have to first persuade the potential diffusers of the merits of the proposal. It may be that people who have already been convinced, and are initiators, will be willing to work extensively to accomplish the diffusion task. In addition to convincing potential members of the necessity for the proposed change, the change agent will have to supply them with information about the proposal. In working with representatives from the mass media, this may mean being willing to supply press releases, suggesting television spots, and answering questions on a radio show. We should note that many diffusion programs fail because the original change agent, the persuasive communicator, selects an appropriate diffusion set, but fails to follow up on the even more important task of making sure that all members of the set are informed about the problem, its definition and dimensions. Diffusion cannot be accomplished with willing but uniformed people.

STAGE 7: DEFINING THE NEED FOR A CHANGE

Defining need begins when the process of social action is first started. As the initiating sets are formed, the legitimizers contacted, and the diffusion sets made, the change agent will have

to explain through persuasion why the change is desirable. Change almost never occurs in the absence of a feeling that there is a need for the change. Why should I vote for increased taxes, if I do not understand what the additional money is going to be spent for? Why should I become interested in abortion reform? Stating that legalized abortion is "only right" is not a sufficient answer for most people. Why should students sit on faculty governing committees? If you can't show me that some benefit will come to me from approving the change, why should I vote for your proposal?

Defining need must go beyond convincing the key members of a campaign. Eventually everyone who will have to vote on the issue, or decide on the issue, will have to be convinced of the merits of the proposal. This means that at some time it will be necessary to convince the general public of the necessity for the change. This is one of the functions to be assumed by the diffusion sets. Obviously, when dealing with larger groups of individuals, persuasion will have to take a different form than when dealing with an interpersonal persuasion situation. You may find that you can work with some subgroups of the general public but that others can be reached only through the mass media.

Various techniques have been developed to reach large segments of the general public in the most economical manner. Earlier chapters have already discussed some of these. Some specific tactics which other communicators have found successful in past social action campaigns follow.

Basic Education For social changes that are very new or that might be considered "far out," a campaign to educate the public up to the point where it can accept the new idea may be necessary. For example, many medical authorities consider it desirable to have a dental service unit attached to the general hospital. This may require some basic medical education because the public may not be educated enough to properly evaluate a proposal in this field. Similarly, in underdeveloped countries, we know that spraying puddles of water to eliminate mosquitoes will help to eradicate malaria, but if villagers do not know that mosquitoes carry malaria, or even know that germs and viruses cause disease, it may be difficult to obtain cooperation in a spraying program. Again, a program in basic education is necessary.

We should introduce one note of caution into this discussion of basic education. There is always a chance that when a group has raised its information level through a program of basic education, it may identify other possible solutions to a problem than those desired by a persuasive communicator. There are few social problems that have only one possible solution. When the level of general knowledge is low, however, it is often the case that only a single possible solution will be seen to a problem. On the other hand when a number of people have a lot of information about a problem, there are likely to be many possible solutions suggested, and the one finally adopted may not be the one desired by a communicator. The energy crisis is an excellent example of this phenomenon. The last few years have seen an explosion of suggested solutions for the energy crisis. Patent applications have increased tremendously in just a short time. If someone had tried to convince an audience fifteen years ago about a proposed solution to a problem associated with energy, there might have been no competing solutions. Today, people know far more about energy, there are far more ideas in the system, and the task of any persuasive communicator who wishes to argue for a single solution is also far more difficult.

Demonstrations or Trials

Nothing is quite as persuasive as seeing a successful demonstration of a new idea. Obviously, a city cannot build a trial civic center in order to see whether it is a good idea, but it can put on a series of teenage dances in an unused building in order to show that there are uses for a civic center. It can also send groups of citizens and officials to other communities which have such facilities in order to report on their success.

A demonstration must be successful if it is to prove persuasive. In fact, such a trial ought to succeed better than the measure that may be passed later. For this reason, the change agent must work with great care to insure the success of the program and to be able to show the public that the trial was successful. A failure may doom the entire program, even if the failure of the demonstration is not related to the eventual success of the program.

Questionnaires or Surveys

Many people refuse to accept social changes until they have been assured that the majority favors the change. We tend to think of ourselves as a nation of people who will always side with the underdog. Actually, there is more evidence to suggest that the majority of the public waits until a trend seems to appear before agreeing with a proposition. The use of a well-designed questionnaire and adequate survey techniques may produce results that can be used to persuade "fence-sitters" to accept the proposed change.

Of course, there is always a danger that a questionnaire will determine that the general population does *not* favor a particular proposal. In such a situation, the persuasive communicator would be in the position of wishing that the survey had never been conducted. Any opposition to the proposal will seize on the results to bolster their side of the controversy. In any kind of situation where it is suspected that the results might not be in favor of the proposal, the questionnaire should not be used to check directly on the attitude of the public toward a proposed social change. Rather an indirect set of questions is designed. For example, if the persuasive communicator is interested in convincing a community to build a community swimming pool, instead of asking directly whether the public favors a tax increase to be used to construct a pool, the survey might ask whether the public is in favor of providing more summer recreation for school children. That evidence is then used to support the request for funds for a pool. Instead of asking whether the community wishes to increase taxes for a new addition to the hospital emergency room, the survey might ask whether there is sentiment in favor of better methods of saving lives. The communicator moves from the results of that question to advance the suggestion that what will help save lives is an addition to the hospital emergency room.

There is an old adage that attempts to disparage surveys and other statistical measures by suggesting that, "Figures don't lie, but liars can figure." Despire the adage, however, a well-designed survey can provide much basic data about the predispositions of a community and can lead to successful efforts at definition of the need for a proposed social change.

The Spirit of Competition

Although the spirit of competition may not be an inherited characteristic, it is a strong motivating force for many groups in the United States. We frequently talk about "keeping up with the Joneses" when describing the motivations of an individual. On a community or institutional level, the competition motive can be evoked by pointing to a similar community or institution that has adopted a particular change as a valid reason for your community to do the same. Institutions in our society seem to have a drive to have everything that the next institution has. Thus, almost all large universities now include some form of student participation in academic government. Almost all cities have Little League baseball diamonds and programs. Many of these programs have been established at the instigation of leaders who did not wish Othertown to be better than Ourtown.

Part of the strategy which can be used by a diffusion set is to suggest that a change must be made in order to provide parity with another institution. Faculty argue for raises on the basis of comparisons of their salaries with the salaries of others. Students argue for higher grades by comparing average grades in one school to those in another. In order to be persuasive, however, comparisions must be made that are meaningful. To argue that a city of 25 thousand inhabitants needs the same budget as a town of 100 thousand is not very persuasive. Comparison of communities of comparable size, however, is an effective technique.

Some cautions should go with the suggestion of this technique. There are clearly cycles in the strength of the spirit of competition motive. For example, during the 1950s it was easy to get foreign countries to adopt a new idea by suggesting that it was in practice in the United States. During the 1970s the opposite result was likely to occur. There has been a rise in nationalistic feelings, and a consequent attempt to reject comparisons with the United States. Some of the same feelings are also present in the United States. Many communities are rejecting the attempt to be just like every other community in the United States, and are tyring to find things that will give them a unique appearance. Attempting to appeal to a spirit of competition would be difficult in such a situation. A careful assessment of the community needs to be made before attempting to construct a set of persuasive messages.

Development Committees

Many communities have citizens who form groups known as "program development committees," or "planning boards," or "citizen's advisory boards." Frequently, the function of such groups is to diffuse information, with a formal seal of approval, to the remainder of the community. The change agent can go to such groups with proposed changes and use the group as a diffusion set. When the community does not have such a group, the change agent may find it helpful to organize one.

There is some risk in using an already established program development committee as a diffusion set charged with defining the need of programs for a community. The risk arises from the fact that a committee already given some formal authority may decide to make major changes or modifications in the ideas advanced by the change agent. Such changes might work in the direction of improving the proposal, but they might also result in changes not desired by the change agent. Once given to such a committee, however, the change agent is bound to accept the results as they emerge from the committee. This risk has to be weighed against the benefits gained from the influence such groups can have with the general population.

Channeling Complaints

This technique has been widely used in social action campaigns. Within any community there are always individuals who voice some dissatisfaction with the current state of affairs. They may object to current school programs, the lack of intramural facilities on a college campus, or the lack of a lunch counter in a factory. Complaints seem to be a natural part of society, and complaints can frequently be *channeled* to suit the desires of the persuasive communicator. An example will help clarify this technique. Imagine that you are the president of a local theatre group. Although you have a very active group, the facilities that you have to use for your productions are totally inadequate. They are small, cramped, and not always available. After surveying the situation, you decide that the best solution is to build a new civic center that will have facilities for theatrical productions. In order to obtain the necessary funds, you will need the help of a large segment of the population who will have to support a bond issue. At this point, you are going to be able to start 'channeling gripes." You find that there are some citizens who are complaining that teenagers have nothing to do in the town, and are getting into trouble. You point out to those people that the new civic center can be used for

teenage dances and other activities. You go to the conductor of the local symphony, who has been complaining that there is not a decent place to perform, and suggest that your proposal will help meet the needs of the symphony. You go to the local Chamber of Commerce, whose members have been complaining about the lack of business, and talk about the number of jobs that will be created by the building of a new civic center.

To each of these people or groups, the persuasive communicator has indicated that a complaint may be alleviated by adopting the social change desired by the communicator. Care must be taken to insure the fairness of making the tie between the complaint and the proposed change.

This technique of attempting to channel complaints toward the acceptance of some proposed solution has proven to be a very valuable one. We should note that there are almost always people who have complaints about the current state of affairs, so the technique can be used over and over again as new ideas are proposed and new solutions to problems are identified.

Use of Past Programs

We indicated earlier that social change takes place against a backdrop of prior social situations. The past social situations will undoubtedly have produced a number of programs designed to solve past problems. Frequently, the persuasive communicator can use past actions as a framework for future actions. In fact, sometimes the actual organizations developed in the past can be used as the framework for new programs. For example: a group of students wish to add students to the academic governance machinery at their university. They might point to the prior addition of students to faculty committees on an ad hoc basis as a justification for their idea, suggesting that the proposed change is not a far out proposal, but simply an extension of past policies. At a national level, there have recently been proposals for massive federal aid to school systems. Government spokesmen have not emphasized the newness of these proposals. Instead, they point to past programs of public aid to schools in construction grants and experimental programs, and suggest that their new proposals are simply a logical extension of past programs.

This technique works because many people are afraid of the new and the novel. They worry about radical social change, and attempt to resist it. If a proposal can be attached to an old, established institution or program, however, the potentially radical nature of the proposal is diffused, and the proposal becomes "progress" and not "revolution."

This technique is one that can be utilized most effectively if the change agent is able to plan ahead of time. Many programs can be presented to a community in an unfinished or open-ended form so that when the first part of the program is completed, the change agent is ready to advance another part of the program. In such a fashion, the demonstration of public need for the new portion of the program is attached to an older program.

Readiness to Exploit a Crisis

Social action is not an automatic process through which any new idea is easily introduced into an institution, community, state, or nation. Frequently, a change agent *will* get all of the appropriate people in agreement. Initiating sets and diffusion sets will be established and working. A number of people will become interested in the idea, and the appropriate legitimizers will have indicated support for the proposal, but the bulk of the population simply remains uninterested, and the proposal languishes as a result of massive disinterest.

This situation should not mean a complete abandonment of the idea. Rather, a waiting game may have to be played in this situation, with the people advocating change ready to move when conditions change. Sometimes, the occurrence of a crisis within the community or society will make it possible to introduce a new

idea successfully. In Indiana, for example, a group of people had been suggesting changed safety regulations for a number of years. Their proposals included suggested changes in the location of fire exits and in the regulations regarding the ways in which doors should open in public buildings. The group had been unsuccessful in getting the changes adopted by city officials or the state legislature. Then a theatre fire occurred in which a number of people lost their lives. The group was ready. They immediately reintroduced their proposals and were successful in getting them adopted almost immediately. They had taken advantage of a crisis.

In Iran, there had been people who wished to change the government for many years. The support wasn't there, and the group bided its time. When the support began to be manifest, people were ready both in and out of the country to mobilize that support, and to advance their ideas. They were ready to exploit a crisis.

No one should wait for a theatre fire in order to introduce some new legislation. Nor does anyone wish to manufacture a crisis in order to get ideas across, but the good change agent is always ready to exploit a crisis when it occurs and to make a persuasive link between the crisis and a proposed program.

Each of these eight techniques, and others that you might think of, may be used by a change agent and those who work with an agent to help the public become aware of the need for a proposal. The motivating principle behind this stage in the social action process is that people who feel something is needed to make life better are more willing to take some action or agree to a new idea. The person who sees no need for a change is a contented person and very difficult to reach through persuasion.

STAGE 8: OBTAINING A COMMITMENT TO ACTION

In earlier chapters, we pointed out the strong link between an individual's public commitment to an action and his eventually taking that action. Persuasion is far more likely to be successful if the individual has been asked to make a public commitment to some action. There is ample evidence, from research and past social action campaigns, to demonstrate the necessity of obtaining public commitments from those individuals who are going to be needed to make any program a success. In any social action program, there are likely to be some things that everyone will have to do. Some individuals will have to engage in telephone solicitation. Some will have to contribute money. Some will have to contribute time. Others will have to be willing to go to the polls and vote on a proposal. Getting an agreement that there is a need for change may be easy, but when the time for action is at hand, the easily obtained agreement may vanish because of an unwillingness of people to actually put time and effort into implementing the proposal. Before action is taken, the relevant members of a social action campaign must have committed themselves to the action.

Commitment may take several forms. It may be merely an agreement in support of the change agent. It may be an agreement to vote for a bond issue, or it may involve a pledge of money or a promise to work in the campaign. Churches planning a building program usually collect pledges from their members ahead of time. They have learned the hard way that mere agreement on the need for a new church is not sufficient to justify breaking ground.

It is certainly the case that individuals may fail to live up to even those promises to which they have publicly committed themselves. In the previously cited research studies there were significant numbers of people who did not live up to their commitments, but the research also shows dramatic differences between those who had committed themselves and those who had not. The communicator, acting as a change agent or working through the other members of the group, should not stop persuasive efforts until it has been possible to secure the various kinds of commitments that will be necessary to carry out the entire plan.

We must also note the difference between commitment and *public* commitment. It may be easy to get someone to agree to support a proposal and to work for a program when we "make a pitch" to the person in an interpersonal setting. If there are no other people present to witness the act of commitment, however, the pressure to follow that commitment with action is not very strong. On the other hand, if an individual agrees to do something, and that agreement is in the presence of many other people, there is far stronger pressure to fulfill the promise. Even being able to get an individual to commit to some action is helpful, but obtaining a public commitment is far more important if real effort is going to be needed from the person.

STAGE 9: DEFINING GOALS

For many reasons, it is a bit unfair to place this stage so late in our analysis of social action. Identifying and defining goals is something that occurs throughout the social action process. The originator of an idea has goals in mind when the idea first occurs. The members of the initiating sets and the diffusion sets have goals when they agree to join the campaign. We discuss it here because of its importance when considering the larger public that will be affected by a proposed change. When a proposal cannot be placed in operation without the cooperation of large sections of the public, it is essential that those goals relevant to that segment be identified and defined.

It may seem unnecessary to discuss this function separately, since varying goals will have been set by those interested during the process. Nevertheless, studies of successful social action campaigns seem to indicate that if future success is to be secured, the various social systems that will be affected by a change must undertake the process of developing a set of goals for themselves, or must accept a set of goals offered to them by the change agent. It is important to note that various groups may agree to quite different sets of goals that can be accomplished by a particular proposal. For example, consider the case of the community contemplating the development of a mass transportation system. Members of the city department concerned with street and road maintenance may find the proposal desirable since it contributes to the elimination of heavy traffic from automobiles, and thus, to cheaper maintenance activities. Members of a model cities board in the same city probably are not much concerned about street maintenance. They see the transportation system as an effective way of allowing their constituents to get to jobs in the suburbs, thus raising the quality of life for the citizens in the neighborhoods with which they are concerned. Local labor unions see the system as a source for new jobs, and that fits in with their overall goals. The change agent must be able to analyze the relevant groups in the larger community and show them that the proposals will help meet some of their goals.

Goals may be explicitly stated in a step separate from the definition of a need, or they may be more effectively included as a portion of the persuasive messages that help to define the need. Regardless of how such an identification and definition occurs, social action campaigns show that this function is an important one.

STAGE 10: AGREEING ON THE METHODS

Many social action situations involve the possibility of using more than one solution to the original problem. Consider the situation in which a college campus is faced with a sudden increase in vandalism and theft from dormitories. Once the decision has been made that a problem exists, and that some steps must be taken to alleviate the situation, there will remain the problem of deciding exactly how the problem is best solved. Additional police could be hired. The campus could be closed to all outsiders. A system of undercover agents could be placed within the dormitories. A system of

self-locking doors could be installed so that rooms would be automatically locked when the student leaves the room. Any of these methods could possibly serve as a deterrent to additional theft, but from the standpoint of the students who are to be served, each of them is probably not equally desirable. And from the standpoint of the administration which has to administer and fund any solution, not all solutions are equally desirable. At some point in the social action process, the relevant groups will have to make decisions regarding the methods to be used to solve the problem.

In actual campaigns, there frequently seems to be a blurring of the stages from defining a need through securing commitment and the formation of goals and methods to be used. The persuasive communicator can sometimes accomplish several of these tasks in the same message or in only a few messages. Individuals who agree with the message received from a diffusion set suggesting the need for some action are also likely to agree that a specific set of methods is the best way to accomplish those goals. The fact that these steps are not easily separated in practice should not lead us to ignore any of the functions. It has happened in many campaigns that the people responsible for the idea do obtain general agreement from a group of receivers, and then think that the work is done. The result is that the community fails to implement the idea while arguing over the methods to be used, and the problem is never solved.

The role of the persuasive communicator is clear. Once a particular set of means begins to stand out as the most practical way of handling the problem, the persuasive communicator will have to find ways of making the means appear most attractive to the group concerned.

STAGE 11: CONSTRUCTING A FORMAL PLAN OF WORK

Whenever someone gets an idea for a change in an institution, community or society, there are going to be some steps that will be necessary for implementing the idea. Perhaps a law will need to be changed, a zoning change made, money raised, or land bought. In most cases, the persuasive communicator should have researched the situation and determined just how a change might be accomplished. The persuasive communicator, however, will be spending much of the time in the early parts of a campaign in securing the necessary cooperation from those groups and individuals who will be involved in the initiation, diffusion and legitimization phases of the campaign. There is typically little time devoted to the details of a plan of action. Nevertheless, when the larger public has finally committed itself to the idea, when a vote has been taken, there does have to be a formal *plan of work* detailing the steps that have to be followed if the idea is finally to be implemented.

In Michigan, a group was successful in getting an issue on the ballot to raise the drinking age from eighteen to twenty-one years of age. The ballot proposal passed by a fairly comfortable margin. After the election, however, it was discovered that the petitioners had failed to specify any penalties for the possession or use of alcohol by minors. Thus there was no formal plan of work to implement the new constitutional provision. As a result, many communities passed ordinances which treated possession of alcohol by a minor much like a parking violation, with minimal fines of five dollars or less. Clearly, this is not what the originators of the petition drive had in mind when they started their campaign. If a plan of action had been decided upon before the election, there might have been some opportunity to have the action steps closer to the wishes of the original change agents.

The formal plan of work will include decisions about financing, operational steps to be taken in implementation, the time sequence that has to be followed, and most important, the specific tasks which each individual associated with the implementation will have to perform. Making these decisions will result in an organizational structure charged with actually carrying out the operations. This structure will provide for appropriate lines of authority, a detailed task description for each individual, and the relation of the operational group to other community groups and institutions.

The plan of work is important to the change agent. What will really happen in any social action campaign ultimately depends on the people who are doing the actual work. The idea for a new civic center may have been the idea of a very persuasive communicator who had finally induced the city to build the new building, but the building will actually exist only as the result of the work of architects, contractors, and laborers combining their efforts to carry out the idea. The change agent must be willing to accept the responsibility of seeing that an effecive plan of work is generated and transmitted to all relevant people and groups who are going to do the actual work.

STAGE 12: FORMALLY LAUNCHING THE PROGRAM

If all has gone well in a social action campaign, it will eventually be introduced and started. Many social action programs will include a formal *launching* ceremony as a part of the project. A bottle of champagne is broken over the hull of a new ship, the mayor and the city council dig the first shovels of dirt for the new civic center, the president of a university gives a dinner just before the meeting at which student representatives are to finally join the faculty committees, and the hospital has an open house to show off its new X-ray facilities. There will be some formal, public recognition of the beginning of a proposed social change.

For small projects, a formal launching is certainly not necessary, but when the opportunity does present itself, there is real merit in having some kind of public ceremony. Not only does it remind the public that their earlier decisions are about to be implemented, but it also provides an occasion for the recognition of the efforts of those who have put in their time and energy on the project. Such recognition may insure the cooperation of such individuals for future projects.

STAGE 13: ACTION STEPS

For minor social changes, the actual steps to be taken will have been carefully described in the formal plan of work, and the change agent need only follow the plan of work that has been developed. For major social action programs, however, it may be that the plan of work merely cites a sequence of programs to be followed rather than a set of details for each separate action step necessary. In such a complex system, one action step will be followed by an evaluation and then by a series of decisions concerning the next step to be undertaken. It may also happen that in a complex set of programs, completing one step will lead to radical changes in future plans, and the entire social action process will have to be started all over again. For example, imagine that there is a program to renovate the downtown area in a city. One block has been torn down, and new buildings constructed. An analysis of this part of the process indicates that the project cost almost twice as much as the original estimates. At this point, the original plan of action may have to be changed, and other plans made.

It is very likely that the individual reading this book will not soon become heavily involved in the massive type of social action campaign which will eventually require the expenditures of millions of dollars and many man hours of work. The number and complexity of the actions that might be involved in these very complex kinds of social change projects require extremely detailed kinds of plans and the flexibility to make changes in those plans. The model we have outlined *is* appropriate to such large-scale social action projects, but everyone should realize that all progress, no matter how small, is made through the efforts of people

working together to make the world a better place in which to live. Our own efforts and our own ideas may be small, but if we do become better communicators, our ideas will broaden and our efforts will have to be increased. In complex social action situations, the change agent and the persuasive communicator play a special role. They must take care to keep all the relevant social systems informed of the progress of the campaign. Failure to keep up the interest of the public in a complex campaign may result in disinterest that can prevent the rest of the plan from being adopted.

Every persuasive communicator is working toward the point at which actions will be taken to implement proposals. We must remember, however, that the task is not complete simply because the action has started.

STAGE 14: EVALUATION

The evaluation stage has been placed last, but evaluation is not a single stage. Evaluation will occur at frequent intervals during the entire social action process. Decisions are made, and changes are suggested. An idea is proposed, and it is evaluated by everyone who comes into contact with the idea. Evaluation is not always formal in nature. Any of the individuals involved in social action, whether it is the person who originated the idea, those involved in legitimizing the proposal or the people charged with diffusion, will be making evaluations. Any individual who decides that the campaign is not progressing well, or that it is not accomplishing what it should accomplish, may withdraw support or suggest modifications.

In addition to these informal evaluations, however, there is a definite place for formal evaluation of the effects of a campaign. A formal evaluation is one way of finding out whether a change that has been introduced is actually accomplishing what it was intended to accomplish. Such an evaluation may also indicate the next steps to be taken in a complex series of social changes. Evaluation ought to be built into any proposal for planned social change.

The functions to be completed for any evaluation of a social action campaign include:

1. Obtaining an agreement on campaign goals
2. Evaluating the degree to which goals were accomplished
3. Evaluating the adequacy of the planning that went into the campaign, with particular attention to the adequacy of the plan of work
4. Evaluating the efficiency of the groups involved in the campaign, with particular attention paid to the talents that might have been uncovered during the campaign
5. Assessing the adequacy of the communication structure and methods used during the campaign
6. Measuring the degree to which the change actually met the needs which were established at the beginning of the campaign.

Evaluation efforts can be very complex, and consume thousands of dollars, as would be the case when the federal government wants to test a new drug that has been proposed. But evaluation can be very simple in most cases, and consist simply of one or more people attempting to answer the kind of questions posed above. In most cases, the answers to such questions, if answered honestly and completely, will provide adequate evaluation.

There is one not immediately obvious advantage to having an evaluation. While the evaluation is, and should be concentrated on the proposed change, a successful project tends to bring credit to the change agent. It may increase credibility for future ideas. An evaluation will frequently identify and credit the persuasive communicator in ways that would not occur if an evaluation had not been done. Evaluation, then, helps in planning for future efforts, identifies the strong and weak elements of a program, and allows us to give credit, or blame, where credit or blame is due. It is an essential part of the social action process.

SUMMARY

The social action construct that has been described here is obviously only a construct. It cannot be followed blindly. It is not a foolproof scheme for changing the hearts and minds of men. In actual practice, the change agent will have to take into account local conditions, and adapt the model to those conditions. Nevertheless, use of this model has resulted in a number of highly successful social action campaigns. In 1972, a small group of students, townspeople, and local ministers established an organization to aid the victims of the war in Bangladesh. Their goal was to conduct a national drive to collect millions of dollars for the victims of the war. The plan they eventually evolved was based largely on the social action construct we have discussed at length. And the program was a success. They eventually had workers all over the United States volunteering their efforts, and millions of Americans contributing funds for their project. This was *planned* social change, change which could not have come about without the efforts of persuasive speakers, campaign workers, and all of the other people and resources that a major campaign takes.

In discussing the social action construct, an attempt has also been made to look carefully at the role of the persuasive communicator. The role is extensive, and at every stage in the process there is a need for persuasive communication. At times, attitudes will have to be changed. Perceptions may have to be modified before people see and understand the needs that the communicator points out. Behavior will have to be modified, votes secured, monies collected, and actions taken. Social action is, first and foremost, a communication process. Unless effective communication is secured, actions will not follow. And the trained persuasive communicator becomes crucial to the process.

We should note, however, that social action does not occur in a vacuum. Most proposed changes have opponents, and opponents frequently have their own ideas which they would like to see put into action. Opponents may also know about social action, and opposing legitimizers, opposing diffusion sets, and opposing change agents may be at work in many of the situations described. In this event, the end result may well be determined by those who have learned the lessons best, by the group that is the best organized, by the group that has developed the most effective communication and the best persuasive speakers and writers.

In final review, the steps in the social action construct as we have discussed it are:

1. The Prior Social Situation.
   What has happened before a change is proposed is important to the final shape of any possible change.
2. Defining the Underlying Problem.
   If we don't know exactly what the problem is, we cannot expect to solve the problem.
3. Locating Relevant Groups and Institutions.
   Not everyone will be of help in solving a problem. The trick is to locate those who will be of help.
4. Using Initiating Sets.
   Some people are important from the very beginning, and special efforts must be made to find those people.
5. Using the Power Base.
   It is extremely important to get the agreement of those who wield power in a community.
6. Getting the Word Out to Everyone in the System.

If people never find out that there is a problem, they will never be willing to do anything about the problem.
7. Defining the Need for a Change.
   If you can't tell me why a community needs to change, I am not likely to vote in your favor.
8. Obtaining a Commitment to Action.
   People are not always lazy, but they certainly work better when they have publicly committed themselves to work.
9. Defining Goals.
   Everyone in the community should know specifically what it is that we are after.
10. Agreeing on the Methods.
    If we cannot get agreement on the methods, everyone is likely to show up with a hammer, when what we need is a saw.
11. Constructing a Formal Plan of Work.
    It never hurts to write down what everyone is supposed to do.
12. Formally Launching the Program.
    Cutting a ribbon may seem silly, but it gives everyone a chance to mark the beginning of change.
13. Action Steps.
    Every social change project involves decisions and actions, taken over time, by many people.
14. Evaluation.
    Every social change project has the potential for success and for failure. Evaluation can help us tell which type or effect a project is going to have.

We can alter the sequence of these stages, we can accomplish some of them alone, and others only with the people with whom we are working. We can be concerned with social action campaigns that affect the lives of millions of people, or have an idea that concerns only a handful of people. But if persuasive communication is to help the world we live in, we cannot ignore what we know about social action.

FOOTNOTES

1. H. W. Simons, "Persuasion and Social Conflicts: A Critique of Prevailing Conceptions and a Framework for Future Research," (Mimeographed paper prepared for the Annual Meeting of the Speech-Communication Association, San Francisco, Calif., December, 1971).

2. S. D. Alinsky, *Rules for Radicals*, (New York: Random House, 1971).

3. John (Klempner) Bear, "People Who Write In: Communication Aspects of Opinion-Letter Writing," (Ph.D. dissertation, Michigan State University, 1966).

4. P. A. Miller, "The Process of Decision Making within the Context of Community Organization," *Rural Sociology*, vol. 17 (1952), pp. 153–61.

5. C. P. Loomis, "Toward a Theory of Systemic Social Change," *Rural Sociology in a Changing Society*. Proceedings of the North Central Rural Sociology Committee Seminar. (Columbus, Ohio: Ohio Agricultural Extension Service, Ohio State University, 1959), pp. 12–48.

6. H. F. Kaufman, "Health Programs and Community Action," Mississippi Agricultural Experiment Station, Preliminary Reports in Community Organization, No. 1, 1954.

7. C. R. Hoffer, "Social Action in Community Development," *Rural Sociology*, vol. 23 (1958), pp. 43–51.

8. C. Sower *et al.*, *Community Involvement*, (New York: Free Press of Glencoe, 1957).

9. P. A. Miller, "Process of Decision Making," pp. 153–61.

10. E. M. Rogers and F. Floyd Shoemaker, *Communication of Innovations: A Cross-Cultural Approach*, (New York: Free Press, 1971).

11. G. M. Beal, "Social Action: Instigated Social Change in Large Social Systems," in J. H. Copp, eds., *Our Changing Rural Society: Perspectives and Trends*, (Ames, Iowa: Iowa State University Press, 1964), pp. 233–64.

12. P. A. Miller, "Process of Decision Making," pp. 153–61.

BIBLIOGRAPHY

Abelson, R. P., and G. S. Lesser. "The Measurement of Persuasibility in Children." In I. L. Janis and C. I. Hovland, eds., *Personality and Persuasibility*, pp. 141–66. New Haven, Conn.: Yale University Press, 1959.

Abelson, R. P., and M. J. Rosenberg. "Symbolic Psycho-logic: A Model of Attitudinal Cognition." *Behavioral Science*, 3 (1958): 1–13.

Addington, D. W. "The Effect of Vocal Variations on Ratings of Source Credibility." *Speech Monographs*, 38 (1971): 242–47.

Adorno, T. W. *The Authoritarian Personality*. New York: Harper and Row, 1950.

Alinsky, S. D. *Rules for Radicals*. New York: Random House, 1971.

Andersen, K. E. "An Experimental Study of the Interaction of Artistic and Non-Artistic Ethos in Persuasion." Ph.D. dissertation, University of Wisconsin, 1961.

Andersen, K. E. *Persuasion Theory and Practice*. Boston: Allyn & Bacon, 1971.

Appelbaum, R. F., and K. W. Anatol. "The Factor Structure of Source Credibility as a Function of the Speaking Situation." *Speech Monographs* 39 (1972): 216–222.

Asch, S. E. "Effects of Group Pressure upon the Modification and Distortion of Judgment." In H. Guetzkow, ed., *Groups, Leadership and men*. Pittsburgh, Pa.: Carnegie Press, 1951.

Atkin, C. "Telephone Survey of Students at Michigan State University." East Lansing, Mich.: Michigan State University, 1971.

Back, K. "Influence through Social Communication." *Journal of Abnormal and Social Psychology* 36 (1951): 9–23.

Bales, R. F., and E. F. Borgatta. "Size of Group as a Factor in the Interaction Profile." In A. P. Hare; E. F. Borgatta; and R. F. Bales, eds., *Small Groups: Studies in Social Interaction*, pp. 495–512. New York: Alfred A. Knopf, 1965.

Ball, S., and G. Bogatz; *The First Year of Sesame Street: An Evaluation*. Princeton: Educational Testing Service, 1971.

Ballantine, B. *Wild Tigers and Tame Fleas*. New York: Holt, Rinehart and Winston, 1958.

Baron, R. L. "Attitude Change through Discrepant Actions: A Functional Analysis." In A. G. Greenwald; T. C. Brock; and T. M. Ostrom, eds., *Psychological Foundations of Attitudes*, pp. 297–326. New York: Academic Press, 1968.

Barrett, J. H. *Gerontological Psychology*, Springfield, Ill.: Charles C. Thomas, 1972.

Bassett, R. "Opinion Differences within the Family." *Public Opinion Quarterly* 13 (1949): 118–20.

Beal, G. M. "Social Action: Instigated Social Change in Large Social Systems." In J. H. Copp, ed., *Our Changing Rural Society: Perspectives and Trends*, pp. 233–64. Ames, Iowa: Iowa State University Press, 1964.

Bear, John (Klempner). "People Who Write In: Communication Aspects of Opinion-Letter Writing." Ph.D. dissertation, Michigan State University, 1966.

Beighley, K. D. "An Experimental Study of the Effects of Four Speech Variables on Listener Comprehension." *Speech Monographs* 19 (1952): 249–58.

Bem, D. *Beliefs, Attitudes, and Human Affairs*. Belmont, Calif.: Brooks Cole Publishing Co., 1970.

Bem, S. L. "Androgyny vs. the Tight Little Lives of Fluffy Women and Chesty Men." *Psychology Today*, 9 (1975), pp. 58–62.

Berelson, B.; P. F. Lazarsfeld; and W. N. McPhee. *Voting: A Study of Opinion Formation during a Presidential Campaign*. Chicago: University of Chicago Press, 1954.

Berlo, D. K. *The Process of Communication*. New York: Holt, Rinehard and Winston, 1960.

Berlo, D. K.; J. Lemert; and R. Mertz. "Dimensions for Evaluating the Acceptability of Message Sources." Mimeographed. East Lansing, Mich.: Michigan State University, 1966.

Berlyne, D. E. *Conflict, Arousal, and Curosity*. New York: McGraw-Hill, 1960.

Bettinghaus, E. "Cognitive Balance and the Development of Meaning," *Journal of Communication* 13 (1963): 95–105.

Bettinghaus, E. *The Nature of Proof*. New York: Bobbs-Merrill Co., 1972.

Bettinghaus, E. "The Operation of Congruity in an Oral Communication Situation." Ph.D. dissertation, University of Illinois, 1959.

Bettinghaus, E. "The Operation of Congruity in an Oral Communication Situation." *Speech Monographs* 28 (1961): 131–42.

Bettinghaus, E.; and J. R. Baseheart. "Some Specific Factors Affecting Attitude Change." *The Journal of Communication* 19 (1969): 227–38.

Bettinghaus, E.; G. R. Miller; and T. Steinfatt, "Source Evaluation, Syllogistic Content, and Judgment of Logical Validity by High- and Low-Dogmatic Persons." *Journal of Personality and Social Psychology* 16 (1970) 238–44.

Bettinghaus, E. "A Survey of Pre-Teen Age Smoking Behavior." Lansing, Mich.: Commission on Youth, State of Michigan, 1970.

Birdwhistell, R. L. *Kinesics and Context*. Philadelphia: University of Pennsylvania Press, 1970.

Blau, P. M. *Exchange and Power in Social Life*. New York: John Wiley & Sons, 1964.

Bowers, J. W. "Some Correlates of Language Intensity." *Quarterly Journal of Speech* 50 (1964): 415–20.

Brehm, J. W., and A. R. Cohen. *Explorations in Cognitive Dissonance*. New York: John Wiley & Sons, 1962.

Brooks, R. D., and T. M. Scheidel. "Speech as Process: A Case Study." *Speech Monographs* 35 (1968): 1–7.

Bryant, D., and K. Wallace. *Fundamentals of Public Speaking*. New York: Appleton-Century-Crofts, 1953.

Burgoon, J. "Ideal Source Credibility: A Reexamination of Source Credibility Measurement." *Central States Speech Journal* 27 (1976): 200–206.

Burgoon, M., and E. Bettinghaus. "Persuasive Message Strategies." In M. Roloff and G. R. Miller, eds., *Persuasion: New Directions in Theory and Research* 8. Beverly Hills: Sage Publications.

Burgoon, J., and T. Saine. *The Unspoken Dialogue: An Introduction to Nonverbal Communication*. Boston: Houghton Mifflin Co., 1978.

Burgoon, M., and M. Ruffner. *Human Communication*. New York: Holt Rinehart and Winston, 1978.

Burgoon, M., and D. Stewart. "Empirical Investigation of Language Intensity: I. The Effects of Sex of Source, Receiver, and Language Intensity on Attitude Change." *Human Communication Research* 1 (1975): 244–48.

Burgoon, M.; J. Heston; and J. McCroskey. *Small Group Communication: A Functional Approach*. New York: Holt, Rinehart & Winston, 1974.

Cantril, H., and Allport. *The Psychology of Radio*. New York: Harper and Row, 1935.

Carmichael, C. W. "Frustration, Sex and Personality." *Western Speech* 34 No. 4 1970: 300–307.

Cartwright, D. "The Nature of Group Cohesiveness." In D. Cartwright and A. Zander, eds., *Group Dynamics*, pp. 182–91. New York: Harper and Row, 1968.

Chaffee, S. H. "The Interpersonal Context of Mass Communication." In F. G. Kline and P. J. Tichenor, eds., *Current Perspectives in Mass Communication Research*, p. 107. Beverly Hills: Sage Publications, 1972.

Chaffee, S. H., and M. J. Petrick. *Using the Mass Media: Communication Problems in American Society*. New York: McGraw Hill, 1975.

Chadwick-Jones, J. K. *Social Exchange Theory: Its Structure and Influence in Social Psychology*. New York: Academic Press, 1976.

Chapanis, N., and A. Chapanis. "Cognitive Dissonance: Five Years Later." *Psychological Bulletin* 61 (1964): 1–22.

Chertkoff, J. M., and Conley. "Opening Offer and

Frequency of Concession as Bargaining Strategies." *Journal of Personality and Social Psychology* 7 (1967): 185–93.

Chomsky, N. *Aspects of the Theory of Syntax*. Cambridge: M.I.T. Press, 1965.

Chu, G. C., and W. Schramm. *Learning from Television*. Washington: National Association of Broadcasters, 1967.

Cialdini, R.B., et al. "Reciprocal Concessions Procedure for Inducing Compliance: The Door in the Face Technique." *Journal of Personality and Social Psychology* 31 (1975): 206–15.

Cohen, A. R. "Some Implications of Self-esteem for Social Influence." In I. L. Janis and C. I. Hovland, eds., *Personality and Persuasibility*. pp. 102–121. New Haven, Conn.: Yale University Press, 1959.

Colburn, C. "An Experimental Study of the Relationship between Fear Appeal and Topic Importance in Persuasion." Ph.D. dissertation, University of Indiana, 1967.

Coleman, J.; E. Katz; and H. Menzel, *Medical Innovation:* A Diffusion Study. New York: Bobbs-Merrill Co.. 1966.

Cronkhite, G., and J. Liska. "A Critique of Factor Analytic Approaches to the Study of Credibility." *Communication Monographs* 43 (1976): 91–107.

Crutchfield, R. B. "Conformity and Character." *American Psychologist* 10 (1955): 191–98.

Crutchfield, R. B. "The Measurement of Individual Differences in Conformity to Group Opinion among Officer Personnel." Institute of Personality Assessment and Research, University of California at Berkeley, *Research Bulletin*, 1954.

Crutchfield, R. B. "Personal and Situational Factors in Conformity to Group Pressures." *Acta Psychologica* 15 (1959): 386–88.

Cushman, D., and G. R. Miller. "New Directions in Forensics: Two Useful Communication Constructs." *American Forensics Association Journal*, in press.

Cutlip, S. "Content and Flow of AP News—From Trunk to TTS to Reader." *Journalism Quarterly*, Fall 1954, pp. 434–46.

Cyert, R. M., and J. G. March. *A Behavioral Theory of the Firm*. Englewood Cliffs, N.J.: Prentice-Hall, 1963.

Darnell, D. "The Relation between Sentence Order and the Comprehension of Written English." *Speech Monographs* 30 (1963): 97–100.

Deutschmann, P. "The Sign-Situation Classification of Human Communication." *Journal of Communication* 7 (1957): 63–73.

DiVesta, F. J., and J. C. Merwin. "The Effects of Need-oriented Communications on Attitude Change." *Journal of Abnormal and Social Psychology* 60 (1960): 80–85.

Dodge, J. S. "A Quantitative Investigation of the Relation between Meaning Development and Context." Ph.D. dissertation, University of Illinois, 1955.

Dubin, R., and R. A. Hedley. *The Medium May be Related to the Message: College Instruction by TV*. Eugene, Ore.: University of Oregon Press, 1969.

Eagly, A. H. and S. Himmelfarb. "Current Trends in Attitude Theory and Research." In S. Himmelfarb and A. H. Eagly, eds., *Readings in Attitude Change*, p. 595–601. New York: John Wiley & Sons, 1974.

"Effects of Segregation and the Consequences of Desegregation: A Social Science Statement." The *Minnesota Law Review* 37 (1953): 435.

Ehinger, D., and W. Brockriede. *Decision by Debate*. New York: Dodd, Mead & Co., 1963.

Ekman, P., and W. Friesen. "The Repertoire of Nonverbal Behavior: Categories, Origins, Usage, and Coding." *Semiotica* 1 (1969): 49–98.

Elms, A. C., and I. L. Janis. "Counter Norm Attitude Induced by Consonant versus Dissonant Conditions of Role Playing." *Journal of Experimental Research in Personality* 1 (1965): 50–60.

Emerson, R. M. "Power-Dependence Relations." *American Sociological Review* 27 (1962): 31–41.

Farace, R. V.; P. R. Monge; and H. M. Russell. *Communicating and Organizing*. Reading, Mass.: Addison-Wesley Publishing Co., 1972.

Feather, N. T. "Acceptance and Rejection of Arguments in Relation to Attitude Strength, Critical Ability, and Intolerance of Inconsistency." *Journal of Abnormal and Social Psychology* 59 (1964): 127–37.

Festinger, L. *The Theory of Cognitive Dissonance*. Stanford, Calif.: Stanford University Press, 1957.

Festinger, L. Informal Social Communication." *Psychological Review* 57 (1957): 271–82.

Festinger, L., and J. M. Carlsmith. "Cognitive Consequences of Forced Compliance." *Journal of Abnormal and Social Psychology* 58 (1959): 203–210.

Fisher, S. C. *Relationships in Attitudes, Opinions, and Values Among Family Members*. University of California Publications in Culture and Society, vol. 2 (1948), no. 2.

Fowler, H. *Curiosity and Exploratory Behavior*. New York: Macmillan Co., 1965.

Freedman, J. L. and S. C. Fraser. "Compliance Without Pressure: The Foot-in-the-Door Technique." *Journal of Personality and Social Psychology* 4, no. 2 (1966): 195–202.

Gerbner, C. "The Interaction Model: Perception and Communication." In J. Ball and F. Byrnes, eds.,

Research, Principles and Practices in Visual Communication, pp. 4–15. East Lansing, Mich.: National Project in Agricultural Communication, 1960.

Gilbert, G. M. "Stereotype Persistence and Change among College Students." *Journal of Abnormal and Social Psychology* 46 (1951): 245–54.

Glanzer, M., and R. Glasser. "Techniques for the Study of Group Structure and Behavior: Empirical Studies of the Effects of Structure in Small Groups." In A. P. Hare; E. F. Borgatta; and R. F. Bales, eds., *Small Groups: Studies in Social Interaction*, pp. 400–426. New York: Alfred A. Knopf, 1965.

Goldstein, M. "The Relationship between Coping and Avoiding Behavior and Response to Fear Arousing Propaganda." *Journal of Abnormal and Social Psychology* 59 (1959): 252.

Golembiewski, R. T. *The Small Group: An Analysis of Research Concepts and Operations*. Chicago: University of Chicago Press, 1962.

Gould, J., and W. L. Kolb, eds., *A Dictionary of the Social Sciences*. New York: Free Press of Glencoe, 1965.

Greenberg, B. S., and J. R. Dominick. "Racial and Social Class Differences in Teen-Agers' Use of Television." *Journal of Broadcasting* 13 (1969): 331–44.

Greenberg, B. S., and G. R. Miller. "The Effects of Low-Credible Sources on Message Acceptance." *Speech Monographs* 33 (1966): 135–36.

Gulley, H., and D. K. Berlo. "Effects of Intercellular and Intracellular Speech Structure on Attitude Change and Learning." *Speech Monographs* 23 (1956): 288–97.

Haefner, D. P. "Some Effects of Guilt-Arousing and Fear-Arousing Persuasive Communications on Opinion Change." Ph.D. dissertation, University of Rochester, 1956.

Haiman, F. S. "The Effects of Ethos in Public Speaking." *Speech Monographs* 16 (1949): 192.

Hare, A. P. "Interaction and Consensus in Different Sized Groups." *American Sociological Review* 17 (1952): 261–67.

Hare, A. P., and R. Bales. "Seating Position and Small Group Interaction." In A. P. Hare; E. F. Borgatta; and R. F. Bales, eds., *Small Groups: Studies in Social Interaction* pp. 427–533. New York: Alfred A. Knopf, 1965.

Harms, L. S. "Listener Judgments of Status Cues in Speech." *Quarterly Journal of Speech* 47 (1961): 164–68.

Harris, T. G. "Achieving Man: A Conversation with David C. McClelland." *Psychology Today* 4, No. 8 (1971): 36.

Harrison, R. P. *Beyond Words: An Introduction to Nonverbal Communication*. Englewood Cliffs, N.J.: Prentice-Hall, 1974.

Hartmann, G. "A Field Experiment on the Comparative Effectiveness of 'Emotional' and 'Rational' Political Leaflets in Determining Election Results." *Journal of Abnormal and Social Psychology* 31 (1936): 99–114.

Harvey, I. G. "An Experimental Study of the Influence of the Ethos of The Introducer as it Affects the Ethos and the Persuasiveness of the Speaker." Ph.D. dissertation, University of Michigan, 1968.

Hayakawa, S. I. *Language in Thought and Action*. New York: Harcourt Brace Jovanovich, 1964.

Heider, F. "Attitudes and Cognitive Organization." *Journal of Psychology* 21 (1946): 107–112.

Heider, F. *The Psychology of Interpersonal Relations*. New York: John Wiley & Sons, 1958.

Hess, R. D., and J. Torney. *The Development of Political Attitudes in Children*. New York: Anchor Books, 1967.

Hewgill, M., and G. R. Miller. "Source Credibility and Response to Fear Arousing Communications." *Speech Monographs* 32 (1965): 95–101.

Hilgard, E. R. *Theories of Learning*. New York: Appleton-Century-Crofts, 1956.

Hilyard, D. "One-sided versus Two-sided Messages: An Experiment in Counterconditioning." Ph.D. dissertation, Michigan State University, 1965.

Himmelhoch, J. "Tolerance and Personality Needs." *American Sociological Review* 15 (1950): 79–88.

Hoffer, C. R. "Social Action in Community Development." *Rural Sociology* 23 (1958): 43–51.

Homans, C. G. *The Human Group*. New York: Harcourt Brace Jovanovich, 1950.

Homans, C. G. *Social Behavior: Its Elementary Forms*. New York: John Wiley & Sons, 1964.

Hovland, C. I.; et al. *The Order of Presentation in Persuasion*. New Haven, Conn.: Yale University Press, 1961.

Hovland, C. I.; I. Janis; and H. H. Kelley. *Communication and Persuasion*. New Haven, Conn.: Yale University Press, 1953.

Hovland, C. I.; A. A. Lumsdaine; and F. D. Sheffield. *Experiments in Mass Communication: Studies in Social Psychology in World War II*, vol. 3. Princeton, N.J.: Princeton University Press, 1949.

Hovland, C. I., and W. Weiss. "The Influence of Source Credibility on Communication Effectiveness." *Public Opinion Quarterly*, 16 (1961): 635–50.

Howes, D., and C. E. Osgood. "On the Combination of Associative Probabilities in Linguistic Context." *American Journal of Psychology* 64 (1954): 241–58.

Hull, C. L. *A Behavior System: An Introduction to Be-*

havior Theory Concerning the Individual Organism. New Haven, Conn.: Yale University Press, 1952.

Jacob, M.A. "The Structure and Functions of Internal Communication in Three Religious Communities." Ph.D. dissertation, Michigan State University, 1972.

Jacobson, W. D. *Power and Interpersonal Relations*. Belmont, Calif.: Wadsworth Publishing Co., 1972.

James, R. W. "Preexisting Attitudes of College Students to Instructional Television." *AV Communication Review* 12 (1964): 325–336.

Janis, I. L. "Personality Correlates of Susceptibility to Persuasion." *Journal of Personality* 22 (1954): 504–518.

Janis, I. L., and P. B. Field. "Sex Differences and Personality Factors Related to Persuasibility." In I. L. Janis and C. I. Hovland, eds., *Personality and Persuasibility*, pp. 55–68. New Haven, Conn.: Yale University Press, 1959.

Janis, I. L., and S. Feshback. "Effects of Fear-Arousing Communications." *Journal of Abnormal and Social Psychology* 48 (1953): 78–92.

Janis, I. L., and J. B. Gilmore. "The Influence of Incentive Conditions on the Success of Role Playing in Modifying Attitudes." *Journal of Personality and Social Psychology* 1 (1965): 17–27.

Janis, I. L., and B. T. King. "The Influence of Role Playing on Opinion Change." *Journal of Abnormal and Social Psychology* 49 (1954): 211–18.

Janis, I. L. and L. Mann. "Effectiveness of Emotional Role-Playing in Modifying Smoking Habits and Attitudes." *Journal of Experimental Research in Personality* 1 (1965): 84–90.

Janis, I. L., and D. Rife. "Persuasibility and Emotional Disorder." In I. L. Janis and C. I. Hovland, eds., *Personality and Persuasibility*, pp. 121–37. New Haven, Conn.: Yale University Press, 1959.

Jersild, A. "Modes of Emphasis in Public Speaking." *Journal of Applied Psychology* 12 (1928): 611–20.

Johennsen, R. L. "The Emerging Concept of Communication as Dialogue." *Quarterly Journal of Speech* 57 (1971): 373–82.

Jones, E. E., and K. E. Davis. "From Acts to Dispositions: The Attribution process in Person Perception." In L. Berkowitz ed., *Advances in Experimental Social Psychology*, vol. 5. New York: Academic Press, 1965.

Katz, E., and P. F. Lazarsfeld. *Personal Influence*. New York: Free Press of Glencoe, 1955.

Kaufman, H. F. "Health Programs and Community Action: Mississippi Agricultural Experiment Station, Preliminary Reports in Community Organization, No. 1, 1954.

Kelley, H. H. "Two Functions of Reference Groups." In H. Prohansky and B. Seidenberg, eds., *Basic Studies in Social Psychology*, pp. 210–14. New York: Holt, Rinehart and Winston, 1965.

Kelley, H. H. "Attribution Theory in Social Psychology." In D. Levine ed., *Nebraska Symposium on Motivation*, vol. 15. Lincoln, Neb.: University of Nebraska Press, 1967.

Kelman, H. C. "Processes of Opinion Change." *Public Opinion Quarterly* 25 1961.

Kelman, H. C.; R. M. Baron; J. P. Sheposh; J. S. Lubalin; J. M. Dabbs; and E. Johnson. *Studies in Attitude Discrepant Behavior*. Manuscript, Department of Psychology, Harvard University, 1969.

King, B. T. "Relationships between Susceptibility to Opinion Change and Childrearing Practice." In I. L. Janis and C. I. Hovland, eds., *Personality and Persuasibility*, pp. 201–221. New Haven, Conn.: Yale University Press, 1959.

Knapp, M. *Nonverbal Communication in Human Interaction*. 2nd Edition. New York: Holt, Rinehart and Winston, 1978.

Knower, F. H. "Experimental Studies of Changes in Attitudes: I. A Study of the Effect of Oral Argument." *Journal of Social Psychology* 6 (1935): 315–47.

Knower, F. H. "Experimental Studies of Changes in Attitude: A Study of the Effect of Printed Argument on Changes in Attitude." *Journal of Abnormal and Social Psychology* 30 (1936): 522–32.

Krech, D.; R. Crutchfield; and E. Ballachey. *Individual in Society*. New York: McGraw-Hill, 1962.

Kumata, H. "A Factor Analytic Investigation of the Generality of Semantic Structure Across Two Selected Cultures." Ph.D. dissertation, University of Illinois, 1957.

Langton, K. P. *Political Socialization*. New York: Oxford University Press, 1969.

Lazarsfeld, P.; P. B. Berelson; and H. Gaudet. *The People's Choice*. New York: Columbia University Press, 1948.

Lazarsfeld, P., and R. Merton. "Mass Communication, Popular Taste and Organized Social Action." In L. Bryson, ed., *The Communication of Ideas*. New York: Harper and Row, 1948.

Leavitt, H. J. "Some Effects of Certain Communication Patterns on Group Performance." *Journal of Abnormal and Social Psychology* 36 (1951): 38–50.

Lefford A. "The Influence of Emotional Subject Matter on Logical Reasoning." *Journal of General Psychology* 34 (1946): 127–51.

Lenneberg, E. H. *Biological Foundations of Language*. New York: John Wiley & Sons, 1967.

Leventhal, H., and S. I. Perloe. "A Relationship Between Self-esteem and Persuasability." *Journal of*

Abnormal and Social Psychology 62 (1962): 385–88.

Lewan, P. C., and E. Stotland. "The Effects of Prior Information on Susceptibility to an Emotional Appeal." *Journal of Abnormal and Social Psychology* 62 (1961): 450–53.

Lipset, S. M., and J. J. Linz. "The Social Bases of Political Diversity in Western Democracies." Unpublished manuscript reported in B. Berelson, and G. Steiner, *Human Behavior: An Inventory of Scientific Findings*. New York: Harcourt Brace Jovanovich, 1964.

Loomis, C. P. "Toward a Theory of Systemic Social Change." *Rural Sociology in a Changing Society*. Proceedings of the North Central Rural Sociology Committee Seminar, pp. 12–48. Columbus, Ohio: Ohio Agricultural Extension Service, Ohio State University, 1959.

Lott, B. "Secondary Reinforcement and Effort: Comment on Aronson's 'The Effect of Effort on the Attractiveness of Rewarded and Unrewarded Stimuli.'" *Journal of Abnormal and Social Psychology* 67 (1963): 520–22.

Luce, R. D., and H. Raiffa. *Games and Decisions*. New York: John Wiley & Sons, 1957.

Lund, F. H. "The Psychology of Belief: IV. The Law of Primacy in Persuasion." *Journal of Abnormal and Social Psychology* 20 (1925): 183–91.

Lynd, R. S., and H. M. Lynd. Middletown: *A Study in Contemporary American Culture*. New York: Harcourt, Brace Jonanovich, 1929.

Lynd, R. S., and H. M. Lynd. *Middletown in Transition: A Study in Cultural Conflicts*. New York: Harcourt Brace Jonanovich, 1937.

McClelland, D. *The Achieving Society*. Princeton, N.J.: D. Van Nostrand Reinhold Co., 1961.

McClelland, D., et al. *The Achievement Motive*. New York: Appleton-Century-Crofts, 1953.

McCroskey, J. C. *An Introduction to Rhetorical Communication*. Englewood Cliffs, N.J.: Prentice-Hall, 1968.

McCroskey, J. C., and R. E. Dunham. "Ethos: A Confounding Element in Communication Research." *Speech Monographs* 32 (1966): 456–63.

McEwen, W. J., and B. S. Greenberg. "The Effects of Message Intensity on Receiver Evaluation of Source, Message and Topic." *Journal of Communication* 13 (1963): 94–105.

McGuire, W. "Cognitive Consistency and Attitude Change." *Journal of Abnormal and Social Psychology* 60 (1960): 345–53.

McGuire, W. "The Current Status of Cognitive Consistency Theories." In S. Feldman, ed., *Cognitive Consistency*. New York: Academic Press, 1966.

McQuail, D. *Towards a Sociology of Mass Communications*. London: Macmillan & Co., 1969.

Maccoby, E.; R. Matthews; and A. Morton. "Youth and Political Change." *Public Opinion Quarterly* 18 (1954): 23–30.

Markham, D. "The Dimensions of Source Credibility of Television Newscasters." *Journal of Communication* 18 (1968): 57–64.

Mehrabian, A. *Silent Messages*. Belmont, Calif.: Wadsworth Publishing Co., 1971.

Mehrabian, A. "Significance of Posture and Position in the Communication of Attitude and Status Relationships." *Psychological Bulletin* 71 (1969): 365.

Mehrabian, A., and S. E. Ferris. "Inference of Attitudes from Nonverbal Communication in Two Channels." *Journal of Consulting Psychology* 31 (1967): 248–52.

Mehrabian, A., and M. Wiener. "Decoding of Inconsistent Communications." *Journal of Personality and Social Psychology* 6 (1967): 109–114.

Merton, R. K. *Mass Persuasion: The Social Psychology of a War Bond Drive*. New York: Harper and Brothers, 1946.

Merton, R. K. *Social Theory and Social Structure*. New York: Free Press of Glencoe, 1949.

"Middletown Revisited." *Time*, Oct. 16, 1978, pp. 106–9.

Miller, G. R. *An Introduction to Speech Communication*. New York: Bobbs-Merrill Co., 1972.

Miller, G. R. "Counter-Attitudinal Advocacy: A Current Appraisal." In C. D. Mortensen, and K. K. Sereno, eds., *Advances in Communication Research*. pp. 105–152. New York: Harper and Row, 1973.

Miller, G. R. and M. Burgoon. "Persuasion Research: Review and Commentary." In B. D. Ruben, ed., *Communication Yearbook II*. New Brunswick, N.J.: Transaction Books, 1978.

Miller, G. R., and M. Burgoon. *New Techniques of Persuasion*. New York: Harper and Row, 1973.

Miller, G. R., and M. Hewgill. "The Effect of Variations in Nonfluency on Audience Ratings of Source Credibility." *Quarterly Journal of Speech* 50 (1964): 36–44.

Miller, G. R. and J. Lobe. "Opinionated Language, Open- and Closed-Mindedness and Responses to Persuasive Communications." *Journal of Communication* 17 (1967): 333–41.

Miller, P. A. "The Process of Decision-making within the Context of Community Organization." *Rural Sociology* 17 (1952): 153–61.

Monge, P. R.; J. A. Edwards; and K. K. Kirste. "The Determinants of Communication and Communication Structure in Large Organizations: A

Review of Research." In B. D. Ruben, ed., *Communication Yearbook II*. New Brunswick, N.J.: Transaction Books, 1978.

Monroe, A. H., and D. Ehninger. *Principles of Speech Communication*. 7th Brief ed., Glenview, Ill.: Scott, Foresman and Co., 1975.

Morgan, C. and H. H. Remmers. "Liberalism and Conservatism of College Students as Affected by the Depression." *School and Society* 41 (1935): 780–84.

Munn, N. L. *Psychology: Fundamentals of Human Adjustment*, 3rd ed. Boston: Houghton Mifflin Co., 1956.

Nerbonne, G. P. "The Identification of Speaker Characteristics on the Basis of Aural Cues." Ph.D. dissertation, Michigan State University, 1967.

Newcomb, T. M. "An Approach to the Study of Communicative Acts." *Psychological Review* 60 (1963): 393–404.

Newcomb, T. M. "Attitude Development as a Function of Reference Groups." In H. Prohansky and B. Seidenberg, eds., *Basic Studies in Social Psychology*, pp. 215–25. New York: Holt, Rinehart and Winston, 1965.

Newcomb. T. M. "Attitude Development as a Function of Reference Groups: The Bennington Study." In E. E. Maccoby; T. H. Newcomb; and E. L. Hartley, eds., *Readings in Social Psychology*, pp. 265–75. New York: Holt, Rinehart and Winston, 1958.

Nunnally, J. C., and H. M. Bobren, "Variables Governing the Willingness to Receive Communications on Mental Health." *Journal of Personality* 27 (1959): 275–90.

Opubor, A. " 'Vocal' Communication: The Effects of Rate (Speed) and Intensity (Loudness) on Response to Spoken Messages." Ph.D. dissertation, Michigan State University, 1969.

Osgood, C. E. *Method and Theory in Experimental Psychology*. New York: Oxford University Press, 1953.

Osgood, C. E.; P. H. Tannenbaum; and G. Suci, *The Measurement of Meaning*. Urbana, Ill.: University of Illinois Press, 1957.

Osgood, C. E.; E. E. Ware; and C. Morris. "Analysis of the Connotative Meanings of a Variety of Human Values as Expressed by American College Students." *Journal of Abnormal and Social Psychology* 62 (1961): 62–73.

Paul, I. H. "Impressions of Personality, Authoritarianism, and the Fait Accompli Effect." *Journal of Abnormal and Social Psychology* 53 (1956): 338–44.

Pearce, W. B. and B. J. Brommel. "Vocalic Communication in Persuasion." *Quarterly Journal of Speech* 58 (1972): 298–306.

Pearce, W. B. and F. Conklin. "Nonverbal Vocalic Communication and Perception of a Speaker." *Speech Monographs* 38 (1971): 235–41.

Pervin, L. A. "Performance and Satisfaction as a Function of Individual-Environment Fit." In N. S. Endler, and D. Magnusson, eds., *Interactional Psychology and Personality*. Washington, D.C.: Hemisphere Publishing Corp., 1976, pp. 73–74.

Peterson, T. D. "The Relationship Between Certain Attitudes of Parents and Children." In H. H. Remmers, ed., *Further Studies in Attitudes*. Lafayette, Ind.: Purdue University Studies in Higher Education, series 2, vol. 37, (1937): 127–44.

Petrie, C. "Informative Speaking: A Summary and Bibliography of Related Research." *Speech Monographs* 30 (1936): 79–91.

Pliner, P.; H. Hart; J. Kohl; and D. Saarl. "Compliance without Pressure: Some Further Data on the Foot-in-the-Door Technique." *Journal of Experimental Social Psychology* 10 (1974): 17–22.

Powell, F. A. "Open- and Closed-mindedness and the Ability to Differentiate Source and Message." *Journal of Abnormal and Social Psychology* 65 (1962): 61–64.

Random House Dictionary of the English Language, The. New York: Random House, 1967.

Robert, H. M. *Robert's Rules of Order Revised*. New York: Scott, Forseman and Co., 1951.

Roberts, W. R. "Rhetorica." In W. D. Ross, ed., *The Works of Aristotle*, Vol. 11. New York: Oxford University Press.

Robinson, J. P. "Mass Communication and Information Diffusion." In F. G. Kline, and P. J. Tichenor, eds., *Current Perspectives in Mass Communication Research*, pp. 71–94. Beverly Hills: Sage Publications, 1972.

Rogers, E. M. "Incentives in the Diffusion of Family Planning Innovation." *Studies in Family Planning* 2 (1971): 241–48.

Rogers, E. M., and D. K. Bhowmik. "Homophily-Heterophily: Relational Concepts for Communication Research." Paper presented at the Association for Education in Journalism. Berkeley, Calif. (August 1969).

Rogers, E. M., and F. F. Shoemaker. *Communication of Innovations: A Cross-Cultural Approach*. New York: Free Press of Glencoe, 1971.

Rohrer, J. H., and M. Sherif. *Social Psychology at the Crossroads*. New York: Harper and Row, 1951.

Rokeach, M. *The Open and Closed Mind*. New York: Basic Books, 1960.

Rokeach, M. "Persuasion that Persists." Psychology

Today, September 1971, pp. 68–92.

Rokeach, M. *Beliefs, Attitudes and Values*. San Francisco: Jossey-Bass, 1968.

Rokeach, M., and L. Mezie. "Race and Shared Belief as Factors in Social Choice." *Science*, January 1960, pp. 167–72.

Rokeach, M., and G. Rothman. "The Principle of Belief Congruence and the Congruity Principle as Models of Cognitive Interaction." *Psychological Review* 72 (1965): 128–42.

Rosenberg, M. J., and C. I. Hovland. "Cognitive, Affective, and Behavioral Components of Attitudes." In C. I. Hovland, and M. J. Rosenberg, eds., *Attitude, Organization and Change*. New Haven, Conn.: Yale University Press, 1960.

Rosnow, R. L., and E. J. Robinson. *Experiments in Persuasion*. New York: Academic Press, 1967.

Rossi, P. H., and A. S. Rossi. "Some Effects of Parochial School Education in America." *Daedalus*, Spring 1961, pp. 300–328.

Ruechelle, R. C. "An Experimental Study of Audience Recognition of Emotional and Intellectual Appeals in Persuasion." *Speech Monographs* 25 (1958): 58.

Sanford, A. C.; G. T. Hunt; and H. J. Bracey. *Communication Behavior in Organizations*. Columbus, Ohio: Charles E. Merrill Publishing Co., 1976.

Scheidel, T. M. *Persuasive Speaking*. Glenview, Ill.: Scott, Foresman and Co., 1967.

Scheidel, T. M. "Sex and Persuasibility." *Speech Monographs* 30 (1963): 353–58.

Schramm, W. "How Communication Works." In W. Schramm, ed., *The Process and Effects of Mass Communication*, pp. 3–26. Urbana, Ill.: University of Illinois Press, 1954.

Schramm, W. *Big Media, Little Media: Tools and Technologies for Instruction*. Beverly Hills: Sage Publications, 1977.

Sears, D. O., and R. P. Abeles. "Attitudes and Opinions." *Annual Review of Psychology* 20 (1969): 253–288.

Sencer, R. "An Investigation of the Effects of Incorrect Grammar on Attitude and Comprehension in Written English Messages." Ph.D. dissertation, Michigan State University, 1965.

Shannon, C., and W. Weaver. *The Mathematical Theory of Communication*. Urbana, Ill.: University of Illinois Press, 1949.

Shaver, Kelly G. *An Introduction to Attribution Processes*. Cambridge, Mass.: Winthrop Publishers, 1975.

Sherif, M. "A Study of Some Social Factors in Perception." *Archives of Psychology*, No. 7 (1935).

Sherif, M., and C. W. Sherif. *An Outline of Social Psychology*. New York: Harper and Row, 1956.

Short, J. F., and F. Strodtbeck. *Group Process and Gang Delinquency*. Chicago: University of Chicago Press, 1965.

Siegel, A. E., and S. Siegel. "Reference Groups, Membership Groups, and Attitude Change." *Journal of Abnormal and Social Psychology* 55 (1957): 360–64.

Simons, H. W. "Persuasion and Social Conflicts: A Critique of Prevailing Conceptions and a Framework for Future Research." Mimeographed paper prepared for the Annual Meetings of the Speech-Communication Association, San Francisco, Calif. (December, 1971).

Simons, H. W. *Persuasion: Understanding, Practice and Analysis*. Reading, Mass.: Addison-Wesley Publishing Co., 1976.

Slater, P. E. "Contrasting Correlates of Group size." *Sociometry* 21 (1958): 129–39.

Snyder, M. and M. R. Cunningham. "To Comply or not Comply: Testing the Self-perception Explanation of the "Foot-in-the-Door Phenomenon." *Journal of Personality and Social Psychology*, vol. 31, no. 1, (1975): 64–67.

Sower, C.; et al. *Community Involvement*. New York: Free Press of Glencoe, 1957.

Star, S., and H. Hughes. "Report of an Educational Campaign: The Cincinnati Plan for the United Nations." *American Journal of Sociology* 55 (1950): 389–400.

Steinfatt, T.; G. R. Miller; and E. Bettinghaus. "The Concept of Logical Ambiguity and Judgments of Syllogistic Validity." *Speech Monographs* 41 (1974): 317–28.

Suci, G. J. "A Comparison of Semantic Structures in American Southwest Culture Groups." *Journal of Abnormal and Social Psychology* 61 (1960): 25–30.

Tannenbaum, Ph.D. "Mediated Generalization of Attitude Change via the Principle of Congruity." *Journal of Personality and Social Psychology* 3 (1966): 493–99.

Tannenbaum, P. H., and R. W. Gengel. "Generalization of Attitude Change through Congruity Principle Relationships." *Journal of Personality and Social Psychology* 3 (1966): 209–304.

Tannenbaum, P. H. "The Congruity Principle: Retrospective Reflections and Recent Research." In R. P. Abelson; E. Aronson; W. J. McGuire; T. J. Newcomb; M. J. Rosenberg; and P. H. Tannenbaum, eds., *Theories of Cognitive Consistency: A Sourcebook*, pp. 52–71. Chicago: Rand McNally, 1968.

Thibaut, J. W., and H. H. Kelley. *The Social Psychology of Groups*. New York: John Wiley & Sons, 1959.

Thistlethwaite, D. L., and J. Kamenetzky. "Attitude Change through Refutation and Elaboration of Audience Counterarguments." *Journal of Abnormal and Social Psychology* 51 (1955): 3–12.

Thistlethwaite, D. L.; J. Kamenetzky; and H. Schmidt. "Factors Influencing Attitude Change through Refutative Communication." *Speech Monographs* 23 (1956): 13–25.

Thomas, E. J., and C. F. Fink. "Effects of Group Size." In A. P Hare; E. F. Borgatta; and R. F. Bales, eds., *Small Groups: Studies in Social Interaction*. New York: Alfred A. Knopf, 1965.

Thompson, E. "An Experimental Investigation of the Relative Effectiveness of Organizational Structure in Oral Communication." *Southern Speech Journal* 26 (1960): 59–69.

Thompson, W. N. *Quantitative Research in Public Address and Communication*. New York: Random House, 1967.

Toulmin, S. *The Uses of Argument*. New York: Cambridge University Press, 1958.

Travers, R. N. W. "The Transmission of Information to Human Receivers." *AV Communication Review* 12 (1964): 373–85.

Trager, G. L. "Paralanguage: A First Approximation." *Studies in Linguistics* 13 (1958): 1–12.

Triandis, H. C., and C. E. Osgood. "A Comparative Factorial Analysis of Semantic Structures in Monolingual Greek and American College Students." *Journal of Abnormal and Social Psychology* 57 (1958): 187–96.

Troldahl, V., and R. Van Dam. "Face-to-Face Communication about Major Topics in the News." *Public Opinion Quarterly* 29 (1965–66): 626–34.

Tryon, R. C. "Identification of Social Areas by Cluster Analysis: A General Method with an Application to the San Francisco Bay Area." *University of California Publications in Psychology*, 1955.

Vacchiano, R.; P. Strauss; and Hockman. "The Open and Closed Mind: A Review of Dogmatism.: *Psychological Bulletin*, Vol. 71, No. 4 (1969): 261.

Weiss, W. "Emotional Arousal and Attitude Change." *Psychological Review* 6 (1960): 267–80.

Werner, H. and E. Kaplan. "Development of Word Meaning through Verbal Contest: An Experimental Study." *Journal of Psychology* 29 (1950): 251.

Westley, B. H., and M. S. MacLean, Jr. "A Conceptual Mode for Communication Research." *Journalism Quarterly* 34 (1957): 31–38.

Weston, J. R. "Argumentative Message Structure and Message Sidedness and Prior Familiarity as Predictors of Source Credibility." Ph.D dissertation, Michigan State University, 1967.

Whittaker, J. O. "Parameters of Social Influence in the Autokinetic Situation." *Sociometry* 27 (1964): 88–98.

Whyte, W. F. *Street Corner Society*. Chicago: University of Chicago Press, 1955.

Windes, R., and A. Hastings. *Argumentation and Advocacy*. New York: Random House, 1965.

Zajonc, R. B. "Cognitive Theories in Social Psychology." In G. Lindzey, and E. Aronson, eds., *The Handbook of Social Psychology*, pp. 320–411, 2nd ed., Vol 1. Reading, Pa.: Addison-Wesley, 1968.

ADDITIONAL REFERENCES

Allen, R. K. *Organizational Management Through Communication*. New York: Harper and Row, 1971.

Baker, L. L., and G. Wiseman. "A Model of Intrapersonal Communication." *Journal of Communication* 16 (1966): 172–79.

Barnlund, D. *Interpersonal Communication: Survey and Studies*. Boston: Houghton Mifflin Co., 1968.

Bass, B. M. *Leadership, Psychology, and Organizational Behavior*. New York: Harper and Row, 1960.

Beal, G. M. "How Does Social Change Occur?" In *Prospects for the Years Ahead*. Ames, Iowa: Iowa Agricultural Experiment Station Special Report 21, 1957.

Berkowitz, Leonard, ed., *Advances in Experimental Social Psychology*, vol. 1, 2, 3. New York: Academic Press.

Berkowitz, L. "Sex and Violence: We Can't Have It Both Ways." *Psychology Today*, December 1971, p. 14.

Bossart, P., and F. J. DiVesta. "Effects of Context, Frequency, and Order of Presentation of Evaluative Assertions on Impression Formation." *Journal of Personality and Social Psychology* 4 (1966): 538–44.

Brehm, J. W. *A Theory of Psychological Reactance*. New York: Academic Press, 1966.

Broadbent, D. C. *Perception and Communication*. New York: Pergamon Press, 1958.

Bureau of Applied Social Research. *The Effects of Oil Progress Week: A Summary of a Supplemental Report*. New York: Bureau of Applied Social Research, Columbia University, 1952.

Byrne, D., and O. London. "Primacy-recency and the Sequential Presentation of Attitudinal Stimuli." *Psychonomic Science* 6 (1966): 193–94.

Campbell, J. H., and H. W. Hepler, eds. *Dimensions in Communication*. Belmont, Calif.: Wadsworth Publishing Co., 1965.

Cannell, C., and J. MacDonald. "The Impact of Health News on Attitudes and Behavior." *Journalism Quarterly* 33 (1956): 315–23.

Chapple, E., and C. Coon. "The Equilibrium of Groups." In A. P. Hare; E. F. Borgatta; and R. F. Bales, eds. *Small Groups: Studies in Social Interaction*. New York: Alfred A. Knopf, 1965.

Cherry, C. E. "Some Experiments on the Recognition of Speech with One and Two Ears." *Journal of the Acoustical Society of America* 25 (1953): 975–79.

Coch, L., and J. R. P. French, Jr. "Overcoming Resistance to Change." *Human Relations* 1 (1948): 512–32.

Cohen, A. R. *Attitude Change and Social Influence*. New York: Basic Books, 1964.

Cronkhite, G. "Autonomous Correlates of Dissonance and Attitude Change." *Speech Monographs* 33 (1966): 393–99.

Cahl, R. A. *Who Governs? Democracy and Power in an American City*. New Haven, Conn.: Yale University Press, 1961.

Cillehay, R. C.; C. Insko; and B. M. Smith. "Logical Consistency and Attitude Change." *Journal of Personality and Social Psychology* 3 (1966): 646–54.

Di Solvo, V.; C. Monroe; and B. Morse. *Business and Professional Communication*. Columbus, Ohio: Charles E. Merrill Publishing Co., 1977.

Dominick, J. R., and B. S. Greenberg. "Blacks on TV: Their Presence and Roles.: Mimeographed report, Michigan State University, 1969.

Downs, C.; W. Linkugel; and D. M. Berg. *The Organizational Communicator*. New York: Harper and Row, 1977.

Edwards, H. T. "Power Structure and Its Communication Behavior in San Jose, Costa Rica." Master's thesis, Michigan State University, 1963.

Emerson, R. M. "Mount Everest: A Case Study of Communication Feedback and Sustained Group Goal-Striving." *Sociometry* 29 (1966): 213–27.

Feldman, S. *Cognitive Consistency*. New York: Academic Press, 1956.

Gerson, W. M. "Mass Media Socialization Behavior: Negro-white Differences." *Social Forces* 45 (1966): 40–50.

Goffman, E. *Interaction Ritual*. Garden City, N.Y.: Doubleday and Co., 1967.

Goldhaber, G. M. *Organizational Communication*. Dubuque, Iowa: Wm. C. Brown Co., 1974.

Greenbaum, C. W. "Effect of Situational and Personality Variables on Improvisation and Attitude Change." *Journal of Personality and Social Psychology* 4 (1966): 260–69.

Griffin, K., and L. Ehrlich. "The Attitudinal Effects of a Group Discussion on a Proposed Change in Company Policy." *Speech Monographs* 30 (1963): 377–79.

Hage, J. T. "Organizational Response to Innovation: A Case Study of Community Hospitals." Ph.D. dissertation, Columbia University, 1963.

Hall, E. T. *The Hidden Dimension*. New York: Doubleday and Co., 1966.

Hall, E. T. *The Silent Language*. New York: Doubleday and Co., 1959.

Hamblin, R. S., et al. "Group Morale and Competence of the Leader." *Sociometry* 25 (1961): 295–311.

Herzog, H. "What Do We Really Know about Daytime Serial Listeners." In P. F. Lazarsfeld, and F. Stanton, eds., *Radio Research, 1942–1943*. New York: Duell, Sloan and Pearce, 1944.

Himmelweit, H.; A. N. Oppenheim; and P. Vince. *Television and the Child*. New York: Oxford University Press, 1958.

Hoffer, E. *The True Believer*. New York: Harper and Row, 1951.

Hovland, C. I., and I. Janis, eds. *Personality and Persuasibility*. New Haven, Conn.: Yale University Press, 1959.

Hull, C. L. *Essentials of Behavior*. New Haven, Conn.: Yale University Press, 1951.

Hunter, F. *Community Power Structure*. Chapel Hill, N.C.: The University of North Carolina Press, 1953.

Huseman, R. C.; James M. Lahiff; and J. D. Hatfield. *Interpersonal Communication in Organizations*. Boston: Holbrook Press, 1976.

Huseman, R. C.; C. M. Logue; and D. L. Freshley. *Readings in Interpersonal and Organizational Communication*, 3rd ed. Boston: Holbrook Press, 1977.

Jacques, E. "Interpretive Group Discussion as a Method of Facilitating Social Change." *Human Relations* 1 (1948): 538–49.

Joslyn, W. D., and T. J. Bunta. "Modifying Speed of Group Decision Making without Awareness of Group Members." *Psychonomic Science* 6 (1966): 297–98.

Karlins, M. and H. I. Abelson. *Persuasion: How Opinions and Attitudes are Changed*, 2d ed. New York: Springer, 1970.

Kendall, P., and K. Wolf. *The Personification of Prejudice as a Device in Educational Propaganda*. New York: Bureau of Applied Social Research, Columbia University, 1946.

Kiesler, C. A.; B. E. Collins; and N. Miller. *Attitude Change*. New York: John Wiley & Sons, 1969.

Klapper, J. T. *The Effects of Mass Communication*. New York: Free Press, 1960.

Klein, J. *Working With Groups: The Social Psychology of Discussion and Decision*. London: Hutchinson and Co., 1961.

Koehler, J. W.; K. W. E. Anatol; and R. L. Applebaum. *Organizational Communication: Behavioral Perspectives*. New York: Holt, Rinehart and Winston, 1976.

Krauss, R. M., and S. Weinheimer. "Concurrent Feedback, Confirmation, and the Encoding of Referents in Verbal Communication." *Journal of Personality and Social Psychology* 4 (1966): 343–46.

Landsberger, H. A. "The Horizontal Dimensions in Bureaucracy." *Administrative Science Quarterly* 6 (1961–62): 299–332.

Lawrence, L. C., and P. C. Smith. "Group Decision and Employee Participation." *Journal of Applied Psychology* 39 (1955): 334–37.

Lazarsfeld, P. "Some Remarks on the Role of the Mass Media in So-called Tolerance Propaganda." *Journal of Social Issues 3* (1947): 17–25.

Levine, J., and J. Butler. "Lecture vs. Group Decision in Changing Behavior." *Journal of Applied Psychology* 36 (1952): 29–33.

March, J. G., and H. A. Simon. *Organizations*. New York: John Wiley & Sons, 1958.

March, J. G., ed. *Handbook of Organizations*. Chicago: Rand McNally and Co., 1965.

McLuhan, M. *Understanding Media*, 2d ed. New York: McGraw-Hill, 1964.

Mannheim, B. "Reference Groups, Membership Groups and the Self Image." *Sociometry* 29 (1966): 265–79.

Marais, H. L. "Attitudes of Bantic Mine Workers toward a Communication Medium." *Psychological Reports* 19 (1966): 107–111.

Miller, G. R. "On Defining Communication: Another Stab." *Journal of Communication* 19 (1966): 88–98.

Miller, G. R., and T. R. Nilsen, eds. *Perspectives on Argumentation*. Chicago: Scott, Foresman and Co., 1966.

Miller, G. R. *Speech Communication: A Behavioral Approach*. New York: Bobbs-Merrill Co., 1966.

Miller, G. R., and M. A. Hewgill. "Some Recent Research on Fear-Arousing Message Appeals." *Speech Monographs* 33 (1966): 377–91.

Miller, P. A. *Community Health Action*. East Lansing, Mich.: Michigan State University Press, 1953.

Newcomb, T. M.; R. H. Turner; and P. E. Converse. *Social Psychology: The Study of Human Interaction*. New York: Holt, Rinehart and Winston, 1965.

Nutton, J. M. "Attitude Change after Rewarded Dissonant and Consonant 'Forced Compliance': A Critical Replication of the Festinger and Carlsmith Experiment." *International Journal of Psychology* 1 (1966): 39–57.

Osgood, C. E., and T. A. Sebeok. *Psycholinguistics: A Survey of Theory and Research Problems*. Bloomington, Ind.: Indiana University Press, 1965.

Osgood, C. E., and P. H. Tannenbaum. "The Principle of Congruity in the Prediction of Attitude Change." *Psychological Review* 62 (1955): 42–55.

Peterson, T.; J. Jensen; and W. L. Rivers. *The Mass Media and Modern Society*. New York: Holt, Rinehart and Winston, 1965.

Podell, J. E., and H. Amster. "Evaluative Concept of a Person as a Function of the Number of Stimulus Traits." *Journal of Personality and Social Psychology* 4 (1966): 333–36.

Polsby, N. *Community Power and Political Theory*. New Haven, Conn.: Yale University Press, 1963.

Powell, F. A. "Latitudes of Acceptance and Rejection and the Belief-Disbelief Dimension: A Correlational Comparison." *Journal of Personality and Social Psychology* 4 (1966): 354–457.

Presthus, R. *Men at the Top: A Study of Community Power*. New York: Oxford University Press, 1964.

Rogers, E. M. and R. A. Rogers. *Communication in Organizations*. New York: Free Press, 1976.

Rosenberg, M. and C. Hovland, eds. *Attitude, Organization and Change*. New Haven: Yale University Press, 1960.

Rosnow, R. L. " 'Conditioning' the Direction of Opinion Change in Persuasive Communication." *Journal of Social Psychology* 69 (1966): 291–303.

Saporta, S., ed. *Psycholinguistics: A Book of Readings*. New York: Holt, Rinehart and Winston, 1961.

Sargent, L., and T. Webb. "The Radical Speaker on the University Campus: A Study in Attitude Change." *Journal of Communication* 16 (1966): 199–212.

Schramm, W., ed. *The Science of Human Communication*. New York: Basic Books, 1963.

Shaw, M. E. *Group Dynamics: The Psychology of Small Group Behavior*. New York: McGraw-Hill, 1971.

Smith, A. G. *Communication and Culture*. New York: Holt, Rinehart and Winston, 1966.

Spaulding, C. B. "Relative Attachment of Students to Groups and Organizations." *Sociology and Social Research* 50 (1966): 421–35.

Stewart, D. K. "Communication and Meaning." *Journal of Psychology* 65 (1966): 95–100.

Toulmin, S. *The Uses of Argument*. New York: Cambridge University Press, 1958.

Vacchiano, R. B.; D. C. Schiffman; and A. Crowell. "Attitude Change as a Function of Intensity Training, Dogmatism, and Authoritarianism." *Psychological Reports* 19 (1966): 359–62.

Van Mondfrans, A. P. "An Investigation of the Interaction between the Level of Meaningfulness and Redundancy in the Content of the Stimulus Material and the Mode of Presentation of the Stimulus Material." Master's thesis, University of Utah, 1963.

Warner, W. L., and W. E. Henry. "The Radio Day Time Serial: A Symbolic Analysis." *Genetic Psychology Monographs* 37 (1948): 3–71.

Watzlawick, P.; J. H. Beavin; and D. D. Jackson. *Pragmatics of Human Communication*. New York: W. W. Norton, 1967.

Weaver, W. W., and N. Garrison. "The Coding of Phrases: An Experimental Study." *Journal of Communication* 16 (1966): 192–98.

Willis, F. N. "Initial Speaking Distance as a Function of the Speaker's Relationship." *Psychonomic*

Science 5 (1966): 221–22.

Wofford, J. E.; E. A. Gerloff; and R. C. Cummins. *Organizational Communication: The Keystone to Managerial Effectiveness*. New York: McGraw-Hill, 1977.

Zagona, S., and M. R. Harter. "Credibility of Source and Recipient's Attitude: Factors in the Perception and Retention of Information on Smoking Behavior." *Perceptual and Motor Skills* 23 (1966): 155–168.

Zajonc, R. B. "The Concepts of Balance, Congruity, and Dissonance." *Public Opinion Quarterly* 29 (1960): 280–96.

Zimbardo, P., and E. B. Ebbensen. *Influencing Attitudes and Changing Behavior*. Reading, Mass.: Addison-Wesley Publishing Co., 1969.

Zimmerman, C., and R. Bauer. "The Effect of an Audience upon What is Remembered." *Public Opinion Quarterly* 20 (1956): 238–48.

Zippel, B., and R. D. Norman. "Party Switching, Authoritarianism, and Dogmatism in the 1964 Election." *Psychological Reports* 19 (1966): 667–70.

INDEX OF SUBJECTS

INDEX OF NAMES